T0213084

Using Microsoft Dynamics AX

Andreas Luszczak

Using Microsoft Dynamics AX

The New Dynamics 'AX 7'

5th Edition

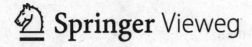 Springer Vieweg

Andreas Luszczak
Vienna, Austria

ISBN 978-3-658-13621-5   ISBN 978-3-658-13622-2 (eBook)
DOI 10.1007/978-3-658-13622-2

Library of Congress Control Number: 2016944400

Springer Vieweg
© Springer Fachmedien Wiesbaden 2009, 2012, 2013, 2015, 2016
The 4th edition of the book was published with the title „Using Microsoft Dynamics AX 2012".

Printed on acid-free paper

Springer Vieweg is a brand of Springer Nature
The registered company is Springer Fachmedien Wiesbaden GmbH

Preface

Reading this Book

The primary purpose of this book is to provide you with a good knowledge of the standard application concept and functionality, enabling you to run business processes in Microsoft Dynamics AX. This book is primarily designed for end users, students, and consultants interested in learning how to use Dynamics AX.

Going beyond the operations on the user interface, you will learn how the different parts of the application work together. As a result, you will also take advantage from learning the end-to-end application concept if you are a system administrator, developer, IT executive, or experienced consultant not knowing the complete application already.

Actually working in an application is the best way to learn it. This book therefore includes exercises building up on each other in a comprehensive case study. If you need support with the exercises, a free download of sample solutions is available.

Dynamics AX is a very comprehensive business solution, making it impossible to cover all parts of the application in a single book. In order to provide a profound understanding of the core application, this book addresses the primary functionality in supply chain (including trade and logistics, and production control) and in finance management. It shows the application, but does not cover tasks in system administration and development.

Microsoft Dynamics AX Version

This book is based on Microsoft Dynamics AX released in March 2016 and updated in May 2016. It is an update of my previous book editions on Dynamics AX 2012.

Microsoft Dynamics AX in the current release officially hasn't got a version number, it is just called "Microsoft Dynamics AX" without version. The internal build version of this release is 7.0. Since the label "Dynamics AX" does not always make clear if an instruction refers to the latest release or generally applies to all releases, descriptions in this book use the name 'AX 7' when pointing out specific items of the latest release.

Applicable Settings

In Dynamics AX, you can individually choose the language of your user interface. Descriptions and illustrations in this book refer to the language "EN-US" (United States English). Whereas it is obvious that the Dynamics AX client displays different labels when choosing languages like Spanish or Russian, there are also differences when selecting British English. For example, the label for the field "Sales tax" is "VAT" in British English. Other differences between your application and the descriptions in the book are possibly caused by permission settings, by local features, or by specific modifications and features in your application.

In order to benefit from the explanations, it is recommended to access a working environment of Dynamics AX. A separate test application, where you can execute the exercises, is required to avoid an impact on actual company data.

For the screenshots in this book, the color theme "High contrast" and a small element size has been selected in the visual preferences of the user options. The illustrations refer to a sample company "Anso Technologies Ltd.", which includes a simple setup limited to the described functionality. In order to grant a flexible choice of the training environment, the tasks in the exercises are specified in a way that you can use the Microsoft standard demo environment ("Contoso Entertainment System USA") or any other test environment.

Available Support

In order to download the exercise guide, which refers to the exercises in this book, and other applicable resources, please access the online service of the publisher or my web site:

http://axbook.addyn.com

If you have comments or questions regarding the book or the exercises, please contact me through this web site or via e-mail to *lua@addyn.com*.

Acknowledgements

Many people have been involved in finalizing this book, directly and indirectly, from the first to the current edition. I want to thank all of them. In particular, I would like to mention Ingo Maresch (Solutions Factory Consulting), Natalija Dajcman (Informio Software), and Finn Nielsen-Friis (AXcademy).

Thank you also to the editor, Sabine Kathke. And finally, my special thanks go to my family – Sonja, Felix and Caroline.

Andreas Luszczak

Table of Contents

1   What is Microsoft Dynamics AX?

Dynamics AX is Microsoft's core business management solution, designed to meet the requirements of mid-sized companies and multinational organizations. Based on a state-of-the-art architecture, Dynamics AX shows comprehensive functionality while ensuring high usability at the same time.

The latest version Dynamics 'AX 7' (officially labeled as "Dynamics AX" without version name) introduces fundamental changes in the system architecture. It is a cloud-based application deployed on the Microsoft Azure platform. An on-premise deployment on customer infrastructure will be available in a later update. Replacing the former Windows client, the new browser-based client supports most operating systems and browsers.

1.1   Axapta and the History of Dynamics AX

Dynamics AX has originally been developed under the name *Axapta* by Damgaard A/S, a Danish software company. Prior to the launch of Damgaard, the founders – Erik and Preben Damgaard – have already been co-founders of PC&C, the company which has developed Navision (now Dynamics NAV).

The first official version of Axapta, version 1.0, has been released in March 1998 for Denmark and the USA. Version 1.5, published in October 1998, has added country-specific functionality for several European countries. With the release of version 2.0 in July 1999 and version 3.0 in October 2002, Axapta has been introduced in multiple additional countries while including functional enhancements in many areas of the application.

After signing a merger agreement in November 2000, Damgaard A/S united with the local rival Navision A/S, a successor of PC&C. Microsoft subsequently acquired Navision-Damgaard in May 2002 and accepted the main products of this company, Navision and Axapta, as the core business solutions in the portfolio of Microsoft. Whereas Dynamics NAV (Navision) with its functionality and technology is a solution for small companies, Dynamics AX (Axapta) is the product for mid-sized and large companies.

Microsoft rebranded Axapta to Dynamics AX when releasing version 4.0 in June 2006. Apart from functional enhancements, Dynamics AX 4.0 introduced a redesigned user interface which provided a Microsoft Office-like look and feel.

Dynamics AX 2009, which included role centers, workflow functionality, and an updated user interface as core improvements, has been published in June 2008. Dynamics AX 2009 also provided enhanced functionality, including the multisite foundation and additional modules ensuring an end-to-end support for the supply chain requirements of global organizations.

Dynamics AX 2012, which has been published in August 2011, has shown a further updated user interface with list pages and action panes across the whole application. Role-based security, the accounting framework with segmented account structures, the enhanced use of shared data structures, and other features have facilitated collaboration across legal entities and operating units within the application, and as a result have provided additional support for large multinational enterprises. Updated versions of Dynamics AX 2012 have been released later – the Feature Pack in February 2012 (adding industry features for retail and process manufacturing), R2 in December 2012 (adding data partitions, additional country features, and Windows 8 support), and R3 in May 2014 (adding the advanced warehouse and transportation management solution).

Microsoft Dynamics 'AX 7' has been published in March 2016 with a first update, primarily containing technical improvements, in May 2016. Whereas this version does not contain a multitude of functional updates if compared to Dynamics AX 2012 R3, it shows a completely new cloud-based application platform and user experience.

1.2   Dynamics AX Product Overview

Microsoft Dynamics AX is an adaptable business management solution, which is easy to use and nevertheless supports the complex requirements of multinational companies.

When accessing Dynamics AX for the first time, most people feel comfortable from the very beginning because its intuitive user interface. This user experience helps to start working in Dynamics AX easily and efficiently, supported by a tight integration to other Microsoft cloud services. Dashboards, which are the start page when opening Dynamics AX, grant an easy and fast access to all required areas.

1.2.1   Functional Capabilities

An end-to-end support of business processes across the whole organization enables the integration of organization units (like companies and departments) and of business partners (like customers and vendors).

Multi-language, multi-country, and multi-currency capabilities, the organization model for managing multiple hierarchies of operating units and legal entities, and the option to manage multiple sites within one legal entity provide the option to manage complex global organizations within a common database.

The functional capabilities of Dynamics AX include following main areas:

➢ **Sales and marketing**
➢ **Supply chain management**

- ➢ **Production**
- ➢ **Procurement and sourcing**
- ➢ **Service management**
- ➢ **Financial management**
- ➢ **Project management and accounting**
- ➢ **Human capital management**
- ➢ **Business intelligence and reporting**

In addition to the core ERP solution, industry-specific functionality for manufacturing, distribution, retail, services, and the public sector, which are included in the standard application, provides a broad industry foundation.

Local features are available in order to comply with country-specific requirements. By default, applicable local features are controlled by the country/region of the primary address of the company (legal entity).

In order to support data analysis, the integrated reporting features and the option to embed business intelligence reports and visualizations grant a fast and reliable presentation of business data. Business intelligence features are not only available to users in finance administration, but also for users in all other areas of Dynamics AX who need to analyze their data.

1.2.2   Implementation

In the current release, Microsoft Dynamics AX is only available as cloud-based solution on Microsoft Azure. A later update will support on-premise deployments.

Microsoft Dynamics Lifecycle Services, which are a Microsoft Azure-based portal solution including a collaborative environment and continuously updated services for managing the Dynamics AX deployment, are the starting point for a Dynamics AX implementation.

Microsoft usually does not sell Dynamics AX directly to customers, but offers an indirect sales channel. Customers purchase licenses from certified partners, who offer their services to support the implementation of Dynamics AX. This support includes application consulting, system setup, and the development of enhancements and functional modifications.

Additional resources including Dynamics AX product information, customer stories and online demos are available on the global Microsoft Dynamics AX web page *http://www.microsoft.com/en-us/dynamics/erp-ax-overview.aspx* and on a local web page accessible through the Microsoft homepage of your country.

1.2.3   Data Structure

When using Dynamics AX (or any other business software), you are working with data which describe transactions (e.g. item transactions). As a prerequisite for these transactions, you need to manage data which describe objects (e.g. customers). Including the data specifying the configuration, there are three types of data:

> ➢ **Setup data**
> ➢ **Master data**
> ➢ **Transaction data**

Setup data determine the way business processes work in Dynamics AX. You can, for example, choose in the setup whether to apply warehouse locations or serial numbers. Apart from modifying programmable objects, setup is the second way to adapt the application according to the requirements of an enterprise. Setup data are entered when initially setting up the system. Later modifications of core setup data need to be checked carefully.

Master data describe objects like customers, main accounts, or products. They do not change periodically, but at the time related objects change – for example when a customer changes the delivery address. Master data are entered or imported initially before a company starts working in the application. Depending on the business, you have to update master data only occasionally later on.

Transaction data are continuously updated when processing business activities. Examples for transaction data are sales orders, invoices, or item transactions. Dynamics AX generates transaction data with every business activity. Registering and posting of transaction data complies with the voucher principle.

1.2.4   Voucher Principle

If you want to post a transaction, you have to start by registering a voucher with a header and one or more lines. Every voucher is processed in two steps:

> ➢ **Registration** – Entering the voucher (creating the initial document)
> ➢ **Posting** – Posting the voucher (creating the posted document)

Vouchers are based on master data like main accounts, customers or products. It is not possible to post a voucher as long as it does not comply with the rules defined by setup data and the Dynamics AX-internal business logic (e.g. enforcing that an item transaction has to include a serial number if serial number control is active). Once a voucher is posted, it is not possible to change it any more.

Examples for vouchers in Dynamics AX are orders in sales and in purchasing, or journals in finance and in inventory management. After posting, the posted documents are packing slips, invoices, ledger transactions, or inventory transactions.

Note: Some minor vouchers like quarantine orders show an exception regarding the voucher structure – they do not consist of a header and separate lines.

2 Getting Started: Navigation and General Options

One of the core principles of Microsoft Dynamics AX is to grant an intuitive and smooth user experience. But business software has to be in line with business processes, which may be quite complex.

2.1 User Interface and Common Tasks

Before we start to go through business processes and case studies, we want to take a look at the general functionality in this chapter.

2.1.1 Logon and Authentication

Microsoft Dynamics AX in version 7.0 is a cloud-based solution, requiring to logon with a Microsoft Azure Active Directory user account (Microsoft Office 365 account). In order to log on, open a supported web browser like the Internet Explorer or Google Chrome and access the web address (URL) of your Dynamics AX application. The browser then shows the logon dialog, where you have to enter your Azure Active Directory user and password.

After logging on, the user-ID in Dynamics AX, the current company (legal entity), and the language derive from your user options, which you can change within the client.

Parameters in the web address of the Dynamics AX application can override the user settings and provide additional options. The web address *https://XXX.com/?&cmp=FRSI&lng=fr* (XXX.com = Dynamics AX URL) for example provides access to the company "FRSI" in French language.

If you want to log off from Dynamics AX, click the user name (or the button ◾) on the right-hand side of the Dynamics AX navigation bar and select *Sign out*.

2.1.2 Navigation

There are four ways to access pages and forms in Microsoft Dynamics AX:

➢ **Dashboard and workspaces**
➢ **Navigation pane**
➢ **Navigation search**
➢ **Favorites**

The Dynamics AX dashboard (see section 2.1.3) is the default initial page when accessing Microsoft Dynamics AX. Since it contains all workspaces which are available to the current user, you can use the dashboard for navigating to workspaces. From the workspaces you can subsequently access list pages and detail forms.

2.1.2.1 Navigation Pane

Whereas workspaces and favorites contain a limited number of menu items for frequent use, the navigation pane provides access to all items for which you have got appropriate permissions.

In order to show the complete navigation pane, press the keyboard shortcut *Alt+F1* or click the button ▤ (*Navigation pane*) on the left-hand side of the Dynamics AX client. If all modules and menu items are shown, the Dynamics AX navigation pane includes following elements (see Figure 2-1):

➢ **Navigation bar** [1]
➢ **Navigation pane** [2]
➢ **Favorites** [3]
➢ **Recent** [4]
➢ **Workspaces** [5]
➢ **Modules** [6]
➢ **Menu** for the selected module [7]

If you want to show the navigation pane permanently, click the button ⊞ (*Pin*) on the top right-hand side of the navigation pane. In case you want to collapse the navigation pane after pinning it open, click the button ◁ (*Collapse*) then shown on the top right-hand side of the navigation pane.

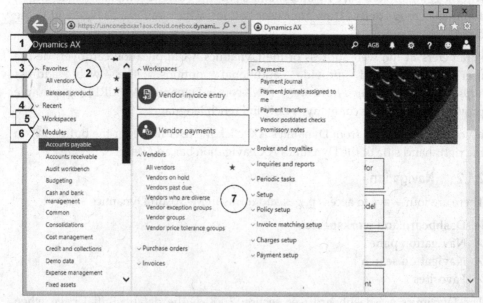

Figure 2-1:   Navigation pane and menu in Dynamics AX

2.1.2.2 Modules and Menu Structure

The structure of the modules complies with functional areas like *Accounts payable* or *Production control* and refers to standard roles in the industry. The modules

Organization administration and *System administration* include basic settings and tasks which are not related to a specific functional area.

The *Common* module contains menu items not related to a functional role, but relevant for all users. This includes the *Global address book* (see section 2.4), the *Work items* (workflow management, see section 10.4.2), the *Cases* (see section 10.5.2), the *Activities* (referring to sales and marketing), and the *Document management* (see section 10.5.1).

After selecting a module, the menu shows all accessible menu items of this module. The particular folders and menu items, which are depending on the individual module, comply with a common basic structure.

The first folder in the menu is the folder *Workspaces*, containing all workspaces related to the selected module. This folder is not shown if the selected module does not include a workspace. Below the workspaces, there are several folders and menu items providing access to pages for frequent tasks in the particular module (e.g. the vendor management in the *Accounts payable* module).

The folder *Inquiries and reports* contains items for reporting and analysis. Inquires show the result directly on the screen, whereas reports generate a printout on paper. If you do not need a printed hard copy, you can select to display a print preview or to save the report to a file.

The folder *Periodic tasks* contains items, which are not used frequently – for example the menu items for month end closing or summary updates.

Depending on the module, one or more *Setup* folders provide access to configuration data of the particular module. Configuration data are entered when initially setting up a company (legal entity). Later on, configuration data are only updated if necessary because of changes in the business processes. Some settings should not be changed without a deep knowledge of the Dynamics AX functionality. For this reason, the permissions for the *Setup* folders usually are set in a way that regular users cannot edit sensible configuration data.

2.1.2.3 Recent Pages

The folder *Recent* in the navigation pane shows the last workspaces and pages which you have visited. Dynamics AX automatically adds menu items to this folder from your browsing history, which makes it easy to go back to a form recently visited.

2.1.2.4 Navigation Search

The navigation search provides the option to directly access menu items by typing part of the name (similar to the search feature in Windows 8/10).

In order to use the navigation search, click the button ▣ (*Search*) in the navigation bar and enter the page title or navigation path in the search field. You can limit the entered text to the first characters of the words of a page title or navigation path.

For example, typing "al pu" in the navigation search shows the page *All purchase orders* as first result. Selecting a menu item in the navigation search results will open the related page.

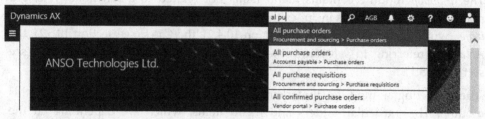

Figure 2-2:   Using the navigation search

2.1.2.5 Favorites and Shared Links

Whereas modules and related menu items in the navigation pane show a uniform structure, the Dynamics AX favorites provide the option to collect menu items according to your particular requirements.

If you want to add a workspace or a page to your Dynamics AX favorites, open the navigation pane to show the particular menu item and click the empty star ☆ on the right of the menu item. A full star ★ on the right of the menu item then indicates that it is included in the favorites.

Once a menu item is added to the favorites, it automatically shows in the favorites area at the top of the navigation pane. If you want to remove an item from the favorites, click the star ★ on the right of the menu item in the favorites pane.

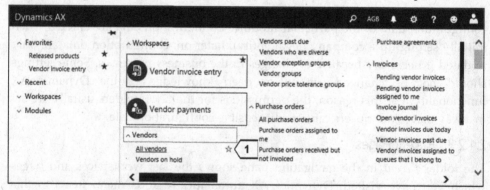

Figure 2-3:   Managing favorites in Dynamics AX

Apart from the favorites within Dynamics AX, you can use shared links to access Dynamics AX forms. In every list page or form, there is the button *OPTIONS/Share/Get a link* in the action pane. A dialog then shows the web address of the current form, which you can copy and send to other users of your Dynamics AX application. Of course you can also use this link together with general features of your browser and add it to the browser favorites or the browser start page tiles.

2.1.2.6 Switching the Current Company

If you want to switch from one legal entity to another, open the lookup for switching companies by clicking the company field in the navigation bar. After selecting a company in the lookup, Dynamics AX immediately switches to the other company.

Figure 2-4:   Switching the current company

2.1.2.7 New in Dynamics 'AX 7'

With the browser-based interface replacing the Windows client, there are completely new options for navigating Dynamics AX. Apart from minor modifications in the menu structure, which eliminate the rigid structure of the *Common* and the *Setup* folder in various modules, core changes include the dashboard (replacing the role center), the workspaces, and the navigation search. There is no Dynamics AX address bar, but you can use the address bar of your browser. The favorites now do not support creating a personal menu structure.

2.1.3   Elements of the User Interface

Microsoft Dynamics AX contains following types of standard pages:

➤ **Dashboard**
➤ **Workspaces**
➤ **List pages**
➤ **Detail and transaction forms**
➤ **Journals, inquiries and setup forms**

This section explains the elements available in these pages.

2.1.3.1 Dashboard

As start page in Dynamics AX, the dashboard displays all your workspaces to give an overview of the work you should do by. Clicking a workspace tile, e.g. *Budget planning* in Figure 2-5, provides access to the related workspace.

The default dashboard contains following areas (compare Figure 2-5):

➤ **Navigation bar** [1] – Described below
➤ **Company banner** [2] – As specified in the company setup (see section 10.1.4)
➤ **Navigation pane** [3] – Collapsed in Figure 2-5
➤ **Calendar** and **Work items** [4]
➤ **Workspaces** [5]

The calendar in the dashboard highlights the *Session date*, which is used as default value for the posting date in the current session. The initial value for the session date is the current date, but through the dashboard calendar (or the menu item

Common> Common> Session date and time) you can temporarily set it to a different date.

The work items pane below the calendar in the dashboard refers to the workflow management (see section 10.4.2).

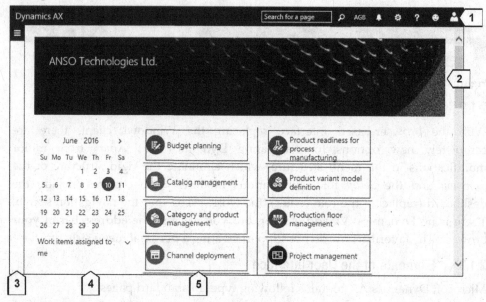

Figure 2-5: Dynamics AX dashboard

When working in a workspace or a form, you can always return to the dashboard (initial page) by clicking the button Dynamics AX on the left side of the navigation bar.

Note: In your user options, you can select to use an alternative page (e.g. the employee self-service portal) as initial page instead of the dashboard.

2.1.3.2 Navigation Bar

The navigation bar at the top of every Dynamics AX form contains following buttons for global Dynamics AX features (see Figure 2-6):

➢ **Go to dashboard** [1] – Return to the initial page
➢ **Navigation search** [2] – See section 2.1.2
➢ **Company select** [3] – See section 2.1.2
➢ **Show messages** [4] – See section 2.1.4
➢ **Settings** [5] – User options and other general settings
➢ **Help** [6] – See section 2.1.6
➢ **Feedback** [7]
➢ **User** [8] – For signing out

Apart from the *User options* (see section 2.3.1), the options in the button ⚙ (*Settings*) include the *Task recorder* (see section 10.5.3) and the Dynamics AX product information (button *About*).

Figure 2-6:   Navigation bar in Dynamics AX

2.1.3.3 Workspaces

Workspaces are designed as starting point for the daily work in Dynamics AX. They are pages which collect all the information and functionality required to perform a specific job. The workspace *Purchase order receipt and follow-up* (see Figure 2-7) for example shows a list of delayed receipts in the center. In addition, it provides access and indicates the number of not invoiced orders, and it includes other data areas through tiles on the right and on the left.

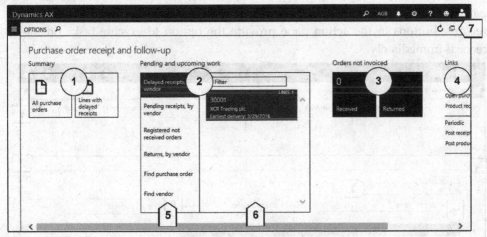

Figure 2-7:   Workspace for purchase order receipt and follow-up

You can view and access all workspaces, for which you have got appropriate permissions, from the dashboard and from the navigation pane. The workspace panorama then contains the following panes (compare Figure 2-7):

➢ **Summary pane** [1]
➢ **Tabbed list pane** [2]
➢ **Optional further panes** [3]
➢ **Related links** [4]

The tabbed list pane [2] in the center of a workspace is the main place for the daily work. After selecting a list in the left area [5] of this pane, the grid in the right [6] displays the related list of records. The filter field above the grid provides the option to apply a record filter. Clicking a key field shown as link in the grid immediately opens the related detail form. Depending on the particular workspace, there are buttons for executing actions in the action pane [7] and – if applicable – in the toolbar above the grid in the tabbed list pane.

The summary pane [1] on the left-hand side contains tiles for starting new tasks or accessing pages which are important in connection with the selected workspace (e.g. purchase orders in Figure 2-7). Tiles in this pane – like tiles in general – are rectangular buttons which open pages (like a menu item button) and optionally show data like counts or key performance indicators.

Depending on the particular workspace, there are further panes [3] to the right of the tabbed list pane, which contain tiles, charts, or graphs. The right-most pane [4] in the workspace contains links to pages which are related to the selected workspace.

2.1.3.4 List Page

A list page, like the customer page in Figure 2-8, shows the list of records of a particular table. While list pages are primarily designed for viewing and selecting records, buttons in the action pane provide the option to execute tasks on these records immediately.

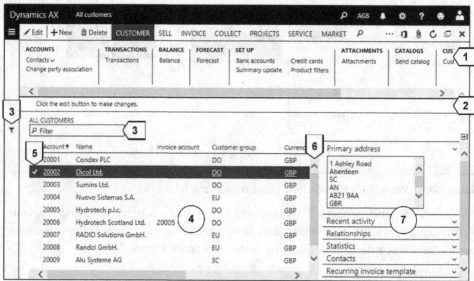

Figure 2-8:   Customer list page as an example of a list page

List pages have a common structure, containing different elements and features depending on the data shown in the particular page. The common structure includes following basic elements:

- ➢ **Action pane** [1] – Contains the action buttons
- ➢ **View/Edit mode banner** [2] – Displays in view mode, indicating that editing data is not possible in this mode
- ➢ **Filter options** [3] – Filter button and quick filter field (see section 2.1.5)
- ➢ **Grid** [4] – Displays the list of records
- ➢ **Grid check boxes** [5] – Enable selecting multiple or – if selecting the checkbox in the header line – all records

➤ **Scroll bar** [6] – Scroll through records or press the shortcut keys *PgUp, PgDn, Ctrl+Home* and *Ctrl+End*

➤ **FactBoxes** [7] – Show a summary of additional information related to the selected record (e.g. the primary address of the selected customer)

Clicking the button *Edit* in the action pane changes the page mode to edit mode, which gives the option to immediately update record data.

If the full action pane is displayed and you need additional space, you can collapse it by clicking the button ⌃ (*Collapse*) on the bottom right of the action pane. Once collapsed, the action pane will expand automatically when clicking an action pane tab (e.g. *CUSTOMER* in Figure 2-8). In order to show the full action pane permanently, click the button ⊞ (*Pin open*) on the bottom right of the action pane when expanded.

If a page does not show the FactBoxes pane and you want to view it, click the button ⊟ (*Show*) top right of the grid. By clicking the button ⊟ (*Hide*) at the same place you can hide the FactBoxes again. A general setting for activating or deactivating the FactBoxes pane is available in the system administration (*System administration> Setup> Client performance options*).

List pages do not automatically refresh, if data displayed on the screen change in the database (e.g. if somebody is working on the records displayed in the list). In order to refresh a list page, press the keyboard shortcut *Shift+F5* or click the button ⟳ (*Refresh*) in the action pane (or use the refresh options of your browser).

2.1.3.5   Action Pane and Action Search

The action pane contains buttons for activities referring to the selected record (like entering the order of a customer) and buttons for access to related detail forms (displaying more information). The number and functionality of buttons, which can show on show on multiple tabs (e.g. the action pane tabs *CUSTOMER* or *SELL* in Figure 2-8), is depending on the particular page. If the window size does not allow to show all action pane tabs, the button ⋯ provides access to the tabs not shown immediately.

On the top right of the action pane, there are buttons for general options including *Open in Microsoft Office* ⬛ (see section 2.2.2), *Attach* ▣ (document handling, see section 10.5.1), *Refresh* ⟳ , *Open in new window* ▣ (described later in the current section), and *Close* ✕.

The action search provides the option to directly access buttons in the action pane by typing part of the name. In order to use the action search, click the button ⌕ (*Search*) in the action pane (or press the shortcut key *Alt+Q*) and enter the action title or action pane button path in the search field. Like in the navigation search, you can limit the entered text to the first characters of the words of the name. As an example for using the action search, you can quickly access the customer balance from the customer list page by pressing the shortcut key *Alt+Q*, typing "b", and pressing the *Enter* key.

2.1.3.6 Detail Form for Master Data

Unlike list pages, which are designed for viewing a list of records, detail forms are there for inserting and modifying individual records.

Clicking a key field shown as link in the grid of a list page (or pressing the *Enter* key when the field is active) opens the related detail form. Alternatively, you can access a detail form by clicking the button *Page options/Change view/Details view* on tab *OPTIONS* in the action pane of a list page.

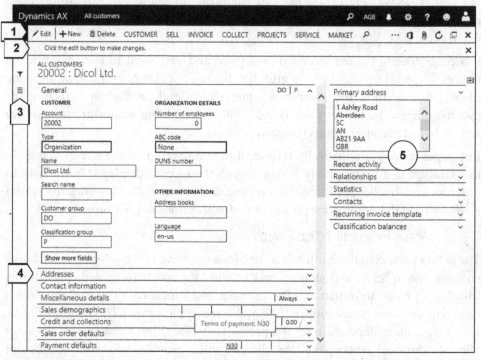

Figure 2-9:   Elements of a detail form on the example of the customer detail form

Detail forms have got a structure which is similar to list pages, and like in list pages the specific elements and functions are depending on the particular form. Figure 2-9 shows the customer detail form (accessed from the list page *Accounts receivable> Customers> All customers*) as example for the structure of detail forms.

The common structure of detail forms includes the following basic elements:

➤ **Action pane** [1] – Collapsed in Figure 2-9.
➤ **View/Edit mode banner** [2] – Indicates whether you are in view mode
➤ **Filter button** and **List button** [3] – Open a pane for entering a filter and/or displaying a list of records

> **Fast tabs** [4] – Group fields according to their functional area and show summary fields, which display core data directly on the tab. In Figure 2-9, the fast tab *Invoice and delivery* for example shows the terms of payment "N30". You can expand fast tabs by clicking the particular tab. A right-hand click on a tab provides the option to expand or collapse all tabs at the same time.
> **FactBoxes** [5] – Show additional information (like in a list page)

The button ▤ (*Show/Hide list*) [3] provides the option to view a list of records in detail forms. After clicking this button in a detail form, Dynamics AX displays a navigation list pane on the left-hand side of the form. Selecting a record in the navigation list immediately shows the related detail data, which makes it easy to move from one record to the next.

Section 2.1.4 later in this book contains more information on editing records, working with fast tabs, and other options available in list pages and detail forms.

In order to return from a detail form to the list page, use the *Back* button of your browser, or press the shortcut *Alt+Back Arrow* (or the *Esc* key), or click the button ☒ (*Close*) in the action pane.

2.1.3.7 Detail Form for Transaction Data

In addition to the detail forms for master data as described above, Dynamics AX contains detail forms for transaction data (like the sales order form in Figure 2-10).

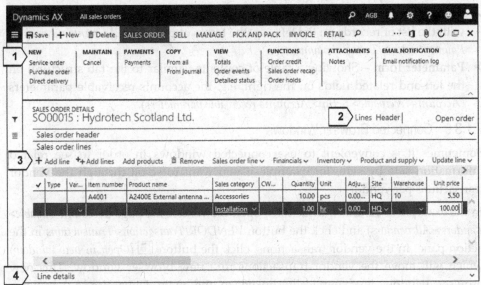

Figure 2-10: Sales order form as example of a transaction detail form

Clicking a key field shown as link in the grid of the particular list page (e.g. the sales order list page *Sales and marketing> Sales orders> All sales orders*) opens the transaction detail form similar to opening a master data detail form from a list page as described above. When accessing a transaction detail form, it shows the *Lines* view where you can view or edit the lines.

In the **toolbar** [3] of the tab *Lines*, there are buttons for executing actions on the selected line – for example deleting a line by clicking the button *Remove*. The **action pane** [1] at the top of the form provides the option to execute actions at header level – for example deleting a complete order by clicking the button *Delete*.

If you want to edit details not shown in the line grid, expand the fast tab **Line details** [4]. In order to structure the field display, the line details tab contains multiple sub-tabs.

The lines view shows basic header data in the tab *Header*. Clicking the button **Header** [2] below the action pane (or pressing the shortcut key *Ctrl+Shift+H*) opens the header view, which contains all fields of the header record. In the header view, the button *Lines* below the action pane (shortcut key *Ctrl+Shift+L*) takes you back to the lines view.

2.1.3.8 Inquiries and Setup Forms

In comparison to detail forms, inquiries and setup forms show a simple layout. Dynamics AX contains following simple forms:

➢ **Simple list** – Plain grid without fast tabs, e.g. the customer groups (*Accounts receivable> Setup> Customer groups*).
➢ **Simple list and Details** – Detail form always showing a navigation list pane with the list of records on the left, e.g. the terms of payment (*Accounts receivable> Payment setup> Terms of payment*).
➢ **Parameter form** – Showing a table of contents (similar to the tab structure) on the left and related fields on the right, e.g. the accounts receivable parameters (*Accounts receivable> Setup> Accounts receivable parameters*).

2.1.3.9 Connected Browser Windows

Sometimes it is convenient to use connected windows in order to see related information side by side, for example if you want to scroll through the vendor transactions per vendor.

In the example of vendor transactions, open the vendor list page (*Accounts payable> Vendors> All vendors*) and click the button *VENDOR/Transactions/Transactions* in the action pane. In the vendor transactions, click the button 🖳 (*Open in new window*) which will move the vendor transactions to a new browser window. This new browser window is dynamically linked to the main Dynamics AX browser window, which shows the previous form (the vendor list page in the example). Moving from one vendor to another in the main window then automatically updates the data shown in the new transaction window.

2.1.3.10 New in Dynamics 'AX 7'

Based on the design principles required for the browser-based user interface, the new release has a "flat" design. This means that all forms show in the main browser window (not opening a separate window per form like in AX 2012).

Client forms now include the action search and the edit mode in list pages. The navigation list pane in detail forms replaces the AX 2012 grid view. There is no command bar, no preview pane, and no status bar. General options of the former command bar are now available in the navigation bar, form-specific features in the tab *OPTIONS* of the action pane. Cues in AX 2012 role centers are replaced by tiles in workspaces.

2.1.4 Working with Records

Microsoft Dynamics AX supports working with the mouse, but also offers extensive support for keyboard usage. Apart from shortcut keys, the navigation search and the action search enable fast data entry without using the mouse. An overview of shortcut keys for executing basic operations in Dynamics AX is included in the appendix of this book.

2.1.4.1 Viewing Records

When accessing a menu item from the navigation pane or through a tile in a workspace, Dynamics AX shows the appropriate list page.

List pages are the starting point for working on items, giving you the possibility to search and filter records. Buttons in the action pane of the list page provide the option to edit, delete, and insert data according to your permissions.

Whereas a list page only contains a limited number of fields, the detail form shows all available fields of the record. In order to access the detail form after selecting a line in the list page, click the key field shown as link in the grid.

Fast tabs on detail forms expand by clicking them or by pressing the *Enter* key. If you want to collapse an individual tab, click the tab header again or press the shortcut key *Alt+0*. Further options are available through a right-hand click on a tab. If you select to expand all tabs, you can scroll through the complete record (e.g. with your mouse wheel). Some tabs contain less important fields, which are not shown immediately when expanding the tab. The link *Show more fields* in such tabs provides the option to show these fields.

2.1.4.2 Edit/View Mode

When accessing a list page, it always opens in view mode which prevents data to be changed unintentionally. Detail forms usually also open in view mode, but this is depending on the settings of the form. In view mode, a banner below the action pane indicates that editing data is not possible.

If you are in view mode and want to edit a record, switch to the edit mode by clicking the button *Edit* in the action pane or by pressing the *F2* key. If you already change to the edit mode in a list page and access the related detail form afterwards, the detail form will open in edit mode. In order to return to the view mode, press the *F2* key again or click the button *OPTIONS/Edit/Read mode* in the action pane.

If you want to start a particular form always in edit mode, click the button *OPTIONS/Personalize/Always open for editing* in the action pane of the form. In case you want to set your general default mode to *Edit* or *View*, choose the appropriate setting on the tab *Preferences* of your user options.

2.1.4.3 Inserting Records

In order to insert a record in a list page or a detail form, press the shortcut key *Alt+N* or click the button *New* in the action pane. In some workspaces, you can also create records (there is an appropriate button in the action pane in this case).

A *Quick create* dialog (see Figure 2-11) then shows on the right-hand side of the form. This dialog contains the core fields of the record, making it possible to insert records in a fast way. After clicking the button *Save* at the bottom of the dialog, Dynamics AX opens to the related detail form where you can enter additional data. Depending on the page, the *Save and open* button contains additional options – e.g. for switching to the sales quotation form immediately when creating a customer.

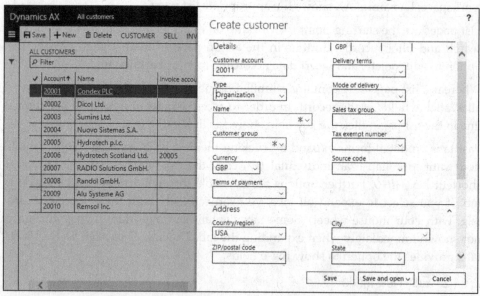

Figure 2-11: *Quick create* dialog for entering a new customer

If no *Quick create* dialog is available for a particular page, Dynamics AX takes you to the related detail form showing an empty record for entering data (except if you apply a template as described in section 2.3.2).

In the lines of a transaction form (e.g. the sales order lines), you can create a new record by simply pressing the *Down Arrow* key from the last line of the grid.

2.1.4.4 Editing Data

Before you can edit a record in a list page or detail form, you have to make sure that you are in the edit mode. In order to switch between the fields of the form, you can use the mouse, the *Tab* key, or the *Shift+Tab* shortcut key.

If you have started to insert a record which contains a mandatory field and you want to stop, you might have to delete the record as described below even if you did not enter anything. Alternatively, you can close the form without saving by pushing the *Esc* key. If you are in a *Quick create* dialog, click the button *Cancel* at the bottom.

You can manually save a record in list pages and detail forms by clicking the button *Save* in the action pane or by pressing the shortcut key *Alt+S* (or *Ctrl+S*). But it is not required to save a record explicitly. Dynamics AX saves every change of a record automatically when leaving the record – switching to another record, or closing the form using the *Back* button of the browser, or the button ☒ (*Close*) in the action pane of the form. If you close a form pressing the *Esc* key, a dialog asks whether you want to save the changes.

If you have entered or modified data and do not want to save the update, press the shortcut key *Ctrl+Shift+F5* or click the button *OPTIONS/Edit/Revert* in the action pane. Reversing restores the record from the database and is only available as long as you do not save the record (manually or by moving to another record).

Another option not to save changes is to close the form by pressing the *Esc* key or the shortcut key *Alt+Shift+Q* (as long as you did not save the record already).

2.1.4.5 Deleting Data

In order to delete the content of an input field, press the *Delete* key. If you want to delete a complete record, click the button *Delete* in the action pane or press the shortcut key *Alt+F9* after selecting the particular record.

In some cases, Dynamics AX shows an error message preventing you from deleting a record – e.g. if there are open transactions.

2.1.4.6 Elements in a Detail Form

When entering data in a form, you have to distinguish between following elements as shown in Figure 2-12 on the example of the bank accounts detail form (*Cash and bank management> Bank accounts*):

➢ **Field group** [1] – Groups fields by functional area to provide a logical structure.
➢ **Mandatory field** [2] – Shows a red frame and the *required field indicator* ✱, requiring data input before you can save the record.

➤ **Slider** [3] – Sliders (as shown in Figure 2-12) and checkboxes are used in fields with a binary choice (Yes/No). In order to select a checkbox or set a slider to "Yes", click it with the mouse or press the *Space bar* key once the cursor is on the field.

➤ **Date field** [4] – The format of date and number fields is specified on the tab *Preferences* of your user options. Date fields show the calendar icon ▦ for selecting a particular date. If entering a date manually, you don't have to type date separators like "." or "/". For a date in the current year, simply enter the day and month (e.g. "0523" if using the US date format). In order to insert the current date, simply type "t" (or "d" for the session date).

➤ **Lookup field with a fixed list of values** [5]

➤ **Lookup field with a related main table** [6]

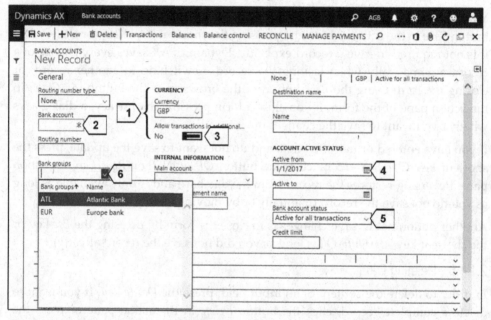

Figure 2-12:   Types of fields on the example of the bank account detail form

2.1.4.7 Lookup Fields and Table Reference

In a lookup field, you can only enter or select a value which is included in a predefined list of values. Related to the setup of this list of values, there are two types of lookup fields:

➤ **Lookup fields with a related main table**, which contains permitted values – e.g. *Bank groups* in Figure 2-12.

➤ **Lookup fields with a fixed list of values**, which is given by Dynamics AX enumerable types (*Enums*) – e.g. *Bank account status* in Figure 2-12.

In edit mode, all lookup fields show the lookup button ⌄ in the right part of the field. In view mode, lookup fields with a related main table show as a link (similar to Internet links).

When typing characters in a lookup field, the value lookup opens automatically and applies the typed characters as filter on the ID (key field of the relevant table). In many lookups, the filter also applies to the column *Name*. If you enter for example "E" in a lookup field, the lookup form automatically pops up showing all records starting with "E" in the key field or the name.

If you want to manually open a value lookup, click the lookup button ⌄ or press the shortcut key *Alt + Down* once the cursor is on the field.

In the lookup form, you can select a record by clicking it, or by pressing the *Enter* key once the appropriate line in the lookup is active. If a value lookup contains multiple lines and you want to reduce the number of displayed lines, you can use the grid column filter and the sorting options as described in section 2.1.5. In the example shown in Figure 2-12, you can enter a filter on the bank group name by clicking the column header field *Name* in the lookup.

Apart from value lookup, the table reference of fields with a related main table also provides the option to directly access the detail form of the related main table. If you want to insert a new bank group in the form shown in Figure 2-12 for example, you can open the bank group form directly from the *Bank group* field.

In edit mode, you have to do a right-click on the field label (and not on the field itself) to open the context menu, where you can choose the option *View details* to access the detail form related to a lookup field.

In view mode or in non-editable fields, the table reference displays as a link providing the option to access the related detail form with a simple mouse click (alternatively you can right-click the field label and select the *View details* option).

After opening the referenced detail form, you can edit records the same way as if accessing from the navigation pane. Apart from using the table reference as an easy way to insert and edit related data, you can apply it to view the details of related records – for example directly accessing a sales order from a line in the invoice inquiry (*Accounts receivable> Inquiries and reports> Invoices> Invoice journal*).

2.1.4.8 Product Information Dialog

In some forms like the sales order or the purchase order form, selecting the option *View details* or clicking the link in the item number field does not show the item form (released product form), but the product information dialog. This dialog displays the core data of the item. In many cases, these data are sufficient and you don't need to access the details in the released product form. But if you need, click the link in the field *Item number* of the dialog to access to released product detail form.

2.1.4.9   Segmented Entry Control

A special kind of lookup applies to ledger account fields, for example in the lines of financial journals. Since the ledger account is one field with multiple segments (the main account and applicable financial dimensions), a specific control for the lookup and data entry applies – the segmented entry control (see section 9.3.2).

2.1.4.10 Message Bar and Message Center

If there is an issue with the operation you are executing in Dynamics AX (e.g. if you try to delete a record which has got related transactions), an error message immediately displays in the message bar below the action pane of the form.

If an asynchronous operation (e.g. document posting, or validation, or processing a batch job) generates an error or warning, the message is sent to the message center. The button ■ (*Show messages*) in the navigation bar then indicates the number of unread notifications. Clicking this button shows all recent messages, and for messages with extensive details (e.g. error messages when posting a document) you can click the link *Message details* to view more information (see Figure 2-13).

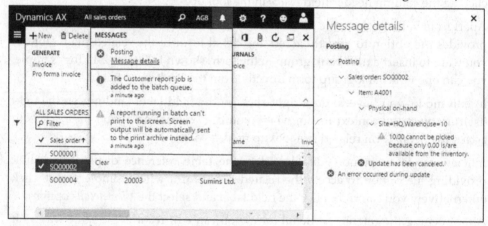

Figure 2-13:   Viewing notifications in the message center

2.1.4.11 New in Dynamics 'AX 7'

The browser-based user interface has required changes in the form layout. There are new shortcuts, sliders replace most checkboxes, the value lookup opens automatically in lookup fields, and the message center replaces the Infolog.

2.1.5   Filtering and Sorting

In order to work efficiently in tables that contain numerous records, it is crucial to find the records in demand quickly. Dynamics AX includes features for filtering and sorting in list pages and in detail forms for this purpose.

2.1.5.1 Quick Filter

In list pages, the quick filter is the easiest way to filter records. When entering characters in the quick filter field, a drop dialog automatically displays where you can select on which column you want to apply the filter.

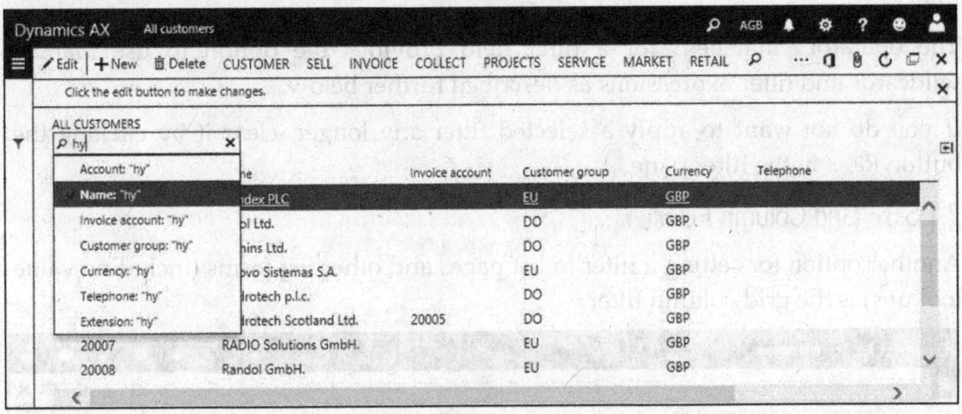

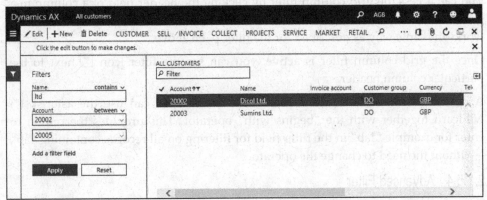

Figure 2-14: Quick filter showing the drop dialog for the filter column

After pressing the *Enter* key or clicking the search button ⌕ on the left-hand side of the quick filter field, the filter applies and the page only shows records which begin with the characters entered in the filter field.

Figure 2-14 shows an example for entering a filter in the quick filter. The filter for customers with a name beginning with the characters "hy" is not yet executed.

2.1.5.2 Filter Pane

The filter pane, which is not only available in list pages but also in detail forms, provides the option to use multiple filter criteria in parallel.

Figure 2-15: Filter pane in a list page

In order to show the filter pane in a form, click the filter button ▼ on the left-hand side or press the shortcut key *Ctrl+F3*. Then enter the required characters for filtering in the appropriate filter field of the filter pane. In the operator selection on the right side above the filter field, you can choose whether to apply these characters with a "begins with", "contains", "is one of", or other operator. If you want to filter on additional or other fields, click the link *Add a filter field* in the filter pane and select the appropriate field. Clicking the button *Apply* finally applies the filter.

The operator "matches" for a filter field provides the option to use manual wildcards and filter expressions as described further below.

If you do not want to apply a selected filter any longer, clear it by clicking the button *Reset* in the filter pane.

2.1.5.3 Grid Column Filter

Another option for setting a filter in list pages and other list forms (including value lookups) is the grid column filter.

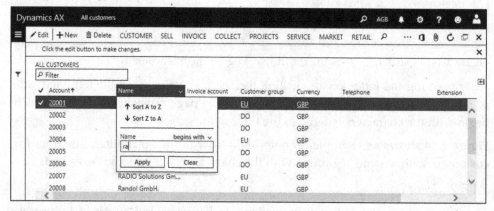

Figure 2-16:   Entering a grid column filter in a list page

You can access the grid column filter by clicking the header field of a column in a grid. In the drop dialog, you can enter the filter in the filter field. The operator works the same way as described for the filter pane above.

Once the grid column filter is active, you can see the filter icon ▼ next to the particular column header.

A special feature in the grid column filter is that you can use the asterisk (*) wildcard together with the "begins with" operator. This provides the option to enter for example "*ab" in the filter field for filtering on all records containing "ab" – without the need to change the operator.

2.1.5.4 Advanced Filter

If you have to enter complex filter criteria, you can access the advanced filter in list pages and in detail forms by pressing the shortcut key *Ctrl+Shift+F3* or by clicking the button *OPTIONS/Page options/Advanced Filter/Sort* in the action pane.

The advanced filter opens in a separate dialog on the right. Like the filter pane, the advanced filter provides the option to set a filter on fields which do not show in the list page or detail form.

If you need to enter a criterion on a field which is not shown in the advanced filter dialog, insert a record in the filter dialog by pushing the shortcut *Alt+N* or clicking the button *Add*. In the new filter line, enter the criterion in the columns *Table*, *Derived table*, *Field* and *Criteria*. The fields *Table* and *Derived table* of a new line by default contain the base table of the filtered page. In case of simple criteria, you don't have to change it.

The lookup button ⊡ in the column *Field* opens a value lookup, where you can select the table field. In the column *Criteria* next to the column *Field*, enter the filter criterion. If the field selected in the filter line is a lookup field, you can open a value lookup.

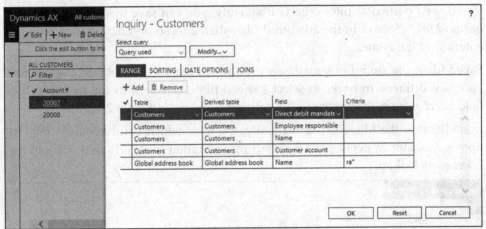

Figure 2-17:   Entering filter criteria in the advanced filter dialog

Once you have finished entering the filter criteria, close the advanced filter dialog by clicking the button *OK*. The filter then applies and the page only shows matching records.

2.1.5.5 Filter Expressions

When entering characters in the quick filter field of a list page, Dynamics AX shows records beginning with these characters.

All other filter options support further filter criteria in order to provide more precise filtering definitions. The table below shows an overview of the most important filter expressions:

Table 2-1:   Important filter expressions

Meaning	Sign	Example	Explanation
Equal	=	EU	Field content to match "EU"
Not equal	!	!GB	Field content not to match "GB"
Interval	..	1..2	Field content from "1" to "2" (incl.)
Greater	>	>1	Field content more than "1"
Less	<	<2	Field content less than "2"
Connection	,	1,2	Field content to match "1" OR "2"; Connects "Not equal" (e.g. "!1,!2") criteria with AND
Wildcard	*	*E*	Field content containing "E"
	?	?B*	First character unknown, followed by a "B", other characters unknown

2.1.5.6 Saving a Filter

If you need particular filter criteria frequently, you can save them by clicking the button *Modify/Save as* in the advanced filter dialog. A second dialog then requires entering a filter name.

Saved filters are stored in your *Usage data*, which means that nobody else can use your saved filters. In order to select a saved filter, choose it in the lookup of the field *Select query* in the advanced filter dialog as shown in Figure 2-18.

In addition to the filters saved manually, the filter which you have used the last time is available in every page by selecting the option *Previously used query* in the *Select query* lookup.

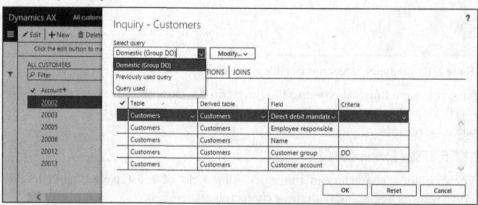

Figure 2-18:   Selecting a saved filter in the advanced filter dialog

2.1.5.7 Sorting

In addition to the filtering options, the grid column filter in list pages – accessible by clicking the appropriate column header – provides sorting options. If you open a detail form after sorting the list page, the detail form will use the sorting selected in the list page.

Alternatively, you can specify sorting criteria in the advanced filter dialog. The advanced filter dialog contains the tab *Sorting* for this purpose, where you can enter applicable sorting criteria with table name and field name in one or more lines (similar to a filter criterion).

2.1.5.8 Distinguish Value Lookup

When using a filter, you should not confuse it with the value lookup shown in section 2.1.4. Whereas the value lookup supports entering a value into a field, the filter features described here are used to select records from the table displayed in the grid.

2.1.5.9 New in Dynamics 'AX 7'

The quick filter, the new filter pane, and the grid column filter in this release replace the filter by grid and the filter by selection in Dynamics AX 2012.

2.1.6 Help System

If you need help on functional questions, you can access the Microsoft Dynamics AX Help system available throughout the whole application. In the help system, there are two areas of help content:

> **Wiki articles** – Links to public Microsoft help text and videos
> **Task guides** – From the Microsoft Dynamics Lifecycle Services (LCS)

Whereas task guides give a description on how to use Dynamics AX in business processes, the wiki articles explain standard features and functionality.

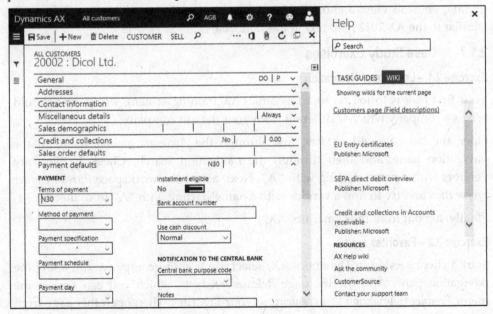

Figure 2-19: Dynamics AX help referring to the customer form

Basic parameters for the help system are specified in the system parameters (*System administration> Setup> System parameters*, tab *Help*).

2.1.6.1 Accessing Help

In order to access help, click the button ▣ (*Help*) in the navigation bar. The help pane then displays task guides and wikis referring to the particular form (see Figure 2-19). After switching to the tab *Wiki*, you can access the help text by clicking the link to the particular Wiki article which opens in a new browser tab.

The search field at the top of the help pane provides options which are similar to the features of search engines in the Internet. Abstracts in the search results help to recognize relevant text easily.

In order to close the help pane, press the *Esc* key or click the button ☒ (*Close*) on the top right of the help pane.

2.1.6.2 Custom Help with Task Guides

Using the task recorder (see section 10.5.3) you can create recordings based on the business processes in your company. After saving a recording to a Microsoft Dynamics Lifecycle Services (LCS) Business Process Library, it will be available on the *Task guides* tab of the help pane.

2.1.6.3 New in Dynamics 'AX 7'

The architecture of the help system has completely changed, containing links to Wikis and task guides instead of the help server. With the Dynamics AX May 2016 update, you can view a short field help if pointing the mouse over a field label (similar to the AX 2012 help text in the status bar).

2.1.7 Case Study Exercises

Exercise 2.1 – Logon and Navigation

Your first task is to log on to a Dynamics AX training system, where you should access a company which is different from your default company.

Open the list page *All vendors*, first through the *Accounts payable* menu in the navigation pane, and then through the navigation search. Check if there are vendors with a name starting with "A". Next, access the workspace *Purchase order preparation* and try to find a vendor with a name starting with "A" from there.

Finally, log out from the Dynamics AX.

Exercise 2.2 – Favorites

Start a client session in Dynamics AX, select the training company, and show the navigation pane. Add the list page *Released products*, which you can find in the menu *Product information management*, to your favorites. Then open this page from the favorites.

Exercise 2.3 – Detail Forms

As an example of detail forms in Dynamics AX, access the vendor detail form through the vendor list page (*Accounts payable> Vendors> All vendors*). In this form you want to view the vendor in the third line of the list page. Show an example of a field group and a lookup field with and without main table.

Then show an example of a slider and a checkbox field. What can you tell about fast tabs and FactBoxes? How do you proceed if you want to edit the vendor? Is there an option to edit multiple vendors in this form?

Exercise 2.4 – Inserting Records

Create a new vendor without applying record templates. For the beginning, the only data for the vendor are the name "##-Exercise 2.4 Inc." (## = your user ID) and any vendor group.

Notes: If the number sequence for vendor accounts is set to "Manual", you have to enter the vendor number manually. If the *Accounts payable parameters* require entering a sales tax group or a tax-exempt number (VAT registration number), access the tab *Invoice and delivery* and enter the required information there.

Exercise 2.5 – Lookup Fields

You want to update the vendor of exercise 2.4. Searching a *Buyer group* in the lookup of the appropriate field on the tab *Miscellaneous details* of the vendor form, you notice that the required group is not available. Create a new buyer group ##-P (## = your user ID) using the *View details* option. Then select the new group in your vendor record.

Exercise 2.6 – Filtering

In order to get some exercise with filtering, enter a few filters in the vendor list page as given below. Use the quick filter and the grid column filter for the first and the second filtering task. For the other filtering tasks, use the filter pane and the advanced filter.

Use following criteria one after the other and clear the filter after each task:

➢ All vendors with a name starting with "T"
➢ All vendors assigned to the vendor group selected in exercise 2.4
➢ All vendors with a name containing "in"
➢ Vendors with a number from US-101 to US-103 or higher than US-108
  (use a similar filter if these vendor accounts do not exist)
➢ Vendors with a number ending with "1" and a name containing "of"
➢ Vendors with an "e" on the second character of the name
➢ Vendors with a name not starting with "C"

Once you have finished the filtering tasks given above, open the advanced filter dialog and select vendors, who do not have *Terms of payment* "Net 30 days".

2.2   Printing and Reporting

Depending on your requirements, there are several options for viewing and analyzing data. Apart from printing Dynamics AX standard reports and using the Microsoft Office integration, you can apply Business Intelligence tools (including Microsoft Power BI) and the Management Reporter (for financial reports).

2.2.1   Printing of Documents

In Dynamics AX, there are following ways to print documents:

➢ **Browser page printing** – Printing any list page or form as a web page using the printing page features of your browser
➢ **Standard report preview download** – Printing a report to the screen (print preview) and exporting a PDF or Word file from there
➢ **Standard report direct printing** – Directly sending a standard report to a local or network printer

The option of printing Dynamics AX pages from your browser, which works like printing any other web page, does not require any print setting in Dynamics AX.

Standard reports are formatted documents based on Microsoft SQL Server Reporting Services (SSRS). When printing a standard report, you can either download a file from the print preview, or send the document directly to a local or network printer. If you want to send documents directly to a printer, you have to configure the Document Reporting Services.

Note: When printing a list page or form, there may be different results depending on the selected browser (Internet Explorer, Google, Chrome, or other).

2.2.1.1   Document Reporting Services Setup

Document Reporting Services are hosted in Microsoft Azure. If you want to connect your printers to the Azure services, you have to install the _Document Routing Agent_ on one or more client computers in your network.

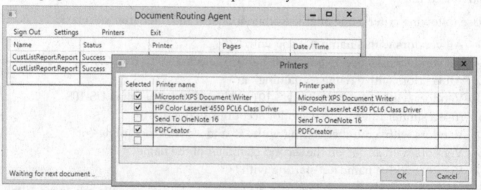

Figure 2-20:   Selecting printers in the Document Routing Agent

In order to install the *Document Routing Agent*, open the form *Organization administration> Setup> Network printers* and click the button *OPTIONS/Application/ Download document routing agent installer*. After installing the application, open the *Document Routing Agent* on your client desktop and click the *Settings* button in the toolbar. Enter the *Dynamics AX URL* (the same URL which you use to access Dynamics AX in the browser) and the Azure AD Tenant (Domain name of the Azure Active Directory / Microsoft Office 365 account). Then click the button *OK* and the button *Sign In*. Finally click the button *Printers* and put a checkmark in front of the printers which you want to use in Dynamics AX.

In the Dynamics AX network printer form (*Organization administration> Setup> Network printers*), you can now view the printers which have been enabled by one or more *Document Routing Agents*. Once the form is in edit mode, select the option "Yes" in the column *Active* for all printers to be used in the current company.

2.2.1.2   Printing Standard Reports

In each Dynamics AX module, there are standard reports in the folder *Inquiries and reports*. In addition, some list pages and detail forms also provide the option to run a standard report by clicking the appropriate button – e.g. a customer account statement by clicking the button *COLLECT/Customer balances/Statements* in the customer list page (*Accounts receivable> Customers> All customers*).

In order to explain how to print a report in Dynamics AX, the description below shows the example of printing a standard report from the menu. After selecting the menu item, Dynamics AX shows the report dialog where you can enter filter criteria and print destinations. Figure 2-21 for example shows the report dialog of the customer list (*Accounts receivable> Inquiries and reports> Customers> Customer report*) after a filter on the group "DO" has been entered.

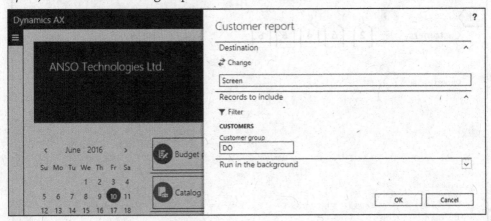

Figure 2-21:   Report dialog for the customer list

Filter criteria are not directly entered in the report dialog, but in a filter dialog which you can access by clicking the button *Filter* on the tab *Records to include* of the report dialog. The filter dialog for reports works similar to the advanced filter in list pages and detail forms. Apart from entering filter criteria on the tab *Range*, you can enter sorting criteria on the tab *Sorting*. After closing the filter dialog, the selected filter shows in the report dialog.

The button *Change* on the tab *Destination* of the report dialog opens the print destination settings, where you can select the destination for the printout. Table 2-2 below shows the available options for the print destination.

Table 2-2: Print destinations for reports

Destination	Explanation
Print archive	Saves the report selection to the print archive
Screen	Shows a report preview on the screen
Printer	Prints the report to the selected printer (available printers are specified in the network printer form as described above)
File	Saves the report content to a CSV, Excel, HTML, XML, or PDF file
E-mail	Saves the report content to a file and sends it to an e-mail recipient (the recipient has to be entered manually)

Once you have finished entering the print destination and the filter criteria in the report dialog, print the report by clicking the button *OK* in the report dialog. The settings used when printing the report are automatically stored in the user options. They show by default when printing the selected report again. You can change the filter criteria and the print destination as required then.

2.2.1.3 Print Preview

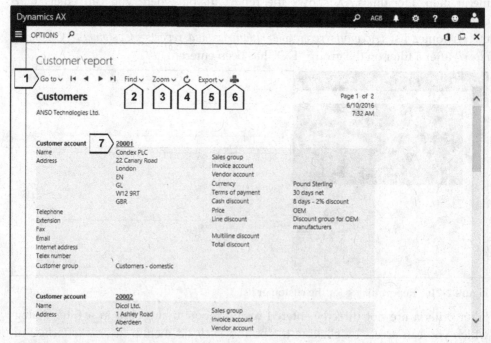

Figure 2-22: Print preview options

If you select the screen as print destination, Dynamics AX shows a print preview on the screen. The preview includes following options (see Figure 2-22):

> **Scroll** [1] between pages by entering the page number (button *Go to*) or clicking the button for the first page ⏮, previous page ◀, next page ▶, or last page ⏭
> **Find** [2] text in the report
> **Zoom** [3] in and out
> **Refresh** [4] the preview in order to retrieve current data
> **Export** [5] the preview to different file formats including XML, CSV, PDF, HTML, TIFF, Excel or Word
> **Print** [6] the preview
> **Link** [7] which provides access to the detail form for selected fields

2.2.1.4 Print Archive

The print archive allows saving a report within Dynamics AX. You can save to the archive either by selecting the print archive as print destination in the report dialog or – if choosing a different print destination – by setting the slider *Save in print archive* to "Yes".

When saving to the archive, the report selection is stored in the print archive which makes it possible to reprint the report later. If you want to access your print archive, open the form *Common> Inquiries> Print archive*. In order to access the print archives of all users, open the form *Organization administration> Inquiries and reports> Print archive*.

2.2.1.5 Post and Print

When posting an external document (e.g. an invoice or a packing slip), you also want to print the document in most cases. Posting dialogs therefore contain a parameter for printing the related document – e.g. the slider *Print invoice* when posting a sales invoice. The buttons *Select* (filter selection) and *Printer setup* (printer selection) in posting dialogs provide the option to specify filter criteria and print destinations as described for standard reports above.

In case the printout of a posted document is required at a later date (e.g. if you have missed to set the slider *Print* to "Yes" when posting), you can still print it in the inquiry of the particular posted document. If you want to (re-)print a sales invoice for example, open the sales invoice journal (*Accounts receivable> Inquiries and reports> Invoices> Invoice journal*) and click the button *INVOICE/Document/ View/Original preview* in the action pane after selecting the invoice.

2.2.1.6 Batch Processing

If you do not need to view the results of a particular report or a periodic activity immediately, you can switch to the tab *Run in the background* in the report dialog and submit the report to a batch process. After setting the slider *Batch processing* to

"Yes" and – if required – selecting a *Batch group*, specify the starting time and repetitions for the batch job by clicking the button *Recurrence*.

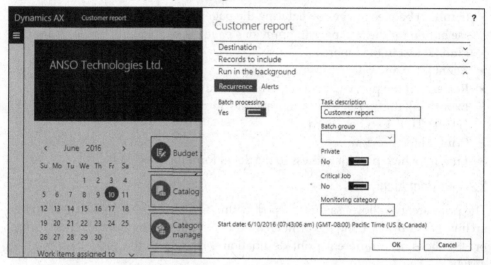

Figure 2-23:   Batch processing selection in a report dialog

As a prerequisite for batch processing, at least one batch server has to be set up and started. You can set up the batch server in the menu item *System administration> Setup> Server configuration*. If you want to categorize batch jobs, you can use batch groups (*System administration> Setup> Batch group*).

Batch processing is a background process on the batch server, except for client and private tasks which require running the periodic activity *Organization administration> Periodic> Batch processing* on a client.

If you want to check and to edit the status of batch jobs, open the form *System administration> Inquiries> Batch jobs*.

2.2.1.7 New in Dynamics 'AX 7'

As a result of the browser-based interface, the regular printing features of the browser replace the AX 2012 auto-report features for printing information in Dynamics AX pages and forms. In addition, the cloud-based architecture requires the Document Routing Agent for connecting printers to the Azure services.

2.2.2   Microsoft Office Integration

The Microsoft Office integration in Dynamics AX provides an easy way for data interaction with Microsoft Office. This data interaction includes:

➢ **Static export** – Export data from Dynamics AX to Microsoft Excel
➢ **Opening and editing** – Update data in Dynamics AX from Microsoft Office

By use of document templates, you can easily create your own Excel workbooks for editing Dynamics AX data in Excel.

2.2.2.1 Static Export to Excel

The static export to Excel, which provides the option to retrieve data from Dynamics AX for viewing them in an Excel workbook, is available in most list pages and detail forms.

As a prerequisite for the static export, open the respective form in Dynamics AX and select lines for the export by marking the appropriate grid check boxes leftmost in the grid. Instead of using the grid check boxes, you can also select lines by clicking them directly in the grid while holding the *Ctrl* key. The *Shift* key selects multiple consecutive lines, and the grid check box in the header line selects all lines of the grid.

The button *Open in Microsoft Office* 🔲 / *Export to Excel* in the action pane of list pages then provides the option to export the list to Microsoft Excel. Alternatively, you can right-click in the grid of a list page to open the context menu where you can choose the option *Export all rows* or *Export marked rows*.

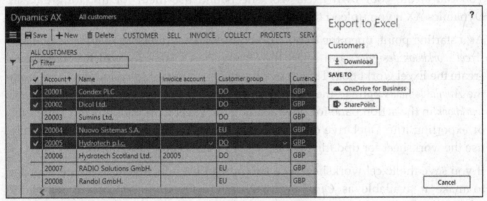

Figure 2-24:   Choosing the export location when exporting to Excel

In the export dialog (see Figure 2-24) you can subsequently select whether you want to download the Excel workbook content to your local computer or if you want to export to OneDrive or SharePoint using Excel Online.

2.2.2.2 Opening Data in Excel

Unlike the static export, which just retrieves data from Dynamics AX to Excel, the option *Open in Microsoft Office* supports updating and inserting data from Excel to Dynamics AX. It is available in most list pages and detail forms. In order to start editing data in Excel, open the respective form in Dynamics AX, click the button 🔲 (*Open in Microsoft Office*) in the action pane and select the appropriate option below the heading *Open in Excel*. In some forms, for example in the general journals (*General ledger> Journal entries> General journals*), there is a dedicated button in the action pane for opening in Excel.

In the *Open in Excel* dialog you can subsequently select if you want to download the Excel workbook for working on your local computer or if you want to open it in OneDrive or SharePoint using Excel Online.

Microsoft Excel then displays the data connector in the task pane, where you have to sign in with your Azure Active Directory account before retrieving data. In Excel you can subsequently edit and insert data (button *New*), also working temporarily offline in Excel if required.

Clicking the button *Refresh* in the Excel worksheet retrieves current data from Dynamics AX, including new lines for new records. In order to transfer data from Excel to Dynamics AX, click the button *Publish*. In case incorrect data are going to be published, an error message in the Excel task pane shows the issue (click the button ▶ at the bottom of the pane to see the details) and prevents the update.

2.2.2.3 Using Document Templates

You can create your own Excel worksheets and use them for updating data in Dynamics AX if you upload them as document templates.

As a starting point, open the Excel workbook designer (*Common> Office integration> Excel workbook designer*) and select the Dynamics AX table for which you want to create the Excel workbook. Then move the fields you want to include in Excel from the *Available fields* pane to the *Selected fields*. In the next step, click the button *Create workbook* in the action pane for downloading the Excel workbook to your computer or exporting it to OneDrive or SharePoint. After signing in, you can immediately use the worksheet for updating Dynamics AX data as described above.

If you save the Excel worksheet, you can upload it as document template in order to make it available as *Open in Excel* option. Open the document templates (*Common> Office integration> Document templates*) for this purpose, click the button *New* in the action pane and upload the Excel file which you have saved in the previous step. The new template then shows as additional option in the button 🔲 (*Open in Microsoft Office*) of the related Dynamics AX form.

2.2.2.4 New in Dynamics 'AX 7'

As a result of the cloud-based architecture, the AX 2012 Copy/Paste functionality is not available any more. The Microsoft Office integration has completely changed, now providing additional options.

2.2.3   Case Study Exercise

Exercise 2.7 – Printing

Print a vendor list (*Accounts payable> Inquiries and reports> Vendor reports> Vendors*), selecting a print preview as print destination. Then print the vendor list again, filtering on any vendor group of your choice and choosing a PDF-file as print destination.

2.3 Advanced Options

Before you can log on to Microsoft Dynamics AX, a Dynamics AX user with appropriate permissions has to be set up for you. In some areas of the application, a worker record (see section 10.2.2) assigned to your user is required additionally.

2.3.1 User Options and Personalization

Options for personally adjusting the Dynamics AX user interface are available in the user options. In addition, personalization provides enhanced features for individually configuring every single form.

2.3.1.1 User Options

The user options are a form controlling core personal settings in Dynamics AX. You can access your user options by clicking the button ⚙/*Options* in the navigation bar (or accessing the menu item *Common> Setup> User options*) if you have got appropriate permissions. System administrators can access your user options from the user management (*System administration> Users> Users*, button *User options*).

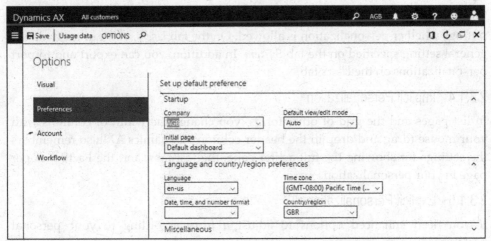

Figure 2-25: Managing preferences in the user options form

Main settings in the user option form as shown in Figure 2-25 include following preferences for your workspace:

> **Language** – Language of the user interface
> **Country/region** – Default value for country/region when entering an address
> **Company** – Default-company when logging on
> **Default view/edit mode** – Start all detail forms in view mode or in edit mode
> **Document handling** – See section 10.5.1
> **Sign out after** (tab **Account**) – Minutes of inactivity for closing your session
> **Visual** tab – Color theme and element size
> **Workflow** tab – Settings for workflow management (see section 10.4)

2.3.1.2   Usage Data

The button *Usage data* in the action pane of the user options opens a form, which shows detailed settings of a user. These settings include filter settings, form settings, and record templates (user templates), which have been stored automatically or manually.

In the usage data, you can switch from the tab *General* to the other tabs if you want to view the usage data in a particular area. Clicking the button *Data* after selecting a usage data record shows the record details. It is not possible to modify usage data, but you can delete usage data records by clicking the button *Delete* or pressing the shortcut key *Alt+F9*. Clicking the button *Reset* on the tab *General* deletes all your usage data.

2.3.1.3   Setup for Personalization

Apart from modifications in the development environment, which apply to all users, changes of the user interface in list pages and forms are also possible at personal level. For this purpose, each user with appropriate permissions in Dynamics AX can adjust forms according to his personal requirements.

The personalization setup (*System administration> Setup> Personalization*) contains settings whether personalization is allowed. On the tab *Users*, you can override the general setting specified on the tab *System*. In addition, you can export and import personalizations on the *Users* tab.

2.3.1.4   Implicit Personalization

In list pages and the grid of other forms, you change the width of columns with your mouse (drag and drop in the header column). Dynamics AX also remembers the settings for showing the full action pane, the fast tabs, and the FactBoxes per page in your personalization.

2.3.1.5   Explicit Personalization

If you need enhanced options to adjust a form according to your personal preferences, you can use the element personalization window and the personalization toolbar. These options are available in every list page, detail form, workspace, and dashboard.

In order to access the element personalization window, right-click an element (e.g. a field shown in a list page) and choose the option *Personalize* in the context menu. The personalization window then provides the option to override several standard settings – for example by entering a personal field label, hiding the element, or preventing to edit the field content.

The personalization toolbar, which you can access by clicking the link *Personalize this form* in the element personalization window or by clicking the button *OPTIONS/Personalize/Personalize this form* in the action pane, provides additional options.

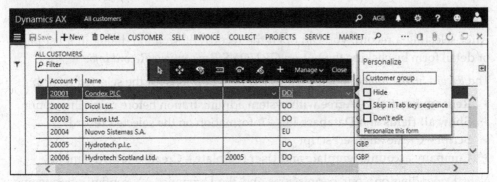

Figure 2-26: Element personalization window and personalization toolbar in a list page

In the personalization toolbar, you can personalize the form by clicking the appropriate button, and then selecting the field or other element to which you want to apply the selected action. Options in the personalization toolbar include *Select* ![icon] (shows the element personalization window as described above), *Move* ![icon] (change the location of an element), *Hide* ![icon], *Summary* ![icon] (in detail forms, shows the field as summary field on the fast tab), *Skip* ![icon] (skip in the tab sequence), *Edit* ![icon] (prevents editing), and *Add* ![icon] (add a table field to display in the form). If you add a field, you have to select the page area where you want to add the field before a dialog shows where you can select one or multiple table fields.

Settings in the personalization apply immediately. The button *Manage* in the personalization toolbar provides the option to reset the form to the standard layout (button *Manage/Clear*) and to export or import the personalization.

Apart from changing the layout of a form, personalization includes the option to add a list page to a workspace by clicking the button *OPTIONS/Personalize/Add to workspace* in the action pane. After selecting the appropriate *Workspace* and the *Presentation* (tile or list) you have to click the button *Configure* and to select some options in a subsequent dialog. When you are finished, the list page shows as additional list or tile in the selected – now personalized – workspace.

In the workspace, the element personalization window for tiles includes the additional option to pin a tile to the dashboard. If you select this option, the dashboard shows the selected form which means that you can directly access it from the dashboard.

2.3.1.6 New in Dynamics 'AX 7'

The browser-based user interface has required a completely new personalization functionality. The new personalization only stores changes to the standard, making it possible to keep personalization even if there are modifications or AX updates.

2.3.2 Record Information and Templates

The record information dialog in Dynamics AX provides access to data and to general features not directly shown in a particular list page or detail form.

2.3.2.1   Options in the Record Information Dialog

After selecting a record, you can open the record information dialog in a list page or detail form by clicking the button *OPTIONS/Page options/Record info*.

The *Record information* dialog provides following options for the selected record:

➢ **Rename key field** – Agree with system administration before using this option
➢ **Show all fields** and **Database log** – Information on the selected record
➢ **Script** – Create an insert script
➢ **Company accounts template** and **User template** – Create a record template

<u>Note</u>: Depending on your permissions and the Dynamics AX configuration, some options might not be available.

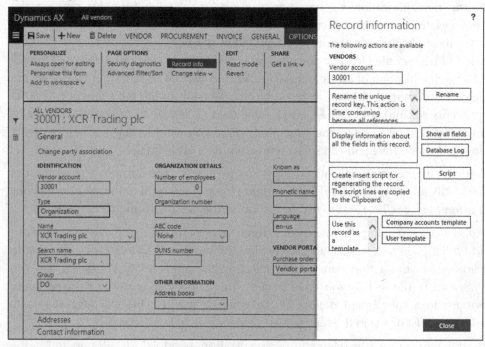

Figure 2-27:   The record information dialog in the vendor detail form

2.3.2.2   Renaming

You can rename the key field of a record by clicking the button *Rename* in the record information dialog. Renaming then opens a second dialog for entering the new field content.

Processing a request for renaming may be a time-consuming activity, because Dynamics AX has to update all references. If you want to modify a vendor number for example, the update does not only include the vendor table itself, but also the vendor transactions, the purchase orders, and all other tables which contain the vendor number. You have to take into account, that references are only updated within Dynamics AX. Other applications and external partners like customers or vendors have to receive the appropriate information separately.

Renaming therefore is an exceptional activity, usually with restricted access secured by appropriate permission settings.

2.3.2.3 Show All Fields and Database Log

The button *Show all fields* in the record information dialog displays the content of all fields of the selected record. Choose this option if you want to know the content of fields not shown in a particular list page or detail form.

The button *Database log* in the record information dialog shows a log file of all changes to the selected record. As a prerequisite, logging for the particular table has to be enabled in the form *System administration> Setup> Database log setup* or in the development environment.

2.3.2.4 Record Templates

Record templates help creating new records by copying the content of fields from a template created before. As an example, it might be useful to set up a' different template in the vendor table for domestic vendors and for foreign vendors, which initialize the record with correct posting groups when creating a new vendor.

When working with record templates, you have to distinguish between two types of templates:

> **User templates** – Only available to the current user
> **Company accounts templates** – Available to all users

A user template is only available to the user who has created it. You can create a user template by clicking the button *User template* in the record information dialog. A second dialog then opens where you enter the name and a short description of the template. The template then is a copy of the record which you have selected when opening the record information dialog.

User templates are stored in your usage data, where it is not possible to modify them later. If a user template is not required any more, you can delete it in the usage data (button ⚙ /*Options* in the navigation bar> button *Usage data*> tab *Record templates*). Alternatively, you can delete a user template by pressing the shortcut key *Alt+F9* in the template selection dialog as shown in Figure 2-28.

Unlike user templates, company accounts templates are available to all users. You can create a company accounts template by clicking the button *Company accounts template* in the record information dialog.

If you want to access a company accounts template later, open the form *Common> Setup> Record templates*. On the tab *Overview* of the record templates form, select the table to which the template belongs. Then switch to the tab *Templates* where you can view and delete the system template.

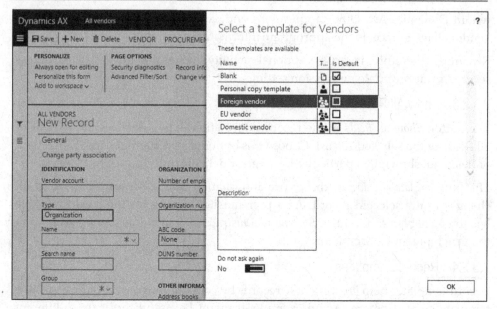

Figure 2-28:   Selecting a template in the template dialog

If there are templates for a table, they display in a template selection dialog when inserting a new record in the particular table. Figure 2-28 for example shows the dialog displayed when creating a new vendor in the vendor detail form (*Accounts payable> Vendors> All vendors*) once there is a vendor template.

In the template dialog, select the appropriate template and click the button *OK*. Company account templates show the icon ▓ whereas user templates show the icon ▣. In the far right column, you can optionally select one line to make it the default template. If you set the slider *Do not ask again* at the bottom of the template dialog to "Yes", Dynamics AX applies the default template without showing the dialog when inserting further records. If you want to show the template dialog when creating new records again, click the button *Show template selection* which then displays in the record information dialog.

2.3.3   Case Study Exercises

Exercise 2.8 – User Options

You want to access your user options in order to check your user name and e-mail address. In the visual options, select the high-contrast color theme and a small element size. The training company should be the *Start company accounts* when logging in to Dynamics AX the next time.

Exercise 2.9 – Record Templates

Create a new user template based on the vendor which you have entered in exercise 2.4. In order to learn how to use templates, insert a new vendor applying this template afterwards.

2.4   Global Address Book

Dynamics AX contains a common table for all business partners of your enterprise
– internal and external relationships, companies and persons. This common table is
the global address book, using the label "parties" for the business partners. Parties
in the global address book are shared across companies and include customers,
sales leads, vendors, organization units, employees, and other contacts.

2.4.1   Party and Address

When creating a new customer, vendor, or any other kind of party, Dynamics AX
inserts a record in the global address book. A party may contain one or more
(postal) addresses and contact information data. A party therefore is not the same
as an address – a party is an organization or person characterized by its name.

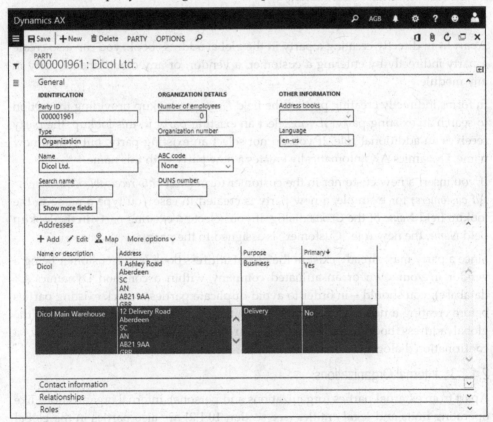

Figure 2-29:   Managing a party with multiple addresses in the party detail form

Depending on permission settings, you can access all parties in the global address
book (*Common> Common> Global address book*). The party detail form accessed from
the global address book shows details like name, addresses, and contact data.

2.4.1.1 Creating Parties in the Global Address Book

You can insert a new party directly in the global address book by clicking the button *New* in the action pane. In the new party record, the *Party ID* usually derives from the appropriate number sequence. The lookup field *Type*, which contains the alternative options "Organization" and "Person", controls the fields which display in the party form (e.g. showing the field *First name* only for persons).

After entering the party name in the field *Name* (for an organization) or in the fields *First name* and *Last name* (for a person), you can enter additional data. These data include the postal address on the tab *Addresses* and contact data like e-mail addresses and phone numbers on the tab *Contact information*. Section 3.2.1 shows – on the example of the vendor management – in more detail how to manage postal addresses and contact information.

2.4.1.2 Indirectly Creating Parties

Apart from directly creating a party in the global address book, you can also create a party indirectly by entering a customer, a vendor, or any other kind of party in any module.

In forms indirectly creating parties, the field *Name* is a lookup providing the option to search an existing party. If you select an existing party in this lookup, the party receives an additional role. If you do not select an existing party, but type a new name, Dynamics AX automatically creates a new party with this name.

If you insert a new customer in the customer form (*Accounts receivable> Customers> All customers*) for example, a new party is created in case you type a name in the lookup field *Name* of the *Create* dialog. If you select an existing party in the lookup field *Name*, the new role "Customer" is assigned to the party.

Since a party may already exist in the global address book (e.g. a customer being a vendor in your own or an affiliated company within a common Dynamics AX database), you should – in order to avoid duplicate parties – check existing parties before creating a new party record. In case the duplicate check is activated in the global address book parameters and you enter a duplicate party anyhow, a confirmation dialog shows the existing record before saving the new party.

2.4.1.3 Internal Organizations

Apart from external parties (organizations and persons), internal organizations like operating units and legal entities (see section 10.1.2) are also parties in the global address book. You can recognize internal organizations by the *Type* (e.g. "Legal entities"). Party types reserved for internal organizations are not available when manually inserting a party directly in the global address book.

2.4.2   Address Book

An address book is a collection of party records. You can set up one or more address books in the form *Organization administration> Global address book> Address books*, e.g. one for sales and one for purchasing.

The global address book is the collection of all parties in all companies of a Dynamics AX system (see Figure 2-30).

In order to link a party to one or more address books, put a checkmark in front of the address books which display in the lookup of the field *Address books* on the tab *General* of the party detail form.

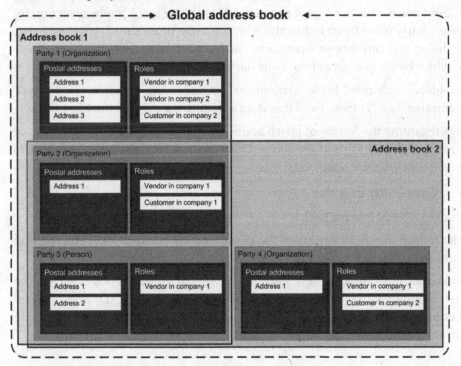

Figure 2-30:   Conceptual structure of the global address book

You can use address books for filtering addresses – e.g. using the filter field *Address books* in the global address book list page – and as a basis for security settings in the extensible data security framework.

2.4.2.1   Roles

A role (e.g. "Vendor" or "Customer") describes the relationship between a party and your enterprise. A party can refer to one or more roles in one or more companies. There are two ways of assigning a role to a party:

➤ **Indirectly** – Entering a record in other areas like the customer list page automatically creates a party with the appropriate role.

➤ **Directly** – Clicking an appropriate button in the action pane of the global address book (e.g. *PARTY/New/Customer*) after selecting a party creates a record in the selected area (e.g. customer record) and assigns the related role.

The roles of a party are shown on the tab *Roles* of the party detail form.

2.4.2.2 Address Book Parameters

If the duplicate check is activated in the global address book parameters (*Organization administration> Global address book> Global address book parameters*, slider *Use duplicate check)*, a dialog shows duplicate party records whenever you try to create a party (directly or indirectly) with the name of an already existing party. In the dialog you can choose whether to use the existing party or to create a new party, which by chance has got the same name as the existing party.

Other global address book parameters include the default party type ("Organization" or "Person") and the name sequence for persons (first/last name).

Settings regarding the format of postal addresses and available ZIP/postal codes or cities are specified in the address setup (*Organization administration> Global address book> Addresses> Address setup*).

2.4.3   Case Study Exercise

Exercise 2.10 – Global Address Book

In order to learn the functionality of the global address book, check if you can find the party record of your vendor from exercise 2.4.

The next task is to insert a new party in the global address book. Fields to be entered include the name "##-Exercise 2.10" (## = your user ID) and a postal address in London. The new party becomes a vendor in your company. What do you do in Dynamics AX?

3 Purchase Management

The primary responsibility of purchasing is to provide your company with goods and services from suppliers. Including tasks in previous and subsequent areas, the complete procurement process covers following activities:

➢ Determining material requirements in operations planning
➢ Processing purchase requisitions, requests for quotations, and purchase orders
➢ Posting item receipts and purchase invoices

3.1 Business Processes in Purchasing

Before we start to go into the details, the lines below give an overview of the business processes in purchasing.

3.1.1 Basic Approach

Starting point for procurement are correct master data, in particular the data on vendors and products. When purchasing services or non-inventoried commodities, you can use procurement categories instead of products.

3.1.1.1 Master Data and Transactions in Purchasing

Vendor and product records are master data, only occasionally updated after initially creating the individual records. In the course of the purchasing process, planned and actual purchase orders (transaction data) receive default values from vendor and product records (master data), which you can override in the transaction – for example if agreeing on special payment terms in a purchase order.

Modifying data in a transaction does not update the related master data. If you agree with a particular vendor to change for example the payment terms in general, you have to update the payment terms in the vendor record.

Based on correct master data, the purchasing process – including required predecessor and successor activities – consists of six steps as shown in Figure 3-1.

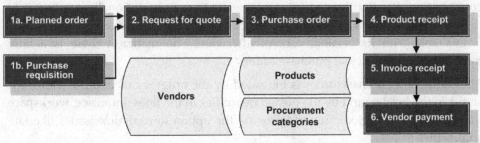

Figure 3-1:   Purchase order processing in Dynamics AX

3.1.1.2 Material Requirements, Purchase Requisition, and Request for Quotation

The identification of material requirements usually is the first step in the purchasing process. Depending on the particular product and the company-specific circumstances, there are two ways for processing material requirements:

> ➢ **Automatically** – Generating planned orders
> ➢ **Manually** – Entering purchase requisitions

The required basis for generating accurate planned orders within operations planning (master planning, see section 6.3) are accurate figures on inventory quantity, sales orders, purchase orders and forecasts on the one hand, and appropriate item coverage settings on the other.

Purchase requisitions – unlike planned orders, which are created automatically by master planning – are manually entered, internal documents asking the purchase department to acquire specific items (like consumables and office supplies). A purchase requisition runs through an approval process workflow before it is released as a purchase order.

Requests for quotation are sent to vendors in order to receive information on prices and delivery times. The purchasing department can enter requests for quotation either manually, or generate them from planned purchase orders or purchase requisitions.

3.1.1.3 Purchase Order

You can create purchase orders either manually or by transferring planned orders, purchase requisitions, or requests for quotation. A purchase order consists of a header, containing fields which are common to the whole order (e.g. vendor data), and one or more lines, containing the required items.

Once you have completed entering the order, you have to start the approval process (in case change management is active). After approval – or without approval if change management does not apply – you can optionally post a purchase inquiry and send it to the vendor for validation purposes.

Before you can continue with order processing, you have to post a purchase order confirmation. Posting the confirmation means to save it, optionally sending it to the vendor electronically or as printed document. The purchase order confirmation is available with its original content afterwards, no matter if there is a later modification on the actual purchase order.

The status of a purchase order is indicated by the order status and the document status in the header, and by the posted quantities in the lines. Inquiries, workspace information, and periodic reports provide the option to recognize issues like late shipments.

3.1.1.4 Product Receipt, Invoice Receipt, and Vendor Payment

Once the goods or services actually arrive, you should record the product receipt in Dynamics AX. Posting the product receipt increases the physical quantity in inventory and reduces the open quantity in the purchase order.

Together with the item delivery, or at a later time, the vendor submits an invoice. When registering the invoice in the vendor invoice form, invoice control features support matching the invoice with the purchase order and the product receipt. If an invoice is not related to a purchase order, you can enter it in the vendor invoice form or in an invoice journal (see section 9.3.3).

Based on posted invoices, you can record payments to vendors either manually or through a payment proposal. Payment proposals include due date and cash discount period calculation. Payment processing is independent from purchase orders and usually a responsibility of the finance department. You can find a description on vendor payments in section 9.3.4 later in this book.

3.1.1.5 Ledger Integration and Voucher Principle

Because of the deep finance integration in Dynamics AX, all inventory and vendor transactions in purchasing are posted to ledger accounts specified in the setup as described in section 9.4.

In order to keep track of the whole business process, Dynamics AX comprehensively applies the voucher principle to transactions: You have to register a transaction in a document (voucher), before you can post it. After posting, it is not possible to modify the document any more. Figure 3-2 shows an overview of the documents in purchase order processing.

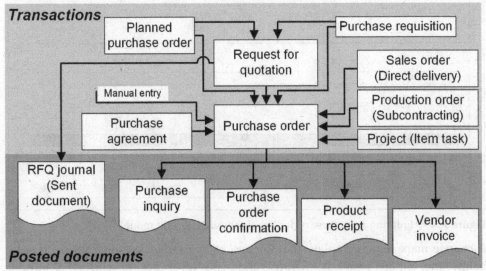

Figure 3-2: Transactions and posted documents in purchasing

3.1.2   At a Glance: Purchase Order Processing

In order to provide an overview of the main steps in purchase order processing, this section shows the basics. In the example, we create an order starting in the *Purchase order preparation* workspace and post all transactions directly in the purchase order form. Of course you can also create the order from the vendor form, or directly in the purchase order list page.

In the *Purchase order preparation* workspace, which you can access from the dashboard or from the *Workspaces* folder of the *Procurement and sourcing* menu, click the button *New purchase order* in the action pane. The *Create purchase order* dialog shows next, where you have to select a vendor in the *Vendor account* field (you can trigger the search there by starting to type the first characters of the vendor name). Clicking the button *OK* in the dialog creates a purchase order header with default data like language or currency from the selected vendor.

The purchase order detail form then opens in lines view. If you are in view mode, switch to the edit mode by clicking the button *Edit* or by pressing the *F2* key. On the tab *Purchase order lines*, you can start to enter an order line with item number, quantity, and price. When selecting the item, Dynamics AX initializes the quantity, the price, and other fields like the site with appropriate default values. If you want to enter a second line, press the *Down Arrow* on the keyboard or click the button *Add line* in the toolbar. Clicking the button *Header* (or *Lines*) below the action pane switches between the lines view (see Figure 3-3) and the header view.

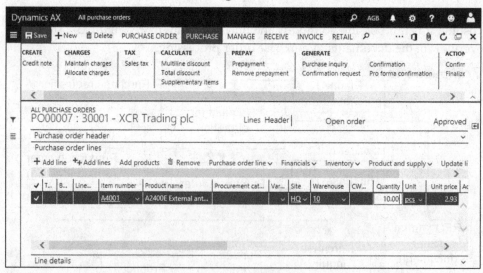

Figure 3-3:   Entering a purchase order line (Lines view, in edit mode)

If change management applies, the *Approval status* (shown on the right-hand side below the action pane) is "Draft" and you have got to click the button *Workflow/Submit* in the action pane after entering all order lines. After approval – or without change management immediately – the *Approval status* is "Approved".

Next, post the purchase order confirmation by clicking the button *PURCHASE/ Generate/Confirmation* (or *PURCHASE/Actions/Confirm*) in the action pane. If you want to print the purchase order, set the sliders *Posting* and *Print purchase order* in the posting dialog to "Yes". The button *Printer setup* in the dialog provides the option to select a printer for the printout (compare section 2.2.1).

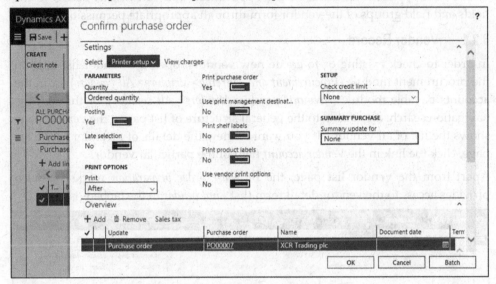

Figure 3-4:   Confirming and printing the purchase order

When receiving the item, post the product receipt by clicking the button *RECEIVE/ Generate/Product receipt* in the action pane of the purchase order form. Posting the product receipt work similar to the purchase order confirmation described above. But unlike purchase order confirmation, the product receipt usually is not printed. If there is no prior item arrival registration, select the option "Ordered quantity" in the lookup field *Quantity* and enter the vendor's packing slip number in the column *Product receipt* on the tab *Overview* of the posting dialog before clicking *OK*. The product receipt increases the physical quantity in inventory and changes the order status to "Received".

If you want to post the invoice receipt directly from the purchase order form, click the button *INVOICE/Generate/Invoice* in the action pane of the order form. Containing an action pane and FactBoxes, the form for vendor invoice posting is different from the other posting dialogs. In order to check the totals there, view the appropriate FactBox on the right of the form or click the button *Totals* in the action pane. After entering the vendor invoice number in the field *Number* (*Invoice identification*), post the invoice by clicking the button *Post*. Invoice posting generates an open vendor transaction to be paid and changes the order status to "Invoiced".

Note: If you want to quit the invoice form without saving, delete the invoice there and do not simply close the form (which would save a pending invoice).

3.2   Vendor Management

Vendor records are required in purchasing and in accounts payable. According to the deep integration of Dynamics AX, there is only one record for each vendor, which then applies to all areas of the application. You can restrict access to the fields and field groups of the vendor form through appropriate permissions.

3.2.1   Vendor Record

In order to check existing or to create new vendors, open the vendor list page in the procurement module (*Procurement and sourcing> Vendors> All vendors*), or in the accounts payable module (*Accounts payable> Vendors> All vendors*), or through the navigation search. According to the general structure of list pages, the vendor page shows the list of all vendors. If you want to view the details of a vendor in the list page, click the link in the *Vendor account* field of the particular vendor.

Apart from the vendor list page, the *Purchase order preparation* workspace also provides access to the vendor detail form (list *Find vendor* in the tabbed list pane).

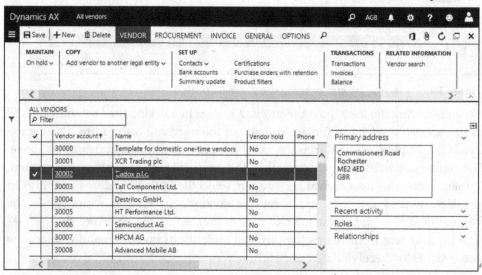

Figure 3-5:   Selecting a vendor in the vendor list page

In the vendor detail form, you can switch to the edit mode by clicking the button *Edit* in the action pane or by pressing the *F2* key. If you are in edit mode in the list page before accessing the detail form, the detail form will open in edit mode.

The vendor detail form contains numerous fields which are used as default values in purchase orders. The following description covers core data in the vendor record, additional information is available in the online help.

3.2.1.1 Creating a Vendor

If you want to create a new vendor, insert a record in the vendor list page or in the detail form by pushing the shortcut key *Alt+N* or by clicking the button *New* in the action pane. If there are templates for vendors in your company (see section 2.3.2), you can populate fields of the new record by choosing a template.

Depending on settings of the related number sequence, a unique vendor number in the field *Vendor account* is assigned automatically or has to be entered manually.

3.2.1.2 Global Address Book Integration

In the vendor detail form, the field *Type* in the field group *Identification* determines if the vendor is a company (organization) or a person. Depending on the type, the *General* tab shows different fields – e.g. *First name* and *Last name* for the type "Person".

Vendors are parties in the global address book. For this reason, the field *Name* is a lookup field providing the option to select an existing party from the global address book when creating a new vendor. If you enter the name of a new vendor manually, a dialog displays in case an existing party has got exactly the same name and the duplicate check is activated in the global address book parameters. This dialog provides the option to link the vendor to an existing party or to create a new party, which by chance has got the same name.

After saving the vendor record, you can access the related party in the global address book through the table reference (*View details*) on the vendor name field.

As an alternative to the vendor form, you can create new vendors in the global address book (*Common> Common> Global address book*, see section 2.4) in order to reduce the risk of duplicate party records. In the global address book, it is easy to check if a new vendor already is a party (e.g. being a vendor in an affiliated company) before creating the new vendor. If the vendor is a party, convert the party to a vendor in your company by clicking the button *PARTY/New/Vendor* after selecting the record. If not, create the party record before converting it to a vendor.

3.2.1.3 General Data

The search name in the vendor record is initialized with the vendor name, but you can modify it. Mandatory fields in the vendor form (apart from the name) are the vendor group in the lookup field *Group* (usually controlling ledger integration, see section 3.2.3), and the currency on the tab *Purchasing demographics* (initialized with the accounting currency).

Further core fields on the tab *General* are the *Language*, specifying the language for printing purchase orders or other documents, and – in case address books are used, especially for access control – the *Address books* linked to the vendor.

The display field *Vendor hold* on the tab *Miscellaneous details* shows whether the vendor is blocked. If you want to change the hold status, click the button

VENDOR/Maintain/On hold in the action pane. If you select the vendor hold status "All", it is not possible to enter or to post any purchase order or other transaction for the vendor. The options "No" and "Never" enable all transactions ("Never" prevents automatic blocking of the vendor after a period of inactivity).

3.2.1.4 Input Tax

Tax settings for the vendor have to be entered on the tab *Invoice and delivery*, where the *Sales tax group* (*VAT group*) determines the tax duty depending on the vendor location. A correct sales tax group is necessary to distinguish between domestic vendors, who charge sales tax or VAT, and foreign vendors, who do not. The setup of sales tax groups and tax calculation is depending on your company and its location. Section 9.2.6 contains more information on the tax setup in Dynamics AX.

If your company is located within the European Union and you need to record the VAT registration number of vendors for tax purposes, enter it in the *Tax exempt number* (*VAT number*) field below the sales tax group. Since it is a lookup field, you have to insert a new tax-exempt number in the main table (*View details* in the context menu, or *Tax> Setup> Sales tax> Tax exempt numbers*) before selecting it in the vendor record.

The *Tax exempt number requirement* and *Mandatory tax group* settings in the accounts payable parameters (*Accounts payable> Setup> Accounts payable parameters*, tab *General*) determine if you have to enter a tax exempt number and/or a sales tax group when creating a vendor.

3.2.1.5 Settings for Delivery and Payment

The field *Delivery terms* on the tab *Invoice and delivery* of the vendor detail form specifies the usual delivery terms of the particular vendor. You can access the setup of required delivery terms including text in foreign languages in the form *Procurement and sourcing> Setup> Distribution> Terms of delivery*.

The tab *Payment* of the vendor detail form contains settings on payment terms and cash discount. More details on these settings are available in section 3.2.2.

3.2.1.6 Postal Address

Address data display on the tab *Addresses* of the vendor detail form. Dynamics AX provides the option to maintain multiple addresses per vendor. Addresses and contact data are stored in the global address book party record which is linked to the particular vendor. For this reason, address and contact data are shared with all other roles of the party (e.g. if the vendor also is a customer or a vendor in another company in Dynamics AX).

If you want to enter an additional postal address of a vendor, click the button *Add* in the toolbar of the tab *Addresses*. In the *New address* dialog, enter the identification (*Name or description*) of the address – for the primary address usually the vendor name. In the primary address of a vendor, make sure the slider *Primary* is (and the slider *Private* is not) set to "Yes".

The *Purpose* in the address dialog determines, for which transactions the current address is used as default value. For a primary address, choose the purpose "Business". If entering a second address, choose an alternative purpose – for example the option "Payment" identifying an alternative payee. One postal address can have multiple purposes at the same time. If no specific address is specified for a particular purpose, the primary address applies.

You can view the available standard address purposes and set up additional purposes in the form *Organization administration> Global address book> Address and contact information purpose*.

Another important setting in a postal address is the *Country/region*, which is the basis for the address format on the one hand and for reports to the authorities – including sales tax and Intrastat reports – on the other.

After selecting the country code, only postal codes of this country show in the lookup of the *ZIP/postal Code* field. Depending on the settings in the address setup (*Organization administration> Global address book> Addresses> Address setup*, tab *Parameters*), postal codes are validated in the ZIP/postal code table when entering an address. If ZIP/postal code validation is activated, you have to insert a new postal code in the ZIP/postal code table before you can enter it in an address. You can access the postal code table on the tab *ZIP/postal codes* of the address setup form, or through the table reference (*View details*) on the ZIP/postal code field.

Clicking the button *More options/Advanced* in the toolbar of the tab *Addresses* in the vendor form provides access to the address details. The tab *Contact information* there contains contact data, which are specific to the particular address (e.g. the phone number of the alternate payee) and not general contact data of the vendor.

3.2.1.7 Contact Information

In order to enter general contact data of a vendor (e.g. the vendor telephone number or the general e-mail address), click the button *Add* in the toolbar on the tab *Contact information* of the vendor detail form.

On the tab *Purchasing demographics* of the vendor detail form, you can select a main contact person in the field *Primary contact*. If you want to select a new main contact, enter the data of this person first (button *VENDOR/Set up/Contacts/Add contacts* in the action pane of the vendor form).

3.2.1.8 Features in the Vendor Form

Clicking the buttons in the action pane of the vendor list page or detail form provides access to various inquiries and activities on the selected vendor:

➢ **Action pane tab** *VENDOR*:
  ○ *Contacts* – Managing vendor contact persons
  ○ *Bank accounts* – Managing vendor bank accounts for payment
  ○ *Transactions* – Showing vendor invoices and payments
  ○ *Balance* – Showing the total of open liabilities
➢ **Action pane tab** *PROCUREMENT*:
  ○ *New/Purchase order* – Entering an order, see section 3.4.2
  ○ *Related information/Purchase orders* – Viewing current orders
  ○ *Agreements/Trade agreements, Purchase prices, Discounts* –
    Viewing purchase prices and discounts, see section 3.3.3
  ○ *Agreements/Purchase agreements* – Blanket orders, see section 3.8.1
➢ **Action pane tab** *INVOICE*:
  ○ *New/Invoice* – Entering a vendor invoice, see section 9.3.3
  ○ *Settle/Settle transactions* – Settling invoices, see section 9.2.5
  ○ *Related information/Invoice* – Viewing posted invoices

3.2.1.9 One-time Vendor

One-time vendors provide the option to keep master data of regular suppliers separate from vendors, who supply items rarely or only once.

The accounts payable parameters (*Accounts payable> Setup> Accounts payable parameters*, tab *General*) include the vendor number of a vendor used as template for one-time vendors. In addition, a separate number sequence for one-time vendors is available on the tab *Number sequences* of the parameters.

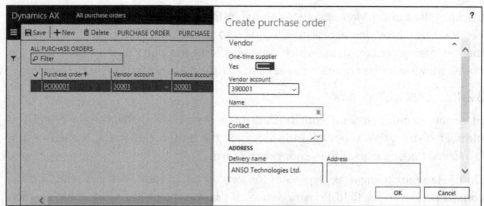

Figure 3-6:   Creating a one-time vendor in a new purchase order

If these parameters are set up for one-time vendors, set the slider *One-time supplier* in the dialog shown in Figure 3-6 to "Yes" (instead of choosing an existing vendor) when creating a purchase order in the list page *Procurement and sourcing> Purchase orders> All purchase orders*. Create an order selecting "Yes" in the *One-time supplier* automatically generates a new vendor.

In the vendor record of these vendors, the vendor account number derives from the number-sequence for one-time vendors, and the checkbox *One-time supplier* on the tab *Vendor profile* of the vendor form is selected. Clearing this checkbox transforms a one-time vendor to a regular vendor (keeping the one-time vendor number).

3.2.2 Payment Terms and Cash Discount

Unlike other business applications, which include cash discount settings in the payment terms, Dynamics AX clearly distinguishes payment terms and cash discount providing two different fields for these settings.

Payment terms and cash discounts in Dynamics AX are shared between vendors and customers. The related administration forms therefore are available in both menus – the accounts payable menu and the accounts receivable menu. The calculation of the due date and the cash discount date starts from the document date, which you can enter in the invoice. If you leave the document date empty, Dynamics AX applies the posting date as the start date for due date calculation. But especially in purchase invoices, the document date may deviate from the posting date.

You can modify the due date and the cash discount date when posting an invoice or when settling it in the settle transactions form (see section 9.2.5).

3.2.2.1 Terms of Payment

In order to edit the payment terms, open the form *Accounts payable> Payment setup> Terms of payment* in the accounts payable menu (or *Accounts receivable> Payment setup> Terms of payment* in the accounts receivable menu). If you want to edit a record, make sure that you are in edit mode.

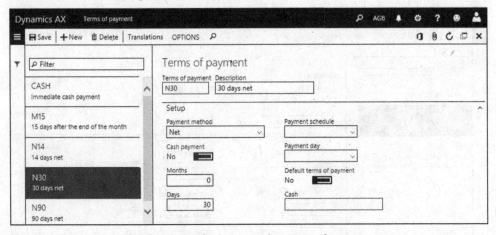

Figure 3-7:   Settings for due date calculation in the terms of payment

The left-hand pane in this form shows the list of payment terms with ID and description. The settings for due date calculation of a particular payment term are shown on the right-hand side.

The lookup field *Payment method* on the tab *Setup* determines the start date for due date calculation: "Net" means starting from the document date, "Current month" means starting from month end. The period length for due date calculation is specified by the number of *Days* and *Months*. If required, there is also the option to choose a payment schedule.

The button *Translations* provides the option to enter a longer text in the own language and in foreign languages. If there is a payment terms text in the language selected in a particular document, this text will be printed on external documents (e.g. the printed purchase order) instead of the content in the field *Description* of the payment terms.

3.2.2.2 Cash on Delivery

If you need payment terms for cash on delivery, choose the *Payment method* "COD", set the slider *Cash payment* to "Yes", and select the appropriate petty cash main account number in the field *Cash*. When posting an invoice referring to these payment terms, Dynamics AX immediately posts the payment and settles the invoice with the petty cash account of the payment terms.

3.2.2.3 Cash Discount

Similar to the payment terms setup, the cash discount setup is included in the accounts payable menu as well as in the accounts receivable menu (*Accounts payable> Payment setup> Cash discounts* and *Accounts receivable> Payment setup> Cash discounts*).

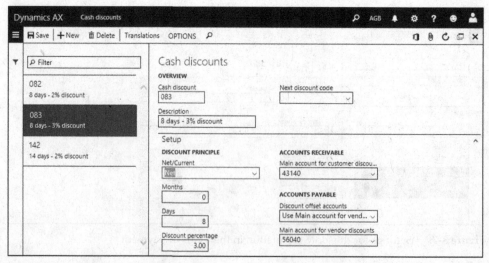

Figure 3-8:   Setting up a cash discount

Setting up cash discounts works like setting up payment terms, but you have to add a cash discount percentage and settings for posting the cash discount to the general ledger.

Cash discounts are in common for accounts payable and accounts receivable, but different settings for posting the cash discount are required for vendors and for customers (the settings apply at the time when posting the payment):

> **Accounts receivable** – *Main account for customer discounts*
> **Accounts payable** – The main account is depending on the lookup *Discount offset accounts* in the cash discount and contains following options:
>   o *Use main account for vendor discounts* – Posting to the *Main account for vendor discounts* entered in the field below
>   o *Accounts on the invoice lines* – Posting to the accounts of the invoice lines (offsetting part of the invoiced expense amount with the cash discount)

3.2.3 Ledger Integration

Whenever posting an invoice in purchasing, the invoice automatically posts in finance in parallel. The postings in finance refer to two different areas: The general ledger on the one hand, and subledgers for accounts payable, sales tax, inventory, and others on the other hand.

3.2.3.1 Subledger and General Ledger

When posting vendor invoices, credit notes, or payments, Dynamics AX posts vendor transactions in accounts payable. In parallel to this subledger posting, Dynamics AX posts transactions in the general ledger as described in section 9.4. There are two different areas of settings which are relevant for assigning main accounts to purchasing transactions:

> **Assignment of products to main accounts** – The inventory posting setup (see section 9.4.2), which refers to the vendor and the item (or the procurement category), contains settings for main accounts applicable when receiving the physical product (or service) and the invoice.
> **Assignment of vendors to main accounts** – The posting profiles contain settings for applicable summary accounts related to the vendor.

Both assignment dimensions, the item and the vendor dimension, are not only available at the level of individual items and vendors, but also at group level.

3.2.3.2 Settings for Vendor Transactions

Vendor groups (*Accounts payable> Vendors> Vendor groups*) are a primary setting for vendor transactions. In addition to the ID and the description, you can optionally enter a *Default tax group* (for the input tax) in the vendor group. When creating a vendor, the default tax group is the default for the sales tax group of the vendor.

Vendor posting profiles (*Accounts payable> Setup> Vendor posting profiles*) control the assignment of vendors to summary accounts. As a prerequisite for posting purchase transactions, at least one posting profile has to be specified in your company. In addition, the default posting profile for regular purchase transactions has to be entered in the accounts payable parameters (*Accounts payable> Setup> Accounts payable parameters*, tab *Ledger and sales tax/Posting*).

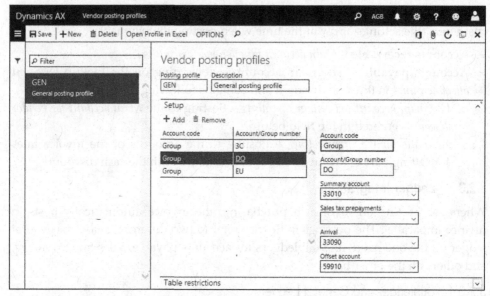

Figure 3-9:   The vendor posting profiles form

The *Summary account* field on the tab *Setup* in the posting profile contains the main accounts used as summary accounts for vendors. The assignment of summary accounts is available at three different levels as specified in the *Account code*:

➢ **Table** – Assigning a summary account to a particular vendor (enter the vendor number in the *Account/Group number* field)
➢ **Group** – Assigning a summary account to a vendor group (enter the vendor group in the *Account/Group number* field)
➢ **All** – Assigning a general summary account (the *Account/Group number* field remains empty)

If settings are entered at multiple levels, Dynamics AX applies the most appropriate setting. The search for this setting starts with the vendor number, the specification level "All" has got the lowest priority.

If you have to use alternative profile settings for special purposes like prepayment, you can set up additional posting profiles with account assignments which are different from the settings in the default posting profile. In order to apply one of the additional posting profiles to a specific transaction, you can choose it in the transaction (e.g. for a purchase order on the tab *Setup* of the header view in the purchase order detail form). For prepayment, the posting profile is specified in the accounts payable parameters.

3.2.4 Case Study Exercises

Exercise 3.1 – Terms of Payment

Your company wants to establish new terms of payment "60 days net", which you want to enter in Dynamics AX with a code P-## (## = your user ID). In addition, a new cash discount D-## for "14 days with 3 percent discount" is required.

Be sure to enter the values for due date and cash discount date calculation correctly. When registering the cash discount in Dynamics AX, choose main accounts similar to the accounts in existing cash discounts.

Exercise 3.2 – Vendor Record

The responsible department accepts a new domestic vendor, who wants to ship items to your company. Enter a new record for this vendor in Dynamics AX without applying a template, including the name (starting with your user ID) and a primary address of your choice. Select an appropriate vendor group and a sales tax group. For this vendor, the terms of payment and the cash discount entered in exercise 3.1 apply.

Exercise 3.3 – Ledger Integration

You want to find out about ledger integration. To which summary account in the general ledger will an invoice from your new vendor post?

3.3 Product Management in Purchasing

Purchasing includes physical products and intangible goods (e.g. services, fees, licenses). For both types of items, you have to ensure correct and complete master data in line with the following purposes:

> **Identification** – Clearly describe the item to make sure that the vendor ships the right product
> **Internal settings** – Multiple settings in the item master data control the way the particular item works in Dynamics AX

When purchasing inventoried items, product records (items) are required master data. When purchasing intangible goods, you can either use product records (including detail data, e.g. prices) or procurement categories (without details).

Along with a short introduction of the basics in product management, this section primarily contains an explanation of the product data necessary for purchasing. A more general description of product management is available in section 7.2.

3.3.1 Procurement Category

Product categories are groups of similar products and services, used in a simple or a multilevel hierarchy structure. Depending on the hierarchy type, a category hierarchy contains procurement categories, sales categories, or other categories.

By assigning products to product categories, you can establish a hierarchical structure of products. Depending on the requirements, you can set up multiple hierarchies in parallel and assign every item to a different category in each hierarchy.

In addition, you can apply product categories for purchasing independently from items. If purchasing a service or intangible item not tracked in inventory, you can simply enter a product category (instead of an item number) in the purchase order line.

3.3.1.1 Category Hierarchies and Product Categories

You can access category hierarchies in the list page *Product information management> Setup> Categories and attributes> Category hierarchies*. If you want to set up a new hierarchy, click the button *New* in the action pane and enter a name and a description for the new hierarchy. Dynamics AX then shows the category hierarchy detail form, where you can enter the categories of the new hierarchy.

In order to assign a category hierarchy to a hierarchy role, open the form *Product information management> Setup> Categories and attributes> Category hierarchy role association*. You can assign a hierarchy to each applicable role (*Category hierarchy type*) in the lines there, including the role "Procurement category hierarchy" for purchasing and "Sales category hierarchy" for sales. Depending on your requirements, select the same or different hierarchies for the different roles.

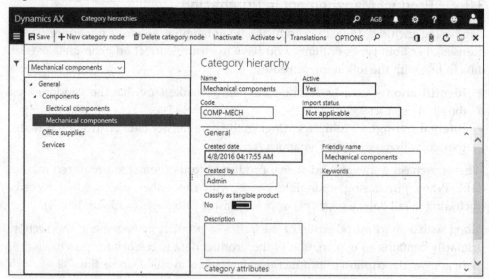

Figure 3-10:   Editing a product category in the category hierarchy form

If you want to edit purchasing-related category data for a category used in procurement (hierarchy role "Procurement category hierarchy"), open the *Procurement categories* form as described further down this section.

If you want to view the structure of an existing hierarchy, click the link in the *Name* field of the particular hierarchy. In the category hierarchy detail form, you can click the button *Edit* in the action pane to edit the structure.

In order to add a new category or a new category folder, select the parent node in the tree structure on the left and click the button *New category node* in the action pane. In the new category, enter at least the *Name*, the *Code*, and the *Friendly name* (see Figure 3-10).

3.3.1.2 Procurement Categories

Procurement categories are product categories which belong to the hierarchy of the type "Procurement category hierarchy". They are available in the lines of purchase transactions (purchase orders, purchase requisitions, purchase agreements), where you can select a procurement category instead of a product number.

You can manage purchasing-related settings of the product categories in the procurement categories form (*Procurement and sourcing> Procurement categories*). An important setting there is the item sales tax group on the tab *Item sales tax groups*.

As a prerequisite for using procurement categories in purchase transactions, the inventory posting setup (see section 9.4.2) has to include settings for the particular categories (*Inventory management> Setup> Posting> Posting*, tab *Purchase order*, option *Purchase expenditure for expense*).

3.3.2 Basic Product Data

In order to support large multi-company enterprises, the structure of product data in Dynamics AX has got two levels:

> **Shared products** – Common to all companies
> **Released products** – Holding company-specific item data

The data structure of shared products applies to all implementations. But in a small enterprise with only one company, it is possible to manage the products directly in the released product form. When creating a new released product there, Dynamics AX automatically generates a related shared product in the background.

3.3.2.1 Shared Products

The aim of shared product records is to establish a common table containing all products (items) of all companies working together in a Dynamics AX database. Apart from product number and name/description, shared products do not contain extensive information.

You can access the shared products in the list page *Product information management> Products> All products and product masters*. The all products page shows all items at enterprise level, and includes regular products, configurable products, and service items.

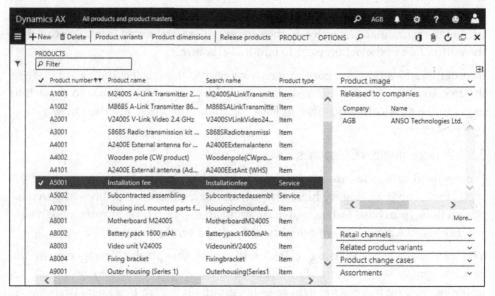

Figure 3-11:   Selecting an item in the all products list page

If you want to enter a new product, click the button *New* in the action pane of the all products list page. In the *Create product* dialog, enter following data:

➢ **Product type** – "Item" for stocked products, "Service" for services
➢ **Product subtype** – "Product" for regular items, "Product master" for configurable items with variants (see section 7.2.1)
➢ **Product number** – To be entered manually, if no automatic number applies from the number sequence
➢ **Product name** – Short description in system language
➢ **Search name** – Internal text for searching the item
➢ **Retail category** – Categorization in retail business, only if applicable (shows if there is a category hierarchy with the role "Retail product hierarchy")
➢ **Catch weight** – Only set to "Yes" for catch weight items (see section 7.2.1)

In order to create a regular stocked item, choose the *Product type* "Item" and the *Product subtype* "Product". For intangible items (e.g. services), choose the *Product type* "Service". Alternatively, you can also choose the *Product type* "Item" for an intangible item if linking it to an item model group for non-inventoried items in the released product (see section 7.2.1).

After clicking the button *OK* in the *Create* dialog, Dynamics AX shows shared product detail form. The detail form then contains further optional settings.

Apart from the product name and the description in the system language (default language specified in the system parameters) entered in the field *Description*, you can enter item descriptions in foreign languages after clicking the button *PRODUCT/Languages/Translations* in the action pane.

By clicking the button *PRODUCT/Set up/Product categories* in the action pane of the shared product, you can access the category assignment and link the product to categories. Hierarchies are optional if there is the need to create hierarchical product structures.

The button *PRODUCT/Set up/Dimension groups* in the action pane of the shared product form provides access to the inventory dimension assignment. Available inventory dimensions are divided into three dimension groups:

> ➤ **Product dimension group** – Only available for the product subtype "Product master", specifying if there are different configurations, sizes, colors, or styles
> ➤ **Storage dimension group** – Specifying if the inventory of the item is tracked at the level of site, warehouse, location, inventory status, or license plate
> ➤ **Tracking dimension group** – Specifying if batch or serial numbers apply

You can leave the dimension groups in the shared product empty. Dimension groups not entered in the shared product have to be entered in the related released products. You want to specify dimension groups at released product level, if different dimension settings per company are required (for example if only one company in your enterprise uses locations).

3.3.2.2 Releasing a Product

Before you can actually register transactions for a new shared product, you have to release it by clicking the button *Release products* in the action pane of the shared product page. The selected product then shows in the *Release products* wizard. After switching to the *Select companies* page of the wizard, put a checkmark in front of all applicable companies. Then confirm the selection by clicking the button *Finish* on the last page.

If applicable (e.g. in a single-company implementation), you can skip creating a shared product and immediately create a new product in the released products page by clicking the button *New* in the action pane. If creating a released product this way, the *New released product* dialog creates a shared product in parallel.

3.3.2.3 Managing Released Products

Released products (*Product information management> Products> Released products*), also labeled "Item" in some areas of Dynamics AX, contain the item details. Apart from directly accessing the released product form, you can also use the *Released product maintenance* workspace to access the released products.

In the shared product form, you can access a related released product by clicking the link in the *Item number* field on the right-hand side of the FactBox *Released to companies* (selecting the appropriate company) and then clicking the link in the field *Item number* of the product information dialog.

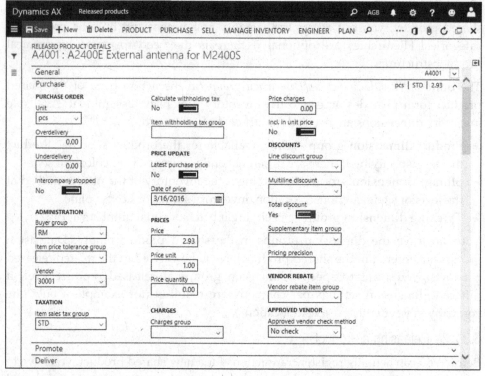

Figure 3-12: Released order detail form with the tab *Purchase* expanded

After releasing a new product, you have to populate the following mandatory fields in the released product from:

➢ **Item group** (tab *Manage costs*) – Linking main accounts for ledger integration
➢ **Item model group** (tab *General*) – Specifying item handling and inventory valuation
➢ **Dimension groups** (button *PRODUCT/Set up/Dimension groups*) – Required if not specified in the shared product
➢ **Unit of measure** – For purchasing, sales, and inventory

The default for the inventory unit of measure (tab *Manage inventory*) is specified in the inventory parameters. You can enter other units for sales (tab *Sell*) and for purchasing (tab *Purchase*) if there is an applicable unit conversion.

In addition to the mandatory fields, you should enter the *Item sales tax group* for purchasing on the tab *Purchase*, and for sales on the tab *Sell*.

In the field *Price* on the tab *Manage costs*, you can enter a base cost price for the item as applicable. If the item applies standard cost valuation (according to selected item model group), click the button *MANAGE COSTS/Set up/Item price* in the action pane and enter/activate a cost price per site as described in section 7.3.3.

3.3.2.4 Purchasing Related Data and Default Order Settings

The tab *Purchase* in the released product form contains core purchasing information, including the item sales tax group already mentioned. The *Buyer group* provides the option to specify the purchasing responsibility for the item.

The lookup field *Approved vendor check method*, initialized with a default value from the corresponding field in the item model group, controls if you can purchase the item only from approved vendors. If you decide to use approved vendors for the item (with the option "Warning only" or "Not allowed"), enter allowed vendors after clicking the button *PURCHASE/Approved vendor/Setup* in the action pane.

Clicking the button *PLAN/Order settings/Default order settings* in the action pane of the released product form provides access to the order settings for the product at company level. An important field in the default order setting form is the *Default order type*. If the default order type is "Purchase order", the item is to be purchased from vendors (if no other setting applies from the item coverage). The tab *Purchase order* in the default order settings contains settings which are specific for purchasing – including default values for lot size (field *Multiple*), order quantity (field *Standard order quantity*), and purchase site. Selecting the checkbox *Stopped* on this tab blocks the item for purchase transactions.

The site specific order settings, accessible by clicking the button *PLAN/Order settings/Site specific order settings* in the released product form, enable overriding the default order settings at site level (sites represent subsidiaries within a company as described in section 10.1.5). After creating a record with the particular site in the site specific order settings, you can enter a default warehouse for purchasing, inventory, and sales as applicable. If you want to override the default order settings for quantity and lead time, set the slider *Override* in the site-specific order settings to "Yes".

When entering an order, default values from the order settings apply (e.g. for the order quantity). You can override the default values in the order line afterwards.

3.3.2.5 Item Coverage

The primary setting for item coverage is the *Default order type* in the default order settings. On the tab *Purchase* of the released product detail form, the field *Vendor* determines the main vendor for purchasing the item.

Coverage groups contain settings for requirements planning (see section 6.3.3). For the applicable coverage group, a general default is specified in the master planning parameters (*Master planning> Setup> Master planning parameters*, field *General coverage group*). You can override this default group with a specific coverage group for the selected item on the tab *Plan* of the released product detail form.

After clicking the button *PLAN/Coverage/Item coverage* in the action pane of the released product form, further settings for the item – including a minimum and a maximum quantity – are available in the item coverage form. In addition, the item coverage contains the fields *Planned order type* (overriding the default order type) and *Vendor account* (overriding the main vendor specified in the released product form). Depending on the dimension groups, coverage settings are required at inventory dimension level (e.g. per warehouse).

3.3.3 Purchase Price Setup

The base functionality for pricing is the same in purchasing and in sales. Pricing includes a multi-stage calculation of prices and discounts, which starts at the base price in the released product form and continues with trade agreements for vendor groups and individual vendors.

Since sales uses discount calculation on a larger scale than purchasing in many companies, the section below focuses on price calculation. You can find details on discount calculation in section 4.3.2.

Apart from discounts deducted immediately, Dynamics AX also supports vendor rebate contracts specifying a discount depending on the purchasing volume in a given period (see section 4.9.2).

3.3.3.1 Base Purchase Price

The base purchase price is specified in the field *Price* on the tab *Purchase* of the released product form. This price is the price per purchase unit (field *Unit* on the tab *Purchase*). The *Price unit* gives the quantity which is the basis for this price – the price unit "100" for example means a price for hundred units (e.g. for screws).

If you want to record different base purchase prices per site (subsidiary), click the button *MANAGE COSTS/Set up/Item price* in the action pane. In the item price form, you can enter and activate a price per site as shown in section 7.3.3 (applying the *Price type* "Purchase price").

Purchase order lines apply the base price, if there is no applicable trade agreement for the particular vendor and item. Since prices (and price charges) in the released product form show in the currency of your company, Dynamics AX converts the prices to the currency of the order if the order is in a foreign currency.

3.3.3.2 Price Charges

In order to record charges (like fees and freight), which are added to the base price, you can optionally enter *Price charges* on the tab *Purchase* of the released product.

If the slider *Incl. in unit price* is set to "No", the amount entered in the field *Price charges* adds to the total of an order line independently from the quantity. With this setting, purchasing for example 10 units of an item with a *Price* of USD 3.00 and *Price charges* of USD 1.00 gives a unit price in the purchase order line of USD 3.00 and a line amount of USD 31.00. The price charges do not show in a separate field on printed purchasing documents.

If the slider *Incl. in unit price* is set to "Yes", Dynamics AX adds the price charges to the unit price. In this case, the field *Price quantity* is the quantity basis for allocating the price charges to the unit price. With this setting, purchasing for example 10 units of an item with a *Price* of USD 3.00, a *Price quantity* of 0.00 (or 1.00), and *Price charges* of USD 1.00 gives a unit price in the purchase order line of USD 4.00 and a line amount of USD 40.00.

In addition to the general price charges in the released product form, site-specific price charges are available in the item price form (accessible by clicking the button *MANAGE COSTS/Set up/Item price* in the action pane of the released product).

When working with charges, do not confuse price charges specified in the item record (released product form) with charges transactions assigned to charges codes, which are managed separately in orders. Details on charges management in orders are available in section 4.4.5.

3.3.3.3 Trade Agreements for Purchase Prices

Trade agreements give to option to specify more advanced settings on prices and discounts. You can view the trade agreements on the purchase prices of a product by clicking the button *PURCHASE/View/Purchase prices* in the action pane of the released product form. Trade agreements show following levels:

> ➢ **Period of validity** – *From date* and *To date*, referring to order entry or delivery (controlled by the *Date type* on the tab *Prices* in the procurement parameters)
> ➢ **Quantity** – Column *From* and *To* (for quantity-dependent prices)
> ➢ **Unit of measure** – Column *Unit*
> ➢ **Currency** – Currency of the price
> ➢ **Vendor dimension** – Column *Account code* and *Account selection* (Individual vendor, vendor group, or all vendors)

In addition to the detail levels mentioned above, trade agreements also include the option to specify prices at inventory dimension level. You need this option if prices are different per site, or per warehouse, or depending on product dimensions like size or color. In order to control the dimension columns displayed in the purchase prices form, click the button *Inventory/Display dimensions* in this form. As a prerequisite for using dimensions in pricing, the dimension group of the particular item has to include the selected dimensions in the price search (see section 7.2.2).

The price search runs from the most specific to the general agreement, in other words from vendor prices to vendor group prices and finally to general prices. If the checkbox *Find next* in the right-most column of the trade agreements is selected, Dynamics AX searches for the lowest price in trade agreements – a lower group price overrides a higher vendor-specific price. You can stop this search by clearing the checkbox *Find next* (setting the slider *Find next* to "No" when entering the respective trade agreement journal line).

3.3.3.4 Registering New Trade Agreements

If you want to set up a new purchase price agreement, enter and post a journal in the form *Procurement and sourcing> Prices and discounts> Trade agreement journals*. Alternatively, you can access the trade agreement journals by clicking the button *PURCHASE/Trade agreements/Create trade agreements* in the released product.

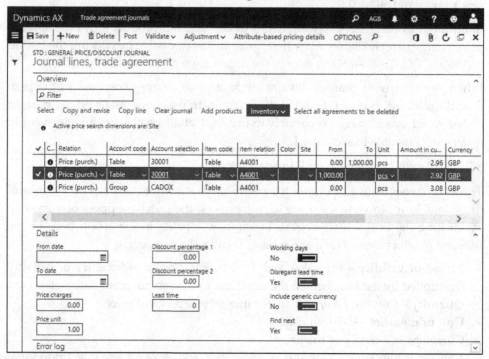

Figure 3-13:   Registering purchase prices in the trade agreement journal lines

A trade agreement journal consists of a header and at least one line. The lookup field *Show* in the upper pane of the trade agreement journal list page provides the option to select whether to view only open journals, or to include posted journals.

In order to register a new journal, click the button *New* in the action pane and select a journal name. Then click the button *Lines* to access the journal lines form, where you can insert journal lines. When entering a purchase price, make sure the option "Price (purch.)" is selected in the column *Relation*. The *Account code* determines if the price is for a vendor ("Table"), for a vendor price group ("Group"), or for all vendors. In a price agreement line, the column *Item code* has to show the option "Table" along with the product number in the *Item relation*.

Apart from the fields in the grid on the tab *Overview* of the journal lines, the tab *Details* contains additional data of the selected record (including validity dates, price unit, and lead time).

When entering an order line, the values for price, price unit, and lead time of the applicable trade agreement override the default values from the released product.

In order to know the applicable inventory dimensions for pricing, check the information text on the tab *Overview*. In Figure 3-13, this information tells that price agreements for the selected item can be entered at site level. You can control which dimensions show in the journal lines by clicking the button *Inventory/Display dimensions* in the toolbar of the tab *Overview*.

After entering the journal lines, click the button *Post* in the action pane to activate the agreement.

3.3.3.5 Updating or Deleting Existing Trade Agreements

In case there is a new price for an item, you would usually just record a new trade agreement with the price, the from-date, and the to-date.

If you want to edit (e.g. update of the to-date of the old agreement) or delete an active agreement, open the trade agreement inquiry – for example by clicking the button *PURCHASE/View/Purchase prices* (or the button *PURCHASE/Trade agreement/ View trade agreements*) in the action pane of the released product. After selecting one or more trade agreement lines, click the button *Edit selected lines* in the action pane. In the confirmation dialog, select a journal name for the new journal (used for the update) and click the button *OK*.

The new trade agreement journal contains one line per original trade agreement line, which is connected to the original trade agreement. Edit the data in the line(s) according to your requirements before clicking the button *Post* to update the agreement. If you want to delete the agreement instead of updating it, click the button *Select all agreements to be deleted* in new trade agreement journal (toolbar on the tab *Overview*) and post the journal.

3.3.3.6 Required Setup for Pricing

As a prerequisite for creating trade agreements, you have to set up at least one trade agreement journal name (*Procurement and sourcing> Setup> Prices and discounts> Trade agreement journal names*). The column *Relation* there specifies the default value for the column *Relation* in the agreement journal lines.

Trade agreements are only used for price calculation, if the appropriate combination of levels is activated in the price/discount activation (*Procurement and sourcing> Setup> Prices and discounts> Activate price/discount*).

If you want to enter prices at group level, you have to set up the required vendor price groups (*Procurement and sourcing> Prices and discounts> Price/discount groups> Vendor price/discount groups, Show* "Price group"). In the vendor detail form, select the appropriate price group on the tab *Purchase order defaults*. When selecting a vendor in a purchase order, the vendor price group applies as default in the order. You can override the price group in the order header afterwards (*Procurement and sourcing> Purchase orders> All purchase orders*, tab *Price and discount* in the header view of the detail form).

3.3.4   Case Study Exercises

Exercise 3.4 – Procurement Categories

Your company purchases a new kind of services, for which you want to set up appropriate product categories in the procurement category hierarchy. Enter a new category node "##-services" containing the categories "##-assembling" and "##-fees" (## = your user ID). This procurement category applies the item sales tax group which refers to the standard tax rate.

Exercise 3.5 – Product Record

In order to process purchase orders in the following exercises, you want to set up a new product. Enter a new shared product with the product number I-## and the name "##-merchandise" (## = your user ID). It should be a regular stocked product without variants or serial/batch numbers. You want to track inventory per site and warehouse. Choose the appropriate dimension groups in the shared product.

Then you want to release the product to your test company. In the released product, select an appropriate item group for merchandise and an item model group with FIFO-valuation. The item does not require approved vendors.

The item sales tax group for sales and for purchasing should refer to the standard tax rate. The unit of measure for the item is "Pieces" in all areas, and the main vendor is the vendor of exercise 3.2. The base purchase price and the base cost price is USD 50 and the base sales price is USD 100.

Enter default quantities (*Multiple* 20, *Min. order quantity* 40, *Standard order quantity* 100) and select the main site for purchasing and sales in the *Default order settings*. In the *Site specific order settings*, enter the main warehouse of the main site.

Note: If the number sequence for product numbers is set up for automatic numbering, you don't have to enter a product number.

Exercise 3.6 – Trade Agreement

You agree upon a lower price for the new item with your main vendor. Enter a trade agreement for the vendor of exercise 3.2, which specifies a purchase price of USD 45 for the item of exercise 3.5. There is no minimum quantity and no end date for this price.

3.4   Purchase Order Management

An order is a definite promise to deliver goods or services on agreed terms. For this reason, purchase orders have to include at least following details: Vendor (name, address), commercial terms (currency, payment terms, terms of delivery), products (identification, quantity, unit of measure), prices (price, discount), delivery date, and delivery address.

3.4.1   Basics of Purchase Order Processing

Apart from manually entering a new purchase order, you can generate it automatically from following starting points:

> **Master planning** – Generating a planned purchase order which you can firm, or immediately an actual purchase order (see section 6.3.4)
> **Purchase requisition** – Automatic or manual transfer (see section 3.8.2)
> **Request for quotation** – Accepting a quotation (see section 3.8.3)
> **Purchase agreement** – Creating a release order (see section 3.8.1)
> **Direct delivery** – Purchase order from a sales order (see section 4.8)
> **Subcontracting** – Purchase order from a production order (see section 5.7.2)
> **Project** – Create a purchase order as item task in the project module
> **Purchase journal** – Transfer a purchase order of the type "Journal"

Planned purchase orders are a result of master planning. Depending on the master planning setup (firming time fence), master planning may skip planned orders and immediately create purchase orders.

Purchase requisitions are internal documents requesting to purchase one or more items, entered or initiated by the person who wants the item.

Requests for quotation are required, if you want to obtain and compare quotes from multiple vendors. You can create a request for quotation either automatically from a purchase requisition or a planned order, or enter it manually.

Purchase order processing related to projects is part of the project module, described in the relevant online help and training documentation.

Other ways for creating purchase orders in Dynamics AX are automatic transfers using an import from external applications or the intercompany functionality (purchasing from affiliated companies within a common Dynamics AX database).

3.4.1.1   Approving and Processing Purchase Orders

After creating and – if required – approving a purchase order, you can process the order from the start to the end as shown in Figure 3-14.

If change management applies to a purchase order, you have to submit the order for approval. Depending on the order and the approval workflow, approval can be granted automatically or needs a manual authorization. If change management does not apply, the approval status of the order immediately shows "Approved".

Once the order is approved, you can optionally post a purchase inquiry if you want to process a vendor review. The next – mandatory – step in order processing is to confirm the order. Confirming may include sending a hardcopy or electronic document to the vendor.

Depending on the setup, you can skip all subsequent steps of order processing except posting the vendor invoice.

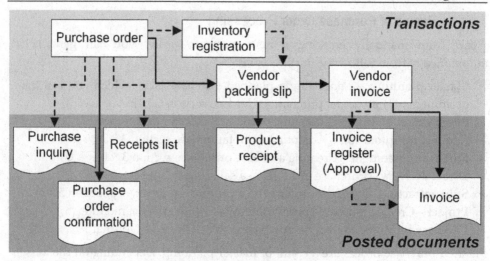

Figure 3-14: Purchase order processing in Dynamics AX

3.4.1.2 Receipts List and Inventory Registration

If your warehouse requires a list of purchased items for information purposes and for preparing the item arrival, you can print a receipts list.

Unlike the receipts list, inventory registration as the next step actually updates the on-hand quantity in inventory. The inventory registration, which includes all required inventory dimensions (depending on the item, e.g. warehouse, serial number, or batch number), is an optional step before posting the product receipt. Depending on the business processes in your warehouse, there are following alternative options to execute the inventory registration:

➢ **Registration form** – Button *Update line/Registration* (in the toolbar of order lines)
➢ **Item arrival journal** – Posting an arrival journal in inventory
➢ **Mobile device transactions** – If using advanced warehouse management

If the checkbox *Registration requirements* is selected in the item model group of the purchased product, inventory registration is not optional, but a mandatory step before posting the product receipt.

3.4.1.3 Product Receipt

When posting the product receipt, Dynamics AX posts inventory transactions and – depending on the setup – general ledger transaction. You can access the product receipt posting dialog either from the related purchase order, or from the appropriate menu item in the procurement module, or from the posted item arrival journal in inventory.

3.4.1.4   Vendor Invoice

Once you receive the vendor invoice, you can enter it in the purchase order form or in the pending vendor invoice form. If applicable, it is not possible to post the invoice before obtaining an approval through a workflow.

An alternative way for recording the vendor invoice is to enter and post it in an invoice register and a subsequent invoice approval journal (see section 9.3.3).

3.4.1.5   Physical and Financial Transactions

When posting inventory transactions, keep in mind that there are two transaction types: Physical and financial transactions. Generally speaking, physical transactions are packing slips (product receipts) and financial transactions are invoices. You have to distinguish between these transactions, in particular regarding inventory valuation and general ledger posting. Details on this topic are available in section 7.2.4.

3.4.2   Purchase Order Registration

Like all documents, purchase orders consist of a header and one or more lines. The header contains the common data of the order – e.g. the order number, vendor, language, currency, and payment terms. Other fields in the order header, for example the delivery date, provide a default value for the order lines, where you can override them at line level.

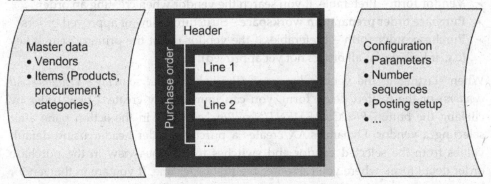

Figure 3-15:   Structure of purchase orders

If you change header data after creating order lines, the procurement parameters (*Procurement and sourcing> Setup> Procurement and sourcing parameters*, button *Update order lines* in the toolbar of the tab *General*) control whether to update existing order lines automatically.

The default value for the *Purchase type* in the purchase order header derives from the *Default values* setting in the procurement parameters (usually "Purchase order" for creating regular purchase orders). You can choose one of the following options for the purchase type in the purchase order then:

➢ **Purchase order** – Regular purchase order

➢ **Journal** – Draft or template, without impact on inventory or finance

➢ **Returned order** – Credit note, see section 3.7

Order lines include the item number or procurement category, description, quantity, price, discount, delivery date, and other data as applicable. When ordering a stocked product, you have to select the item number of the released product. For non-inventoried items (e.g. services), either enter the item number of an intangible item, or skip the item number and select a procurement category.

When creating a new purchase order header or line, Dynamics AX initializes numerous fields with default values from the vendor in the header or the item in a line. Depending on your permissions, you can update the content of fields in the purchase order subsequently. If you agree with your vendor for example on specific payment terms for a particular order, change the terms of payment in the order header. If the new payment terms apply to all future orders, you should also change the terms of payment in the vendor record for receiving the right default value when entering the next order for this vendor.

3.4.2.1 Entering a New Purchase Order

Depending on how you want to proceed, there are different starting points for creating a purchase order:

➢ **Vendor form** – Preferable, if you search the vendor when creating an order

➢ **Purchase order preparation workspace** – Structured view of approved orders

➢ **Purchase order form** – Preferable, if the vendor is not the primary search key (e.g. if looking for all orders not yet approved)

When starting in the vendor list page (*Procurement and sourcing> Vendors> All vendors*) or the related detail form, you can immediately create a new order by clicking the button *PROCUREMENT/New/Purchase order* in the action pane after selecting a vendor. Dynamics AX creates a purchase order header using default values from the selected vendor and switches to the lines view in the purchase order detail form, where you can enter the first order line. If you are in the vendor list page and want to check the existing purchase orders per vendor, click the button *PROCUREMENT/Related information/Purchase orders/All purchase orders* in the action pane of the vendor form. After clicking this button, Dynamics AX shows the purchase order list page filtered on the selected vendor.

The *Purchase order preparation* workspace, which you can access from the dashboard, shows an overview of approved orders on tabbed lists in the center. Clicking a purchase order number shown as link in the grid opens the related purchase order detail form. In the workspace, you can create a new order by clicking the button *New purchase order* in the action pane. The following steps are the same as if creating an order from the purchase order list page described below.

If accessing the purchase order list page through the menu item *Procurement and sourcing> Purchase orders> All purchase orders*, it shows the list of all purchase orders. In order to view the details of a purchase order in the list page, click the link in the *Purchase order* field of the particular order.

If you want to register a new purchase order in the purchase order list page, push the shortcut key *Alt+N* or click the button *New* in the action pane. In the *Create purchase order* dialog, you have to select a vendor in the *Vendor account* field. You can search the vendor by starting to type the first characters of the vendor number (or the name), or by opening the lookup and applying a *Grid column filter* – e.g. in the column *Name* of the lookup.

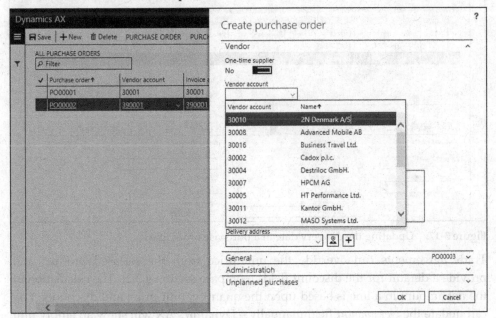

Figure 3-16: Creating a new order in the purchase order list page

After selecting a vendor, the create dialog retrieves various default values from the vendor record. Expanding the tabs *General* and *Administration* in the create order dialog provides access to additional fields of the new order header. If you want to change data like the vendor number, purchase type, or currency, you can update the particular field in the dialog or – after closing the dialog – in the header view of the purchase order detail form.

After clicking the button *OK* in the *Create purchase order* dialog, Dynamics AX creates the purchase order header and switches to the purchase order detail form showing the lines view.

3.4.2.2 Purchase Order Lines

In order to create an order line in the lines view of the purchase order detail form, simply click the first line in the lines pane or click the button *Add line* in the toolbar of the *Purchase order lines* tab and start selecting an item number (released product) or a procurement category. Data from the released product provide default values for numerous fields like the quantity, purchase unit, unit price, site, or warehouse. If site and warehouse are entered in the order header, they take priority over the default values from the item.

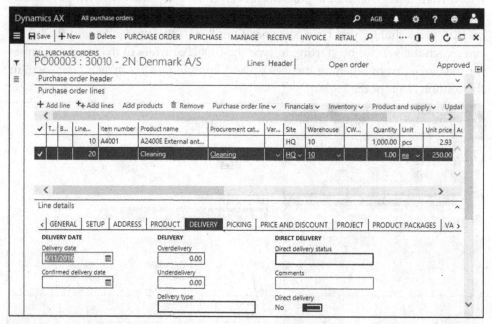

Figure 3-17: Updating the delivery date in a purchase order line

Trade agreements can override the unit price from the released product and provide a default for the discount fields (compare section 4.3.2). The calculation of the net amount in a line is based upon the quantity, unit price, and discounts. You can update the *Net amount* field manually – Dynamics AX will show an empty unit price and discount in this case.

The *Line number* is populated automatically when saving the order line. Numbering of line numbers applies the *Increment* specified in the system parameters (*System administration> Setup> System parameters*).

If you want to view the delivery date and other additional line data, expand the tab *Line details* and switch to the appropriate sub-tab. The delivery date on the sub-tab *Delivery* of the line details receives its default value from the purchase order header, if this date is after the lead time of the item. Otherwise, the default for the delivery date of the line is the lead time added to the session date. You can specify the lead time of an item in the default (and the site-specific) order settings of the item, in the purchase price trade agreements, and in the item coverage form.

3.4.2.3 Inventory Transaction

When entering a line with an inventoried product in a regular purchase order, Dynamics AX creates a related inventory transaction. You can view this transaction by clicking the button *Inventory/Transactions* in the toolbar of the order line. The transaction shows the receipt status "Ordered", and the fields *Physical date* and *Financial date* are empty. In the course of purchase order processing, posting the product receipt and the vendor invoice will update the inventory transaction as shown in section 7.2.4.

3.4.2.4 Intangible Items and Procurement Categories

If you want to order an intangible item (e.g. a particular service), select the item number of a non-inventoried product (item with product type "Service", or linked to an item model group for non-stocked items – see section 7.2.1) and enter the order line like you do for regular inventoried items.

Alternatively, you can skip the item number field in the order line and select a procurement category. The procurement category does not include as many details as the item record. For this reason, you have to manually enter data including quantity, unit, unit price, line text (on the sub-tab *General*) and other details as applicable.

3.4.2.5 Delivery Address

You can specify the delivery address for a purchase order on the tab *Address* in the purchase order header view. The default for this delivery address is your company address as specified on the tab *Addresses* in the legal entities form (*Organization administration> Organization> Legal entities*). If a delivery address is specified for the site or warehouse entered in the order header, the purchase order retrieves the site or warehouse address.

If you want to change the delivery address in a purchase order, you can choose between two options:

> **Select an existing address** – If already available in the global address book
> **Insert a new address** – If the address is completely new

If you want to choose an existing address (e.g. a customer address), click the button ⬚ near the *Delivery address* field on the *Address* tab. The *Address selection* dialog then provides the option to select any address from the global address book.

If you want to enter a completely new address, click the button ⊞ near the *Delivery address* field. In the *New address* dialog, enter the address for delivery (similar to entering a vendor address, see section 3.2.1) and set the slider *One-time* to "Yes".

If different delivery addresses are required at line level, open the sub-tab *Address* on the *Line details* tab in the purchase order lines. In the lines, you can choose existing addresses or create new addresses (like in the header).

Note: If you select the option "Delivery" in the field _Purpose_ of the _New address_ dialog and set the slider _One-time_ to "No", the address is the new main delivery address for your company.

3.4.2.6 Charges and Input Tax

If an order includes additional costs like freight or insurance, you can use charges at order header level or at line level. The functionality of charges in purchasing corresponds to charges in sales (see section 4.4.5). In order to access the charges referring to an order header, click the button _PURCHASE/Charges/Maintain charges_ in the action pane of the purchase order. In order to access the line charges, click the button _Financials/Maintain charges_ in the toolbar of the tab _Purchase order lines_ after selecting the appropriate order line.

Input tax (Sales tax/VAT) is based upon the relation of vendor and item:

➢ **Sales tax group** – The vendor record contains the _Sales tax group_ (VAT group) distinguishing between domestic and foreign vendors. For companies in the European Union, "EU vendors" usually is a third category.

➢ **Item sales tax group** – The item record contains the _Item sales tax group_ (item VAT group) distinguishing between items with a regular tax rate and other items, for which a reduced rate applies (in many countries for example food).

Purchase order header and lines retrieve the tax groups from the vendor and the item. Based on these groups and related settings, the applicable tax is calculated automatically. You can edit the _Sales tax group_ on the tab _Setup_ in the header view. It is copied to the lines, where you can access the _Sales tax group_ and the _Item sales tax group_ on the sub-tab _Setup_ of the _Line details_ tab.

In order to view the calculated sales tax in the purchase order form, click the button _PURCHASE/Tax/Sales tax_ in the action pane of the purchase order.

3.4.2.7 Delivery Schedule

In a purchase order with an item, which you want to receive in multiple deliveries, you have to enter multiple order lines with the same item. In order to support entering and managing order lines with common commercial conditions (price, discounts) but multiple deliveries, you can use the delivery schedule functionality.

Entering a delivery schedule starts by inserting a regular order line with the total quantity of all deliveries. Then click the button _Purchase order line/Delivery schedule_ in the toolbar of the order lines. In the _Delivery schedule_ dialog, enter the lines with quantity and delivery date for the different deliveries. After clicking the button _OK_ in this dialog, Dynamics AX creates additional purchase order lines for the deliveries. Only these lines are included in document posting and item availability calculation. The column _Type_ in the purchase order lines shows whether an order line is the total quantity line or a delivery line.

3.4.2.8 Header View and Lines View

When accessing the purchase order detail form, it shows in lines view. At the top of the page, a header line below the action pane displays the order number and the vendor on the left-hand side, and the order status and the approval status on the right-hand side. After expanding the tab *Purchase order header* in the lines view, it shows selected header fields (e.g. the delivery date).

If you want to access the complete header, click the button *Header* in the line below the action pane of the detail form, or press the shortcut key *Ctrl+Shift+H*. In order to switch from the header view back to the lines view, click the button *Lines* in the line below the action pane or press *Ctrl+Shift+L*.

3.4.2.9 Copying a Purchase Order

As an alternative to manually entering a new purchase order, you can copy an existing order. Since the existing order can have a different purchase type, there is the option to copy an order of the type "Journal" into an actual order for example.

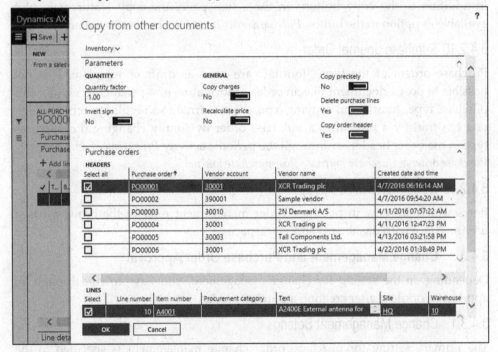

Figure 3-18:   Selecting records in the *Copy from other documents* dialog

If you want to copy an order to a new purchase order, start with inserting a new order header which should receive the copied records. In the new order, click the button *PURCHASE ORDER/Copy/From all* in the action pane. The *Copy from other document* dialog then displays a list of orders on the tab *Purchase orders*, and other documents for copying on the lower tabs. Select the checkbox in the left-most column as shown in Figure 3-18 to mark the records which you want to copy – entire orders in the upper pane, or individual order lines in the lower pane.

When copying an order, be aware of the slider *Delete purchase lines* on the tab *Parameters* If this slider is set to "Yes", all lines of the new order are deleted before inserting the copied lines. This does not matter for a new order, but it might be unwanted if you just want to copy additional lines to an existing order.

Once you have finished selecting order headers and lines (lines can refer to different headers), close the copy dialog by clicking the button *OK*. Dynamics AX copies the selected lines, depending on the slider *Copy order header* including header data like the payment terms (if copying header data, select one header).

In addition to the *Copy from all* button, there is another button for copying in the purchase order form – the button *PURCHASE ORDER/Copy/From journal*. This button is useful if there is a purchase order with posted documents like vendor invoices, and you want to transfer the posted lines into the order again.

In addition to the copy buttons in the action pane, the copy features are also available as option in the button *Purchase order line* of the toolbar in the order lines.

3.4.2.10 Purchase Journal Order

Purchase orders of the type "Journal" are used as draft or template. It is not possible to post a document like an order confirmation or a product receipt for this purchase type. Apart from copying a purchase journal to a regular purchase order, you can transfer a journal to a purchase order by simply changing the purchase type in the order header, or through the periodic activity *Procurement and sourcing> Purchase orders> Purchase journal> Post purchase journal*.

3.4.2.11 New in Dynamics 'AX 7'

Items which are new in purchase order management refer to the browser-based user interface with dashboard and workspaces.

3.4.3   Change Management and Purchase Order Approval

Depending on the setting for change management, you have to run through an approval workflow after creating a purchase order.

3.4.3.1   Change Management Settings

The primary setting for purchase order change management is specified in the procurement parameters (*Procurement and sourcing> Setup> Procurement and sourcing parameters*, tab *General*). Setting the slider *Activate change management* there to "Yes" activates the approval workflow for all future purchase orders.

If the slider *Allow override of settings per vendor* in the procurement parameters is set to "Yes", you can enter deviating settings for particular vendors as applicable. Setting the slider *Override settings* in the vendor detail form to "Yes" (field group *Change management for purchase orders* on the tab *Purchase order defaults*) enables overriding the general setting in both directions: Activating change management only for specific vendors while approval is not required in general, or the other way around.

The purchase order approval process is based on the workflow system (see section 10.4). Procurement workflows are specified in the form *Procurement and Sourcing> Setup> Procurement and sourcing workflows*, where purchase order workflows refer to the template "Purchase order workflow" and "Purchase order line workflow".

3.4.3.2 Approval Status

The purchase order header contains the *Approval status*, displayed in a separate column on the purchase order list page. Depending on the approval workflow, a purchase order shows the following approval status:

> **Draft** – When registering the order, before submitting for approval
> **In review** – After submitting, while the order is waiting for approval
> **Rejected** – After the reviewer rejects approval (resubmit or recall in this case)
> **Approved** – After approval, making it possible to post a confirmation
> **In external review** – After posting the purchase inquiry (optional step)
> **Confirmed** – After posting the purchase order confirmation

In addition, the button *PURCHASE/Actions/Finalize* after posting the invoice provides the option to irrevocably close an order, setting the status to "Finalized". This optional last step, which is necessary when working with budget control and encumbrances, blocks the order for any changes.

If change management does not apply to a purchase order, the order immediately shows the approval status "Approved" and you can continue order processing by confirming the order.

3.4.3.3 Approval Workflow for Purchase Orders

If change management applies to a purchase order, the button *Workflow* shows in the action pane and the initial approval status of the order is "Draft". After entering a new order, you have to submit it for approval by clicking the button *Workflow/Submit*. Approval is also required after modifying an order which has already been approved.

After submitting for approval, the approval status changes to "In review" and the workflow system starts processing the approval workflow in a batch process.

Because of this batch process, it is not possible to post the order confirmation for a purchase order immediately if change management is active. Even if a workflow with automatic approval applies, you have to wait until the workflow system has finished the batch process. If manual approval applies, the responsible has to decide in the work items assigned to him or his queues (see section 10.4.2) whether to approve the purchase order.

3.4.3.4 Request Change

If you want to change a purchase order after approval, click the button *PURCHASE ORDER/Maintain/Request change* in the action pane of the purchase order. After finishing the required changes on the purchase order, you have to submit the order for approval again.

When deciding on the approval of a modified order, the responsible can compare the current purchase order with the last confirmed version by clicking the button *MANAGE/History/Compare to recent versions* in the action pane. Clicking the button *MANAGE/History/View purchase order versions* provides the option to compare all previous versions.

3.4.4 Canceling and Deleting Purchase Orders

There is a difference between canceling and deleting a purchase order; Whereas canceling removes the open quantity expected for future product receipt, deleting completely eliminates the order line or the entire order.

In addition, deleting an order is not possible after posting the order confirmation or – if change management applies – after approval, whereas you can always cancel the order.

3.4.4.1 Canceling an Order or Order Line

You should cancel a purchase order line, if you do not expect any further deliveries for the line.

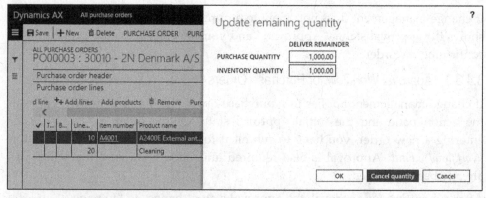

Figure 3-19: The dialog to change or cancel a remaining line quantity

In order to cancel a purchase order line or to change the open line quantity, click the button *Update line/Deliver remainder* in the toolbar of the purchase order lines after selecting the appropriate line. Dynamics AX then shows the *Update remaining quantity* dialog, where you can change or cancel the remaining quantity for deliveries. If you want to cancel the deliver remainder, click the button *Cancel quantity* in the dialog which sets the deliver remainder to zero.

Clicking the button *OK* in the dialog adjusts the deliver remainder in the order line. If there have been prior partial deliveries, canceling has not got an impact on these receipts – you just do not expect any further receipt.

If you want to cancel all lines of an order, cancel the order lines separately one after each other. If the purchase order confirmation has been posted already, you can cancel the complete order by clicking the button *PURCHASE ORDER/Maintain/ Cancel* in the action pane of the order form. After canceling all lines, the order status shows "Canceled".

3.4.4.2 Deleting Purchase Orders and Order Lines

Unlike canceling, which reduces the open quantity of an order line, deleting a purchase order line completely removes it from Dynamics AX. In order to delete a purchase order line, select the record and click the button *Remove* in the toolbar of the order lines, or push the shortcut key *Alt+F9*.

If you want to delete a complete order, click the button *Delete* in the action pane at the top of the detail form or – after selecting the order header – push the shortcut key *Alt+F9*.

Once you have posted the order confirmation or submitted approval, it is not possible to delete the order completely. If you want to delete an order line in an approved order to which change management applies, you have to request a change (button *PURCHASE ORDER/Maintain/Request change*, see section 3.4.3).

Note: If you want to delete an order line, click the *Remove* button in the toolbar – not the button *Delete* in the action pane which deletes the complete order.

3.4.5   Purchase Inquiry and Order Confirmation

After entering the purchase order and – if required – finishing the approval process, the purchase order shows the approval status "Approved". In this status, you can optionally post the purchase inquiry before posting the required purchase order confirmation.

In case you are using the vendor portal in Dynamics AX, post a *Confirmation request* (instead of the purchase inquiry) for vendor validation on the portal.

3.4.5.1 Purchase Inquiry

The purchase inquiry is an optional document, which you can send to the vendor for validation purposes. It does not create physical or financial transactions. After posting the purchase inquiry, the approval status of the order is "In external review".

In order to post the purchase inquiry, click the button *PURCHASE/Generate/ Purchase inquiry* in the action pane of the purchase order. In the posting dialog for the purchase inquiry, you can select settings for posting and printing as described for the purchase order confirmation below.

If the vendor wants you to apply changes on the purchase order, you can update the order and – if change management applies – approve the changes through the approval workflow before posting another purchase inquiry for the same order.

3.4.5.2 Purchase Order Confirmation

The purchase order confirmation is a mandatory document, which you have to post before you can record the product receipt. In parallel to posting the order confirmation, you usually print it (physically or electronically) and send it to the vendor.

Confirming a purchase order means to save it unchanging and separately from the current purchase order. The confirmation is an evidence of the document which has been sent to the vendor. It does not create physical or financial transactions.

In order to confirm a purchase order, click the button *PURCHASE/Generate/ Confirmation* in the action pane of the purchase order form after selecting the particular order. Alternatively, you can click the button *PURCHASE/Actions/ Confirm* executing the same functionality without showing the posting dialog.

The option to confirm a purchase order is also available on applicable tabs in the tabbed list pane of the *Purchase order confirmation* workspace and the *Purchase order preparation* workspace.

3.4.5.3 Posting Dialog for Order Updates

When posting an update of the purchase order (e.g. a purchase order confirmation), the posting dialog shows following options:

➤ **Parameters / Quantity** – "Ordered quantity" is the only option for the purchase order confirmation, posting the total quantity of all lines. Additional options are available for other transactions (e.g. for the receipts list described later).
➤ **Parameters / Posting** – If set to "Yes", the order confirmation is posted. If set to "No", the output is a pro forma document.
➤ **Print options / Print** – When selecting multiple orders for a summary update, the option "Current" prints documents separately while posting, whereas "After" starts printing after the last document has been posted.
➤ **Print options / Print purchase order** – If set to "Yes", the document is printed. Otherwise, posting is without printing (reprinting is possible nevertheless).
➤ **Print options / Use print management destination** – If set to "Yes", print settings specified in the form *Procurement and sourcing> Setup> Forms> Form setup* (button *Print management* on the tab *General*) or in the vendor form (button *GENERAL/Set up/Print management*) are used. Otherwise, print settings specified by clicking the button *Printer setup* in the toolbar of the posting dialog apply.

In order to finally post the document, click the button *OK* in the posting dialog. If the slider for printing in the posting dialog is set to "Yes", Dynamics AX prints the document on a printer or saves a file as specified in the printer selection.

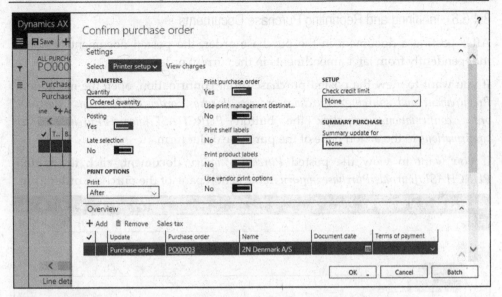

Figure 3-20:   Selecting to print in the purchase order confirmation dialog

3.4.5.4 Pro Forma Document

In the posting dialog, you can select to print a document while setting the slider *Posting* to "No". Dynamics AX generates a pro forma document in this case. A pro forma document, which can be required for purposes like customs declaration, is not a posted document. For this reason, it is not possible to reprint or display the document independently from the purchase order once printing is finished.

Another way to generate a pro forma confirmation is to click the button *PURCHASE/Generate/Pro forma confirmation* in the action pane of the purchase order. In the posting dialog for pro forma documents, the setting of the slider *Posting* is always "No".

3.4.5.5 Summary Update

Apart from posting a document through the appropriate button in the purchase order form, you can run a periodic activity for summary updates.

The summary order confirmation (*Procurement and sourcing> Purchase orders> Purchase order confirmation> Confirm purchase orders*) shows the same posting dialog as the button for order confirmation in the purchase order. But whereas a filter selecting the current order automatically applies when accessing the posting dialog from a purchase order, the summary update requires manually entering a filter. You can do this by clicking the button *Select* in the toolbar on the tab *Settings* of the posting dialog, which opens an advanced filter for selecting purchase orders.

After closing the filter dialog, the selected orders show on the tab *Overview* of the posting dialog. If you do not want to post a particular order listed there, simply delete the appropriate line before posting the document by clicking the button *OK*.

3.4.5.6 Inquiring and Reprinting Purchase Documents

After posting a document in the purchase order, the posted document is stored independently from later amendments in the current order.

If you want to view the posted purchase order confirmation, open the menu item *Procurement and sourcing> Purchase orders> Purchase order confirmation> Purchase order confirmations* or click the button *PURCHASE/Journals/Purchase order confirmations* in the action pane of the purchase order form.

If you want to view the posted *Purchase inquiry* document, click the button *PURCHASE/Journals/Purchase inquiry* in the action pane of the purchase order form.

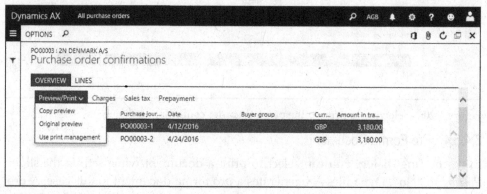

Figure 3-21: Selecting to reprint in the purchase order confirmation inquiry

The order confirmation inquiry form shows all posted purchase order confirmations on the tab *Overview*. After selecting an order confirmation header on this tab, the tab *Lines* displays the related order lines.

If you want to display a print preview of the posted order confirmation, click the button *Preview/Print/Copy preview* or *Preview/Print/Original preview* in the inquiry form. From the preview, you can reprint the document. Alternatively, you can print one or more order confirmations directly in the order confirmation inquiry by clicking the button *Preview/Print/Use print management* (printing to the printer specified in print management).

3.4.5.7 New in Dynamics 'AX 7'

Items which are new in purchase order confirmation refer to the new vendor portal using the confirmation request.

3.4.6 Case Study Exercises

Exercise 3.7 – Purchase Order

In order to avoid processing purchase order approval, make sure change management does not apply to your vendor entered in exercise 3.2.

You want to order your item (entered in exercise 3.5) from your vendor (entered in exercise 3.2). Enter the purchase order in the *Purchase order preparation* workspace.

Which quantity and which price show in the order line, where do they come from? Order two hours of the procurement category "##-assembling" (entered in exercise 3.4) for a price of USD 100 in a second order line.

After closing the purchase order from, you want to display all orders referring to your vendor. How do you proceed and how many orders display?

Exercise 3.8 – Order Confirmation

Post and print the purchase order confirmation for the order which you have created in exercise 3.7. Printing should be to a PDF file.

Then change the quantity in the first order line of exercise 3.7 to 120 units. How do you proceed? When posting the order confirmation, display a print preview.

3.5 Item Receipt

Once an ordered item arrives at your warehouse, you want to post an item receipt which makes the item available in inventory.

3.5.1 Basics of Item Receipts

The *Purchase order receipt and follow-up* workspace helps to make sure that required items arrive in time. It shows the delayed and pending receipts on the tabbed lists in the center and provides fast access to a filtered list of backorder purchase lines.

Apart from the workspace, there are particular inquiries and reports designed to review open purchase order lines. These inquiries include:

➢ *Procurement and sourcing> Purchase orders> Purchase order follow-up> Backorder purchase lines*: List page showing open order lines with a confirmed delivery date before or on the *To date* entered in the filter area of the list page.

➢ *Procurement and sourcing> Purchase orders> Purchase order follow-up> Open purchase order lines*: Inquiry showing all open order lines (use the filter pane, the grid column filter, or the advanced filter to select relevant records).

You can optionally print a receipts list to prepare the expected item receipt. This list is just an optional information for the vendor and/or the responsible in your warehouse. Independently from the receipts list, the warehouse responsible can also use the arrival overview form for viewing and preparing expected receipts.

Item receipt in inventory then includes two consecutive steps (see Figure 3-22):

➢ **Inventory registration** – You can record the inventory registration, which preliminarily increases the on-hand quantity in inventory, directly from the order line, or through an item arrival journal, or through mobile device transactions in the advanced warehouse management.

➢ **Product receipt** – The product receipt posts the final physical inventory transaction and – depending on the setup – general ledger transactions for the item receipt. Inventory registration before the product receipt is optional.

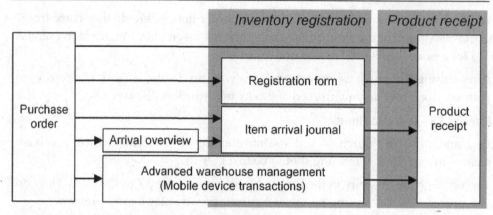

Figure 3-22: Options for processing the item receipt

Whereas you can execute the inventory registration no matter if the purchase order confirmation has been posted before, posting the product receipt requires a prior purchase order confirmation.

Depending on the particular requirements and the setup, it is possible to skip the inventory registration and/or the product receipt for a purchase order. If you skip posting the product receipt, Dynamics AX will post it when you post the vendor invoice.

3.5.2   Receipts List

The way of posting the receipts list is similar to posting the purchase order confirmation: If you want to generate a receipts list, you have to access a posting dialog for posting and printing. The receipts list is optional, and it does not create inventory or financial transactions.

In order to post and print a receipts list, open the purchase order and click the button *RECEIVE/Generate/Receipts list* in the action pane after selecting the appropriate order. Alternatively, you can access the posting dialog for summary update (*Procurement and sourcing> Purchase orders> Receiving products> Post receipts list*) and enter a filter by clicking the button *Select*.

The receipts list is not a very common document, but you can use it ˋfor information purposes regarding an expected item receipt.

3.5.3   Inventory Registration

Inventory registration is a preliminary step before posting the product receipt. The options, which are available for inventory registration, are depending on the warehouse policy.

Referring to the required level of detail, Dynamics AX supports two core warehouse policies:

> **Basic approach** – No pallet management and no detailed tracking of transactions within the warehouse required
> **Advanced warehouse management** – Detailed planning and tracking of warehouse work with pallets or other handling units

Depending on the warehouse policy, there are following ways for processing the inventory registration:

> **Basic approach**
> o **Registration form** – From the order line (e.g. for entering serial numbers)
> o **Item arrival journal** – In inventory, avoiding the purchase order form
> o **Arrival overview** – Generating item arrival journals
> **Advanced warehouse management**
> o **Mobile device** – Recording transactions on the mobile devices portal

Inventory registration is only possible for stocked items (as specified in the item model group). The item model group of the purchased item further controls whether you have to post registration before posting the product receipt (*Inventory management> Setup> Inventory> Item model groups*, checkbox *Registration requirements* on the tab *Inventory policies*).

For order lines containing a procurement category or a non-stocked item, inventory registration is not available. You can only post a product receipt for these lines.

This section covers the inventory registration process in the basic approach for warehouse management. Section 8.1.2 contains a description on how to process item receipts if using the advanced warehouse management.

3.5.3.1 Registration in a Purchase Order Line

If it is required to register the item quantity before posting the product receipt, the usual way is to post an item arrival journal or – if using advanced warehouse management – to register mobile device transactions.

But you can also record the inventory registration independently from these advanced options, for example if you need to split the transaction of a single order line into lines with different locations, batch numbers, or serial numbers.

In order to access the item registration from the purchase order form, click the button *Update line/Registration* in the toolbar of the tab *Purchase order lines* after selecting the appropriate order line.

The inventory registration form contains two areas: The *Transactions* tab shows the status of the inventory transaction(s) linked to the order line. The *Registration lines* tab is used to post the registration.

When accessing the inventory registration from a purchase order line, the tab *Transactions* initially shows a single inventory transaction, which has been created when entering the order line. This transaction is split into multiple lines if you post partial deliveries, or if you split the line manually. When registering inventory dimensions like different batch or serial numbers (if applicable), you can split a line by clicking the button *Split* or *Create serial numbers* in the toolbar of the tab *Transactions*.

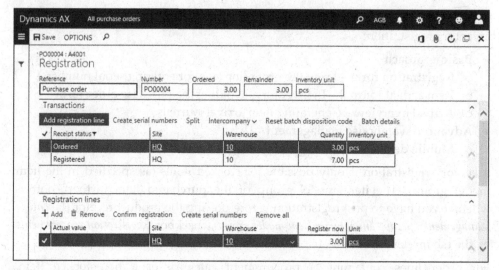

Figure 3-23:   Registering a receipt in the inventory registration form

In order to record and post the inventory registration, insert appropriate lines in the tab *Registration lines*. As an alternative to manually inserting a record by clicking the button *Add* in this tab, you can click the button *Add registration line* in the toolbar of the tab *Transactions* (see Figure 3-23).

Before posting the registration by clicking the button *Confirm registration* on the tab *Registration lines*, you can change the warehouse, the quantity, and applicable inventory dimensions as required. In a partial registration, which is recorded by entering a smaller than the original quantity on the tab *Registration lines* before posting, the inventory transaction splits into two lines – one for the registered quantity, and one for the remaining quantity.

If you have already started a registration on the tab *Registration lines* and you want to cancel it before posting, click the button *Remove all*. Clicking this button restores the registration as it has been before starting the current registration.

3.5.3.2 Registration Status

Once the inventory registration is posted, the recorded quantity shows the status "Registered" and is available in inventory. After registration, you can transfer, sell, or consume the registered quantity as required in your company.

The *Line quantity* form (button *GENERAL/Related information/Line quantity* in the action pane of the order) shows the posted quantity in the column *Registered*.

Unlike product receipt and invoice posting, which generate voucher documents containing unchanging transactions, inventory registration is a preliminary transaction. If you reset an inventory registration, there is no posted transaction of the original registration any more.

The only transaction which you can still view after resetting a registration is the posted item arrival journal (if registration has been posted through an item arrival journal) or transactions in the advanced warehouse management (if the registration has been posted on mobile devices).

3.5.3.3   Item Arrival Journal

If it is required to register item receipts in the warehouse separately from posting vendor packing slips (product receipts) in the office, you can use item arrival journals. Posting an item arrival journal generates the same transactions in inventory and in purchasing as the registration directly in the purchase order line.

You can access the item arrival journals in the form *Inventory management> Journal entries> Item arrival> Item arrival*. Registering and posting an item arrival journal works similar to other inventory journals (see section 7.4.2).

3.5.3.4   Arrival Overview

The form *Inventory management> Inbound orders> Arrival overview* provides an overview of expected item arrivals. On the tab *Arrival options* and *Arrival query details* of the form, you can enter filter criteria like the date range of expected receipts (*Days back, Days forward*), the warehouse, or the vendor (*Account number*). Clicking the button *Update* in the action pane applies the selected criteria. If you want to use the same filter criteria repeatedly, click the button *Arrival overview profiles* or *New arrival overview profile* and create one or more profiles with appropriate filter settings. On the tab *Arrival options* of the arrival overview, you can subsequently select an *Arrival overview profile name*.

After selecting receipts for arrival (column *Select for arrival* on the tab *Receipts* or the tab *Lines*), click the button *Start arrival* in the toolbar of the tab *Receipts*. Starting the arrival creates – but does not post – an item arrival journal for the selected lines with the journal name selected on the tab *Arrival options*.

In order to post the arrival journal, open the item arrival journals (*Inventory management> Journal entries> Item arrival> Item arrival*). Alternatively, you can click the button *Journals/Show arrivals from receipts* in the toolbar of the arrival overview tab *Receipts* after selecting the receipt, for which you have started the arrival.

The button *Journals/Product receipt ready journals* in the arrival overview shows posted arrival journals, for which the product receipt (see section 3.5.4 below) has not been posted yet.

3.5.3.5 Reversing an Inventory Registration

In order to reverse (cancel) a registration, which has been posted through an item arrival journal or through the registration form, open the registration form in the purchase order after selecting the appropriate order line.

On the tab *Transactions* of the registration form, click the button *Add registration line* after selecting the particular transaction. Then post the transaction like a regular inventory registration, but with a negative quantity.

3.5.4 Product Receipt

Posting the product receipt (vendor packing slip/delivery note) generates the physical inventory transaction, which finally receives the item in an unchanging voucher document.

3.5.4.1 Posting Dialog for Product Receipts

The way to post a product receipt is similar to a purchase order confirmation. You can access the posting dialog by clicking the button *RECEIVE/Generate/Product receipt* in the purchase order form after selecting the appropriate order.

The posting dialog shows the familiar format. The applicable option in the lookup field *Quantity* on the tab *Parameters* is depending on the prior process:

➢ **Registered quantity** – Select this option, if an inventory registration (item arrival) has been posted before posting the product receipt. Dynamics AX applies the registered (not yet received) quantity as default for the posting lines.
➢ **Registered quantity and services** – In addition to the registered quantity of inventoried items, Dynamics AX applies the ordered quantity for order lines referring to product categories and non-inventoried items.
➢ **Ordered quantity** – Dynamics AX applies the total remaining quantity.
➢ **Receive now quantity** – Dynamics AX applies the quantity of the order line column *Receive now*.

The posting quantity shows in the column *Quantity* on the tab *Lines* in the lower area of the posting dialog. If required, you can change the quantities there before posting.

The other parameters in the posting dialog are similar to the purchase order confirmation parameters (see section 3.4.5), except for the following options:

➢ **Product receipt** – Column on the tab *Overview* of the posting dialog, in which you have to enter the packing slip number of your vendor.
➢ **Print product receipt** – Slider on the tab *Parameters* of the posting dialog, which is usually set to "No" because you probably don't print your own document when receiving the vendor's packing slip.

If an exclamation mark (!) shows in front of a product receipt record on the tab *Overview* of the posting dialog, it indicates an issue with posting. A possible reason is that the selected quantity in the posting dialog is "Registered quantity", but there has not been an inventory registration before the product receipt. Selecting the quantity "Ordered quantity" in the posting dialog usually solves this problem.

3.5.4.2 Summary Update and Other Options for Posting

Similar to the option in the purchase order confirmation, the posting dialog for product receipts is also available as a periodic activity for summary updates. In the posting dialog for summary update (*Procurement and sourcing> Purchase orders> Receiving products> Post product receipt*), you have to enter a filter by clicking the button *Select*. After closing the filter dialog, you can collect multiple purchase orders into one collective product receipt by clicking the button *Arrange*. More information on arranging orders to collective documents is available in section 4.6.2 of this book.

An alternative way to access the product receipt posting dialog is available, if an item arrival journal (see section 7.4.2) has been posted for the purchase order. In this case, you can post the product receipt by clicking the button *Functions/Product receipt* in the action pane of the item arrival journal. If a *Packing slip* number has been entered on the tab *Journal header details* of the item arrival journal before posting, it applies as default value for the *Product receipt* number in the product receipt posting dialog.

3.5.4.3 Canceling a Product Receipt

You can cancel a posted product receipt using the *Cancel* feature in the product receipt inquiry form.

In order to access the product receipt inquiry, click the button *RECEIVE/Journals/ Product receipt* in the action pane of the purchase order form. After selecting the appropriate receipt, click the button *Cancel* in the toolbar of the tab *Overview*. If you just want to reduce the posted quantity, click the button *Correct* in the product receipt inquiry.

Canceling and correcting a product receipt does not change the original transaction, but posts a new transaction offsetting the original one.

3.5.4.4 Ledger Integration and Settings for Product Receipt Posting

If ledger integration is activated for the product receipt, Dynamics AX posts accrual transactions in the general ledger in parallel to the inventory transactions. These ledger transactions are reversed when posting the related invoice.

There are two relevant settings for posting product receipts to the general ledger:

➢ **Accounts payable parameters** – The slider *Post product receipt in ledger* on the tab *General* has to be set to "Yes" for enabling ledger posting.
➢ **Item model group** – The checkbox *Post physical inventory* on the tab *Costing method & cost recognition* in the item model group of the item has to be selected.

Independently from the parameter setting, product receipt transactions of items with the inventory model "Standard costs" are always posted to the ledger.

Apart from the setting on ledger integration, the item model group contains two more relevant settings for product receipts: The checkbox *Registration requirements* in the item model group controls, if you have to post the inventory registration before posting the product receipt. The checkbox *Receiving requirements* controls, if you have to post the product receipt before posting the vendor invoice.

3.5.4.5 New in Dynamics 'AX 7'

Since the old "Warehouse Management II" module is not supported in the new release, items referring to this functionality (e.g. pallets) have been removed.

3.5.5 Partial Delivery and Over/Under Delivery

You have to post a partial delivery, if you do not receive the entire quantity of a purchase order line in one shipment, but split into multiple shipments. In case the checkbox *Prevent partial delivery* on the tab *Line details* (sub-tab *General*) of the purchase order line is selected, it is not possible to post partial deliveries.

3.5.5.1 Inventory Registration of Partial Deliveries

In inventory registration, you can record partial deliveries in the registration form as described in section 3.5.3 (compare Figure 3-23). If the inventory registration is posted through an item arrival journal, enter the partial quantity in the arrival journal lines. When posting the product receipt related to the inventory registration afterwards, select the option "Registered quantity" in the quantity lookup field of the posting dialog.

3.5.5.2 Product Receipt of Partial Deliveries

If you do not use inventory registration, you can optionally enter a *Receive now* quantity in the purchase order line for preparing the partial product receipt. The *Receive now* quantity shows in a column far to the right on the tab *Purchase order lines* of the purchase order form.

As an alternative to the column in the purchase order lines, you can also enter the *Receive now* quantity on the tab *Receive now* of the *Line quantity* form (see Figure 3-24). In order to access the *Line quantity* form, click the button *GENERAL/Related information/Line quantity* in the action pane of the purchase order.

In the quantity lookup field of the product receipt posting dialog, choose the option "Receive now quantity" referring to this column then.

Alternatively, you can skip the *Receive now* quantity and choose the option "Ordered quantity" in the quantity lookup field of the product receipt posting dialog. In this case, you have to enter the received quantities in the column *Quantity* on the tab *Lines* further down the posting dialog.

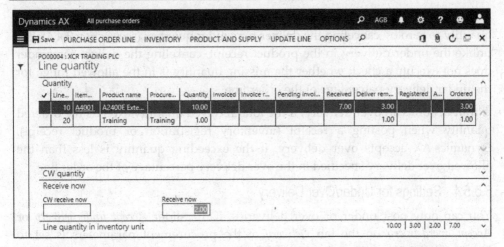

Figure 3-24: Line quantity form for a purchase order after posting a partial delivery

After posting a partial delivery, the quantity open for future product receipts shows in the column *Deliver remainder* of the *Line quantity* form (see Figure 3-24). The total quantity received shows in the column *Received* there.

When receiving further partial deliveries, you can post the product receipts in the same way as described for the first delivery until the total of the received quantity equals the ordered quantity.

3.5.5.3 Processing Under and Over Delivery

If you post the receipt of a quantity, which is less than the ordered quantity, Dynamics AX posts a partial delivery unless you characterize it as under delivery (marking the receipt to be the last for the particular order line). For this purpose, you can select the checkbox in the column *Close for receipt* on the tab *Lines* of the posting dialog (see Figure 3-25) after entering the received quantity in the column *Quantity*.

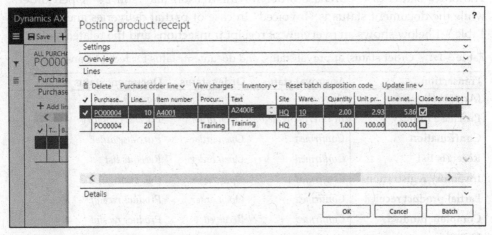

Figure 3-25: Selecting under delivery in the posting dialog for the product receipt

As alternative to the under delivery in the product receipt, you can set the open quantity to zero by canceling the deliver remainder quantity (see section 3.4.4). But unlike the under delivery in the product receipt, canceling the deliver remainder does not execute a check whether the missing quantity is in the allowed range for the under delivery percentage of the order line.

A transaction is an over delivery, if the total received quantity exceeds the ordered quantity when posting a receipt (inventory 'registration or product receipt). Dynamics AX accepts over delivery, if the exceeding quantity is less than the allowed over delivery specified in the over delivery percentage of the order line.

3.5.5.4   Settings for Under/Over Delivery

You can only post under or over deliveries, if the slider *Accept underdelivery* or *Accept overdelivery* on the tab *Delivery* of the procurement parameters is set to "Yes". In the released product form (*Product information management> Products> Released products*), the maximum percentage for over and for under delivery in purchase orders and sales orders is specified on the tabs *Purchase* and *Sell*. The percentages in the released product are a default for the order lines, where you can adjust them in the particular order as needed (tab *Line details*, sub-tab *Delivery*).

3.5.6   Order Status and Inquiries

Posting the item receipt updates the inventory quantity and the order status.

3.5.6.1   Purchase Order Status

The purchase order list page contains the column *Approval status* (see section 3.4.3) and the column *Purchase order status*. The header view of the purchase order detail form additionally shows the *Document status* on the tab *General*. Whereas the order status indicates the order progress as given by the lowest status of the purchase order lines, the document status shows the highest status of a posted document.

The order status of a purchase order for this reason may still be "Open order" while the document status is "Invoiced" in case of partial deliveries and invoices. Table 3-1 below shows an overview of receipt transactions and the related status.

Table 3-1:   Order status, approval status, and document status for receipt transactions

Transaction	Approval status	Order status	Document status
(Approval)	*Approved*	*Open order*	*None*
Purchase inquiry	*In external review*	*Open order*	*Purchase inquiry*
Confirmation	*Confirmed*	*Open order*	*Purchase order*
Receipts list	*Confirmed*	*Open order*	*Receipts list*
Inventory registration	*Confirmed*	*Open order*	(No change)
Partial product receipt	*Confirmed*	*Open order*	*Product receipt*
Complete product receipt	*Confirmed*	*Received*	*Product receipt*

If you click the button *GENERAL/Related information/Postings* in the action pane of the purchase order form, you can access a form showing the last document number of posted documents for the particular order.

At line level, the status shows in the field *Line status* on the sub-tab *General* of the *Line details* tab. In addition, the *Line quantity* form shows the quantity per status.

3.5.6.2 Inventory Transaction Status

Both, the inventory registration and the product receipt, change the on-hand quantity through inventory transactions.

When entering a new purchase order line with an inventoried item, Dynamics AX creates an inventory transaction with the *Receipt* status "Ordered". You can view this transaction by clicking the button *Inventory/Transactions* in the toolbar of the tab *Purchase order lines*.

When posting an inventory registration, the receipt status of the inventory transaction changes to "Registered". The registration date is stored in the field *Inventory date*, which you can view on the tab *General* of the *Transaction detail* form (access by clicking the button *Transaction details* in the inventory transaction). If you reverse the inventory registration, Dynamics AX clears the inventory date.

When posting a product receipt with or without a previous inventory registration, the receipt status of the inventory transaction changes to "Received". The posting date of the product receipt shows in the column *Physical date* of the inventory transaction. The *Financial date* in the inventory transaction remains empty until posting the vendor invoice. Additional detail data of the transaction (e.g. the packing slip number) show on the tab *Updates* of the *Transaction detail* form.

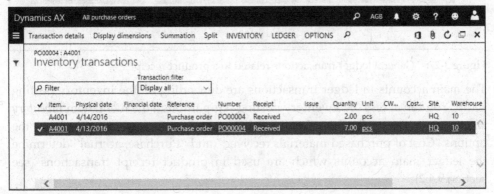

Figure 3-26:   Inventory transactions after posting product receipts

Since reversing a product receipt is only possible by posting an offsetting transaction, the physical date of an inventory transaction never changes after posting the receipt.

In case of partial receipts, the original inventory transaction splits into two transactions with a different status according to the posted quantities. Figure 3-26 for example shows the inventory transactions linked to a purchase order line after posting the product receipts of two partial deliveries.

3.5.6.3 Product Receipt Inquiry

In order to view the posted product receipts, open the form *Procurement and sourcing> Purchase orders> Receiving products> Product receipt* or click the button *RECEIVE/ Journals/Product receipt* in the action pane of the purchase order form.

After selecting a product receipt on the tab *Overview* of the inquiry form, you can switch to the tab *Lines* to view the related receipt lines. The button *Inventory/Lot transactions* in the toolbar of the *Lines* tab provides an alternative access to the inventory transactions.

3.5.6.4 Ledger Transactions and Transaction Origin

In case ledger integration is activated for the product receipt, click the button *LEDGER/Vouchers/Physical voucher* in the action pane of the inventory transaction inquiry if you want to view related general ledger transactions. In order to view all ledger transactions of a complete product receipt, open the product receipt inquiry and click the button *Vouchers* in the toolbar of the tab *Overview* there.

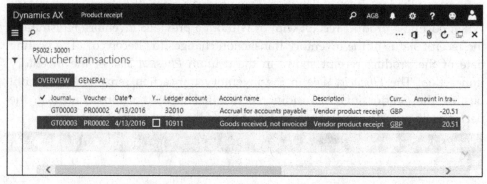

Figure 3-27:   General ledger transactions related to a product receipt

The main accounts in ledger transactions are depending on the inventory posting setup. You can access the inventory posting setup through the menu item *Inventory management> Setup> Posting> Posting*. On the tab *Purchase order* of this form, the options "Cost of purchased materials received" and "Purchase, accrual" determine the ledger main accounts which are used in product receipt transactions (see section 9.4.2).

Note: For source documents like the product receipt, settings on the tab *Batch transfer rules* in the general ledger parameters determine, if transactions in subledgers are posted synchronously to the general ledger, or if they are summarized in a scheduled batch. The general ledger transactions shown for a product receipt are depending on this setting.

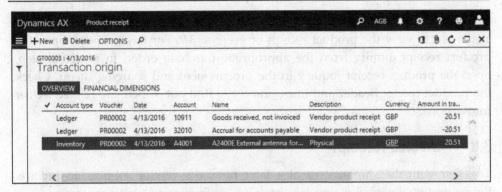

Figure 3-28: Transaction origin form showing all transactions for a product receipt

Clicking the button *Transaction origin* in the action pane of the voucher transactions (in a narrow screen, click the button ⋯ to view all buttons of the action pane) opens the transaction origin form, which shows all related transactions in all modules. Depending on integration settings, the product receipt posts transactions in inventory and in the general ledger. Figure 3-28 for example shows the transaction origin of the transaction selected in Figure 3-27.

3.5.7 Case Study Exercises

Exercise 3.9 – Product Receipt

Your vendor ships the goods and services ordered in exercise 3.7 with packing slip PS309. Before posting the receipt, check following items in the purchase order:

➢ Order status and document status
➢ Inventory quantity of the ordered item (button *Inventory/On-hand*)
➢ Inventory transaction related to the order line of the product

Then post a product receipt for the complete order quantity (120 units for the first line according to exercise 3.8) with to the vendor packing slip number given above. You can post the receipt directly from the purchase order form.

Now review the status of the points in the list above again. What is different after product receipt posting?

Exercise 3.10 – Partial Delivery

You want to order your item (entered in exercise 3.5) from your vendor another time. Enter a purchase order for 80 units and post the product receipt of packing slip PS310 with a partial delivery of 50 units. Then post the product receipt PS311 of a second partial delivery with 10 units.

Do you know how to show the remaining quantity? Check the order status, the inventory quantity, and the inventory transactions like in exercise 3.9. What is different in comparison to exercise 3.9?

Exercise 3.11 – Product Receipt Inquiry

You want to view the product receipt of exercise 3.9. For this purpose, open the product receipt inquiry from the appropriate purchase order. In a second step, open the product receipt inquiry in the procurement and sourcing menu. Check the product receipt header and lines, and try to find out if there are related ledger transactions.

3.6   Invoice Receipt

Together with the shipment or at a later time, the vendor submits an invoice. Before posting the invoice, you can check it in an invoice matching procedure.

Whereas the product receipt changes the preliminary (physical) inventory value, the invoice receipt changes the actual (financial) value. For this reason, posting an invoice receipt does not only increase the open vendor balance, but it also increases the financial value in inventory.

Once all lines of a purchase order are invoiced, purchase order processing is completed. Payment of vendor invoices runs through a separate process shown in section 9.3.4 of this book.

3.6.1   Ways for Processing Vendor Invoices

Apart from invoices related to a purchase order, there are vendor invoices without an order reference. In order to process the different types of invoices, there are following ways:

➤ **Purchase order invoices** – Purchase orders and purchase order invoices include only lines with products or procurements categories.
➤ **Invoices without order assignment** – Depending on whether you want to manually select an offset ledger account, there are two types:
  o **Using non-stocked products or procurements categories** – Posting is similar to purchase order invoice posting, just without purchase order assignment.
  o **Using ledger accounts** – Register and post an invoice journal, usually for specific subjects like office rent or legal services.

3.6.1.1   Invoice Journal and Vendor Invoice Form

If you want to enter an invoice with a manual offset ledger account (usually an expense account), use the invoice journal. Invoice journals (see section 9.3.3) are independent from purchase orders.

If you don't want to enter an offset ledger account, use the vendor invoice form (*Pending vendor invoices*) no matter whether the invoice refers to a purchase order or not. The invoice lines in the vendor invoice form contain products and procurement categories. If the invoice entered in the vendor invoice form does not refer to a purchase order, you can only select non-inventoried items and procurement categories.

If your company wants to apply approval workflows to pending vendor invoices, set up appropriate workflows referring to the template "Vendor invoice workflow" or "Vendor invoice line workflow" in the form *Accounts payable> Setup> Accounts payable workflows*.

3.6.1.2 Purchase Order Invoice

When recording an invoice referring to a purchase order, there are two options depending on approval requirements:

➢ **Vendor invoice form** – Enter and post the invoice in the (pending) vendor invoice form, with or without approval workflow.

➢ **Invoice register journal** – As a preceding step to the vendor invoice form, you can first post the invoice to interim accounts in the invoice register journal, followed by posting in the invoice approval journal (or the invoice pool inquiry) from where you access the vendor invoice form (see section 9.3.3).

If you want to make sure that invoices are approved before posting, you can either use the approval workflow functionality in the pending vendor invoices, or the invoice register journals. From a financial perspective, the difference between the vendor invoice approval workflow and invoice register journal posting is, that the invoice register journal already posts an invoice, which is subject to tax calculation, when starting the approval process.

3.6.1.3 Vendor Invoice and Item Receipt

Vendor invoices related to a purchase order either refer to a previous product receipt, or the physical receipt of the items (or services) and the invoice receipt is one common step.

In the vendor invoice form, you can click the button *Default from* in the action pane. If you select the option "Ordered quantity" or "Receive now quantity", the invoice quantity is not based upon the received quantity. Invoice posting then also posts the receipt of the exceeding quantity (for any quantity of an invoice line exceeding the received quantity of the related order line). If you have not posted the product receipt, invoice posting will also receive the complete quantity in inventory as a result.

Invoice posting without a previous product receipt is useful, if you receive goods or services together with the invoice and do not post a separate item receipt in the warehouse. If you want to post an invoice for an inventoried item this way, the item model group assigned to the item may not show a checkmark in the checkbox *Receiving requirements* (see section 7.2.3).

3.6.2 Vendor Invoice Posting

Entering vendor invoices works independently from purchase orders in a separate list page – the vendor invoice form (*Accounts payable> Invoices> Pending vendor invoices*). This form contains all vendor invoices, which have been entered but not posted yet.

In order to access the detail form from the pending vendor invoice list page, click the link in the *Number* (invoice number) field of the particular invoice or click the *Edit* button in the action pane.

If you want to enter a new pending vendor invoice, there are following ways:

> **Vendor invoice entry workspace**
> **Vendor invoice form**
> **Vendor form**
> **Purchase order form**

The *Vendor invoice entry* workspace gives and overview of chargeable documents (purchase orders and product receipts) and of entered invoices, which have not been posted. You can create a pending vendor invoice by clicking the button *New vendor invoice* there.

If you start in the vendor invoice form, click the button *New* in the action pane to create a new pending invoice. If you rather want to start entering new invoices in the vendor form, click the button *INVOICE/New/Invoice/Vendor invoice* in the action pane of this form.

3.6.2.1   Invoices without Order Reference

Registering an invoice, which does not refer to a purchase order, is similar to entering a purchase order in the purchase order form. After selecting a vendor number, the invoice retrieves numerous default values from the vendor record. You can view and edit the corresponding fields in the header view. But unlike purchase order lines, new lines entered in the lines view of the vendor invoice form may only contain non-stocked items and procurement categories.

When closing the vendor invoice detail form without posting, the invoice is stored for later posting (and approval, if applicable) and shows in the pending vendor invoices. If you want to cancel registration after starting to enter a new invoice, delete the invoice by clicking the button *Delete*.

3.6.2.2   Purchase Order Invoices

If you want to register an invoice which refers to a purchase order, start in the pending vendor invoice form (after creating the invoice from the vendor invoice entry workspace, or from the vendor form, or from the vendor invoice form) and select the vendor number in the field *Invoice account*.

Then select the purchase order number in the lookup field *Purchase order*. If you select the order number before selecting a vendor, Dynamics AX automatically retrieves the correspondent vendor.

If you are working in the purchase order form, you can also register a vendor invoice directly starting there. Clicking the button *INVOICE/Generate/ Invoice* in the action pane of the purchase order form opens the pending vendor invoice form, already referring to the selected order. A similar option is available in the *Vendor invoice entry* workspace, where you can click the button *Invoice now* in tabbed list pane after selecting a purchase order or a product receipt.

Although the vendor invoice form looks different from the other posting dialogs (e.g. the product receipt), it shares similar functionality. Like in the other posting dialogs, it is depending on the preceding process which option to choose in the quantity selection (button *Default from* in the action pane):

➢ **Product receipt quantity** – Common option, applies if a product receipt has been posted before and you want to assign the invoice to the product receipt.

➢ **Ordered quantity** or **Receive now quantity** – If selected, the product receipt is not the default for the column *Quantity* in the invoice lines. For any quantity not yet received, an item receipt is posted in parallel to the invoice.

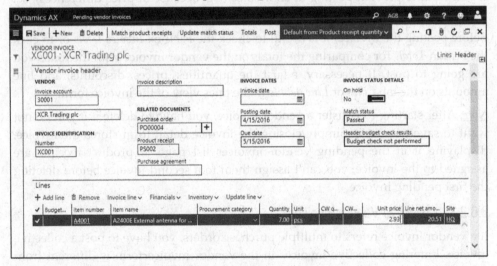

Figure 3-29:   Registering a vendor invoice referring to a purchase order

If you select the option "Product receipt quantity" in the *Default quantity for lines*, the quantity received not invoiced applies as default value in the column *Quantity* on the tab *Lines* of the vendor invoice. In order to check the product receipts covered by the invoice, click the button *Match product receipts* in the action pane of the vendor invoice form. The match dialog then shows the product receipts available for invoicing. Clearing or selecting the checkboxes in the column *Match* there excludes or includes product receipts. If the vendor only invoices a partial quantity of a receipt line, you can update the column *Product receipt quantity to match* in the lower pane of the match dialog. After closing the dialog by clicking the button *OK* and clicking "Yes" in the message bar which asks whether to update the invoice quantity (if applicable), the selected product receipt displays in the column *Product receipt* on the tab *Lines* ("<multiple>", if assigned to multiple receipts).

If the vendor invoice is independent from product receipts (e.g. if there is no prior item receipt), click the button *Default from* in the action pane, select the option "Ordered quantity", and adjust the quantities in the invoice lines as applicable. But be aware that invoice posting in this case also posts the receipt in inventory for any invoice quantity exceeding the received quantity (total quantity, if there is no prior product receipt).

The invoice number (mandatory field *Number* in the field group *Invoice identification*), the *Posting date*, the *Invoice date*, and the *Due date* (receiving the default value from the payment terms calculation) show on the tab *Vendor invoice header* of the lines view. More details are available in the header view, where you can set the slider *Approved* on the tab *Approval* to "No" if you want to exclude an invoice from payment proposals.

If you want to prevent posting of an invoice (e.g. because of price differences), set the slider *On hold* on the tab *General* of the vendor invoice header to "No".

Before posting the invoice, it is useful to check the FactBox *Invoice totals* or to click the button *Totals* for comparing the totals on the vendor invoice with the totals you are going to post. If necessary, adjust the quantities, prices, discounts, and line amounts on the tab *Lines* or *Line details* in the lines view of the invoice form.

<u>Note</u>: After starting to register a vendor invoice, you have to delete it if you do not want to save or post it. Simply closing the invoice detail form stores the invoice, displaying it in the pending vendor invoices list page. If product receipts are assigned to the invoice, you can't assign them to a second invoice before deleting the first pending invoice.

3.6.2.3 Collective Vendor Invoices

If a vendor invoice refers to multiple purchase orders, you have to post a collective invoice. Entering collective invoices in the vendor invoice form is different from registering collective documents for other document types (e.g. collective product receipts).

In the vendor invoice form, click the button ⊞ on the right-hand side of the field *Purchase order* to access the *Retrieve purchase orders* dialog. When selecting purchase orders in the retrieve dialog, pay attention to the option selected in the button *Default from* in the action pane of the vendor invoice form. The option there controls whether you can select a purchase order without a prior product receipt.

In addition, summary update parameters (*Accounts payable> Setup> Summary update parameters*) and settings at vendor level determine required settings in orders collected to a common invoice (similar to accounts receivable, see section 4.6.2).

3.6.2.4 Invoice Matching

The details entered in the vendor invoice form have to match the received invoice exactly. In case the prices, discounts, charges, or other elements in the vendor invoice do not match the purchase order or the product receipt, there are discrepancies which have to be resolved.

Depending on the invoice matching setup, the vendor invoice form shows "Failed" in the field *Match status* on the invoice header (and in the column *Price match* on the tab *Lines*) if the vendor invoice exceeds specified tolerances. In order to view the details, click the button *REVIEW/Matching/Matching details* in the action pane of the vendor invoice form.

Primary settings for invoice matching are available on the tab *Invoice validation* in the accounts payable parameters. Setting the slider *Enable invoice matching validation* to "Yes" activates invoice matching. You can subsequently specify different types of invoice matching and different tolerances:

➢ **Invoice totals matching** – Compares only invoice total fields (invoice amount, sales tax, charges) with the purchase order.
➢ **Price and quantity matching**
   o **Line matching policy** – "Two-way matching" compares the invoice price and discounts with the order line; "Three-way matching" in addition compares the quantity in product receipts.
   o **Match price totals** – Applies to partial deliveries and invoices, comparing the order line with the total of the current invoice line and related partial invoice lines already posted.
➢ **Charges matching** – Separate settings for matching charges.

If allowed in the invoice validation parameters, you can override these validation criteria at vendor level or at item level in the forms of the menu folder *Accounts payable> Invoice matching setup*. In addition, business policies (*Accounts payable> Policy setup*) provide the option to specify matching rules which are different from the standard invoice validation settings.

3.6.2.5 Invoice Posting and Ledger Integration

Once you have finished entering an invoice, you can optionally leave it non-posted and post it at a later time – e.g. if an approval workflow applies. Depending on the invoice matching setup, you have to click the button *Update match status* before posting the invoice. Once you want to post the pending vendor invoice, click the button *Post* in the action pane of the vendor invoice form.

After posting, the invoice shows in the open vendor invoices list page (*Accounts payable> Invoices> Open vendor invoices*) which displays all invoices not yet paid.

Posting a vendor invoice generates general ledger transactions, inventory transactions, vendor transactions, and transactions in other subledgers (e.g. sales tax if applicable). As shown in section 3.2.3, the vendor posting profile specifies which summary account applies to the vendor transaction. Settings for inventory transactions are available in the inventory posting setup – depending on the item and the vendor (see section 9.4.2).

3.6.2.6 New in Dynamics 'AX 7'

Items which are new in vendor invoice processing refer to the browser-based user interface and include minor changes like deprecating the *Cancel* option (*Remove* is available).

3.6.3   Order Status and Inquiries

Like posting the product receipt, posting the vendor invoice updates the order status and the inventory transactions, vendor transactions, and general ledger transactions.

3.6.3.1 Purchase Order Status and Transaction Status

Depending on whether you have posted a partial or a complete invoice, the purchase order shows following status:

➤ **Partial invoice** – Order status "Received" or "Open order", document status "Invoice"

➤ **Complete invoice or last partial invoice** – Order status "Invoiced", document status "Invoice"

If you want to view the impact of the vendor invoice on inventory transactions, click the button *Inventory/Transactions* in the toolbar of the tab *Purchase order lines* after selecting the appropriate order line in the purchase order form.

After posting the invoice, the *Receipt* status of the inventory transaction is "Purchased" and the posting date of the invoice shows in the column *Financial date*. The invoice number shows on the tab *Updates* of the *Transaction detail* form (access by clicking the button *Transaction details* in the inventory transaction).

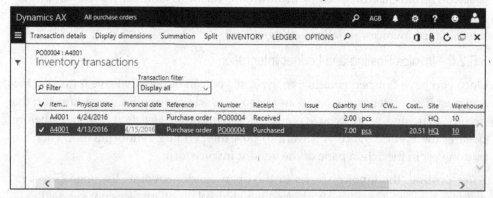

Figure 3-30: Inventory transactions after posting the vendor invoice

The example in Figure 3-30 shows two inventory transactions referring to a purchase order line, of which only one line has been included in invoice posting.

3.6.3.2   Invoice Inquiry

In order to access the posted invoice, open the form *Accounts payable> Inquiries and reports> Invoice> Invoice journal* or click the button *INVOICE/Journals/Invoice* in the action pane of the purchase order form.

After selecting an invoice on the tab *Overview* of the inquiry form, you can switch to the tab *Lines* to view the related invoice lines. The button *Inventory/Lot transactions* on the tab *Lines* opens the inventory transactions described above.

3.6.3.3   Ledger Transactions and Transaction Origin

If you want to view the general ledger transactions related to a vendor invoice, click the button *Voucher* on the tab *Overview* of the invoice inquiry to access the voucher transactions form. Alternatively, you can access the voucher transactions from the inventory transaction inquiry (click the button *Ledger/Financial voucher* there), but in this case only the ledger transactions which refer to the particular inventory transaction display.

The voucher transactions form displays all general ledger transactions referring to the posted invoice. Figure 3-31 for example shows following transactions:

> **Reversing the packing slip transactions** – Accounts 32010 and 10911
> **Vendor summary account transaction** – Posting the vendor balance (Account 33010, specified in the vendor posting profile)
> **Stock account transaction** – Posting inventory items (Account 10310, specified in the inventory posting setup)
> **Input tax transaction** – Posting sales tax (Account 25520, specified in the ledger posting group of the sales tax code)

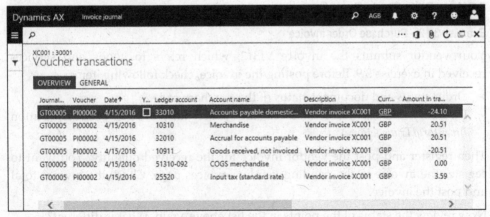

Figure 3-31:   General ledger transactions related to a posted vendor invoice

More information on the vendor posting profile setup is available in section 3.2.3, and on the inventory posting setup in section 9.4.2.

Note: Like for the product receipt, settings on the tab *Batch transfer rules* in the general ledger parameters determine, if vendor invoices are summarized when posting to the general ledger. In this case, not all described transactions are available at the level of an individual invoice.

Clicking the button *Transaction origin* in the action pane of the voucher transactions (in a narrow screen, click the button ⊡ to view all buttons of the action pane) opens the transaction origin form, which shows related transactions for the voucher in all modules.

✓ Account type	Voucher	Date	Account	Name	Description	Currency	Amount in tra...
Ledger	PI00002	4/15/2016	25520	Input tax (standard rate)	Vendor invoice XC001	GBP	3.59
Ledger	PI00002	4/15/2016	51310-092	COGS merchandise	Vendor invoice XC001	GBP	0.00
Ledger	PI00002	4/15/2016	10911	Goods received, not invoiced	Vendor invoice XC001	GBP	-20.51
Ledger	PI00002	4/15/2016	32010	Accrual for accounts payable	Vendor invoice XC001	GBP	20.51
Ledger	PI00002	4/15/2016	10310	Merchandise	Vendor invoice XC001	GBP	20.51
Ledger	PI00002	4/15/2016	33010	Accounts payable domestic t...	Vendor invoice XC001	GBP	-24.10
✓ Vendor	PI00002	4/15/2016	30001	XCR Trading plc	Vendor invoice XC001	GBP	-24.10
Sales tax	PI00002	4/15/2016	25520	Input tax 17.5%	Sales tax	GBP	3.59
Inventory	PI00002	4/15/2016	A4001	A2400E External antenna for...	Financial	GBP	20.51

Figure 3-32:   Transaction origin form, showing all transactions for a journal

Apart from ledger transactions, the transaction origin includes vendor transactions, inventory transactions, and tax transactions as applicable. Figure 3-32 for example shows the transaction origin of the journal line selected in Figure 3-31.

3.6.4   Case Study Exercises

Exercise 3.12 – Purchase Order Invoice

Your vendor submits the invoice VI312, which refers to goods and services received in exercise 3.9. Before posting the invoice, check following items:

➢ Order status and document status of the purchase order
➢ Inventory transaction related to the order line of the product (button *Inventory/Transactions*)

Then register and post the vendor invoice for the received quantity. You want to register the invoice in the pending vendor invoices page. Check the invoice total and post the invoice.

Now review the status of the points in the list above again. What is different?

Exercise 3.13 – Partial Invoice for a Purchase Order

You receive the invoice VI313, which applies to the goods received with packing slip PS310 in exercise 3.10. Post the vendor invoice starting in the purchase order form, making sure that the vendor invoice only contains the items received with packing slip PS310.

Exercise 3.14 – Vendor Invoice Not Related to a Purchase Order

Your vendor now submits the invoice VI314, which contains a line with one hour of the procurement category "##-assembling" (created in exercise 3.4) and a price of USD 105. The invoice does not refer to a purchase order.

You accept this invoice and want to register it in the pending vendor invoices page. Check the invoice total before posting the invoice.

Exercise 3.15 – Invoice Inquiry

You want to view the invoice of exercise 3.12. For this purpose, open the invoice inquiry for the particular order in the purchase order form. As an alternative, choose the appropriate menu path. Check the invoice header and lines as well as the related ledger transactions.

In exercise 3.3, you were looking for the summary account for your vendor. Can you find the ledger transaction for this account? Finally, open the transaction origin form and check, to which modules your invoice has posted.

3.7   Credit Note and Item Return in Purchasing

When receiving a credit note from a supplier, you have to register and post it. Posting a vendor credit note is similar to posting a vendor invoice, except that credit notes require a negative quantity. Like vendor invoices, vendor credit notes are grouped into following types:

➤ **Credit notes for inventoried items** – Returned to the vendor
➤ **Credit notes for intangible goods** – For example services, fees, or licenses

Vendor credit notes referring to inventoried items have to be registered in the purchase order form. When posting a credit note for an inventoried item, Dynamics AX also posts an item return (negative receipt) in inventory if no separate item return has been posted before. If the item model group does not allow a negative physical inventory, posting the return is only possible if the item is still on stock.

Vendor credit notes, which are not related to inventoried items, can be registered in the following way:

➤ **Purchase order** – Order lines with non-stocked items (or procurement categories) and a negative quantity
➤ **Pending vendor invoice** – Invoice lines with non-stocked items (or procurement categories) and a negative quantity
➤ **Invoice journal** – Journal lines with offset ledger accounts (see section 9.3.3)

In case you have to reverse a product receipt, but not an invoice receipt, use the functionality for canceling product receipts (see section 3.5.4).

3.7.1   Crediting Purchase Orders

For an inventoried item, you have to access the purchase order form if you want to post a credit note. If the parameter *Safety level of invoiced orders* in the procurement parameters (*Procurement and sourcing> Setup> Procurement and sourcing parameters,* tab *Delivery*) is not set to "Locked" (and the approval status of the order is not "Finalized"), you can record and post a credit note in the original purchase order. Otherwise, you have to enter a new purchase order for the credit note.

In case invoiced orders are not locked, there are following options to register a credit note with an inventoried item:

➢ **Original purchase order** – Registering a new line in the original order
➢ **New purchase order** – Purchase type "Purchase order" or "Returned order"

3.7.1.1   Credit Note in the Original Purchase Order

If you want to register a credit note in a new line of the original purchase order, access the purchase order in edit mode. Enter a regular order line, but with a negative sign in the column *Quantity*. If you expect a replacement from your vendor, you can enter a second purchase order line with a positive quantity for the replacement.

Depending on change management settings, the order may be subject to approval. Posting the credit note in the pending vendor invoice form after confirming the purchase order works like posting a vendor invoice – after entering the credit note number in the invoice number field you can post the credit note by clicking the button *Post* in the action pane of the vendor invoice form.

If the checkbox *Deductions requirement* in the item model group of the credited item is selected, you have to post a separate – negative – product receipt (item return) before posting the credit note (negative invoice).

3.7.1.2   Returned Order

If you want to use a new order for the credit note, you can enter a regular purchase order (*Purchase type* "Purchase order") with lines containing a negative quantity. Alternatively, you can select the *Purchase type* "Returned order" when creating the order (field on the tab *General* in the *Create purchase order* dialog). If you use the purchase type "Returned order", there are following requirements:

➢ **RMA number** – The return merchandise authorization provided by the vendor has to be entered in the *RMA number* field in the *Create purchase order* dialog.
➢ **Quantity** – Has to be negative in all order lines.
➢ **Return action** – For information purposes, displayed on the sub-tab *Setup* of the purchase order lines (default value in the procurement parameters).

In order to facilitate entering the credit note, you can use the *Create credit note* feature by clicking the button *PURCHASE/Create/Credit note* in the action pane of the purchase order. This feature is also available by clicking the button *Purchase order line/Credit note* in the toolbar of the order lines.

The credit note feature is similar to the copy feature for purchase orders (see section 3.4.2). But unlike the regular copy feature, creating a credit note reverses the quantity sign, creates a reservation in the original order line, and applies inventory marking (exactly offsetting the inventory value of the original line). Depending on whether you add credit note lines to an existing or to a new order, you have to pay attention to the checkbox *Delete purchase lines* in the *Create credit note* dialog.

3.7.1.3 Inventory Marking

In order to avoid unintended changes of inventory value, you can apply inventory marking to assign the value of the returned/credited item to the corresponding original receipt.

For this purpose, select the new order line (credit note line) in the purchase order form and click the button *Inventory/Marking* in the toolbar of the purchase order line. In the marking dialog, select the checkbox in the column *Set mark now* (marking the original order line now returned) and click the button *Apply*. The inventory value of the new line entered for crediting now exactly offsets the inventory value received from the original line.

Without marking, Dynamics AX calculates the outbound inventory value of the credit note according to the item model group of the item, for example applying the FIFO model.

3.7.1.4 Transaction Settlement

In case the original invoice has not been paid and settled yet, you can close the open vendor transaction of the original invoice immediately when posting the credit note.

For this purpose, click the button *INVOICE/Settle/Open transaction* in the action pane of the crediting purchase order. In the *Settle transaction* dialog, select the checkbox in the column *Mark* of the appropriate invoice and click the button *OK*. When posting the credit note, the open vendor transaction of the invoice will be closed.

If you do not settle the invoice when registering the crediting purchase order, the responsible has to settle the invoice and the credit note later in the open transactions (see section 9.2.5).

When working with settlements, take into account that there is no manual settlement if automatic settlement is selected in the applicable vendor posting profile (tab *Table restrictions*) or in the accounts payable parameters (tab *Settlement*).

3.7.2   Inventory Valuation with Separate Credit Notes

If you receive a credit note from a vendor for an item price reduction (e.g. refunding depreciation of damaged goods), there is no actual physical return of an item.

3.7.2.1   Crediting and Re-Invoicing

The easiest way to process such a refund is to register and to post a purchase order containing two lines: One line with a negative quantity and the original price (credit note) and one line with a positive quantity and the new price (invoice).

3.7.2.2   Crediting and Allocating Charges

If this is not suitable, for example if the credited goods have already been shipped, you have to post a credit note which does not directly refer to the item. The credit amount has to be allocated to the item separately in this case. There are two ways to enter this credit note:

> **Vendor invoice form** – Entering an invoice line with negative quantity and an appropriate purchasing category.
> **Invoice journal** – Entering a journal line with negative amount and an appropriate ledger account (see section 9.3.3).

After posting the credit note, you can record a charges transaction to adjust inventory valuation if applicable. For this purpose, select the original invoice in the invoice inquiry (*Accounts payable> Inquiries and reports> Invoice> Invoice journal*) and click the button *Charges/Adjustment* in the toolbar on the tab *Overview*. In the *Allocate charges* dialog, enter a line for the charges transaction then. The lookup *Charges code* in this dialog only shows charges with the *Debit type* "Item" and the *Credit type* "Ledger account". You can offset the balance on the credit ledger account by choosing a charges code referring to the same ledger account which you have used in the credit note. The ledger account on the credit note is either determined by the purchasing category (if posting in the vendor invoice form) or entered as offset account in the invoice journal.

Information on the general use of charges is available in section 4.4.5 of this book, detailed information on the *Allocate charges* form in the online help of this form.

3.7.3   Case Study Exercise

Exercise 3.16 – Credit Note

The goods received in exercise 3.9 show serious defects. You return them to your vendor and receive the credit note VC316. The vendor does not send a replacement. Which ways do you know for registering the credit note?

You decide to register the credit note in the original order. Enter the required data and post the credit note.

3.8 Purchase Agreement, Requisition, and Quotation Request

Purchase orders are the only documents in procurement which you can use as basis for product receipts and vendor invoices. Other documents in purchasing are used for business processes which prepare creating a purchase order.

3.8.1 Purchase Agreement

Purchase agreements provide the option to register and to follow up on blanket orders. Apart from purchase agreements at the level of product number and quantity, there are agreements specifying the total amount per product (and not the quantity), and agreements at the level of product categories or vendor totals.

3.8.1.1 Managing Purchase Agreements

In order to create a purchase agreement, open the form *Procurement and sourcing> Purchase agreements> Purchase agreements* and click the button *New* in the action pane. When entering an agreement, you have to select a *Purchase agreement classification* in the *Create* dialog. Agreement classifications (*Procurement and sourcing> Setup> Purchase agreement classification*) are only used for grouping and reporting purposes and do not refer to a specific functionality.

The header field *Default commitment* in in the dialog determines the level of the agreement:

> **Product quantity commitment** – Product number and quantity
> **Product value commitment** – Product number and value
> **Product category value commitment** – Value of a product category
> **Value commitment** – Total value for a vendor

The header fields *Effective date* (start date of the contract) and the *Expiration date* (end date) on the tab *General* of the dialog are used as default for the agreement lines. After clicking the button *OK* in the dialog, Dynamics AX creates the purchase agreement header and opens the lines view of the purchase agreement detail form.

In the agreement lines, enter line details including the *Item number*, *Quantity*, *Unit price*, and *Discount percent* (or *Net amount* and *Procurement category*, depending on the option selected in the *Default commitment*). If you want to prevent, that the total quantity of related release order lines exceeds the quantity in the agreement, set the slider *Max is enforced* on the sub-tab *General* of the tab *Line details* to "Yes".

Once you have finished entering the agreement lines, you can confirm and print the agreement by clicking the button *PURCHASE AGREEMENT/Generate/ Confirmation* in the action pane. In the *Confirm purchase agreement* dialog, set the slider *Print report* to "Yes" if you want to print the confirmation. In addition, you can set the slider *Mark agreement as effective* to "Yes" if you want to set the *Status* in the agreement header to "Effective".

If the agreement is not set to be effective when posting the confirmation, you have to manually change the *Status* in the agreement header from "On hold" to "Effective" before you can generate a release order.

3.8.1.2˙ Release Orders

In order to create a release order in the agreement form, click the button *PURCHASE AGREEMENT/New/Release order* after selecting a purchase agreement. Dynamics AX shows the *Create release order* dialog, where you select items by entering the *Purchase quantity* and the *Delivery date* for the release order. Clicking the button *Create* in the dialog creates the new release order, which is a regular purchase order of the type "Purchase order".

Instead of creating a release order in the purchase agreement form, you can start by creating a regular order in *Purchase order preparation* workspace or in the purchase order form. On the tab *General* in the *Create purchase order* dialog, select the appropriate *Purchase agreement ID* in order to generate a release order assigned to the agreement. When entering an order line with an item covered by the agreement, Dynamics AX automatically generates a link.

If you create a new purchase order in the vendor form and there is an applicable agreement, a dialog displays which provides the option to select an agreement.

In the release order, you can post the order confirmation, the product receipt, and the vendor invoice like in any other purchase order. When posting the product receipt or the invoice, the related purchase agreement updates the order fulfillment (lines view in the purchase agreement, sub-tab *Fulfillment* on the tab *Line details*).

If you want to check the link to the purchase agreement in an order line, click the button *Update line/Purchase agreement/Attached* in the toolbar. At header level, click the button *GENERAL/Related information/Purchase agreement* in the action pane.

3.8.2   Purchase Requisition

A purchase requisition is an internal document, asking the purchase department to buy requested goods or services. Unlike a planned order, which is created automatically based on an item requirement, a purchase requisition has to be entered manually.

3.8.2.1 Prerequisites for Processing Purchase Requisitions

Before a purchase requisition is transferred to a purchase order, it has to run through an approval process. This approval process is based on the workflow system (see section 10.4).

In order to configure the purchase requisition workflow, open the form *Procurement and Sourcing> Setup> Procurement and sourcing workflows*. Workflows for purchase requisitions refer to the template "Purchase requisition review" and – if necessary for the approval process – "Purchase requisition line review".

Products and categories, which are available in purchase requisitions, have to be registered and activated in an appropriate procurement catalog (*Procurement and Sourcing> Catalogs> Procurement catalog*). In the purchasing policies (*Procurement and Sourcing> Setup> Policies> Purchasing policies*), make sure that this catalog is selected in the policy rule *Catalog policy rule* of the policy which applies to your organization.

3.8.2.2   Entering a Purchase Requisition

You can enter purchase requisitions in the list page *Procurement and Sourcing> Purchase Requisitions> All purchase requisitions*. When clicking the button *New* in the action pane, Dynamics AX shows the *Create* dialog where you should enter a name for the requisition before clicking the button *OK*. Depending on purchasing policy settings, you can enter a purchase requisition line on behalf of a different person or organization by selecting an appropriate *Requester*, *Buying legal entity*, or *Receiving operating unit*.

The way for entering requisition lines depends on the type of the particular item:

> **Internal catalog items** – Choose a regular released product, linked to the current procurement catalog, by selecting it in the *Item number* column.
> **Non-catalog items** – Enter services and new products without item number by registering a *Procurement category* and a *Product name* (description).

Apart from entering lines by choosing an item number or a procurement category directly on the tab *Purchase requisition lines*, you can click the button *Add products* in the toolbar of the lines. In the related *Add products* dialog, click the button *Add to lines* in the middle pane after selecting an item which complies with the filter on procurement categories in the left pane. Clicking the button *OK* at the bottom of the dialog transfers the items to the requisition lines.

3.8.2.3   Approval Workflow

As long as you have not finished entering a purchase requisition, it shows the *Status* "Draft". Once the purchase requisition is complete, click the button *Workflow/Submit* in the action pane to start the requisition workflow. The requisition status switches to "In review" and the workflow system starts processing the submitted requisition in a batch process.

The further approval process is depending on the workflow configuration of the purchase requisition workflow. Section 10.4 in this book contains a brief description on how to configure and to process workflows.

As long as a purchase requisition shows the status "In review", you can create a related request for quotation (see section 3.8.3) by clicking the button *PURCHASE REQUISITION/New/Create request for quotation* in the action pane of the purchase requisition.

3.8.2.4 Creating a Purchase Order

Once a purchase requisition is approved, it shows the status "Approved" and is ready to be released (generating a purchase order). In case purchase requisitions are released automatically, Dynamics AX skips the status "Approved" and immediately switches to "Closed".

In the purchasing policies (*Procurement and Sourcing> Setup> Policies> Purchasing policies*), the policy rule *Purchase order creation and demand consolidation* (in the policy for your organization) determines if purchase orders are generated automatically or if they have to be released manually.

If manual releasing is necessary, click the button *RELEASE/New/Purchase order* in the action pane of the list page *Procurement and sourcing> Purchase requisitions> Approved purchase requisition processing> Release approved purchase requisitions* to release an approved purchase requisition to a purchase order.

3.8.3   Request for Quotation

A request for quotation (RFQ) is an external document which asks vendors to submit a quotation. One common request for quotation can include multiple vendors. Once the quotation from a vendor arrives, register it in a "Request for quotation reply" to prepare a comparison of quotes. If you accept a quote, you can transfer it to an order.

3.8.3.1 Entering a Request for Quotation

You can create a request for quotation manually in the request for quotations form, or generate it from planned purchase orders or purchase requisitions.

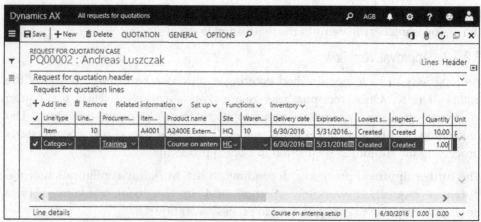

Figure 3-33:   Entering lines in the request for quotation form

In order to create a new request for quotations, click the button *New* in the action pane of the form *Procurement and sourcing> Requests for quotations> All requests for quotations*. In the *Create* dialog, choose the *Purchase type* "Purchase order" for a request referring to a regular purchase order. After entering the delivery date and the expiration date, close the dialog by clicking the button *OK*.

Requests for quotation consist of a header and one or more lines. The header contains common data like the language and the quotation deadline (*Expiration date*). The lines contain the items with quantity and price. Both, header and lines, include the fields *Lowest status* and *Highest status* showing the status ("Created", "Sent", "Accepted", or "Rejected") of the request and related quotations.

Like in the lines of purchase requisitions or purchase orders, a line in the request for quotation either refers to an item number or to a procurement category. In the request for quotation form, the column *Line type* controls whether the line contains an item or a procurement category. Data like delivery date and address in the lines retrieve a default value from the header. By use of the document management (see section 10.5.1) you can add details like data sheets or drawings to the request header or lines.

In order to specify the vendors receiving the request for quotation, switch to the tab *Vendor* in the header view and insert a line for each vendor.

3.8.3.2   Sending the Request to Vendors

After entering the appropriate vendors, click the button *QUOTATION/Process/Send* in the action pane which opens the posting dialog for sending the request. If you want to print the request, click the button *Print* in the toolbar of the posting dialog and set the slider *Print request for quotation* to "Yes". Then click the button *OK* in the posting dialog to post and print the request.

In order to view to which vendors you have sent the request for quotation, you can click the button *QUOTATION/Journals/Request for quotation journals* in the action pane of the request for quotation form afterwards.

3.8.3.3   Request for Quotation Reply

In the action pane of the request for quotation form, you can click the button *QUOTATION/Replies/Set RFQ reply defaults* to specify the fields to be included in a reply. These fields show on the RFQ reply sheet, which you can print when sending the request for quotation (choose the appropriate slider setting in the printing options). The default for the reply field settings is specified in the procurement parameters (*Procurement and sourcing> Setup> Procurement and sourcing parameters*, button *Default request for quotation reply fields* on the tab *Request for quotation*).

Once a vendor replies to a request by sending a quotation, register the quotation (reply) in the form *Procurement and sourcing> Requests for quotations> Requests for quotations follow-up> Request for quotation replies*. Alternatively, you can access the replies by clicking the button *QUOTATION/Replies/Enter reply* in the action pane of the request for quotation form. If accessing the reply form this way, make sure to edit the reply of the right vendor – click the button ▤ (*Show/Hide list*) to display the navigation list pane for this purpose.

In the reply form, enter details of the vendor quote on the tab *Quotation* (for header data) and on the tab *Purchase quotation lines* (for lines data). In order to support data input, you can click the button *REPLY/Process/Copy data to reply* to copy data from the request into the reply fields.

Once you have finished entering the reply, the highest/lowest status of the request and the reply show the status "Received".

3.8.3.4   Approving and Rejecting Vendor Quotations

If you want to compare the different replies (quotes) from your vendors, click the button *QUOTATION/Replies/Compare replies* in the action pane of the request for quotation form to access the *Compare request for quotation replies* form.

In the compare form, you can accept a quotation by selecting the checkbox in the column *Mark* and clicking the button *Accept* in the action pane. Alternatively, you can accept a quotation in the request reply form (button *REPLY/Process/Accept*).

When posting the acceptance, Dynamics AX automatically creates a purchase order. If you accept all lines of a request, Dynamics AX suggests to reject the other replies for the request. Alternatively, you can reject a request by clicking the button *REPLY/Process/Reject* in the reply.

3.8.4   Case Study Exercise

Exercise 3.17 – Request for Quotation

You want to receive vendor quotations for your item. For this purpose, enter a new request in the request for quotations form. This request should contain a line with the item entered in exercise 3.5. The RFQ reply defaults for the request should include the header field *Reply valid to* and the line fields *Quantity* and *Unit price*.

You want to send the request to your vendor of exercise 3.2 and another vendor of your choice. Once you have finished entering the request, choose the option *Send* in order to post and print the RFQ for these vendors.

After a while, you receive quotes with quantities and prices of your choice from both vendors. In order to track the quotes, enter them as request for quotation replies assigned to the original request. Your vendor of exercise 3.2 has submitted the better quote, which you want to accept transferring the RFQ reply to a purchase order. Then send a quote rejection to the other vendor.

4 Sales and Distribution

The primary responsibility of sales and distribution is to provide customers with goods and services. In order to perform this task, sales and distribution processes sales orders from the start (entering the order) through picking and shipping until the end (sending the invoice to the customer).

4.1 Business Processes in Sales and Distribution

Before we start to go into details, the lines below give an overview of the business processes in sales and distribution.

4.1.1 Basic Approach

Starting point for sales and distribution are correct master data, in particular the data on customers and products. When selling services or non-inventoried items, you can use sales categories instead of products.

4.1.1.1 Master Data and Transactions in Sales

Customer and product records are master data, only occasionally updated after initially creating the individual records. In the course of sales order processing, sales quotations and sales orders (transaction data) receive default values from customer and product records (master data). You can override the data in transactions, for example if your customer requires a different delivery address in a particular sales order. If such an update should also apply to future orders, you have to modify the customer record accordingly.

Since the sales process is mirroring the purchasing process, sales order processing is very similar to purchase order processing. Figure 4-1 shows the primary steps of sales order processing (including required predecessor and successor activities).

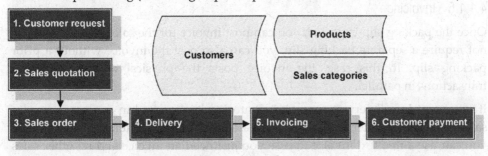

Figure 4-1: Sales order processing in Dynamics AX

4.1.1.2 Sales Quotation

If we disregard prior marketing activities, sales order processing starts with a request from a prospect or customer. Answering this request, the sales team creates a quote and sends it to the potential or actual customer. Based on the sales quotation, Dynamics AX can generate activities for following up on the quotation.

4.1.1.3 Sales Order

If the customer agrees to the proposal and orders the goods or services, you have to create a sales order as the basis for order fulfillment. Like a purchase order, a sales order consists of a header, which primarily contains customer data, and one or more lines, which contain the ordered items (products or sales categories).

Optionally, you can post an order confirmation and send it to the customer electronically or as printed document. Posting the order confirmation stores the confirmation. The order confirmation is available with its original content afterwards, no matter if there is a later modification on the actual sales order.

In order to manage long-term contracts (blanket orders), you can use sales agreements in Dynamics AX. If you want to issue a shipment related to the blanket order later, create a release order with a partial quantity of the sales agreement. Release orders are regular sales orders which are assigned to the agreement.

4.1.1.4 Delivery Management

Depending on the settings of the item, master planning takes care of the material supply (through purchasing or production) and makes sure that you can ship the sales order in time.

Before shipping the item, you can print a picking list to prepare delivery. After finishing the internal shipment procedure, you can post the packing slip. Posting a packing slip without a prior picking list is possible, if your company does not need picking lists.

4.1.1.5 Invoicing

Once the packing slip is posted, you can post invoice for the sales order. If you do not require a separate packing slip, you can also post the invoice without a prior packing slip. In this case, the invoice posts the physical and the financial transactions in parallel.

If you want to sell services or non-inventoried items, you can process a regular sales order (enter order lines with sales categories or service items). Alternatively, you can use a free text invoice in case you just need an invoice and no other sales document. In the lines of a free text invoice, you have to enter ledger main accounts instead of products or sales categories.

4.1.1.6 Customer Payment

Before the due date, your customer has to pay the invoice with or without cash discount deduction. Section 9.3.4 contains a description on how to post the customer payment and to settle the invoice in the customer transactions.

If the customer does not pay in time, you can create payment reminders in Dynamics AX.

4.1.1.7 Ledger Integration and Voucher Principle

Because of the deep finance integration in Dynamics AX, all inventory and customer transactions in sales are posted to ledger accounts specified in the setup as described in section 9.4.

In order to keep track of the whole business process, Dynamics AX comprehensively applies the voucher principle which means that you have to register a document (voucher) before posting the transaction. The transactions in sales order processing are similar to the respective purchasing process transactions.

For your guidance, Figure 4-2 below shows a comparison of purchase and sales documents in order processing.

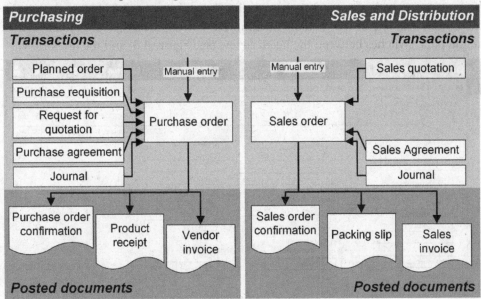

Figure 4-2:   Comparison of purchasing and sales documents

4.1.2   At a Glance: Sales Order Processing

In order to provide an overview of the main steps in sales order processing, this section shows the basics. In the example, we create an order starting in the *Sales order processing and inquiry* workspace and post all transactions directly in the sales order form. Of course you can also create the order from the customer form, or directly in the sales orders list page.

In the *Sales order processing and inquiry* workspace, which you can access from the dashboard or from the *Workspaces* folder of the *Sales and marketing* menu, click the button *New/Sales order* in the action pane. The *Create sales order* dialog shows next, where you have to select a customer in the *Customer account* field (you can trigger the search there by starting to type the first characters of the customer name). Clicking the button *OK* in the dialog creates a sales order header with default data like language or currency from the selected customer.

The sales order detail form then opens in lines view. If you are in view mode, switch to the edit mode by clicking the button *Edit* or by pressing the *F2* key. On the tab *Sales order lines*, you can start to enter an order line with item number (or sales category), quantity, and price. When selecting the item, Dynamics AX initializes the quantity, the price, and other fields like the site with default values. If you want to enter a second line, press the *Down Arrow* on the keyboard or click the button *Add line* in the toolbar. Clicking the button *Header* (or *Lines*) below the action pane switches between the header view (see Figure 4-3) and the lines view.

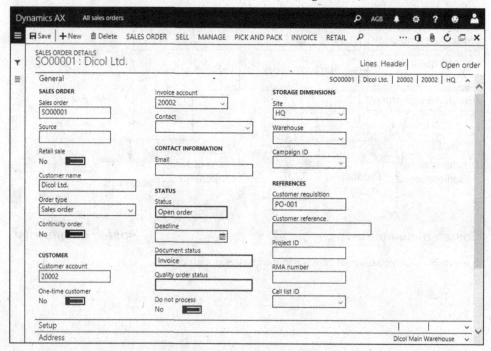

Figure 4-3:   Entering header data in the sales order header view

Note: If the sales order contains only one line, you might need to press the shortcut *Shift+F5* to refresh the form before you can post the order confirmation next.

If you want to print the order confirmation, post it by clicking the button *SELL/ Generate/Confirm sales order* in the action pane. In the posting dialog, make sure that the sliders *Posting* and *Print confirmation* on the tab *Parameters* are set to "Yes" and optionally click the button *Printer setup* to select a printer (compare section 2.2.1).

In order to post the packing slip in the sales order form, click the button *PICK AND PACK/Generate/Post packing slip* in the action pane of the order form. In the posting dialog, choose the option "All" in the field *Quantity* to ship the entire quantity. After making sure the sliders *Posting* and *Print packing slip* are set to "Yes", click the button *OK* to post and print the packing slip. Packing slip posting reduces the physical quantity in inventory and sets the order status to "Delivered".

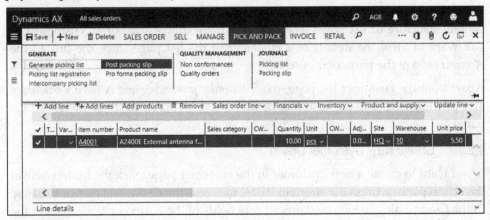

Figure 4-4: Posting the packing slip in the sales order

Posting the sales invoice by clicking the button *INVOICE/Generate/Invoice* in the sales order form is similar to packing slip posting. In order to invoice only shipped items, make sure to choose the option "Packing slip" in the lookup field *Quantity* of the posting dialog. If you select the option "All", invoice posting in parallel ships the deliver remainder quantity (open quantity, which is not included in prior packing slips). Invoice posting generates an open customer transaction to be paid and updates the order status to "Invoiced".

If applicable, you can skip transactions in the process described above. The most streamlined process is to post the invoice immediately after entering the sales order (selecting "All" in the *Quantity* field of the invoice posting dialog).

4.2   Customer Management

Business partners, who receive goods or services, have to be entered as customers in Dynamics AX. As long as the business partner only receives quotations, you can also use a prospect record.

Customer records in sales mirror vendor records in purchasing. In both areas there are list pages and detail forms with similar features. Examples are one-time customers, payment terms, cash discounts, posting profiles, and the global address book integration.

4.2.1   Core Data and Comparison to Vendor Records

In order to edit existing or to create new customers, open the customer list page in the sales module (*Sales and marketing> Customers> All customers*) or in the accounts receivable module (*Accounts receivable> Customers> All customers*). According to the general structure of list pages, the customer page shows a list of all customers. If you want to view the details of a customer in the list page, click the link in the *Account* field of the particular customer.

Apart from the customer list page, the *Sales order processing and inquiry* workspace also provides access to the customer detail form (list *Find customer* in the tabbed list pane).

4.2.1.1   Create New Customer Dialog

If you want to create a new customer in the customer page, click the button *New* in the action pane or press the shortcut *Alt+N* to access the *Create new customer* dialog. In the *Create* dialog, which contains all core fields of the customer record, select the appropriate *Type* ("Person" or "Organization") first. The field *Name* in the dialog is a lookup providing the option either to enter a new name or – if the customer is already a party in the global address book – to select an existing party.

Customer records are linked to the global address book in the same way as vendor records, which is why features like the duplicate check work as described for vendors (see section 3.2.1).

If you want to create a sales order immediately after creating the customer, you can click the button *Save and open/Sales order* in the dialog.

4.2.1.2   Customer Detail Form

In the customer detail form, you can switch to the edit mode by clicking the button *Edit* in the action pane or by pressing the *F2* key. If you are in edit mode in the list page and access the detail form afterwards, the detail form will open in edit mode.

The customer form contains numerous fields, which represent default values for sales orders. Like the vendor group in vendor records, the *Customer group* in customer records is a core setting which controls ledger integration through customer posting profiles (compare section 3.2.3). Further important fields include the *Sales tax group* (VAT group) and the *Delivery terms* on the tab *Invoice and delivery*, the *Currency* on the tab *Sales demographics*, the *Terms of payment* on the tab *Payment defaults*, and settings for blocking (lookup field *Invoice and delivery on hold* on the tab *Credit and collections*).

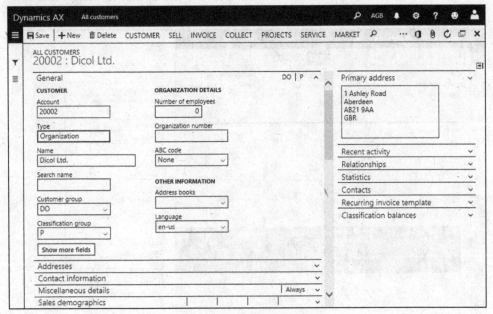

Figure 4-5:   Editing a customer in the customer detail form

Since the structure and the content of the fields in the customer record are very similar to the vendor record, the description below only covers deviations and elements, which primarily refer to customer records and which have not been explained for vendor records.

4.2.1.3 Invoice Account

Sometimes it is necessary to send an invoice to a customer, who is not the order customer – for example if the head office of an affiliated group should receive the invoice for subsidiaries. In order to comply with this situation, select the customer number of the invoice customer in the field *Invoice account* on the tab *Invoice and delivery*. A customer number entered there is the default value for the field *Invoice account* in related sales order headers. If required, you can override the invoice account in the sales order.

Invoices of applicable orders contain the invoice customer instead of the order customer, generating an open customer transaction referring to the customer number of the invoice account. Unless chosen differently in the lookup field *Invoice address* on the tab *Invoice and delivery* of the customer record, the printed invoice shows the address of the invoice account.

4.2.1.4 Alternative Address and Global Address Book Integration

Whereas the invoice account number in the customer form refers to a second customer number (assigning a separate customer record), the customer addresses on the tab *Addresses* of the customer form provide the option to assign multiple postal addresses to a single customer number.

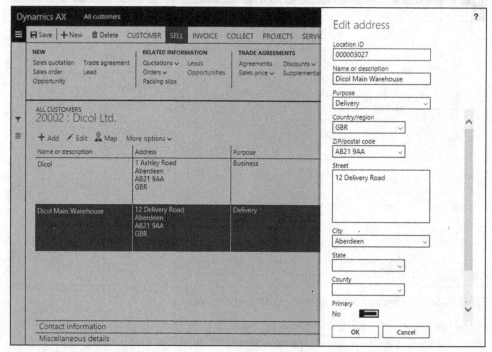

Figure 4-6: Editing a customer delivery address in the address dialog

Like the postal addresses for vendors (see section 3.2.1), customer addresses are shared with the related party in the global address book.

After clicking the button *Add* in the toolbar of the tab *Addresses*, the address dialog displays where you enter the address name and select one or more purposes. For the primary customer address, set the slider *Primary* to "Yes".

If entering an address with the purpose "Invoice", invoices for the customer show this address instead of the primary address. An address with the purpose "Delivery" is the default for the delivery address in sales orders. If you want to ship to an address, which is different from the delivery address or the primary address (default if there is no specific delivery address), select one of the other customer addresses or enter a completely new address in the sales order.

4.2.1.5 Print Management

Base settings for printing options like the destination (printer), the number of copies, or the footer text are available in the accounts receivable print management setup (*Accounts receivable> Setup> Forms> Form setup*, button *Print management* in the toolbar of the tab *General*).

You can override these settings in the print management at customer level (button *GENERAL/Set up/Print management* in the customer form). After selecting the appropriate original or copy document in the left pane of the print management form, choose the option *Override* in the context menu (which opens by a right-hand click) before entering the individual settings. Customer print management settings are transferred to sales orders, where you can override them at order level again.

Print management settings (e.g. a specified printer) apply to documents, if the slider *Use print management destination* in the particular posting dialog is set to "Yes" (compare section 3.4.5).

4.2.1.6 Credit Limit

Many companies want to apply credit limits to customers in sales. For this purpose, the accounts receivable parameters (*Accounts receivable> Setup> Account receivable parameters*, tab *Credit rating*) contain settings which control the usage of credit limits. Depending on these settings, the credit limit check includes only unpaid invoices, or also open packing slips, or additionally open orders, and shows a warning or an error message.

The tab *Credit and collections* in the customer form contains the field *Credit limit* where you can enter the credit limit amount of the customer. If the slider *Mandatory credit limit* is set to "Yes", the credit limit amount applies always. Otherwise, a credit limit amount of zero means unlimited credit.

When you enter (or post, depending on the parameter settings) a sales order, Dynamics AX checks if the customer exceeds the credit limit and either displays an error message (which prevents posting) or a warning.

4.2.1.7 New in Dynamics 'AX 7'

Items which are new in customer management refer to the browser-based user interface. The shipping carrier interface is deprecated.

4.2.2   Case Study Exercises

Exercise 4.1 – Customer Record

A new domestic customer wants to order your items. Create a record for this customer containing the name (starting with our user ID), primary address, and an appropriate customer and sales tax group for domestic customers. In addition, the terms of payment and the cash discount entered in exercise 3.1 apply.

The customer wants you to ship ordered goods to a separate delivery address. Enter a domestic delivery address of your choice for this purpose, which should be the default for orders of this customer.

Exercise 4.2 – Ledger Integration

You want to find out about ledger integration. To which summary account in the general ledger will an invoice for your new customer post?

4.3 Product Management in Sales

Apart from customer records (which are the main data source for sales order headers), products and sales categories (applying to order lines) are the second core area of master data for sales operations.

Product and released product records are required for inventoried items. For intangible items (e.g. services, fees, licenses), you can either use item records (with the product type "Service" or a specific item model group) or sales categories.

The following section primarily contains an explanation of data in the product record which are necessary for sales and distribution. A more general description of product management is available in section 7.2.

4.3.1 Product Data and Sales Category

When entering a sales order line, you have to select either an item number or a sales category to identify the item or service which you are selling.

4.3.1.1 Sales Category

A product category (see section 3.3.1) is a group of similar products or services. You can access the product categories in the category hierarchy form (*Product information management> Setup> Categories and attributes> Category hierarchies*).

Sales categories are product categories which belong to the hierarchy of the type "Sales category hierarchy". You can manage sales-related settings of these product categories in the sales categories form (*Sales and marketing> Setup> Categories> Sales categories*). An important setting there is the item sales tax group on the tab *Item sales tax groups*.

4.3.1.2 Creating a Product

The product record structure in Dynamics AX shows two levels, with the shared products containing data which are common to all companies, and the released products containing company-specific data (see section 3.3.2 and 7.2.1). You can access shared products in the form *Product information management> Products> All products and product masters*. Most sales specific data are included in the released product form (*Product information management> Products> Released products*).

In order to create a new product, open the shared product form and insert a record by clicking the button *New* in the action pane. After closing the *Create* dialog and entering shared product data as applicable, click the button *Release products* in the action pane of the shared product. In the released product, you have to enter at least the item group, the item model group, and– if not specified in the shared product – the dimension groups.

As an alternative to creating a shared product and releasing it, you can create a released product directly in the released product form by clicking the button *New* in the action pane there. In this case, the *New released product* dialog creates a shared product in parallel.

4.3.1.3 Sales Related Data

Core sales data, including the *Item sales tax group* (specifying whether regular sales tax / VAT or a reduced rate applies), are available on the tab *Sell* of the released product form.

After clicking the button *MANAGE INVENTORY/Order settings/Default order settings* in the released product, you can enter settings for order quantities and lot sizes at company level. In order to access the site-specific settings, click the button *MANAGE INVENTORY/Order settings/Site specific order settings* in the released product. If you want to enter quantity settings in the site-specific order settings, set the slider *Override* to "Yes".

Both order setting forms contain data for purchasing, sales, and inventory. Sales-related data show on the tab *Sales order*. Selecting the checkbox *Stopped* there blocks the product for sales transactions.

4.3.2   Sales Price and Discount Setup

In addition to the base sales price, which you can enter directly in the released product form, trade agreements provide the option to manage multiple price lists and discount agreements.

4.3.2.1 Base Sales Prices

The base sales price shows on the tab *Sell* of the released product form. Dynamics AX can automatically update this price based upon the purchase price or the cost price. The field group *Price update* of the tab *Sell* contains settings for this price calculation, including the lookup field *Base price* which provides two options:

➤ **Purchase price** – Sales price based on the base purchase price (tab *Purchase*)
➤ **Cost** – Sales price based on the base cost price (tab *Manage costs*)

The *Sales price model* specifies, if the price calculation refers to the field *Contribution ratio* or to the field *Charges percentage*. The *Sales price model* "None" means that there is no automatic calculation of the base sales price.

The other settings related to the base sales price (including price unit and price charges) are similar to the base purchase price settings (see section 3.3.3).

In addition to the base sales price on the tab *Sell* of the released product form, base prices are available at site level in the item price form. In order to access the item price form, click the button *MANAGE COSTS/Set up/Item price* in the released product. For manufactured items you can run a calculation of sales prices in the item price form based upon the bill of materials and the route (See section 7.3.3).

4.3.2.2 Discount Groups

Apart from the *Base sales price*, the tab *Sell* in the released product form also contains item discount groups for line discount and multiline discount.

Another kind of discounts are total discounts (invoice discounts), which are specified independently from items at order header level. In the released product form, you can exclude particular products from the basis of total discount calculation by setting the slider *Total discount* on the tab *Sell* to "No".

In the customer form, the tab *Sales order defaults* contains the price groups and discount groups (line discount, multiline discount).

4.3.2.3 Structure of Trade Agreements

Trade agreements in sales determine prices and discounts depending on customers and items (released products). Dynamics AX includes the following types of trade agreements for this purpose:

➢ **Sales prices**
➢ **Line discounts**
➢ **Multiline discounts**
➢ **Total discounts** (Invoice discounts)

Section 3.3.3 contains a description of price trade agreements on the example of purchase prices. In addition to the options available in purchasing, the sales trade agreements include the option to apply a *Generic currency* and an *Exchange rate type* specified in the accounts receivable parameters (*Accounts receivable> Setup> Accounts receivable parameters*, tab *Prices*). If a generic currency is specified, prices in trade agreements in this currency (if the slider *Include in generic currency* in the agreement line is set to "Yes") are automatically converted to other currencies if there is no other applicable trade agreement when entering a sales order line.

In the order management, you can assign discounts to the header and to the lines:

➢ **Line and multiline discounts** – Assigned to order lines
➢ **Total discounts** – Assigned to order headers

Discount and price trade agreements can refer to different pricing levels. You can for example enter a price agreement for an individual customer, for a customer discount group, or for all customers.

Line discount agreements can – in addition to the customer dimension – refer to the item dimension: Individual item, item discount group, or all items. Table 4-1 shows the different levels of line discount agreements in the dimension item and customer.

Table 4-1: Discount specification levels for line discounts

	Item number	Item discount group	All items
Customer number	X	X	X
Customer discount group	X	X	X
All customers	X	X	X

As a result, you can enter a line discount agreement for a particular item and a particular customer, and another agreement for an item discount group and all customers.

For multiline discounts, the same principle applies except that you can't enter a multiline discount for an item number.

Trade agreements for prices and trade agreements for total discounts have only got one dimension. Prices are specified per item, which restricts the item dimension to "Item number". Total discounts apply at order header level, which restricts the item dimension to "All items".

4.3.2.4 Managing Line Discount Agreements

In order to view sales line discounts, you can access the line discounts from different menu items depending on the basis of the discount:

➤ **For an item** (including the line discount group of the item) – In the released product form, click the button *SELL/View/Line discount*
➤ **For a customer** (including the line discount group of the customer) – In the customer form, click the button *SELL/Trade agreements/Discounts/Line discount*
➤ **For an item discount group** – In the item discount group form (*Sales and marketing> Prices and discounts> Item discount groups*), click the button *TRADE AGREEMENTS/Sales/View line discount*
➤ **For a customer discount group** – In the customer price/discount group form (*Sales and marketing> Prices and discounts> Customer price/discount groups*), select the option "Line discount group" in the lookup *Show* and click the button *TRADE AGREEMENTS/Sales/View line discount*

When working in line discount agreements, be aware that the column *Discount* shows a discount amount. The discount percentage 1 shows in a separate column and in the footer pane of the form. The discount percentage 2 only shows in the footer pane.

Another important setting for discount calculation is the column *Find next* in the discounts form. The checkbox there should only be selected for discounts, which apply in addition to discounts entered at another level. In the example of trade agreements shown in Figure 4-7, the discount in a sales order line with a quantity of 100 units (or more) would be 17 percent, if the checkbox *Find next* was marked for the 12 percent discount line and if the item is assigned to the item discount group with a discount of 5 percent in the other agreement line.

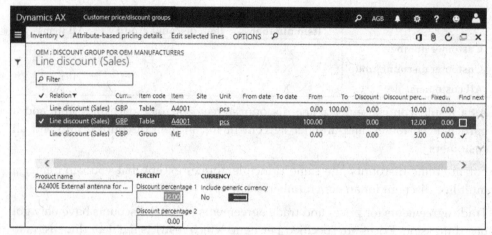

Figure 4-7:   Viewing line discounts for a customer discount group

Like registering a new price agreement (see section 3.3.3), registering a new sales line discount agreement requires to enter and to post a trade agreement journal (*Sales and marketing> Prices and discounts> Trade agreement journals*). After creating a journal by clicking the button *New* in the agreement journal header, click the button *Lines* in the action pane to access the journal lines.

When registering a sales line discount in an agreement journal line, make sure to select "Line discount (Sales)" in the column *Relation*. Line discount agreements (similar to price agreements) include following fields:

➢ **Period of validity** – *From date* and *To date*, referring to order entry or delivery (controlled by the *Date type* on the tab *Prices* in accounts receivable parameters)
➢ **Quantity** – Column *From* and *To* (for quantity-dependent discounts)
➢ **Unit of measure** – Column *Unit*
➢ **Currency** – Currency, for which the discount applies
➢ **Customer dimension** – Column *Account code* and *Account selection* (Individual customer, customer group, or all customers)
➢ **Item dimension** – Column *Item code* and *Item relation* – Individual item, item discount group, or all items

When entering line discounts, you have to keep in mind that discount percentages show in the footer pane of the journal lines.

If you want to enter line discounts at inventory dimension level (e.g. per site or color) and the appropriate dimension column does not show, click the button *Inventory/Display dimensions* in the action pane and select the appropriate dimension. As a prerequisite, the dimension group of the particular item has to include the selected dimension in the price search.

Once you have finished entering the line discounts in the agreement journal, click the button *Post* to activate the agreement.

If you want to update or to delete an active trade agreement, access the trade agreement inquiry form and select the agreement before clicking the button *Edit selected lines*. Like when updating purchase prices (see section 3.3.3), the update or deletion is posted through a new journal which is linked to the selected agreement.

4.3.2.5 Managing Multiline Discounts and Total Discounts

Whereas the line discount calculation is based upon individual order lines, multiline discount calculation includes all lines of a sales order with items which contain the same multiline discount group. You can use multiline discounts, if you want to grant a discount based upon the total quantity of different items. Multiline discount administration works similar to line discount administration.

Unlike line discounts, total discounts (invoice discounts) are not based upon items or item groups. Total discounts refer to a complete invoice and provide the option to enter a discount based upon the invoice total.

4.3.2.6 Required Setup for Prices and Discounts

As a prerequisite for creating trade agreements, set up at least one trade agreement journal name (*Procurement and sourcing> Setup> Prices and discounts> Trade agreement journal names*, also containing purchase trade agreement journal names).

If you want to use trade agreements at group level, you have to create appropriate price and discount groups and assign them to customers and/or released products.

Trade agreements are only used in price and discount calculation, if appropriate combinations in the price/discount activation (*Sales and marketing> Setup> Prices and discounts> Activate price/discount*) are selected.

Within the activated elements, discount calculation searches from the specific definition to the general – first the customer and item number level, then the group level, and finally the general discount level. Depending on the setting in the checkbox *Find next* of the selected trade agreements, only one discount or the total of discounts at multiple levels applies to a particular order line.

If line discount and multiline discount apply to a particular sales order line in parallel, a setting in the accounts receivable parameters (field *Discount* on the tab *Prices*) controls how to calculate the total of line and multiline discount.

4.3.2.7 Ledger Integration

Since discounts have an impact on finance, Dynamics AX includes discount posting in ledger transactions. Relating to ledger transactions and sales revenue calculation, you have to distinguish between line and multiline discounts on the one hand and total discounts on the other hand.

Line and multiline discounts are included in item revenue calculation, therefore reducing revenue and gross margin. Settings for the ledger integration of line and multiline discounts provide the option to either reduce the amount posted to revenue accounts, or to post the discount to separate accounts. Dynamics AX posts to separate accounts, if the inventory posting setup (see section 9.4.2) contains appropriate main accounts (*Inventory management> Setup> Posting> Posting*, tab *Sales order*, option *Discount*).

Unlike line and multiline discounts, total discounts do not reduce the revenue at item level. In addition, it is not possible to post total discounts to different main accounts. The account number for total discount transactions is specified in the accounts for automatic transaction (*General ledger> Posting setup> Accounts for automatic transactions*), where a line for the posting type "Customer invoice discount" contains the appropriate main account.

4.3.3   Case Study Exercises

Exercise 4.3 – Sales Categories

Your company offers installation services to your customers. For this purpose, enter a new category "##-installation" (## = your user ID) in the sales category hierarchy. This sales category applies the item sales tax group which refers to the standard tax rate.

Exercise 4.4 – Price List

Your company requires an additional price list applicable to new sales markets. Enter a new customer price group P-## (## = your user ID) for this price list and attach it to your customer of exercise 4.1.

The new price list should show a price of USD 90.00 for the item of exercise 3.5 starting from the current date. Enter and post this price in a trade agreement journal. Then check if the price shows correctly on your customer.

Exercise 4.5 – Line Discount

You agree with your customer of exercise 4.1 to grant a line discount of 10 percent on all items. Enter and post a trade agreement for this discount, which only applies to your customer. Which setting is required to use the discount in sales order lines?

4.4   Sales Order Management

The first document generated in relation to a sales order often is a sales quote, which you can send to a prospect or customer in reply to a request for quotation. Once the customer orders some goods or services, enter an appropriate sales order. Relating to the functionality and the structure of forms and list pages, sales orders work similar to purchase orders. This section therefore primarily explains subjects in sales, which are different from purchasing.

4.4.1   Basics of Sales Order Processing

Unlike purchase orders, which are primarily based on material requirements known within Dynamics AX, sales orders in most cases originate from sources outside the application. Apart from manually entering a sales order, there are only a few other options to generate a sales order from within Dynamics AX. Possible prior steps to a sales order are:

> **Sales quotations** – After receiving the acceptance from the customer
> **Sales agreements** – Blanket orders are the basis for release sales orders
> **Data import/export framework** – Exchanging data with other applications
> **Intercompany functionality** – Purchase orders in another legal entity
> **Project module** – Creating project sales orders or item requirements

In Dynamics AX, blanket orders are covered by sales agreements (*Sales and marketing> Sales agreements> Sales agreements*), which do not only contain contracts at the level of product number and quantity, but also at the level of the total sales amount for a product, or at the level of the total sales volume for a customer. In order to ship and invoice deliveries related to a sales agreement, you have to create release orders (regular sales orders linked to the sales agreement). The functionality of sales agreement matches the purchase agreements functionality as described in section 3.8.1.

Once you have finished creating a new sales order – either manually or transferring a prior document like the sales agreement – you can post and print the order confirmation. The further proceeding depends on the required transactions in inventory and sales, reflected by settings in Dynamics AX.

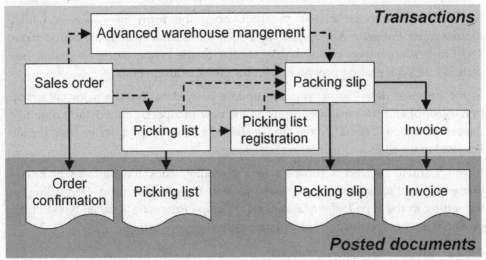

Figure 4-8:   Sales order processing in Dynamics AX

In order to process a sales order in the warehouse, there are following options as shown in Figure 4-8:

> **Packing slip** – Immediately posting the packing slip
> **Picking list** – Posting a picking list before packing slip posting

➢ **Picking list registration** – Registration of the posted picking list before packing slip posting

➢ **Advanced warehouse management** – Using advanced warehouse management functionality (see chapter 8)

In addition, you can execute picking using the pick form in the sales order line. Usually you work this way if you have to register serial numbers or batch numbers, but do not process picking as a separate process in the warehouse.

After posting the packing slip, you can post invoice. If no packing slip is required, you can post the invoice immediately after entering the order.

4.4.2   Sales Quotation

In a sales quotation, the business partner does not need to be a customer – it can be also a prospect. But since sales orders require a customer record, you have to convert the prospect to a customer before you can transfer an accepted quotation to a sales order.

4.4.2.1 Managing Prospects

Prospects are parties – companies or persons – in sales, who are not customers yet. Unlike customers, who are used in accounts receivable transactions, prospects are not included in financial transactions. But they are used in CRM activities like mailings and marketing campaigns, and in sales quotations.

If you want to create a new prospect, open the form *Sales and marketing> Relationships> Prospect> All prospects* and click the button *New* in the action pane. The *Create new prospect* dialog works similar to the create customer dialog (see section 4.2.1), integrating prospects with the global address book.

In the prospect detail form, you can update basic data like the sales tax group (VAT group) and the customer group of the new prospect. Some default data like the prospect type (*Type ID* on the tab *General*) of a new prospect derive from the tab *Prospects* in the sales and marketing parameters.

If you want to convert a prospect to a customer, click the button *GENERAL/ Convert/Convert to customer* in the action pane of the prospect form. Depending on the setting in the type (*Sales and marketing> Setup> Prospects> Relation types*) of the prospect, the prospect is deleted automatically after converting.

4.4.2.2 Processing Sales Quotations

In order to create a new sales quotation, open the quotation form (*Sales and marketing> Sales quotations> All quotations*) and click the button *New* in the action pane. Alternatively, you can create a quotation by clicking the button *SELL/New/ Sales quotation* in the customer form or in the prospect form.

If creating a quotation in the quotation form, the *Create quotation* dialog displays where you have to select the *Account type* ("Customer" or "Prospect"). Depending on the selected account type, enter a customer or a prospect in the appropriate lookup field. Dynamics AX then applies default values from the selected customer or prospect to the sales quotation, which you can override in the *Create* dialog. Clicking the button *OK* in the dialog creates the quotation header and switches to the quotation detail form showing the lines view.

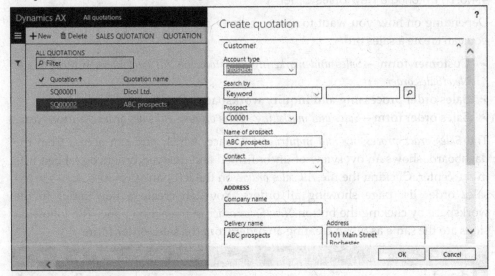

Figure 4-9:   Creating a new quotation for a prospect

In the quotation detail form, you can start to enter a line on the tab *Lines* by clicking the button *Add line* in the toolbar or by simply clicking the first line in the grid. Then select an item number or a sales category and other line details as required.

Clicking the button *QUOTATION/Generate/Send quotation* in the action pane of the quotation form posts and prints the quotation (similar to an order confirmation in a sales order). Depending on the answer of the customer or prospect, click the button *FOLLOW UP*/Generate/*Confirm* in the action pane at a later time to confirm the quotation (automatically generating a sales order).

If the quote refers to a prospect, you have to transfer the prospect to a customer before creating the sales order. For this purpose, the button *FOLLOW UP/Modify/Convert to customer* is available directly in the quotation form.

4.4.3   Sales Order Registration

Like in a purchase order, the order type in a sales order is a core characteristic. The order type in a sales orders can show following order types:

➢ **Sales order** – Regular sales order
➢ **Journal** – Draft or template, without impact on inventory and finance
➢ **Subscription** – Periodic order, remains open after invoicing
➢ **Returned order** – Credit note, see section 4.7.1

The order type "Item requirements" shown as additional option characterizes particular sales orders generated in the Dynamics AX project module, which is beyond the scope of this book. It is not possible to enter orders of the type "Item requirements" manually in sales.

4.4.3.1 Entering a New Sales Order

Depending on how you want to proceed, there are different starting points where you can create a sales order:

> **Customer form** – *Sales and marketing> Customers> All customers*, button *SELL/ New/Sales order*
> **Sales order processing and inquiry workspace** – Button *New/Sales order*
> **Sales order form** – *Sales and marketing> Sales orders> All sales orders*, button *New*

The *Sales order processing and inquiry* workspace, which you can access from the dashboard, shows an overview of unconfirmed and delayed orders on tabbed lists in the center. Clicking the tile *All sales orders* on the left pane provides access to the sales order list page showing all orders. You can create a new order in the workspace by clicking the button *New/Sales order* in the action pane. The following steps are the same as when creating an order from the sales order form.

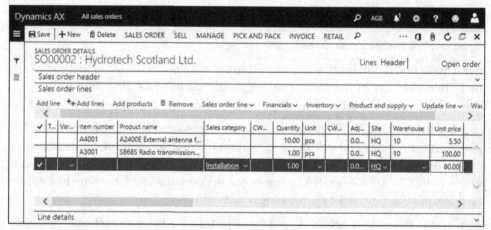

Figure 4-10:   Entering a sales order line with a sales category in the order form

In the *Create sales order* dialog, choose a customer in the *Customer account* field. You can search the customer by starting to type the first characters of the customer number (or the name), or by opening the lookup and applying a *Grid column filter* – e.g. in the column *Name* of the lookup. The sales order then accepts various default values from the selected customer, which you can override in the dialog. Clicking the button *OK* in the dialog finally creates the sales order header and switches to the order detail form in the lines view.

In the sales order detail form, you can start entering a line on the tab *Sales order lines* by clicking the button *Add line* in the toolbar or by simply clicking the first line in the grid. Then select an item number or a sales category and enter other line details as required.

Working in sales orders corresponds to working in purchase orders for the most part. For this reason, you can refer to section 3.4.2 regarding following topics:

> Structure and features in the order form
> Sales tax / VAT (see also section 9.2.6)
> Delivery schedule
> Orders of the type "Journal" (Section 3.4.2)
> Canceling orders (Section 3.4.4)
> Partial delivery, over and under delivery (Section 3.5.5)
> Order status and inquiries (Section 3.5.6 and 3.6.3)

Unlike purchase orders, sales orders do not apply change management and order approval.

When deleting a sales order, following accounts receivable parameters apply:

> **Mark order as voided** (tab *General*) – If set to "Yes", deleted sales orders show in the form *Sales and marketing> Inquiries and reports> History> Voided sales orders*.
> **Delete order line invoiced in total** and **Delete order after invoicing** (tab *Updates*) – If set to "Yes", orders (or order lines) are deleted when posting the invoice.

4.4.3.2 Keyword Search

The keyword search is an enhanced search functionality, available for searching customers, prospects, and items.

Before using the keyword search, you have to set up basic search parameters in the form *Sales and marketing> Setup> Search> Search parameters*. Then select the fields to be included in the search functionality on the tab *Criteria* in this form, or in the form *Sales and marketing> Setup> Search> Define criteria*. Buttons in the toolbar or the action pane specify the search fields for the customer search and the item search.

When creating a new sales order, you can select the option "Keyword" in the lookup *Search by* of the create order dialog to execute a customer search according to the selected criteria.

The item keyword search shows up if you enter part of the product name in the item number field of a sales order line and press the *Tab* key (ignoring the lookup which opens automatically). As a prerequisite for searching by product name, the search criteria setup has to include the product name.

4.4.3.3 Sales Order Hold

Sales order holds provide the option to put an order on hold while giving a reason for the hold. As a prerequisite, you have to set up hold codes (*Sales and Marketing> Setup> Sales orders> Order hold codes*) indicating the different hold reasons.

If you want to set an order hold, click the button *SALES ORDER/Functions/Order holds* in the sales order form. In the order hold form, click the button *New* and select the appropriate *Hold code*. The sales order list page then shows a checkmark in the column *Do not process* for the order and prevents order processing.

In order to clear the hold, open the order hold form by clicking the appropriate button in the sales order again (or accessing the menu item *Sales and marketing> Sales orders> Open orders> Order holds*) and click the button *CLEAR HOLD/Clear holds* in the action pane.

If you do not want to assign the decision to somebody else, click the button *HOLD CHECKOUT/Override checkout* in the order hold form and select the other user in the dialog. The selected user then is the only person who may work on the hold. If you need to override the checkout and transfer it to another user, click the *Override checkout* button again. The checkout is cleared by finally clearing the order hold, or by clicking the button *HOLD CHECKOUT/Clear checkout*.

4.4.3.4 Delivery Address and Invoice Address

The delivery address in a sales order derives from the primary address (or from the delivery address) of the customer. Like in a purchase order (see section 3.4.2), you can override the address on the tab *Address* in the header view or – at line level – on the sub-tab *Address* of the order lines. In this context, settings on the tab *Summary update* in the accounts receivable parameters determine whether posted documents (e.g. invoices) are split based upon different addresses.

Unlike the delivery address, address data for the invoice address are not directly editable in a sales order. The invoice address is the address of the *Invoice account* on the tab *General* in the sales order header view. The default for this invoice account is the invoice account in the customer record, but you can override the invoice account number in an order. If the invoice account field in the customer record is empty, Dynamics AX inserts the order customer number into the invoice account of the order. In case the customer record of the invoice account contains an address with the purpose "Invoice", this address prints on documents instead of the primary address of the invoice customer.

4.4.3.5 Item List

If a customer frequently orders the same products, you can use item lists in Dynamics AX as a copy template with item numbers and quantity.

For this purpose, you can set up multiple item lists in the form *Sales and marketing> Setup> Items> Item list*. If you want to create a new list, click the button *New* and enter the *Item list* ID and the *Description*. Then click the button *Add* in the toolbar of the tab *Items* and add items (including product dimensions as applicable) with their particular default order quantity. The button *Item list generation* in the action pane of this form provides the option to generate a customer-specific item list based on past sales.

In order to use item lists in a sales order, click the button *Sales order line/Copy/From item list* in the toolbar of the order lines. In the *Item list* dialog, select applicable items and optionally override the quantity before clicking *Copy and close*.

4.4.3.6 Delivery Date Control

An important task in sales order management is to determine delivery dates. A number of aspects determine the calculation of delivery dates in sales:

> ➤ **Item availability**
> ➤ **Order entry deadlines**
> ➤ **Sales lead time**
> ➤ **Delivery date control settings**

When discussing delivery dates, you have to keep in mind that Dynamics AX distinguishes between the shipping date and the customer receipt date on the one hand, and between the requested and the confirmed date on the other hand. For this reason, there are four different fields referring to the delivery date on the sub-tab *Delivery* of the tab *Line details* in the sales order lines.

If you want to calculate the delivery date automatically when entering a sales order line, activate the delivery date control on the tab *Shipments* of the accounts receivable parameters. The lookup *Delivery date control* there provides following options for delivery date calculation:

> ➤ **None** – Not applying delivery date control
> ➤ **Sales lead time** – Delivery date based on lead time and calendar settings
> ➤ **ATP** ("Available to promise") – Delivery date based on the item availability
> ➤ **ATP + Issue margin** – Adding the safety margin for the item (specified in the coverage group) to the delivery date calculated from ATP
> ➤ **CTP** ("Capable to promise") – Immediately executing local master planning

If the option "Sales lead time" is selected, delivery date calculation in sales order lines is only based on the applicable sales lead time and calendars. The sales lead time is the number of days required internally until shipping the item. A general default for the sales lead time is specified on the tab *Shipments* of the accounts receivable parameters. The lead time specified there applies as a default to the ship date in the order header. Order lines accept the header ship date, if the calculated delivery date based on the sales lead time of the item is not after the header ship date. You can specify sales lead times at item level in the default order settings, in the site-specific order settings, and in trade agreements for sales prices.

If the option "ATP" is selected, delivery date calculation is based on the item availability within the *ATP time fence* (field group *ATP*). Existing planned orders are included in the ATP calculation, if the slider *ATP incl. planned orders* is set to "Yes". If the quantity entered in a sales order line is not available (the calculation includes the on-hand quantity and the transactions within the ATP time fence), the shipping date is the first day after the ATP time fence. In order to avoid unnecessary delays, the ATP time fence should consequently match the lead time. The ATP offset time settings in the accounts receivable parameters apply to the calculation of delayed demand and to supply transactions, which are scheduled for past periods.

If the option "CTP" is selected, delivery date calculation immediately executes local master planning in the current dynamic master plan (see section 6.3.1) and creates planned purchase and production orders as required. For planned production orders, the delivery date resulting from the planned order includes the delivery time for components.

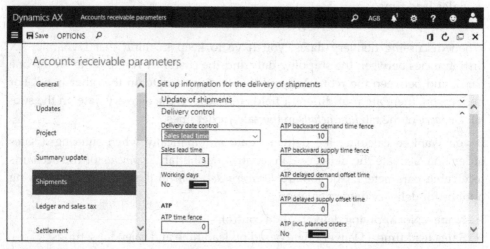

Figure 4-11: Delivery control settings in the accounts receivable parameters

Settings in the lookup *Delivery date control* of the released product (default order settings or site-specific order settings) can override the base settings in the accounts receivable parameters. If you want to activate or deactivate delivery control for a specific sales order or sales order line, you can override the lookup *Delivery date control* on the (sub-)tab *Delivery* of the order header or line.

When determining the delivery date in an order line, the calculation includes following calendar and transport time settings:

➢ *Inventory management> Setup> Inventory breakdown> Warehouses*, tab *Master planning* – *Calendar* of the shipping and the receipt warehouses
➢ *Organization administration> Organizations> Legal entities*, tab *Foreign trade and logistics* – General *Shipping calendar* of the current company
➢ *Sales and marketing> Customers> All customers* – *Receipt calendar* in the customer detail form (tab *Invoice and delivery*) or in the delivery address
➢ *Sales and marketing> Setup> Distribution> Modes of delivery*, button *Transport calendar* – Transport calendar per delivery mode and – optionally – warehouse
➢ *Inventory management> Setup> Distribution> Transport days* – Depending on delivery mode, shipping warehouse, and receipt address or warehouse

Order entry deadlines (*Inventory management> Setup> Distribution> Order entry deadlines*) determine the final time for entering same-day shipments in sales order lines. After the deadline, delivery date calculation starts with the next day.

In case delivery date control is activated, Dynamics AX checks if the item in the order line is available at the entered delivery date. In order to receive a proposal of possible delivery dates, click the link *Simulate delivery date* above the field *Confirmed ship date* on the (sub-)tab *Delivery* in the order header or line.

If necessary, you can deactivate delivery date control by selecting the option "None" in the lookup *Delivery date control* on the order header or line. After deactivating delivery date control, you can enter a date which is not included in the regular dates of possible delivery.

4.4.3.7   Item Availability and Delivery Alternatives

As a prerequisite for shipping a product, it must be available in inventory. You can use manual or automatic reservation (see section 7.4.5) to make sure, that the required quantity is reserved for the order and not available for any other purpose.

Multiple inquiries in the sales order form provide the option to check the availability of an item. If you only want to view the current inventory quantity of an item using the inventory dimensions of the order line (like site/warehouse), click the button *Inventory/On-hand inventory* in the toolbar of the order line.

In order to view the distribution of the item quantity among warehouses and other inventory dimensions, click the button *Overview* in the *On-hand*-form. Clicking the button *Display dimensions* provides the option to select inventory dimensions. If clicking the button *Net requirements*, the net requirements form for displays.

The button *Product and supply/Net requirements* in the toolbar of the sales order line provides the option to access the net requirements form, where you can start local master planning (see section 6.3) in order to calculate possible options for the delivery date. The button *Product and supply/Explosion* in the toolbar of the order line opens the explosion form, which shows the item availability at multiple BOM levels.

In case there are issues to meet the required delivery date in an order line, the delivery alternatives dialog supports selecting other delivery options – warehouses, product dimensions (for product masters), and modes of delivery. You can access the delivery alternatives dialog by clicking the button *Product and supply/Delivery alternatives* in the toolbar of the sales order line. Clicking the button *Select to promise* and *OK* in the delivery alternatives transfers the selected alternative to the order line. The options in the dialog are depending on the setting in the lookup *Delivery date control* (sales lead time, ATP, CTP) on the sub-tab *Delivery* of the order line.

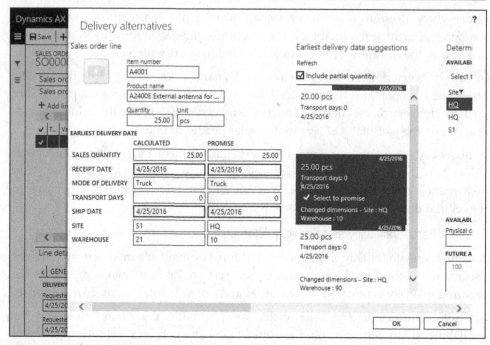

Figure 4-12: Selecting site and warehouse in the delivery alternatives dialog

4.4.3.8 New in Dynamics 'AX 7'

Apart from the delivery alternatives dialog, new items in sales order management refer to the browser-based user interface with workspaces.

4.4.4 Order Price and Discount

Based upon price and discount groups in the customer and order header, products and order lines, and appropriate trade agreements, Dynamics AX determines prices and discounts. Apart from the prices and discounts which apply immediately, trade allowances specifying a discount depending on the sales volume in a period (see section 4.9.1) have an impact on the sales revenue and profitability.

4.4.4.1 Sales Price

The sales price in an order line derives from the base price in the item record, or from applicable trade agreements. Trade agreements for prices at customer level take priority over prices at price group level.

The price group (representing a price list in Dynamics AX) of a customer is specified in the field *Price* on the tab *Sales order defaults* of the customer form. When entering a sales order, the price group of the customer is the default for the price group on the tab *Price and discount* of the sales order header view. If required, you can change the price group in the sales order.

In the sales order lines, you can override the calculated sales price and enter a new price manually.

If you enter a sales price or discount manually, and afterwards modify data in fields of the order line which are among the basis of price calculation (e.g. the ordered quantity), Dynamics AX may override your manual price and discount with the applicable trade agreement. Depending on the accounts receivable parameters (tab *Prices*, include the source "Manual entry" in the list on the sub-tab *Trade agreement evaluation*), Dynamics AX shows a dialog before overriding the manual price or discount.

If the margin percentage (calculated from the sales amount and the cost price) is too low, a margin alert icon shows in the column *Margin alert* of the order lines next to the *Estimated margin %*. As a prerequisite, margin alerts (with a minimum percentage for the acceptable and the questionable margin) have to be enabled on tab *Margin alerts* in the accounts receivable parameters.

4.4.4.2 Discounts

Sales orders apply the discounts from applicable trade agreements for total discounts, multiline discounts, or line discounts as default value. If you want to change a discount group in the order header, select the appropriate group on the tab *Price and discount* of the sales order header.

Since the total discount is a discount at header level, the order header does not only contain the discount group for the total discount, but also the discount percentage.

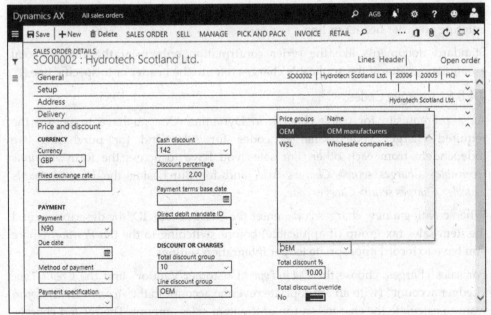

Figure 4-13:   Price and discount groups in the sales order header

The percentage of a line discount shows in a separate column in the sales order lines. In addition, the line discount percentage together with the multiline discount also shows on the sub-tab *Price and discount* in the order line. Apart from the percentage fields, there are fields for the line discount amount and the multiline discount amount – be aware not to confuse percentage and amount fields.

Dynamics AX calculates the line discount for a sales order line whenever saving the line. Unlike the line discount calculation, the multiline discount and the total discount calculation need to be started manually by clicking the button *SELL/ Calculate/Multiline discount* or *SELL/Calculate/Total discount* in the action pane.

For the total discount, you can skip the manual calculation if the slider *Calculate total discount on posting* on the tab *Prices* of the accounts receivable parameters is set to "Yes". In this case, Dynamics AX calculates the total discount whenever printing or posting an order.

If price details are enabled in the accounts receivable parameters (tab *Prices*, slider *Enable price details*), you can view extended price and discount information in the price details form opened by clicking the button *Sales order line/Price details* in the toolbar of the sales order line.

4.4.5   Surcharge Management

Charges in sales and purchase orders provide the option to cover expenses, which are not included in the price shown in order lines – for example fees for freight and insurance.

You can enter charges manually at header level and at line level in a sales order or a purchase order. In addition, there are charges which apply automatically when entering an order header or line.

Standard documents like the order confirmation only print the charges total amount, no matter if the applicable charges refer to the header or to specific lines.

4.4.5.1 Charges Codes

As a prerequisite for using charges in Dynamics AX, you have to set up the required charges codes. Charges codes for sales and for purchasing are independent from each other. For sales you have to access the form *Accounts receivable> Charges setup> Charges code*, and for purchasing the form *Accounts payable> Charges setup> Charges code*.

When creating a new charges code, enter the charges code ID, the description, and the item sales tax group (if applicable) before switching to the tab *Posting*, where you have to record appropriate ledger integration settings.

For sales charges, choose the *Debit/Type* "Customer/Vendor" and the *Credit/Type* "Ledger account" (with an appropriate revenue account in the *Account* field) if you want to calculate the charges on top of the item sales amount. The related charges amount prints separately on documents (e.g. invoices).

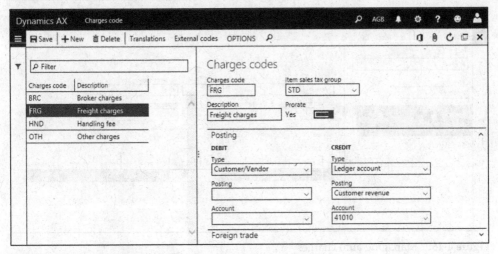

Figure 4-14: Managing charges codes for sales

For purchase charges to be shown separately on the vendor invoice, choose the option "Customer/Vendor" in the *Credit/Type*. In the *Debit/Type*, select "Ledger account" (posting to a separate ledger account) or "Item" (including the charges amount in the inventory value of the item).

In addition to charges with *Debit/Type* (or *Credit/Type*) "Customer/Vendor", which show separately on documents, it is also possible to set up charges codes generating only internal transactions in finance. The codes for these charges only include the types "Ledger account" or "Item" in the *Debit* and the *Credit* transaction.

4.4.5.2 Manual Charges

If you want to apply charges to a sales order or to a purchase order, open the charges transactions form.

At header level, you can access the charges transaction form of a sales order by clicking the button *SELL/Charges/Charges* in the action pane of the sales order form. In purchase orders, click the button *PURCHASE/Charges/Maintain charges* in the action pane. In order to assign line charges in a sales order or purchase order detail form, click the button *Financials/Maintain charges* in the toolbar of the order lines.

In the charges transactions form, first select the appropriate charges code. In the column *Category* you can specify if the charge is a fixed amount, or the calculation is based on the line amount or the line quantity.

4.4.5.3 Auto Charges

If you want to apply charges to sales orders automatically, enter automatic charges in the form *Accounts receivable> Charges setup> Auto charges*. Auto charges apply as default to charges transactions in sales orders, where you can override them.

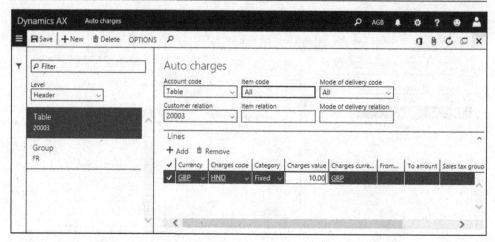

Figure 4-15: Managing auto charges

The header of the auto-charges form contains the lookup *Level* where you can choose whether to apply the charges to order headers or to lines.

The top right pane of the form contains the customers and items to which the charge applies. Line charges can depend on the customer (customer number, group, or all customers), the mode of delivery (mode of delivery, group, or all) and on the item (item number, group, or all). For header charges, the item selection is fixed to "All".

In order to enter the calculation formula for the charge, access the tab *Lines* and – like in a manual charge – select the *Category* specifying if the charge is a fixed amount, or if it is calculated based on the line amount or the line quantity.

As a prerequisite for applying auto charges to sales orders, the sliders *Find auto charges for header* or *Find auto charges for line* on the tab *Prices* of the accounts receivable parameters have to be selected.

For purchasing, similar settings are available in the form *Procurement and sourcing> Setup> Charges> Automatic charges* and in the procurement parameters.

4.4.6   Sales Order Confirmation

Printing an order confirmation requires to post it, which saves the document unchanging and separately from the actual sales order. Within Dynamics AX, it is the evidence of the document which has been sent to the customer.

Like confirming a purchase order, posting a sales order confirmation does not create inventory or financial transactions.

4.4.6.1   Posting Dialog for Sales Order Confirmations

In order to generate an order confirmation, click the button *SELL/Generate/ Confirmation* (or *SELL/Generate/Confirm sales order*) in the action pane of the sales order form. The posting dialog for the sales order confirmation is similar to the posting dialogs in purchasing (see in section 3.4.5). Like there, you can select the printer by clicking the button *Printer setup* or by setting the slider *Use print management destination* to "Yes". Make sure that the sliders *Posting* and *Print confirmation* in the posting dialog are set to "Yes" before clicking the button *OK* to post and print the confirmation finally.

As an alternative to the sales order form, you can access the posting dialog for order confirmations by clicking the button *Confirm* on the tab *Unconfirmed* in the tabbed list pane of the *Sales order processing and inquiry* workspace. Another option for posting order confirmations is the appropriate menu item for summary update (*Sales and marketing> Sales orders> Order confirmation> Confirm sales order*). In the posting dialog for summary update, apply a filter by clicking the button *Select*.

4.4.6.2 Inquiries

Once a sales order confirmation has been posted, the posted document provides the option to display and to reprint the order confirmation independently from later modifications in the actual order. In order to access the posted order confirmations, open the form *Sales and marketing> Sales orders> Order confirmation> Sales order confirmations* or click the button *SELL/Journals/Sales order confirmation* in the action pane of the sales order.

4.4.7 Case Study Exercises

Exercise 4.6 – Sales Order

Your customer (entered in exercise 4.1) orders 20 units of the item created in exercise 3.5. You want to register the sales order starting in the customer form. Which quantity and which price show as default, where do they come from?

Then switch to the header view and check the delivery address and the price group of the current order.

Exercise 4.7 – Charges

Your company wants to invoice a handling fee to customers. Enter a charges code C-## (## = your user ID) with the standard tax rate, selecting the posting type "Customer revenue" and an appropriate revenue account for credit posting.

In the sales order header of exercise 4.6, add this new handling fee as additional charge to the customer with an amount of 10 USD.

Exercise 4.8 – Order Confirmation

Post and print the order confirmation for your order of exercise 4.6 from the *Sales order processing and inquiry* workspace and select to display a print preview. Can you tell which amount shows in the order line and where the confirmation prints the charges?

4.5   Delivery Management

Delivery management includes all activities in the process of picking and shipping the ordered items. Picking, as preparation for shipping, is the internal process of collecting items within the warehouse.

4.5.1   Basics of Picking and Shipping

In order to prepare picking and shipping, you have to check upcoming deliveries continuously. For this purpose, the *Sales order processing and inquiry* workspace shows delayed orders and orders with delivery date changes on tabbed lists in the center. Apart from the workspace, there are particular forms which are designed to review pending shipments:

➢ *Sales and marketing> Sales orders> Open orders> Backorder lines*
➢ *Sales and marketing> Sales orders> Open orders> Open sales order lines*

In addition, pending shipments also show by filtering on the delivery date or the ship date in the posting dialog of picking lists and packing slips.

4.5.1.1   Picking Policy

In Dynamics AX, it is not required to process picking as a separate step. Depending on the setup, you can skip picking and immediately ship an item by posting the packing slip or the invoice.

If you want to process picking, the warehouse policy (distinguishing between the basic approach and the advanced warehouse management) determines the available options. Depending on the warehouse policy, there are following options for the picking process:

➢ **One-step picking**
  o **Pick form** – Manual recording in the pick form
  o **Picking list** – With automatic picking list registration
➢ **Two-step picking**
  o **Order picking** – Picking list, followed by picking list registration
  o **Advanced warehouse management** – Picking wave, followed by mobile device transactions

One-step picking is a process where you perform picking, but do not require confirming the picked quantity. This way of picking is only used in the basic approach for warehouse management.

Two-step picking requires confirming the actually picked quantity. In a warehouse applying the basic approach, this is done by entering the picking list registration (based on the picking list posted before). In a warehouse applying advanced warehouse management, the confirmation is done through mobile device transactions (based on picking wave work generated before).

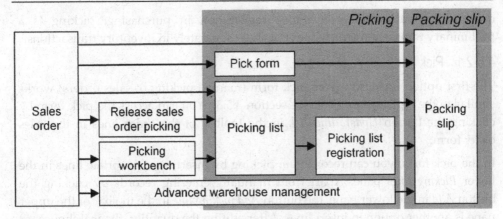

Figure 4-16:   Options for sales order picking in Dynamics AX

This section covers the picking process in the basic approach for warehouse management. In section 8.1.2 you can find a description on how to process picking using advanced warehouse management.

4.5.1.2 Core Settings for Picking

A number of settings control the picking process. Apart from settings relevant for advanced warehouse management, the accounts receivable parameters determine whether to apply one-step or two-step picking in the basic approach for warehouse management:

> **One-step picking** – If the *Picking route status* on the tab *Updates* of the accounts receivable parameters shows the option "Completed", automatic picking list registration is enabled. Dynamics AX then immediately reduces the quantity in inventory when posting the picking list.
> **Two-step picking** – If the *Picking route status* is set to "Activated", Dynamics AX does not change the quantity in inventory when posting the picking list. In this case you have to update the *Picking list registration* subsequently.

Picking is only possible for stocked items (as specified in the item model group). The item model group of the item further controls whether you have to register picking before posting the packing slip (checkbox *Picking requirements* on the tab *Inventory policies* of the item model group).

4.5.1.3 New in Dynamics 'AX 7'

Since the old "Warehouse Management II" module is not supported in the new release, items referring to consolidated picking have been removed.

4.5.2   Pick Form and Picking List

Picking in sales corresponds to inventory registration in purchasing: After picking, the related quantity shows the status "Picked" and is not included in the on-hand quantity any more. Like inventory registration in purchasing, picking is a preliminary transaction which does not show separately in inventory transactions.

4.5.2.1 Pick Form

The first option for picking, the pick form (manual picking of sales orders) works similar to the registration form (see section 3.5.3). You can access the pick form by clicking the button *Update line/Pick* in the toolbar of the order lines in the sales order form.

In the pick form, you can record item picking by inserting appropriate lines in the lower *Picking lines* pane. Apart from manually entering records by clicking the button *Add* in the lower pane, the button *Add picking line* in the toolbar of the upper pane is another option to insert lines. After editing the quantity, the warehouse, or other inventory dimensions in the lower pane as applicable, post the transaction by clicking the button *Confirm pick all* in the toolbar of the lower pane.

4.5.2.2 Picking List

If you need a printed report to support picking in the warehouse, you can post and print a picking list instead of registering the picking transaction in the pick form. In Dynamics AX, there are multiple ways to post the picking list:

➢ **Sales order** – *Sales order* form, button *PICK AND PACK/Generate/Generate picking list* in the action pane
➢ **Summary update** – *Sales and marketing> Sales orders> Order shipping> Generate picking list*
➢ **Release picking** – Starting from the *Release sales order picking* form, see below
➢ **Picking workbench** – Grouping picking lists to batches, see section 4.5.3

After posting and printing the picking list, you can provide the warehouse personnel with a hardcopy of the picking list.

If the warehouse usually picks all items immediately, it is useful to enable one-step picking by setting the parameter *Picking route status* in the accounts receivable parameters to "Completed". In this case, no manual picking list registration is required and the next step in Dynamics AX is to post the packing slip.

4.5.2.3 Picking List Registration

Picking list registration is required after posting a picking list, if two-step picking applies (accounts receivable parameter *Picking route status* set to "Activated").

In this case, you can access the picking list registration form by clicking the button *PICK AND PACK/Generate/Picking list registration* in the action pane of the sales order form. Alternatively, you can access the picking list registration form through the menu item *Sales and marketing> Sales orders> Order shipping> Picking list registration* or the menu item *Inventory management> Outbound orders> Picking list registration*. If starting from the sales order, picking list registration applies a filter on the current order. Otherwise, you have to enter a filter manually to show appropriate orders.

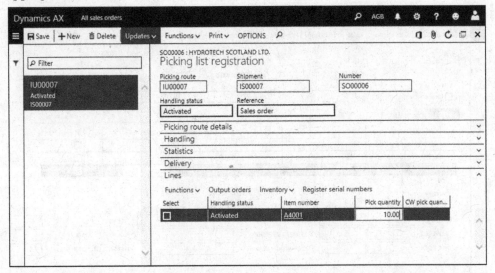

Figure 4-17: Picking list registration accessed from a sales order (tab *General* collapsed)

In the *Lines* tab of the picking list registration form, you can choose the lines which should be updated by selecting the checkbox in the column *Select* (see Figure 4-17). Before confirming the picked quantity of these lines by clicking the button *Updates/Update selected* (or *Updates/Update all* for all lines), adjust the quantity in the *Pick quantity* column as applicable.

4.5.2.4 Release Sales Order Picking

If you want to start picking from an overview with order lines ready for shipping, open the release picking form (*Inventory management> Periodic tasks> Release sales order picking*). The release picking form only includes items which are currently on stock and provides the option to select multiple sales order lines for shipping.

When opening the release picking form, an advanced filter displays for entering filter criteria on order lines. By clicking the button *Select* in the action pane of the release picking form, you can modify this filter as applicable later.

If you click the appropriate option in the button *Activation* on the action pane or enter quantities in the column *Activate now* manually, the items are activated for picking. This activation includes reserving the item quantity.

For the quantities in the column *Activate now*, you can post the picking list by clicking the button *Release for pick* in the action pane. The further proceeding, including one-step or two-step picking, is the same as when posting the picking list directly from the order.

If you want to specify priorities for picking based on the customer, you can enter a *Classification group* on the tab *General* of the customer form. This group displays in the left-most column of the release picking form, which provides the option to filter on this criterion.

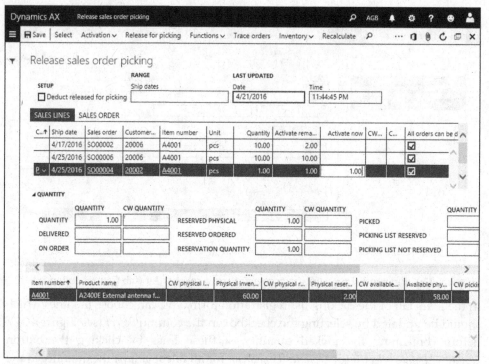

Figure 4-18:   Release sales order picking

4.5.2.5 Reverse Picking Transactions

The pick form is not only used for picking, but also for reversing a pick transaction, which has been posted in the pick form or through a picking list. Similar to registering the original picking transaction, you can access the pick form in the sales order detail form by clicking the button *Update line/Pick* in the toolbar of the order lines after selecting the respective line. In the upper pane of the pick form, click the button *Add picking line* after selecting the appropriate transaction. Posting the reversing transaction by clicking the button *Confirm pick all* works similar to regular picking, but with a negative quantity.

If the original picking transaction has been posted through a picking list, you can alternatively use the picking list registration to reverse picking. In this case, open the picking list registration form by clicking the button *PICK AND PACK/Generate/ Picking list registration* in the action pane of the sales order form. In the picking list registration form, click the button *Functions/Unpick* in the toolbar of the tab *Lines*. In a second step, you have to click the button *Functions/Cancel picking line* in the action pane of the picking list registration form to cancel the picking list itself. You can skip the second step by setting the slider *Cancel unpicked quantity* in the unpicking dialog of the first step to "Yes".

4.5.3 Picking Workbench

The picking workbench is an enhancement for sales order picking in paper-based warehouse processes, which provides the option to group picking lists to batches (picking waves).

Optionally you can apply a boxing logic to collect items in boxes or carts if your picking process includes putting items into boxes. Dynamics AX then suggests boxes of an appropriate size for picking.

You can use the picking workbench as an alternative to the *Release sales order picking* functionality described in section 4.5.2.

4.5.3.1 Setup for the Picking Workbench

As a primary prerequisite, number sequences for the picking workbench have to be specified in the inventory parameters (*Inventory management> Setup> Inventory and warehouse management parameters*). If you want to use the boxing logic, set the slider *Boxing logic* for picking workbench on the tab *General* of the parameters to "Yes".

In the workbench profile (*Inventory management> Setup> Picking workbench> Workbench profiles*), set up one or more profiles used as filtering criteria in the picking workbench.

In the warehouse form (*Inventory management> Setup> Inventory breakdown> Warehouses*), the tab *Picking workbench* contains settings for splitting picking waves (workbench sessions) – e.g. the maximum number of lines per picking list.

If you want to use the boxing logic in the picking workbench, open the form *Inventory management> Setup> Boxing logic> Box definitions* and set up the different boxes which are used in the warehouse with their physical dimensions and weight. The checkbox *Active* controls whether a box is available for picking.

In the released products detail form, the tab *Deliver* contains the slider *Apply boxing logic for picking workbench* which has to be set to "Yes" for items using the boxing logic. The selection of applicable boxes for an item is only based on the physical dimensions and the weight of the item (tab *Manage inventory* of the released product). If the slider *Ship alone* on the tab *Deliver* of the released product is set to "Yes", the item will be picked separately without boxing.

4.5.3.2 Working with the Picking Workbench

Picking processes in the picking workbench are based on sales orders which you have to enter before you can start picking.

In the picking workbench (*Inventory management> Outbound orders> Picking workbench*), you can start the picking process by clicking the button *New* in the action pane. On the tab *Criteria* of the picking workbench form, enter criteria like the *Ship date* of the order line to specify which sales orders should be included in the current picking. In the criteria field *Profile,* you can select a workbench profile providing default values for the criteria fields.

After selecting appropriate criteria, click the button *PICKING SESSION/Generate picking batches* in the action pane of the picking workbench. Depending on the criteria, on settings for splitting picking batches in the warehouse form, and on settings for boxing (box size and item size/weight), Dynamics AX then creates one or more picking batches. Generating picking batches executes picking list posting. The picking lists linked to a picking batch show on the tab *Picking list* in the workbench.

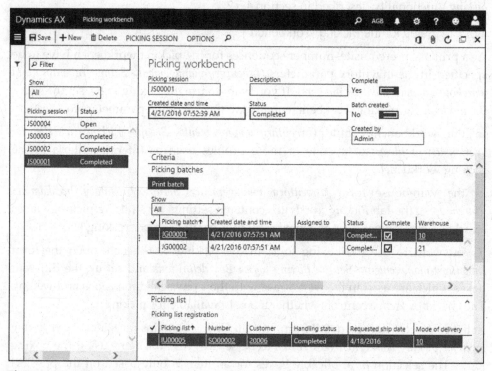

Figure 4-19:   Managing a picking batch in the picking workbench

Printing the picking batch label and the picking list is a required step, which you can do by clicking the button *Print batch* in the toolbar of the *Picking batches* pane in the workbench. For items applying the boxing logics, the selected box name is printed in the picking list header.

After printing all picking lists of a picking batch, select the checkbox *Complete* in the picking batch. The slider *Complete* in the picking session completes all related picking batches.

Depending on whether one-step picking or two-step picking applies to your company (see section 4.5.1), the next step is posting the packing slip (one-step picking) or confirming the picking list (two-step picking).

In case of two-step picking, confirming the picking list through the picking list registration is not different from the regular picking list registration in the basic picking list process. But in addition to the other access options to the picking list registration, the picking workbench contains the button *Picking list registration* to access the picking list registration form directly.

4.5.4   Packing Slip

Posting the packing slip (delivery note) is the last step in the picking and shipping process.

4.5.4.1   Posting Dialog for Packing Slips

You can open the posting dialog for packing slips by clicking the button *PICK AND PACK/Generate/Packing slip* in the action pane of the sales order form or through the menu item *Sales and marketing> Sales orders> Order shipping> Post packing slip*.

The posting dialog shows the familiar format. The applicable option in the lookup field *Quantity* on the tab *Parameters* is depending on the prior process:

➢ **Picked** – Select this option, if picking is executed before posting the packing slip. The picked quantity then is the default for the column *Update* on the tab *Lines* of the posting dialog.
➢ **Picked quantity and non-stocked products** – Includes the ordered quantity of non-stocked products in addition to picked quantity of stocked items.
➢ **All** – The total remaining order quantity applies.
➢ **Deliver now** – The quantity of the column *Deliver now* in the order lines applies.

Make sure that the sliders *Posting* and *Print packing slip* in the posting dialog are set to "Yes" before clicking the button *OK* in order to post and print the packing slip.

Partial deliveries, over deliveries, and under deliveries are available in sales the same way as in purchasing (see section 3.5.5). If you want to learn about the order status and the document status update, you can also refer to the corresponding purchase order status as described in section 3.5.6.

4.5.4.2   Ledger Integration

If ledger integration is activated for packing slip posting, Dynamics AX posts transactions to the general ledger in parallel to the inventory transactions. These ledger transactions are reversed when posting the related invoice.

Following core settings control packing slip posting to the general ledger:

➢ **Accounts receivable parameters** – The slider *Post packing slip in ledger* on the tab *Updates* has to be set to "Yes" to enable ledger posting (not required for standard cost items).
➢ **Item model group** – The checkbox *Post physical inventory* on the tab *Costing method & cost recognition* in the item model group of the item has to be selected.

These settings work similar to the related setting for the ledger integration of product receipts.

4.5.4.3 Transaction Inquiry

If you want to view the inventory transactions in the sales order form after posting the packing slip, click the button *Inventory/Transactions* in the toolbar of the order lines. After posting the packing slip, the issue status of the inventory transaction is "Deducted". The posting date of the packing slip shows in the column *Physical date* whereas the *Financial date* remains empty until posting the invoice. The packing slip number shows on the tab *Updates* of the *Transaction detail* form (access by clicking the button *Transaction details* in the inventory transaction).

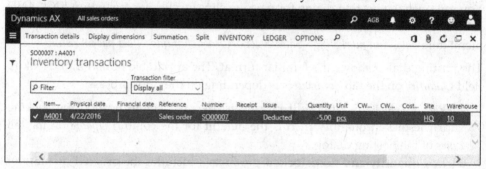

Figure 4-20:   Inventory transaction after packing slip posting

In order to access the posted packing slips, open the form *Sales and marketing> Sales orders> Order shipping> Packing slip* or click the button *PICK AND PACK/Journals/ Packing slip* in the action pane of the sales order form. After selecting a packing slip on the tab *Overview* of the inquiry form, you can switch to the tab *Lines* to view the related packing slip lines.

If you want to view related transactions in the general ledger, open the voucher transactions form by clicking the button *Vouchers* in the action pane of the packing slip inquiry (or the button *Ledger/Physical voucher* in the inventory transactions).

4.5.4.4 Canceling a Packing Slip

You can cancel a posted packing slip using the *Cancel* feature in the packing slip inquiry form (*Sales and marketing> Sales orders> Order shipping> Packing slip*). After selecting the particular packing slip, click the button *Cancel* in the action pane. If you just want to reduce the posted quantity, click the button *Correct*.

4.5.5   Case Study Exercises

Exercise 4.9 – Packing Slip

You want to check which order lines which are available for shipping. The inquiry should not be limited to your orders, but also include other orders available in your company. Which options do you know?

Knowing your order of exercise 4.6 is among the orders to be shipped, you want to post the packing slip. Before posting, check following items in the sales order:

➤ Order status and document status
➤ Inventory quantity of the ordered item (button *Inventory/On-hand inventory*)
➤ Inventory transactions related to the order line (button *Inventory/Transactions*)

Post and print a packing slip for the complete order quantity in the sales order form, selecting a print preview as print destination.

Now review the status of the points in the list above again. What is different after packing slip posting?

Exercise 4.10 – Picking List

Your customer of exercise 4.1 orders another 20 units of the item entered in exercise 3.5. Enter an appropriate sales order.

Your warehouse requires a picking list this time. Post and print a picking list containing 10 units of the ordered item. Can you tell which setting controls if you need to enter picking list registration? If required, update the picking list registration.

Then post the packing slip for the picked items.

Exercise 4.11 – Packing Slip Inquiry

You want to view the packing slip of exercise 4.10. Open the packing slip inquiry from the sales order form. In a second step, open the packing slip inquiry through the appropriate menu path. Check the packing slip header and the lines and try to find out, if there are related ledger transactions.

4.6   Sales Invoice

Posting the sales invoice is the last step in sales order processing. The invoice increases the open customer balance and reduces the financial value of inventory. After invoicing all lines of a sales order, the sales order is completed. Payment of invoices then runs through a separate process in finance (see section 9.3.4).

If you want to invoice inventoried products, you have to process a sales order. But it is not required to go through the complete process including order confirmation, picking, and shipping – you can post the sales order invoice immediately after entering the order.

Free text invoices apply, if you want to post an invoice not referring to products or sales categories. In the lines of a free text invoice, you have to enter ledger accounts instead of item numbers. Free text invoices have no connection to items and no impact on inventory and supply chain management.

4.6.1   Sales Order Invoice

The way of posting a sales invoice is similar to posting the packing slip.

4.6.1.1 Posting Dialog for Sales Order Invoices

You can access the posting dialog for invoices by clicking the button *INVOICE/ Generate/Invoice* in the action pane of the sales order form or through the menu item *Accounts receivable> Invoices> Batch invoicing> Invoice*.

The posting dialog shows the familiar format. The applicable option in the lookup field *Quantity* on the tab *Parameters* is depending on the prior process:

> **Packing Slip** – Usual option, since in most cases a packing slip is posted first and you want to invoice the shipped quantity.
> **All** or **Deliver now** – If selected, Dynamics AX does not initialize the column *Update* in the invoice lines with the shipped quantity. For any quantity not shipped yet, the physical transaction is posted in parallel to the invoice.

If you choose the option "Packing Slip" in the lookup *Quantity*, the button *Select packing slip* in the toolbar on the tab *Overview* of the posting dialog provides the option to select or deselect particular packing slips for invoicing.

Before posting, you can click the button *Totals* on the tab *Overview* of the posting dialog to check the totals. Then make sure that the sliders *Posting* and *Print invoice* in the posting dialog are set to "Yes" before clicking the button *OK* in order to post and print the invoice.

4.6.1.2 Transaction Inquiry

Posting the invoice generates general ledger transactions, inventory transactions, customer transactions, and transactions in other subledgers like sales tax as applicable. Once all lines of an order are completely invoiced, the order status changes to "Invoiced".

If you want to view the inventory transactions in the sales order form after posting the invoice, click the button *Inventory/Transactions* in the toolbar of the order lines. After posting the invoice, the issue status of the inventory transaction is "Sold" and the posting date of the invoice shows in the column *Financial date*.

In order to view the posted sales invoices, open the form *Accounts receivable> Inquiries and reports> Invoices> Invoice journal* or click the button *INVOICE/Journals/ Invoice* in the action pane of the sales order form. Clicking an invoice number shown as link in the grid opens the related invoice detail form where you can view the invoice lines on the tab *Lines*.

If you want to view corresponding transactions in the general ledger, open the voucher transactions form by clicking the button *Voucher* in the invoice inquiry (or the button *Ledger/Financial voucher* in the inventory transactions).

4.6.1.3 Transaction Origin

Clicking the button *Transaction origin* in the voucher transactions form opens the transaction origin form, which shows related transactions for the voucher in all modules. Figure 4-21 for example shows the invoice for an item, which has been shipped with a prior packing slip.

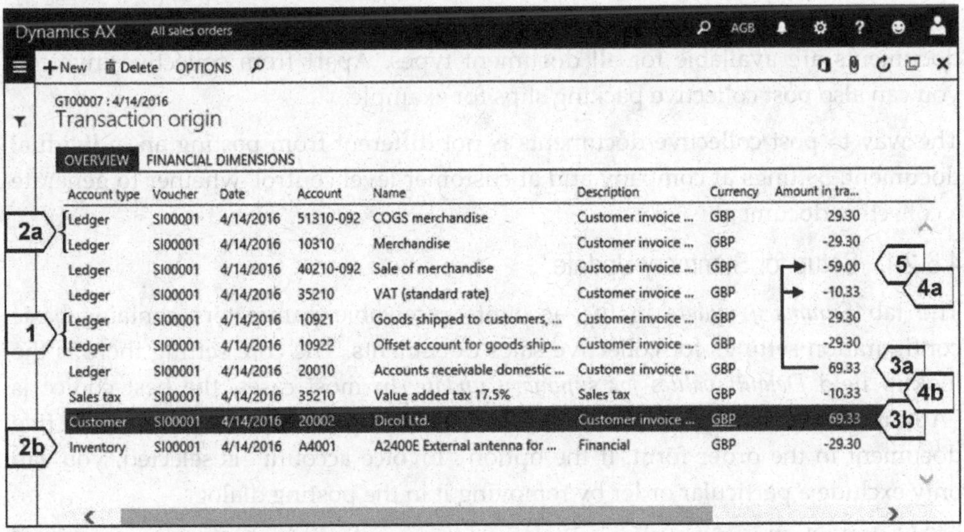

Figure 4-21: Transactions of a sales invoice in the transaction origin form

When classifying the transactions of the invoice shown in Figure 4-21, you have to distinguish between following transactions types:

Table 4-2: Transactions of the sales invoice in Figure 4-21

Transaction	General ledger		Subledger	
Packing slip reversal	Account 10921 offsetting account 10922	[1]		
Inventory	Account 51310 for COGS (cost of goods sold) offsetting stock account 10310	[2a]	Financial inventory transaction for item A4001	[2b]
Customer	Summary account 20010 offsetting tax account 35210 and revenue account 40210	[3a] [4a] [5]	Customer transaction and sales tax transaction	[3b] [4b]

Invoice posting only reverses packing slip transactions, if a prior packing slip has been posted to the general ledger.

The particular ledger accounts in all transactions are depending on the actual procedure and on the applicable setup. For this reason, there may be more or fewer transactions if comparing the transactions in Figure 4-21 with other invoices. For example, there are no sales tax transactions in invoices to foreign countries.

The customer summary account related to the customer transaction is specified in the applicable customer posting profile, which works similar to the vendor posting profile (see section 3.2.3). Apart from the sales tax transaction, settings for the other transactions are available in the inventory posting setup (see section 9.4.2).

4.6.2   Collective Invoice

If you want to post an invoice related to multiple sales orders (e.g. a monthly invoice), you have to post a collective invoice in a summary update. Collective documents are available for all document types. Apart from collective invoices, you can also post collective packing slips for example.

The way to post collective documents is not different from posting an individual document. Settings at company and at customer level control, whether to generate a collective document.

4.6.2.1   Setup for Summary Update

The tab *Summary update* in the accounts receivable parameters contains basic configuration settings for collective sales documents. The core setting there is the lookup field *Default values for summary update*. In most cases, the best choice is "Automatic summary" which allows deselecting orders from a collective document in the order form. If the option "Invoice account" is selected, you can only exclude a particular order by removing it in the posting dialog.

Clicking the button *Summary update parameters* on the sub-tab *Summary update* of the accounts receivable parameters tab *Summary update* displays the summary update parameters form. This form contains a separate tab per document type with the setting, which sales order fields must have the same content to join a collective document.

If the option "Automatic summary" is selected in the parameter field *Default values for summary update*, you have to enabled automatic summary on the particular customers (button *CUSTOMER/Setup/Summary update* in the customer form). The setting on the customer is the default for sales orders, where you can change it after clicking the button *GENERAL/Setup/Summary* in the sales order form.

4.6.2.2   Posting Collective Invoices

In order to post a collective invoice, open the summary update dialog *Accounts receivable> Invoices> Batch invoicing> Invoice*. In most cases, the option "Packing slip" in the lookup field *Quantity* of the posting dialog is the right choice, making sure that the invoice only covers shipped quantities.

In the posting dialog, first click the button *Select* [1] as shown in Figure 4-22 in order to select appropriate sales orders in the advanced filter dialog. After closing the filter dialog, the selected orders show on the tab *Overview* of the posting dialog.

If there are orders which you do not want to invoice, click the button *Remove* in the toolbar of the tab *Overview* to delete the respective lines. Deleting a line in the posting dialog only removes the selection. It does not delete the order or the packing slip, which is why the order will show again, whenever you want to post an appropriate invoice the next time.

If you want to include or exclude particular packing slips from invoice posting, click the button *Select packing slip* [2].

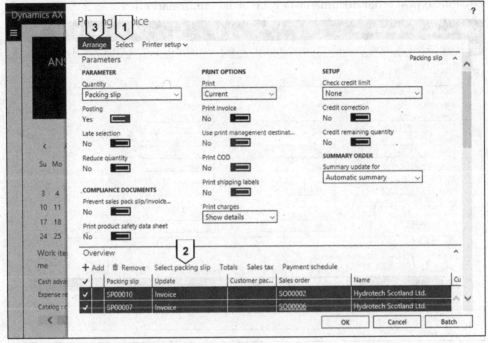

Figure 4-22: Posting a collective invoice receipt

Once you have finished selecting sales orders and packing slips, click the button *Arrange* [3]. Arranging combines the orders into a common invoice according to the summary update parameters. If the setting in the accounts receivable parameters is not suitable when posting a particular invoice, you can choose a different option in the lookup *Summary update for* on the tab *Parameters* before arranging.

In the example shown in Figure 4-22, the *Arrange* feature will merge the two orders into one common line. Clicking the button *OK* in the posting dialog afterwards posts the collective invoice.

4.6.3 Free Text Invoice

Free text invoices are used to invoice a customer for intangible items without order processing. The structure of free text invoices is similar to sales orders: Every free text invoice consists of a header and one or more lines. But instead of product numbers and sales categories, the lines of a free text invoice contain main accounts. Entering a negative invoice amount in the free text invoice creates a credit note. But free text invoices and free text credit notes are not included in item statistics and inventory valuation.

Once you have finished entering the free text invoice, you can post and print it. The invoice is the only document which you can post in a free text invoice, it is not possible to post other documents (e.g. an order confirmation).

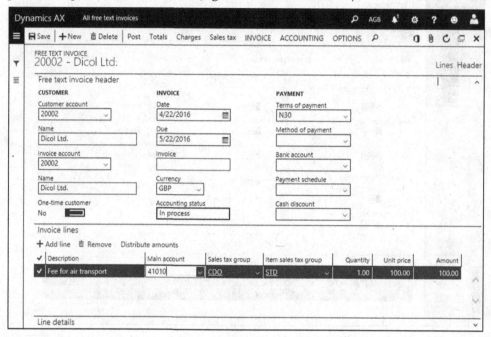

Figure 4-23: Registering an invoice line of a free text invoice

4.6.3.1 Registering Free Text Invoices

In order to enter a free text invoice, open the form *Accounts receivable> Invoices> All free text invoices* and click the button *New* in the action pane. Alternatively, you can access the customer form and create a free text invoice by clicking the button *INVOICE/New/Free text invoice* in action pane there.

Unlike the sales order form, the free text invoice does not show a separate *Create new* dialog when creating a new invoice starting in the free text invoice list page. But it provides the option to select the customer in the lines view, showing the fields *Customer account* and the *Invoice account* on the tab *Free text invoice header*.

Then you can enter the lines with *Description*, *Main account*, and *Amount* (or *Quantity* and *Unit price*). If a line requires a longer description, you can enter it in the invoice text field on the sub-tab *General* of the tab *Line details*. If sales tax (VAT) applies, make sure to choose a correct *Sales tax group* and *Item sales tax group*.

If you sell a fixed asset, enter the *Fixed asset number* on the sub-tab *General* of the tab *Line details*.

In order to update financial dimensions (e.g. department or cost center), switch to the sub-tab *Financial dimensions line* on the tab *Line details* and enter applicable dimension values individually or by selecting a financial dimension default template in the lookup *Template ID*.

4.6.3.2 Posting and Inquiry

In order to post the free text invoice, click the button *Post* in the action pane of the free text invoice form. After posting, you can view the posted invoice by clicking the button *INVOICE/Related information/Invoice journal* in the action pane.

In the inquiry *Accounts receivable> Inquiries and reports> Invoices> Invoice journal*, free text invoices display in parallel to sales order invoices. You can recognize free text invoices in this inquiry by the missing order number and by different invoice numbers (if a separate number sequence applies).

4.6.3.3 Recurring Free Text Invoices

If you want to issue a particular free text invoice periodically, you can use recurring free text invoices. As a prerequisite for this kind of invoices, set up a free text invoice template (*Accounts receivable> Invoices> Recurring invoices> Free text invoice templates*). Then you can assign customers to one or more templates by clicking the button *INVOICE/Set up/Recurring invoices* in the customer form.

In order to generate a periodical free text invoice then, open the menu item *Accounts receivable> Invoices> Recurring invoices> Generate recurring invoices*. The periodic activity generates regular free text invoices, which you can access in the free text invoice form before posting.

4.6.4   Case Study Exercises

Exercise 4.12 – Invoice

You want to invoice the items shipped in exercise 4.9. Before posting the invoice, check following items:

➢ Order status and document status of the sales order
➢ Inventory transaction related to the order line (button *Inventory/Transactions*)

Post and print the invoice directly in the sales order for and check the invoice total in the posting dialog before posting.

Now review the status of the points in the list above again. What is different now?

Exercise 4.13 – Partial Invoice

You want to invoice the items picked and shipped in exercise 4.10. Post and print the invoice in the sales order form, making sure to invoice only shipped items.

Exercise 4.14 – Shipping with Invoice

Your customer of exercise 4.1 orders another unit of the product entered in exercise 3.5. In addition, he wants to order one hour of the installation service entered in exercise 4.3 for a price of USD 110. This time you do not post a packing slip, you want to ship the items with the invoice.

Enter an appropriate sales order and immediately post the invoice. After posting the invoice, review the order status, the document status, and the inventory transaction of the product.

Exercise 4.15 – Invoice Inquiry

You want to view the invoice posted in exercise 4.12. Open the invoice inquiry and check the invoice header and lines as well as the related ledger transactions.

In exercise 4.2, you were looking for the summary account for your customer. Can you find the ledger transaction on this account? Finally, open the transaction origin form and check, to which modules your invoice has been posting.

Exercise 4.16 – Free Text Invoice

You want to invoice specific services, for which no product or sales category is available, to your customer of exercise 4.1. Enter a free text invoice choosing an appropriate revenue account and post the invoice. What is the difference between a free text invoice and a sales order invoice?

4.7   Sales Credit Note and Item Return

Credit notes are documents issued when a customer returns an item to your company and receives a replacement or a financial compensation. You can also post a credit note if the customer does not actually return defective items, or if you have to credit a price variance.

In order to manage customer returns, you can use the return order management in Dynamics AX. In case of a simple return process, you can use regular sales orders instead of return orders.

If a credit note does not refer to the delivered items, you can use a free text invoice.

4.7.1   Return Order Management

Return orders support a proper procedure for item returns, making sure that a customer has to contact you and receives a return merchandise authorization (RMA) before returning a product.

4.7.1.1 Disposition Codes and Required Setup

As a prerequisite for using return orders, you have to set up disposition codes (*Sales and marketing> Setup> Returns> Disposition codes*). The core setting in the disposition code is the field *Action*, which controls the handling of a defective item:

➢ **Credit only** – Credit without item return
➢ **Credit** (or **Scrap**) – Return items and credit
➢ **Replace and credit** (or **Replace and scrap**) – Return items and replace
➢ **Return to customer** – Do not credit

If scrap applies, an item receipt has to be posted anyhow (similar to an item receipt for products returned to stock). But in parallel to the packing slip transaction of the return order, Dynamics AX posts an inventory transaction for scrapping.

Apart from disposition codes, a number sequence with the reference *Area* "Order management" and the *Reference* "RMA number" is required for return orders.

4.7.1.2 Return Order Registration

Return orders are sales orders of the type "Returned order", showing the sales order number in the return order header. But except for return orders referring to the disposition code "Credit only", return orders do not show in the regular sales order form until posting the item arrival.

In order to access return orders from the menu, open the list page *Sales and marketing> Sales returns> All return orders*. When creating a return order by clicking the button *New* in the action pane, you can optionally select a *Return reason code* in the header (used for statistical purposes and to assign charges automatically if applicable).

The *Sales return processing* workspace, which you can access from the dashboard, shows an overview of return orders. Clicking the tile *All return orders* in the left pane provides access to the return order list page. In the workspace, you can create a new return order by clicking the button *New/Return order* in the action pane. The following steps are the same as when creating an order from the return order form.

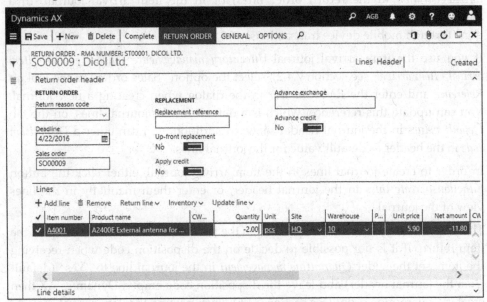

Figure 4-24: Registering an item in the return order form

Clicking the button *RETURN ORDER/Return/Find sales order* in the action pane provides the option to copy posted sales invoice lines into the return order.

Alternatively, you can manually enter return order lines with a negative quantity. The *Disposition code* for a line is available on the sub-tab *General* of the *Line details* tab. But except for disposition codes with the *Action* "Credit only" (crediting without physical return), the disposition code remains empty until the item arrival.

Optionally, you can click the button *RETURN ORDER/Send/Return order* in the return order to print a RMA document which you can send to your customer.

If you want to send an up-front replacement for the returned item to the customer, create an appropriate sales order by clicking the button *RETURN ORDER/New/ Replacement order* in the action pane of the return order.

4.7.1.3 Return Orders without Physical Returns

If you do not want your customer to return the item, choose a disposition code without item return ("Credit only") on the sub-tab *General* of the *Line details* tab in the return order. In this case, you can immediately post the credit note in the sales order form (*Sales and marketing> Sales Orders> All sales orders*) or in the summary update *Accounts receivable> Invoices> Batch invoicing> Invoice*.

4.7.1.4 Return Orders – Item Arrival and Credit Note

Once receiving the items of a return order, you have to record inventory registration. Like the inventory registration in purchasing (see section 3.5.3), the registration for return orders can be done in the registration form (button *Update line/Registration* in the return order lines) or in the item arrival journal. In a warehouse applying advanced warehouse management, inventory registration is done through mobile device transactions.

If you use the item arrival journal (*Inventory management> Journal entries> Item arrival> Item arrival*, see section 7.4.2), select the option "Sales order" in the lookup *Reference* and enter the *RMA number* in the dialog when creating a new journal. You can update this reference, which is a default for the journal lines, on the tab *Default values* in the journal header view. In addition, you can enter a *Disposition code* in the header as default value for the journal lines.

In order to create journal lines in the item arrival journal, either click the button *Functions/Create lines* in the journal header, or enter them manually in the lines view of the journal.

The disposition code has to be specified in the journal lines before you can post the item return. If it is not possible to decide on the disposition code when receiving the item, set the slider *Quarantine management* in the journal line to "Yes" (default from the journal header) and leave the disposition code empty. Dynamics AX then creates a quarantine order (see section 7.4.6) when posting the item arrival. You do not have to enter the disposition code before ending quarantine in this case.

After posting the item arrival journal by clicking the button *Post*, the status of the return order line is updated to "Registered".

Once you have finished inventory registration, you can optionally print a receipt acknowledgement by clicking the button *RETURN ORDER/Send/Acknowledgement* in the return order form.

Then post the packing slip (showing a negative quantity) in the return order form (button *RETURN ORDER/Generate/Packing slip*) or in the sales order form (button *PICK AND PACK/Generate/Packing slip*) and make sure to select an appropriate option in the lookup *Quantity* of the posting dialog.

In order to credit the customer financially, open the sales order form and click the button *INVOICE/Generate/Invoice* in the action pane, or choose the summary update *Accounts receivable> Invoices> Batch invoicing> Invoice*.

4.7.2   Simple Credit Note

If you do not want to process a customer return applying the steps in a return order, you can credit a customer through a regular sales order. Apart from the sales order, the free text invoice is another option for crediting.

4.7.2.1   Credit Note from a Sales Order

Since the order type "Returned order" is not available for manual selection, the order header of a crediting order looks like the header of a regular sales order. In the sales order form, there are following options for crediting:

> **Original order line** – Negative *Deliver now* quantity
> **New order line** – Order line with a negative quantity in the original order
> **New order** – Order line with a negative quantity in a new sales order

The options for registering a new order or a new line are similar to purchasing (see section 3.4.2).

If you want to register a credit note in the original order line, enter a negative quantity in the column *Deliver now* of the respective sales order line. When posting the credit note, choose the option "Deliver now" – which refers to the *Deliver now* column – in the *Quantity* lookup field of the invoice posting dialog.

4.7.2.2   Inventory Valuation for Returned Items

If registering a credit note in a new order or order line, you should select the original invoice number in the lookup field *Return lot ID* (on the sub-tab *Setup* of the tab *Line details*) of the order line before posting. This link ensures that the inventory value of the crediting line exactly matches the inventory value of the original delivery.

Dynamics AX automatically applies the return lot ID, if you create a credit note line by clicking the button *RETURN ORDER/Return/Find sales order* in the return order form, or the button *SELL/Create/Credit note* in the sales order form.

If you do not select a return lot ID, Dynamics AX applies the *Return cost price* on the sub-tab *Setup* of the crediting order line for inventory valuation.

4.7.2.3 Scrapping Items

If you do not want the customer to return a defective item, set the slider *Scrap* on the sub-tab *Setup* of the order line to "Yes". When posting the invoice (credit note), Dynamics AX posts the item receipt and a related inventory loss at the same time. In return orders, the checkbox *Scrap* is controlled by the disposition code.

4.7.2.4 Refunds not Referring to Returns

The free text invoice form (see section 4.6.3) is an option to register and post customer refunds. But if a refund refers to an item, you should not use a free text invoice, since this kind of invoicing is not included in item statistics and inventory valuation.

In case of crediting a price variance, rather enter a new sales order containing one line with a negative quantity and the old price and one line with a positive quantity and the right price. Clicking the button *Inventory/Marking* (see section 3.7.1) provides the option to link these transactions (offsetting the inventory value).

4.7.3   Case Study Exercise

Exercise 4.17 – Credit Note

Your customer complains about defects on the items invoiced in exercise 4.12. You agree to accept an item return and to credit the invoice. Enter an appropriate return order and post the item receipt applying a suitable disposition code. After posting the packing slip return, you want to post and print the credit note.

4.8   Direct Delivery

Direct delivery means shipping goods from a vendor directly to a customer. Avoiding a warehouse in between saves time and expenses for transportation and stocking.

4.8.1   Processing Direct Deliveries

The functionality for direct deliveries in Dynamics AX is based on a purchase order which is created from a related sales order. There are three options for creating this purchase order:

➤ **Create purchase order** – Creating a regular purchase order from the sales order
➤ **Create direct delivery** – Creating a direct delivery from the sales order
➤ **Direct delivery workbench** – Creating a direct delivery from the workbench

Whereas creating a regular purchase order or a direct delivery purchase order from the sales order does not require specific settings, the direct delivery workbench requires marking a sales order line for direct delivery.

4.8.1.1 Regular Purchase Order form the Sales Order

Creating a regular purchase order from the sales order is an option which is useful if you want to process the purchase order separately from other orders, but nevertheless receive and ship it through a warehouse of your company.

When entering the sales order, there is no difference to a regular order. Once you have finished entering the order, create a related purchase order by clicking the button *SALES ORDER/New/Purchase order* in the action pane.

In the *Create purchase order* dialog, you have to select the checkbox *Include* and to choose a vendor (if no main vendor is specified in the item). Processing the purchase order and the sales order works like processing regular orders, including change management for the purchase order.

In the purchase order, the delivery address for the vendor is the warehouse or company address (like in any regular purchase order). You can post the product receipt in your warehouse and then perform picking and shipping to the customer.

4.8.1.2 Direct Delivery from the Sales Order

In case of a direct delivery, the sales order again is not different from regular sales orders. But selecting a separate warehouse for direct deliveries is useful to avoid mixing direct deliveries and regular inventory transactions in the warehouse.

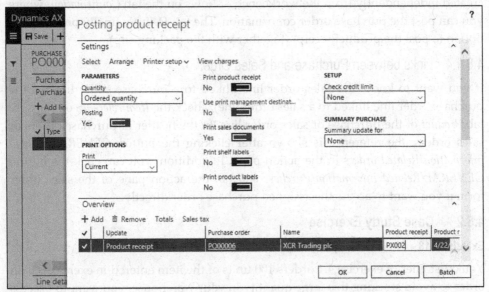

Figure 4-25: Printing a sales packing slip when posting the product receipt

The button *SALES ORDER/New/Direct delivery* in the action pane of the sales order generates a purchase order like the *Create purchase order* option, but creates a tighter link between the orders. The delivery address of the purchase order is the customer address, modifications of the address and other data in the sales order which are relevant to purchasing (e.g. the quantity or the delivery date) are synchronized to the purchase order. In case of changes you have to observe the purchase order change management, at least requiring a confirmation of the modified purchase order.

When posting the product receipt for a direct delivery in purchasing, Dynamics AX automatically posts the related sales packing slip. If you are required to print a packing slip for the customer, set the slider *Print sales documents* in the posting dialog for the product receipt to "Yes" (see Figure 4-25). Invoice posting in sales is independent from the purchase invoice.

4.8.1.3 Direct Delivery Workbench

The direct delivery workbench gives an overview of all sales orders with direct delivery and allows processing the related purchase and sales orders.

In order to use the direct delivery workbench, make sure the slider *Direct delivery* on the sub-tab *Delivery* of the sales order line is set to "Yes" (default from the released product, tab *Delivery*). In addition, the item must have a main vendor.

In the direct delivery workbench (*Procurement and sourcing> Purchase orders> Direct delivery processing> Direct delivery*), the sales order initially shows on the tab *Direct delivery*. Clicking the button *Create direct delivery* in the toolbar of this tab creates the purchase order. This purchase order – like any direct delivery purchase orders created independently from the workbench – shows on the tab *Confirmation*, where you can post the purchase order confirmation. The tab *Delivery* finally provides the option to post the product receipt (together with the packing slip).

4.8.1.4 Links between Purchase and Sales Order

If you want to know the sales order line linked to a purchase order line (or the purchase order line linked to a sales order line), check the *Item reference* on the sub-tab *Product* of the purchase or sales order line. In the header of purchase orders or sales orders, the reference is shown after clicking the button *GENERAL/Related information/Related orders* in the action pane. In addition, you can click the button *GENERAL/Related information/Purchase order* in the action pane of the sales order form if you want to access the assigned purchase order directly.

4.8.2   Case Study Exercise

Exercise 4.18 – Direct Delivery

Your customer of exercise 4.1 orders 100 units of the item entered in exercise 3.5. In order to avoid stocking this large quantity in your warehouse, you want to process a direct delivery. Enter an appropriate sales order and choose the option *Direct delivery* for generating a purchase order to your vendor of exercise 3.2.

Your vendor confirms shipping the item with packing slip PS418. You want to post this product receipt in the purchase order. In the next step, check the status of the sales order, then post and print the sales invoice. After receiving the purchase invoice VI418, post the invoice receipt.

4.9 Trade Allowance and Incentive Management

Customer rebates and trade allowances are contracts, which specify a discount depending on the sales volume. Usually the customer receives a credit note or a payment at the end of a period if the total sales amount or quantity meets the target as agreed in the rebate contract.

Incentive management in Dynamics AX does not only cover customer agreements, but also agreements with vendors, broker contracts, and royalty contracts:

➤ **Customer rebates** – Rebate contracts with customers
➤ **Trade allowances** – Enhancement of the customer rebates
➤ **Vendor rebates** – Rebate functionality in purchasing (similar to sales)
➤ **Broker contracts** – Payment of agents (vendors) based upon the sales revenue with particular customers
➤ **Royalty contracts** – Payment of royalty owners (vendors) based upon the sales volume of particular items

Customer rebate agreements (*Sales and marketing> Customer rebates> Rebate agreements*) with the rebate program type "Rebate" and "TMA" work similar to the bill back trade allowance agreement described below.

4.9.1 Trade Allowance

Trade allowance agreements in Dynamics AX support the calculation and payment of rebates, and the analysis of the profitability of promotions. You can group trade allowances in Dynamics AX into three categories:

➤ **Bill back** – Allowances based upon the posted invoices in a period, paid to the order customer or the invoice customer
➤ **Lump sum** – Allowances paid upfront to an agent (vendor or customer)
➤ **Invoicing rebate** – Allowance immediately deducted from the sales invoice

4.9.1.1 Required Setup for Trade Allowances

As a prerequisite for using trade allowances, you have to set up at least one customer hierarchy containing the customers which are subject to trade allowances. You can access the customer hierarchies in the form *Sales and marketing> Trade allowances> Customer category hierarchy*, where you can click the button *New* to set up a new hierarchy.

In the hierarchy, you can click the button *New category node* in the toolbar of the tab *Categories* to create a multilevel hierarchy structure. In order to assign or to view customers in a category node, click the button *Add/remove customer*.

In the rebate program types (*Sales and marketing> Customer rebates> Rebate program types*), create at least one rebate program type with the *Rebate program type* "Bill back" and the applicable default accrual and expense account.

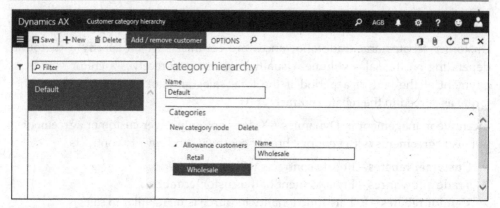

Figure 4-26: Managing customer hierarchy categories

In the merchandising event categories (*Sales and marketing> Setup> Trade allowance> Merchandising event category*), create at least one category per applicable trade allowance type:

➢ **Bill back** – Category with *Default type* "Bill back"
➢ **Lump sum** – Category with *Default type* "Lump sum"
➢ **Invoicing rebate** – Category with *Default type* "Off invoice"

Following parameter settings apply to trade allowances:

➢ **Accounts receivable parameters** – Select an *AR consumption journal* and a *Rebate accrual journal* (usually separate journal names in finance) on the tab *Rebate program*. In addition, set the slider *Rebates at invoicing* to "Yes" if you want to create a rebate transaction immediately when posting an applicable sales invoice. On the tab *Number sequences*, enter number sequences for the *Reference* "Rebate ID" and "Rebate agreement ID".
➢ **Trade allowance management parameters** (*Sales and marketing> Setup> Trade allowance> Trade allowance management parameters*) – Enter required number sequences and optionally select a default *Customer hierarchy* and a *Default rebate program ID*. If working with lump sum allowances, select an *Expense account* or a *Procurement category* for lump sum transactions.

4.9.1.2 Funds and Optional Setup

Trade allowance funds provide the budget for the costs caused by the trade allowances rebates. Although funds are not mandatory for using trade allowances, it is useful to apply them because they are required to check the profitability of sales promotions through rebates. In order to set up trade allowance funds, open the form *Sales and marketing> Trade allowances> Funds> Funds*. When creating a new fund, select the *From date* and the *To date* (specifying the validity period) and enter the budget amount in the field *Fund budgeted*. On the tabs *Customers* and *Items*, select the applicable customers and items for the particular fund. Then activate the fund by changing the *Status* to "Approved".

Trade allowance agreement periods (*Sales and marketing> Setup> Trade allowance> Trade allowance agreement period*) provide the option to specify date intervals which you can use as default when entering trade allowance agreements.

If you want to apply an approval process for trade allowance agreements, you can set up approval workflows in the menu item *Sales and marketing> Setup> Trade allowance> Trade allowance workflows*.

4.9.1.3 Managing Trade Allowance Agreements

Trade allowance agreements specify rebates for customers. In order to create a new agreement, open the menu item *Sales and marketing> Trade allowances> Trade allowance agreements* and click the button *New* in the action pane. Then enter a description and the validity dates (*Order from* and *Order to* is required), which specify the sales orders and invoices included in the rebate calculation. You can optionally select a *Trade allowance agreement period* as default for the validity dates.

In the field group *Analysis*, you have to select the *Unit* before you can specify the sales target of the agreement. This target is given by entering the usual sales quantity without trade allowances in the *Base units*, and the intended increase in the *Lift percent*. The tabs *Customers*, *Items*, and *Funds* in the header view of the trade allowances provide the option to set default values for the trade allowance lines.

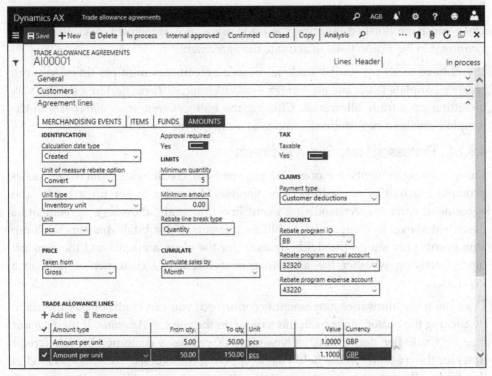

Figure 4-27: Amount calculation settings in a bill back trade allowance agreement line

After switching to the lines view you should make sure that appropriate customers are selected on the tab *Customers*. On the sub-tab *Merchandising event* of the tab *Agreement lines*, add one or more lines with the applicable *Category*. After selecting a merchandising event line, switch to the other sub-tabs and enter event details as applicable. The sub-tab *Amounts* contains the allowance calculation for the selected event line. Depending on whether the particular merchandising event line is linked to a *Category* with the *Default type* "Bill back", "Lump sum", or "Off invoice", this sub-tab shows different fields.

When entering the calculation details for a "Bill back" event, the *Minimum quantity* and *Minimum amount* on the sub-tab *Amounts* specify the minimum sales volume within the period selected in the field *Cumulate sales by* for a customer to be eligible for the allowance rebate. The *Payment type* defines if the order customer is credited, or if the invoice customer is credited, or if the customer receives a payment (reimbursement through accounts payable by paying a vendor who is associated with the customer). The *Trade allowance lines* pane contains the rebate calculation, in the column *Amount type* specifying whether the *Value* is an amount or a percentage. You can enter multiple trade allowance lines in case the allowance percentage or amount is depending on the sales volume. The field *Rebate line break type* in the field group *Limits* determines whether the *From qty* and the *To qty* in the lines are quantities or amounts.

Once you have finished entering the trade allowance agreement, click the button *Confirmed* in the action pane to activate the agreement.

If you have to set up similar trade allowance agreements multiple times, you can create a template (*Sales and marketing> Trade allowances> Templates*) in a similar way to setting up a trade allowance. Clicking the button *Create trade allowances* in the template creates a new trade allowance as a copy of the template.

4.9.1.4 Processing Lump Sum Agreements

Lump sum agreements are one-time payments or credit notes which fund sales promotion activities of customers or vendors. In order to set up a lump sum agreement, enter a merchandising event line in a trade allowance agreement as described above. In comparison to bill back events, the sub-tab *Amounts* for lump sum events only shows the fields *Amount* (for the claim amount) and the *Payment type* (specifying whether the allowance is credited to a customer or paid to a vendor).

Once the trade allowance agreement is confirmed, you can credit or pay the claim by clicking the button *Approve* in the toolbar on the sub-tab *Amounts*. If the *Payment type* is "Customer deductions", Dynamics AX creates a customer invoice (credit note) for the customer in the field *Pay to* (applying the expense account specified in the trade allowance parameters). If the *Payment type* is "Pay using accounts payable", Dynamics AX creates a vendor invoice for the vendor in the field *Pay to* (applying the procurement category specified in the trade allowance parameters).

You can view the customer invoice (or the vendor invoice) in the (open) transactions of the particular customer or vendor.

4.9.1.5 Processing Bill Back Agreements

Bill back agreement rebates are based on sales invoices and apply to the customers and items specified in the agreement. Depending on the slider *Rebates at invoicing* on the tab *Rebate program* in the accounts receivable parameters, Dynamics AX immediately creates rebate entries when posting an invoice. If this slider is set to "No", you have to execute the periodic activity *Sales and marketing> Customer rebate> Rebate update> Calculate rebates* to create rebate entries.

You can manage the rebate entries related to a bill back agreement in the bill back workbench (*Sales and marketing> Trade allowances> Bill back workbench*). At the end of the trade allowance cumulating period, calculate the rebate amounts by clicking the button *Cumulate* in this form or through the periodic activity *Sales and marketing> Customer rebate> Rebate update> Cumulate rebates*. Then approve the rebates by clicking the button *Approve* after selecting the lines for approval in the grid. Finally click the button *Process* to generate rebate transactions. Processing sets the rebate status to "Mark" and posts accrual transactions.

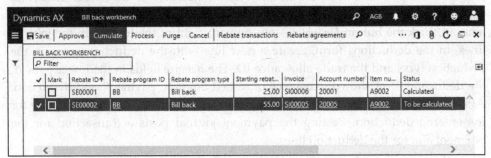

Figure 4-28: Calculating rebates in the bill back workbench

In the next step, access the open transactions of the customers receiving a rebate (button *COLLECT/Settle/Settle transactions* in the action pane of the customer form). In the *Settle open transactions* form, click the button *Functions/Bill back program* and select the checkbox *Mark* in the rebate lines to be credited. If the rebate should be processed as a credit note in sales, click the button *Functions/Create credit note*. In case the rebate is to be paid, click the button *Functions/Pass to AP* to create an open vendor transaction which is included in the next payment proposal.

After crediting or paying the customer, the rebate status shows "Completed".

4.9.1.6 Canceling and Purging Rebates

If you do not want to pay or credit a rebate which is generated from a trade allowance agreement, cancel the rebate after processing it (Status "Mark"). After clicking the button *Cancel* in the bill back workbench and specifying an appropriate filter in the dialog, the status of the selected rebate transaction is set to "Canceled" and related accrual transactions are reversed.

Purging is used to clean up the bill back workbench, deleting all transactions which are finished (status "Completed" or "Canceled").

4.9.1.7 Deductions and One-Time Promotions

You can use trade allowance deductions in case a customer does not want to wait for the rebate payout at period end and just pays a reduced amount indicating the deduction. As a prerequisite for using deductions, following setup is required:

➢ **Deduction journal name** – Select a journal name in the trade allowance parameters for posting the deductions
➢ **Deduction types** – Create at least one type with the related offset account in the form *Sales and marketing> Trade allowances> Deductions> Deduction types*
➢ **Deduction denial reasons** – Create at least one reason in the form *Sales and marketing> Trade allowances> Deductions> Deduction denial reasons*
➢ **Deduction write-off reasons** – Create reasons as applicable in the form *Sales and marketing> Trade allowances> Deductions> Deduction write-off reasons*

Deductions are registered when entering customer payments in the payment journal (*Accounts receivable> Payments> Payment journal*) as described in section 9.3.4. After entering a payment journal line which does not fully match the invoice amount, click the button *Deductions* on the very right of the toolbar in the journal lines. In the deductions form, create a new line with the deduction amount, the deduction type, and the trade allowance ID. The *Balance* fields in the lower pane of the deduction form show the balance of settled amount, payment, and deduction. After closing the deduction form, the payment journal shows an additional line for the entered deduction. Posting the payment journal posts a transaction for the payment and for the deduction lines.

Open deductions display in the deduction workbench (*Sales and marketing> Trade allowances> Deductions> Deduction workbench*). Credit transactions for trade allowances, which are generated by processing the trade allowances for applicable bill back and lump sum agreements, are available for reconciliation in the lower pane of the deduction workbench. In order to match a deduction with a credit transaction in the deduction workbench, select the checkbox *Mark* in the appropriate deduction first, and mark applicable rebate transactions in the lower pane afterwards. Clicking the button *Maintain/Match* in the action pane posts a match transaction in a deduction journal.

In case a deduction is incorrect, click the button *Maintain/Deny* in the action pane of the deduction workbench for reversing the deduction transaction. The denied amount then shows as open customer transaction. The button *Maintain/Split* provides the option to split a deduction line, for example if you want to deny only part of the deduction.

If you want to allow a one-time deduction for an amount exceeding the trade allowance agreement, you can post an additional promotion by clicking the button *Maintain/Settle deduction as one-time promotion*. Click the button *OK* and optionally add a fund in the dialog shown next. The one-time promotion is posted as a lump sum transaction based on the trade allowance template selected as *One-time promotion template* in the trade allowance parameters.

4.9.1.8 Analyzing Trade Allowance Agreements

In the trade allowance agreement form, you can click the button *Analysis* in the action pane to view the results of a trade allowance agreement. In addition, the form *Sales and marketing> Trade allowances> Trade allowance analysis> Trade allowance activity* shows the detailed sales transactions and costs related to an agreement.

4.9.1.9 New in Dynamics 'AX 7'

In the new release, trade allowance management is not a separate module but included in the sales and marketing module. Minor additional changes include the option to apply sales tax/VAT to all trade allowance types.

4.9.2 Vendor Rebate

Rebate and trade allowance agreements are not only available in the sales module. You can also manage rebate agreements with your vendors in Dynamics AX.

The setup of vendor rebate agreements (*Procurement and sourcing> Vendor rebates> Rebate agreements*) is similar to the setup of customer rebate agreements and trade allowance agreements. The form *Procurement and sourcing> Vendor rebates> Rebate claims* is used to process vendor rebates.

The required configuration for vendor rebate agreements is available in the procurement and sourcing parameters, and in the forms of the menu item folder *Procurement and sourcing> Vendor rebates*.

4.9.3 Broker Contract

Broker contracts support agreements with agents (vendors), which require to pay the agent based upon your sales revenue with selected customers and items.

4.9.3.1 Required Setup for Broker Contracts

As a prerequisite for broker contracts, you have to set up at least one charges code (Ledger – Ledger) for broker charges in the accounts receivable charges (*Accounts receivable> Charges setup> Charges code*). This code is used for posting the broker charges when posting a sales invoice.

In the *Accounts payable parameters*, select appropriate journal names and an expense account for the broker claim on the tab *Broker and royalty*. In the *Accounts payable parameters*, select a number sequence for the *Broker claim invoice* on the tab *Number sequences*.

4.9.3.2 Entering and Processing Broker Contracts

Since the broker is a vendor, access the accounts payable module to manage the broker contracts (*Accounts payable> Broker and royalties> Broker contracts*). When setting up a broker contract, select the broker and a default for the charges code in the upper pane of the form. In the lower pane, specify which items and customers are covered by the broker agreement. *Break type* and *Break* in the line determine the minimum quantity or amount for applying a broker charge. Depending on the *Category* selected in the upper pane, the *Charges value* is a percentage or an amount. You can enter multiple lines in the lower pane if there are different charges depending on the sales quantity or amount. The contract is effective once the *Status* is set to "Approved".

When entering a sales order line covered by the broker contract, you can view the calculated broker commission by clicking the button *Sales order line/Broker commission* in the toolbar of the sales order line. Clicking the button *Financials/Maintain charges* in sales order line provides access to the related charges transaction. When posting the sales order invoice, the charges transaction posts an accrual transaction and a broker contract claim.

In the broker claims (*Accounts payable> Broker and royalties> Broker claims*), you can view the claims generated in sales. In order to pay a claim, make sure that the checkbox *Mark* is selected (select it manually in the upper pane or click the button *Mark all*) and click the button *Approve*. Approving posts a reversal of the accrual and a vendor invoice with the broker expense.

4.9.4 Royalty Agreement

Royalty agreements in Dynamics AX support contracts with royalty owners (vendors), which require to pay a fee (e.g. a license fee) to the royalty owner based upon your sales of selected items. Royalty contracts work similar to vendor rebate agreements, but they are based on the customer invoice transactions covered by the royalty agreement.

The required setup for royalty contracts includes settings on the tabs *Broker and royalty* and *Number sequences* in the accounts payable parameters.

Royalty contracts are available in the form *Accounts payable> Broker and royalties> Royalty agreements*. The form *Accounts payable> Broker and royalties> Royalty claims* is used to manage the calculation.

5 Production Control

The primary responsibility of production control is to manufacture finished goods. In order to perform this task, production consumes material and resource capacity (men and machinery). The manufacturing process may cover multiple levels of semi-finished products in the bill of materials of the manufactured product.

5.1 Business Processes in Manufacturing

Depending on the requirements of your company, you can choose to apply following manufacturing concepts in Dynamics AX:

> **Discrete manufacturing** – Core production functionality, including bills of materials (BOMs), resources, routes, and production orders
> **Process manufacturing** – Supports the additional requirements of batch-producing industries like formulas and batch production orders
> **Lean manufacturing** – Supports production flows and Kanbans (completely independent from routes and production orders)

You can apply these concepts in mixed mode, for example using process manufacturing for components and lean manufacturing for finished products.

This book primarily covers the core production functionality used in discrete manufacturing, and gives an overview of process manufacturing. Before we start to go into details, the lines below give an overall picture of discrete manufacturing.

5.1.1 Basic Approach

Like in purchasing and in sales, correct master data are an essential prerequisite for successfully executing production control.

5.1.1.1 Master Data and Transactions in Production Control

The released product record shows the main characteristics of an item. The bill of materials (BOM) then describes the structure of a finished (or semi-finished) item by specifying the components (materials, or lower-level semi-finished items).

Resources (machines or human resources) are another basic element, providing capacity for manufacturing. Routes and operations, which describe the necessary activities to manufacture an item, determine the required resources.

Products, BOMs, resources, and routes are master data, only occasionally updated after initially creating the individual records. In the course of production order processing, planned and actual production orders (transaction data) receive default values from these master data, which you can override in the transaction – for example selecting a non-standard bill of materials in a particular production order.

Figure 5-1 below shows the main steps in production order processing.

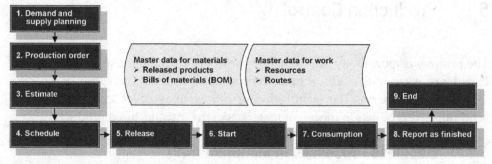

Figure 5-1:   Production order processing in Dynamics AX

5.1.1.2 Demand and Supply Planning

In order to know the required quantity of finished products, the first step in the manufacturing process usually is to run master planning (see section 6.3). Depending on settings for scheduling, the item demand derives from sources like forecasts, sales quotations, sales orders, or settings for a minimum stock.

5.1.1.3 Creating a Production Order

Master planning generates planned production orders for finished and semi-finished products, which you can transfer to actual production orders. Apart from transferring planned orders, following options are available for creating a production order:

➤ **Manual** – Entering an order in the production order form
➤ **Sales order** – Creating a production order from a sales order line
➤ **Pegged supply** – Automatically creating a production order for a semi-finished item (sub-production order) in the production order of a finished item
➤ **Project** – Creating a production order in a project (project accounting module)

A production order consists of an order header, which contains the manufactured item, and order lines. Unlike purchase and sales orders, which only include item lines, production orders contain two different types of lines: BOM item lines and route operation lines. These line types show in separate forms.

After creating a production order, you have to execute all subsequent steps – from estimating to ending – one after the other. Depending on parameter settings, you can skip steps when processing a production order.

5.1.1.4 Estimating and Scheduling

After creating a production order, estimation is the first step in order processing. Estimation determines the quantity and cost of all items and resources which are required to manufacture the product.

Whereas estimation calculates the item quantity and resource capacity demand without timing it, scheduling as the next step calculates exact production dates.

5.1.1.5 Releasing and Starting

Releasing a production order means to hand it over from the front office to the shop floor. At this stage you can print the production papers as required.

Once you want to begin with activities in the shop floor, you have to set the order status to "Started". This status provides the option to consume items and resources. When starting an order, you can print the picking list and post the automatic consumption of items and resource capacity.

5.1.1.6 Production Journals

In the course of the manufacturing process, the shop floor consumes material and resource capacity. Production journals are used to report this consumption. Depending on the requirements, you can post the journals manually or backflush automatically (using estimation data). Alternatively, you can report consumption through terminals and mobile devices in the Dynamics AX *Manufacturing execution*.

5.1.1.7 Reporting as Finished and Ending the Production Order

Once manufacturing is completed for a partial quantity or the entire quantity of the finished product, post a "Report as finished" transaction. The reported quantity of the finished product is then available in inventory. Ending the production order is the last step in production order processing, calculating the actual costs of production and posting financial transactions in the general ledger.

5.1.1.8 Ledger Integration and Voucher Principle

Production journals, which record the consumption of materials and resources and the receipt of finished products, are posting physical transactions to the general ledger already before ending the order (see section 9.4.3).

The voucher principle, which is the general principle for processing transactions in Dynamics AX, also applies to transactions in manufacturing: You have to register a transaction in a journal before you can post it.

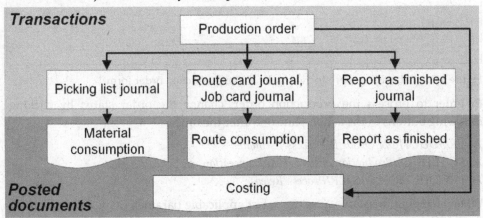

Figure 5-2: Transactions and posted documents in production control

5.1.2   At a Glance: Production Order Processing

In order to provide an overview of the main steps in production order processing, this section shows the basics. In the example, we create an order starting in the *Production floor management* workspace and post all transactions directly in the production order form. Of course you can also create the order directly in the production order list page.

In the *Production floor management* workspace, click the button *Create new/ Production order* in the action pane. The *Create production order* dialog shows next, where you have to select the *Item number* of the manufactured item. Dynamics AX initializes the quantity, BOM, and route in the production order with default values from this item. Clicking the button *Create* in the dialog creates a new production order.

In the production order detail form, click the button *Edit* to switch to the edit mode if you are in view mode. If you want to view or edit the material components or the route operations of the order, click the button *PRODUCTION ORDER/Order details/BOM* (or *PRODUCTION ORDER/Order details/Route*) in the action pane.

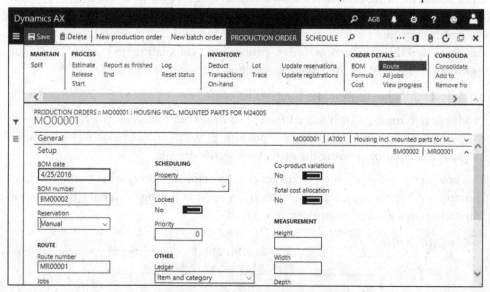

Figure 5-3:   Managing a production order in the production order form

In order to process the production order, change the order status by clicking following buttons in the action pane one after the other:

➢ *PRODUCTION ORDER/Process/Estimate*

➢ *SCHEDULE/Production order/Schedule operations* or *Schedule jobs*

➢ *PRODUCTION ORDER/Process/Release*

When changing the status, you can select applicable parameters on the first tab (or the tab *General*) in the update dialog – e.g. to select the scheduling direction when scheduling, or to print the production papers when releasing. If you skip a step, it is automatically executed with the next step. Once the production order should be processed in the shop floor, click the button *PRODUCTION ORDER/Process/Start* which starts the order and posts automatic material and route consumption as applicable. When starting the order, you can print the picking list.

In order to enter the consumption of items configured for manual posting, click the button *VIEW/Journals/Picking list* in the action pane of the production order. In the journal list page, click the button *Picking list/Create lines* to generate a proposal with picking list lines. Selecting "Remaining quantity" in the lookup field *Proposal* of the *Create lines* dialog initializes the journal lines with the open quantity. You can edit the consumption quantity, the warehouse, and other data in the lines view of the journal detail form (access by clicking the journal ID shown as link in the grid of the journal list page) before you post the journal by clicking the button *Post*.

Depending on the setup and on the scheduling type (*Operations scheduling* or *Job scheduling*) which you have selected when scheduling the production order, you can enter the actual working time consumption either at route level or at job level (button *VIEW/ Journals/Route card* or *VIEW/Journals/Job card* in the action pane of the order). In route card journals and job card journals, there is no proposal initializing the lines with default values when manually entering a journal. Click the button *New* in the action pane of the route card (or job card) journal and select the journal name in the *Create production journal* dialog. After clicking *OK* in the dialog, enter one or more lines with date, operation/job number, resource, hours, and good quantity in the lines view of the journal detail form before clicking the button *Post*.

✓	Journal↑	Name	Journal type▼	Description	Lines	Posted	Production
	MJ00001	PL	Picking list	Picking list	1	☑	MO00001
	MJ00004	PL	Picking list	Picking list	2	☑	MO00001
	MJ00010	PL	Picking list	Picking list		☐	MO00001

Figure 5-4: Picking list journal page with a journal which is not yet posted

If you do not want to post a journal immediately, you can close the journal lines and access the lines view of the journal detail form later again by clicking the journal ID shown as link in the grid of the journal page.

In order to receive the manufactured item in inventory, click the button *PRODUCTION ORDER/Process/Report as finished* in the production order. If you want to ignore missing consumption postings, select the checkbox *Accept error* on the tab *General* of the update dialog. Once all transactions of the production order are posted, close the order by clicking the button *PRODUCTION ORDER/ Process/End*.

5.2   Product Management and Bill of Materials

All material components required for manufacturing have to be entered in the shared and the released product records. Apart from inventoried items like finished products, semi-finished products, and raw material or parts, product records are also necessary for phantom items or purchased services.

The bill of materials (BOM) specifies the materials which are included in a finished product. You can assign one bill of materials or multiple bills of materials to one item, but you can also assign one common bill of materials to multiple items. Multiple bills of materials for one item are required, if the applicable bill of materials is for example depending on the lot size or on the production date.

In case a product has got variants, select the product subtype "Product master" when creating the shared product (see section 7.2.1). Depending on the requirements, you can use product configuration models or configuration groups in Dynamics AX for products which are configured to customer request.

5.2.1   Product Data in Manufacturing

The shared product form (*Product information management> Products> All products and product masters*) and the released product form (*Product information management> Products> Released products*) contain all finished products, semi-finished products, and raw materials or parts. At released product level, you can also use the *Released product maintenance* workspace to access the product management.

Details on general product data are included in section 7.2 of this book. The lines below therefore only cover product data referring to production control. Except for the product type, which is specified in the shared product, these data are included in the released product.

Product change cases (see section 10.5.2) support data maintenance providing the option to collect all products affected by a change. You can then validate, approve, and activate all related bill of materials and route versions in common.

5.2.1.1   Item Model Group, Production Type and Default Order Type

The first essential setting in the released product is the *Item model group* shown on the tab *General* of the released product form. All items used in production control – including finished products, semi-finished products, and raw materials or parts – have to be linked to an item model group for stocked products (see section 7.2.1). Since this setting is also required for non-inventoried BOM-components like subcontractor work, choose the *Product type* "Service" for non-inventoried products in order to avoid inventory control for these items.

In the lookup field *Production type* on the tab *Engineer*, select the option "BOM" for finished or semi-finished products. The production types "Formula" and

"Planning item" provide the option to assign a formula instead of a BOM, which is applicable to process manufacturing.

The production type "None" prevents assigning a BOM to the item. This means you can only purchase the item, not produce it. But you can also purchase an item with another production type, because the default order type – and not the production type – determines the primary sourcing strategy for the item.

Controlling item sourcing, the default order type is an important setting. The lookup field *Default order type* shows on tab *General* in the default order settings, which you can access by clicking the button *PLAN/Default order settings* in the action pane of the released product form. Following options are available for the default order type:

> **Purchase order** – Supply through purchase orders
> **Production** – Supply through production orders
> **Kanban** – Supply through Kanbans (lean manufacturing)

If you need to override the default order type at the level of a specific site, warehouse, or other inventory dimension, open the item coverage form (button *PLAN/Item coverage* in the action pane of the released product). On the tab *General* there, the lookup field *Planned order type* provides the option to override the default order type.

5.2.1.2 Settings for Quantity and Price

Apart from the default order type, the tab *Inventory* in the default order settings contains additional default data for production orders including lot size (field *Multiple*) and order quantity. Site-specific order settings, which you can access by clicking the button *PLAN/Site specific order settings* in the action pane of the released product, possibly override the default order settings at site level.

On the tab *Manage costs* in the released product form, the field *Price* specifies the general cost price of the item. Site-specific cost prices are available in the item price form, which you can by clicking the button *MANAGE COSTS/Set up/Item price* in the action pane of the released product (see section 7.3.3).

If the item model group of the released product applies the valuation model "Standard cost", you have to activate a cost price with a costing version referring to the costing type "Standard cost" in the item price form.

5.2.1.3 Phantom Item

The slider *Phantom* on the tab *Engineer* in the released product form determines the default for the *Line type* when inserting the item as a component in a BOM line. Phantom items are semi-finished products with a bill of materials and (optionally) a route. When estimating a production order, BOM lines of the type "Phantom" are exploded. As a result, the production order contains BOM lines with the components of the phantom item (instead of a line with the phantom item itself).

5.2.1.4 Flushing Principle

The *Flushing principle* on the tab *Engineer* of the released product form controls, if production orders should post automatic consumption of the particular item in BOM lines. It contains three different options:

➢ **Start** – Automatic consumption when starting the production order
➢ **Finish** – Automatic consumption when reporting as finished
➢ **Manual** – No automatic consumption

In the BOM line, you can override the flushing principle specified in the released product record if necessary.

As a prerequisite for automatic consumption based upon the released product or BOM line setting, you have to select the option "Flushing principle" in the lookup *Automatic BOM consumption* on the tab *General* of the update dialog when starting a production order or reporting as finished (see section 5.4.3).

5.2.2   Bill of Materials (BOM)

A bill of materials (BOM) primarily is a list of products with the related quantity. The main purpose of a bill of materials is to determine the components of a manufactured product (finished or semi-finished product).

5.2.2.1 Bill of Materials Structure

In Dynamics AX, components of a manufactured product are not directly assigned to the product, but to a bill of materials. This bill of materials is then separately assigned to the finished product (compare Figure 5-5). The assignment of the bill of materials to the finished product is called "BOM version" in Dynamics AX. One finished product can be assigned to one or multiple bills of materials.

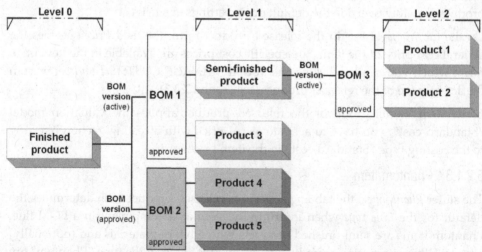

Figure 5-5:   Example of a multi-level product structure with BOMs and BOM versions

Items, which are included as a component in a BOM, can consist of other items and therefore refer to a lower-level BOM. Such items are semi-finished goods, generating a multi-level product structure.

The BOM level (field *Level* on the tab *Engineer* of the released product) shows the number of product levels between the selected product and a finished product. Products, which are not a component in any active BOM show the level "0". Semi-finished products, which only are included in BOMs of finished products, show the level "1", and so on. If a product is included as component in the BOMs of multiple finished products, the field *Level* in the released product shows the deepest level (highest level number) in any applicable BOM structure.

The BOM level is important for master planning (calculate the demand of finished products first, because this determines the demand of components) and for periodic cost calculation (calculate component prices first to use already updated prices for upper levels). You can update the BOM level in the form *Product information management> Periodic tasks> Recalculate BOM level* or in parallel to other periodic tasks.

In order to make use of a bill of materials in production control, the BOM and the BOM version has to be approved. In addition, the BOM version has to be activated if it should apply as a default in production orders and in master planning. An active BOM version has to be unique per date, quantity, and site.

5.2.2.2 Creating Bills of Materials and BOM Versions

You can access bills of materials from following places:

➢ **From the released product** (*Product information management> Products> Released products*, button *ENGINEER/BOM/BOM versions*)
➢ **From the menu** (*Product information management> Bills of materials and formulas> Bills of materials*)

The *Product readiness for discrete manufacturing* workspace is another place, from which you can access (link *Bills of materials* in the pane on the very right) and create (button *NEW/BOM* in the action pane) bills of materials. The functionality in the BOM page then is similar as if accessed from the menu.

Although the BOM form accessed from the menu and the BOM versions form accessed from the released product are used to update the same BOM and BOM version records, the functionality and structure of these forms is different.

Since understanding the data structure is easier if starting from the menu, we start with discussing the BOM form accessed this way. Dynamics AX in this case shows a list page containing all bills of materials. Clicking a BOM ID shown as link in the grid of the list page opens the related detail form in the lines view, where you can see the BOM lines. Clicking the button *Header* below the action pane in the detail form switches to the header view, where you can view the BOM versions (assignment of finished products to the BOM).

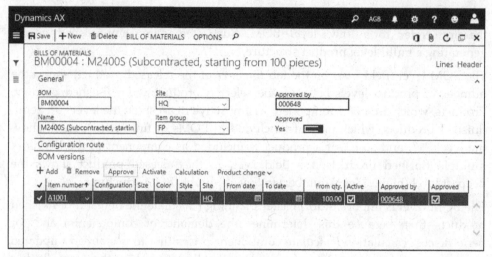

Figure 5-6:   BOM version in the header view of the BOM form (accessed from the menu)

In order to create a new bill of materials, click the button *New* in the action pane of the BOM form. The BOM detail form then opens in lines view, where you want to enter the *Name* of the BOM (e.g. using the product name) on the tab *Bill of materials header*. Depending on the settings of the applicable number sequence, the BOM ID is assigned automatically or has to be entered manually. If the bill of materials is site-specific, enter the site in the field *Site*. Leaving the site empty creates a common bill of materials for all sites.

In order to assign a finished (or semi-finished) product to the BOM, switch to the header view and click the button *Add* in the toolbar of the *BOM versions* tab (see Figure 5-6). In the BOM version line, enter the *Item number* of the finished product. If the BOM is only valid for a particular period, enter the *From date* and the *To date*. If the BOM assignment depends on the lot size, enter a *From qty*. And if the BOM assignment depends on the site, enter the *Site* in the assignment line.

If you want to assign the BOM to a second finished product (which is not very common), enter a second BOM version.

5.2.2.3 BOM Lines

In the lines view of the BOM form, you can view and edit the components (raw materials, parts, and semi-finished products) assigned to the bill of materials.

When inserting a new BOM line by clicking the button *New* in the toolbar of the tab *Bill of materials lines*, enter at least the *Item number* and the *Quantity*. The column *Per series* specifies the quantity of finished items produced with the component quantity in the column *Quantity* – e.g. 5 boxes (*Quantity* and *Unit*) to produce 10 finished products (*Per series*).

If you select the option "Constant" instead of the default "Variable" in the lookup field *Consumption is* (on the sub-tab *Setup* of the *Line details* tab), the consumption is always the same as entered in the field *Quantity*, regardless of the finished good quantity. If you want to specify additional consumption to cover inevitable scrap, enter a percentage in the *Variable scrap* and/or a fixed quantity in the *Constant scrap*.

On the sub-tab *Setup* in the *Line details* tab, you can also select a *Flushing principle* for automatic consumption. If the flushing principle in the BOM line is empty, the setting in the released product record of the BOM line item applies.

In a site-specific bill of materials, you can enter a picking warehouse in the column *Warehouse* of the BOM lines. In bills of materials not referring to a particular site, it is not possible to specify the picking warehouse in the BOM lines. In both cases, you can select the checkbox *Resource consumption* if you want to apply the applicable input warehouse of the resource/resource group as picking warehouse.

The *Line type* on the sub-tab *General* of the *Line details* tab determines the supply strategy of a BOM line with following options:

> **Item** – Semi-finished or purchased item, considered as demand in inventory
> **Phantom** – Virtual semi-finished item, replaced by its components when estimating a production order
> **Pegged supply** – Semi-finished or purchased item, creating a referenced sub-production or purchase order when estimating the production order
> **Vendor** – For subcontracting, works like "Pegged supply"

BOM lines of the line type "Item" generate a demand in inventory. When creating planned production or purchase orders, master planning pools different demands (orders and warehouse replenishment proposals) according to the item coverage settings. The default order type (or the order type in the item coverage) controls, if master planning creates a planned purchase order, production order, or Kanban. There is no fixed link between the order for the semi-finished item and the original production order of the finished product.

Production order scheduling and master planning calculate the item demand in a way that all components have to be available at the start date of the production order. If this does not apply to some components because they are required at a later date, assign components to the respective route operation by entering the operation number in the BOM line. Available operation numbers are depending on the route assigned to the finished item. For this reason, the field *Oper.No.* only got a lookup functionality if accessing the BOM lines from the released product.

Instead of entering all lines in a BOM from scratch, you can copy an existing BOM which is similar to the new BOM by clicking the button *BILL OF MATERIALS/ Maintain/Copy* in the action pane of the BOM form.

5.2.2.4 Approving and Activating

You can only use approved BOM versions in a production order. Once you have finished entering the bill of materials, you can click the button *BILL OF MATERIALS/Maintain/Approval* in the action pane of the BOM form to approve the bill of materials. Clicking the button *Approve* in the toolbar of the tab *BOM versions* in the header view of the detail form approves the BOM version (which is the assignment of the BOM to the finished product).

If approving the BOM version before approving the BOM itself, a slider to approve BOM and BOM version in parallel is displayed in the *Approve version* dialog.

If you want to apply a bill of materials as default in production orders and in master planning, activate the BOM version by clicking the button *Activate* in the toolbar of the tab *BOM versions*. Active BOM versions show a checkmark in the column *Active* and have to be unique per date, quantity, and site.

In order to support approval and activation, the *Product readiness for discrete manufacturing* workspace contains the list *Missing active BOM versions* showing items with the default order type "Production" but no active BOM version.

In addition, product change cases support approval processes by providing the option to approve and activate multiple bills of materials in a case (see section 10.5.2).

You can remove the activation and remove the approval by clicking the button for approval or activation again. In order to remove an approval, set the slider *Remove approval* in the dialog to "Yes".

5.2.2.5 Bills of Materials in the Released Product

Apart from the menu item, the released product form provides another way to access bills of materials. Clicking the button *ENGINEER/BOM/BOM versions* in of a released product with the *Production type* "BOM" opens the BOM version form where you can view the bills of materials assigned to the selected item.

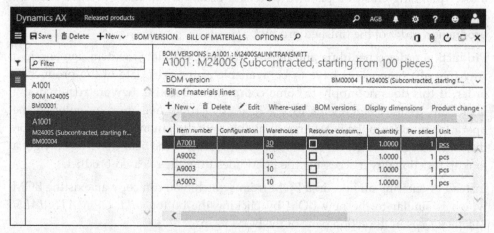

Figure 5-7:   Working in the BOM version form (accessed from the released product)

In the rare case that a bill of materials is assigned to multiple items, you have to keep in mind that modifying a bill of materials in this form in parallel applies to all other items with a BOM version linked to this BOM.

The BOM version form (see Figure 5-7) has got a different structure than the BOM form accessed from the menu: Instead of a header view and a lines view, it has got a tab *BOM version* (containing the fields of the BOM version) and a tab *Bill of materials lines* (containing the BOM lines of the BOM selected in the BOM version).

If you want to enter a new bill of materials in this form, click the button *New/BOM and BOM version* in the action pane. Click the button *New/BOM version* for inserting a BOM version only if you want to assign the item to an existing bill of materials. After entering BOM version details like site, from/to date, and quantity as applicable, you can switch to the tab *Bill of materials lines* where you can insert BOM lines. In order to enter line details, click the button *Edit* in the toolbar of the BOM lines which opens a dialog containing most fields shown of the *Line details* tab in the BOM form accessed from the menu.

If you want to approve a BOM version in the BOM version form, click the button *BOM VERSION/Maintain BOM version/Approve* in the action pane.

5.2.2.6 BOM Designer

The BOM designer is an alternative option for viewing and editing BOMs and BOM versions. You can access it by clicking the button *ENGINEER/BOM/Designer* in the action pane of the released product form, or by clicking the button *BILL OF MATERIALS/MAINTAIN/Designer* in the action pane of the BOM form.

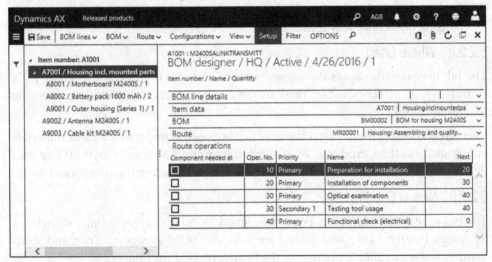

Figure 5-8:   Working in the BOM designer

The BOM designer shows a multi-level structure of the bill of materials in the left pane, and related detail date on tabs in the right pane. In the action pane of this form, there are buttons to edit, insert, and delete BOM lines and to create new bills of materials with the related version. On the tab *Route operations*, you can assign a BOM line to a route operation by selecting the checkbox *Component needed at* (which is a different way of entering the *Oper.No.* in a BOM line).

If you want to change the display settings in the BOM designer, click the button *Setup* in the action pane to access a dialog where you can choose which fields to view in the left pane (e.g. the quantity).

Clicking the button *Filter* in the action pane opens another dialog where you can choose which BOM/BOM version to show. The *Display principle* "Selected/Active" (or "Selected") in the *Filter* dialog provides the option to view a BOM version, which is different from the active BOM version for the selected site, date, and quantity. If you select the display principle "Selected", click the button *BOM/BOM versions* in the BOM designer to access the *BOM versions* form. In the BOM versions form, highlight the BOM version which you want to view and click the button *Select* before closing the form.

5.2.2.7 Block BOM for Editing

Depending on the setup, you can update an approved bill of materials at any time. In some industries, it is required to protect an approved BOM against any changes. For this purpose, there are following settings in the inventory management parameters (*Inventory management> Setup> Inventory and warehouse management parameters*, tab *Bill of materials*):

> **Block editing** – If this slider is set to "Yes", no changes are possible once a BOM is approved (remove approval and re-approve afterwards in this case)
> **Block removal of approval** – If set to "Yes" in parallel to *Block editing*, you can't change a BOM once it is approved

5.2.2.8 Where-Used

The bill of materials shows the components of an item. If you want to know for a component, in which finished or semi-finished products it is included, open the where-used form.

You can access the where-used form, which shows the respective bills of materials and related finished products, by clicking the button *ENGINEER/BOM/Where-used* in the action pane of the released product form after selecting the component item.

5.2.2.9 New in Dynamics 'AX 7'

The bill of materials form has been redesigned in the new release (now showing a list page, header view, and lines view). In the BOM designer, drag and drop features are not available because of the browser-based user interface.

5.2.3 Case Study Exercises

Exercise 5.1 – Components

Your company wants to produce a new finished item, which consists of two components. Enter these components in Dynamics AX, creating an item with the product number I-##-C1 and the name "##-Component 1" (## = your user ID) and an item with the number I-##-C2 and the name "##-Component 2" in the released product form. Variants and serial/batch numbers are not required. Inventory control is at the level of site and warehouse.

For both items, choose applicable settings for product type, product subtype, dimension groups, item group (raw material/parts), and production type. The item model group should refer to the inventory model "FIFO". The unit of measure is "Pieces", and the items are subject to the standard tax rate. Approved vendors are not required.

The base purchase price and the base cost price of both items is USD 100. In addition, choose your vendor of exercise 3.2 as main vendor for the items. The flushing principle should be "Manual". For purchasing and inventory, enter the main site in the *Default order settings* and the main warehouse of the main site in the *Site specific order settings*.

Note: If the number sequence for product numbers is set up for automatic numbering, don't enter a product number.

Exercise 5.2 – Finished Item

For the finished product, create an item with the product number I-##-F (if no automatic number sequence applies) and the name "##-Finished product" in the released product form. Variants and serial/batch numbers are not required. Inventory control is per site and warehouse.

Choose applicable settings for product type, product subtype, dimension groups, item group (finished product), and production type. The item model group should refer to the inventory model "FIFO". The unit of measure is "Pieces", and the item is subject to the standard tax rate.

The base cost price is USD 500 and the base sales price USD 1,000. In the *Default order settings*, make sure that the appropriate *Default order type* is selected and enter the main site in the settings for inventory and sales. Finally enter the main warehouse as default for inventory and sales in the *Site specific order settings*.

Exercise 5.3 – Bill of Materials

After creating item records for the finished item and its components in the exercises above, enter a bill of materials for the finished item of exercise 5.2 starting in the released product form.

The BOM applies to the main site and contains two units of the first and one unit of the second item entered in exercise 5.1. The warehouse for picking the components should be the main warehouse. Once you have finished entering the components, approve and activate the BOM version.

5.3   Resource and Route Management

Resources are the basic entities in a company, which execute the operations in manufacturing. They include working places, personnel, machines, tools, and vendors (subcontractors). Resources provide the available capacity which scheduling and master planning matches with the capacity demand.

Routes are the basis for calculating the capacity demand, specifying the necessary resources and the working time for producing a particular item.

Along with items and bills of materials, resources and routes therefore are the second area of master data required for production control.

5.3.1   Production Unit and Resource Group

Production units represent plants in capacity management. Within a production unit, resource groups collect resources according to the physical organization in the shop floor. Resources within a resource group can have different capabilities and do not need to be interchangeable.

5.3.1.1 Production Units

Production units, which refer to capacity management, are controlled separately from the storage dimension "Site", which refers to material management. They are not included in inventory transactions, but they are available for filtering/sorting in applicable production control forms (e.g. *Production control> Operations> Current operations*). Multiple production units can be linked to one common site.

Setting up production units is optional. If you want to create a production unit, access the form *Production control> Setup> Production> Production units* and enter identification, name, and site of the new production unit. On the tab *General*, you can optionally enter an *Input warehouse*. This warehouse applies as picking warehouse to BOM lines with a checkmark in the checkbox *Resource consumption*.

Resource groups are linked to a production unit by selecting the production unit in the respective field of the resource groups form.

5.3.1.2 Resource Groups and Resource Assignment

Resource groups in Dynamics AX reflect the physical organization of resources with following purpose:

➢ **Structuring** – Establishing a hierarchical organization structure by linking resources, resource groups, production units, sites, and warehouses
➢ **Scheduling** – Capacity planning at resource group level in operations scheduling

Assigning resources to resource groups is date effective, providing the option to adjust the assignment according to organizational and seasonal changes. A resource cannot be linked to more than one resource group at any date.

If a resource is not attached to a resource group a given day, it is not available for production on that day. Resource scheduling only includes resources which are assigned to a resource group.

If you want to edit resource groups, open the form *Production control> Setup> Resources> Resource groups*. In order to create a new resource group, click the button *New* in the action pane and enter the applicable identification, name and site.

On the tab *General* of the resource groups form, optionally assign a production unit. The *Input warehouse* specifies the warehouse for consuming BOM lines, which show a checkmark in the checkbox *Resource consumption* (overriding the default of an applicable production unit).

Settings on the tab *Operation* correspond to equivalent settings on resources in the resource form (see section 5.3.2 below).

The tab *Resources* shows the resources which are a member of the selected resource group. In order to assign an additional resource, click the button *Add* in the toolbar of this tab. The button *View/All* in the toolbar provides the option to view past assignments. Apart from attaching resources to a resource group in the resource group form, you can start in the resource form and select the resource group of a resource there.

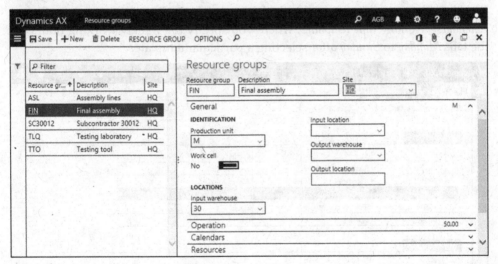

Figure 5-9: Editing a resource group

By setting the slider *Work cell* on the tab *General* in the resource group to "Yes", the resource group refers to lean manufacturing and is not available for operations and production orders in discrete manufacturing. In addition, the tab *Work cell capacity* specifying capacity for lean manufacturing is editable in this case.

5.3.1.3 Working Time Calendar and Templates

The working time calendar assigned to a resource determines the hours of operation. For a resource, capacity calculation includes the working time calendar and the efficiency percentage. For a resource group, the available capacity is the total capacity of its resources

If you want to attach a calendar to a resource group, expand the tab *Calendars* of the resource groups form. Calendar assignment is date effective, providing the option to record a future change of the calendar (button *View/All* in the toolbar to show the *Effective* date) – for example changing the working time of a particular resource group from regular business hours to a 24-hour operation.

Before you can assign a calendar to a resource group, the calendar has to be set up in the form *Production control> Setup> Calendars> Calendars*. If you need to enter a new calendar (for example if a resource group has working times which are different from all existing calendars), insert a new record in the calendar form. In order to assign working days and working hours, click the button *Working times* in the calendar form. The working times form shows calendar days in the upper pane and the hours (which you can update) of the selected day in the lower pane.

You can create working days and related hours by clicking the button *Compose working times* in the working times form. In the *Compose working times* dialog, select a *Working time template* providing the default for the daily working times.

Working time templates are available in the form *Production control> Setup> Calendars> Working time templates*, where you specify the weekly working hours on the tabs *Monday* to *Sunday* after selecting a particular template.

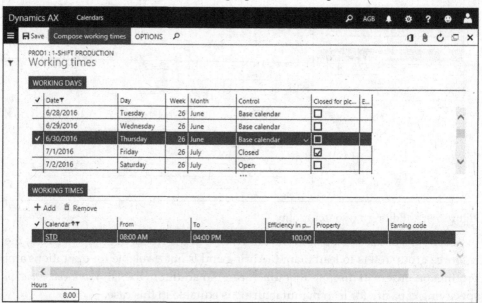

Figure 5-10:   Editing working times in the working times form

The base calendar is an alternative to the working time template for determining working times. In the calendar form, you can select a related *Base calendar* per calendar. If you set the slider *Use base calendar* in the *Compose working time* dialog to "Yes" then, the column *Control* in the working days of the working times form is initialized with the option "Base calendar". This option means that the working time is given by the base calendar. Changing the *Control* to "Open" or "Closed" overrides the working times in the current calendar for the selected day.

Independently from the base calendar functionality, you can override the working times of a particular resource or resource group by clicking the button *RESOURCE/ Maintain/Calendar deviations* in the resource or resource group form and assigning an alternative calendar on a given date (e.g. a calendar without working times if a resource is temporarily not available).

5.3.2   Resource and Capability

Resources are the lowest level for capacity management in Dynamics AX. They are assigned to resource groups according to the organizational hierarchy, and (optionally) to resource capabilities according to the functional abilities.

5.3.2.1   Creating and Editing Resources

In order to edit resources, open the form *Production control> Setup> Resources> Resources*. If you want to insert a new resource, be aware that the resource identification needs to be unique – not only within the resources, but also within resource groups. You can easily distinguish resources from resource groups for example by using a longer identification number for resources.

When creating a resource, you have to select a resource type in the lookup field *Type* in order to distinguish between the different kinds of resources:

➢ **Machine** – General default, for production machines
➢ **Human resources** – Personnel (optionally link a worker record)
➢ **Vendor** – External resource for subcontracting (optionally link a vendor record)
➢ **Tool** – Device, often subject to wear through usage
➢ **Location** – Represents physical space (independent from warehouse locations)
➢ **Facility** – Similar to "Machine", but for a group of machines and people

If you do not need to schedule and to report the activities of a machine and its operating staff separately, you can manage them in a common resource of the type "Facility" or "Machine". If you want to manage tools, enter the tool usage as a secondary operation in routes (see section 5.3.3 below).

On the tab *Calendars* of the resources form you can assign a calendar to a resource (similar to assigning a calendar to a resource group).

The *Resource groups* tab provides the option to view and to update the resource group assignment. In order to change the group assignment, click the button *Add* in the toolbar of this tab or the button *RESOURCE/Maintain/Add to resource group* in the action pane of the form.

5.3.2.2   Operation Settings on the Resource

The unit of time for scheduling a resource is hours. If you need a different unit of time for a resource, enter a conversion factor in the field *Hours/time* on the tab

Operation of the resource form. If the time in route operations is in minutes for example, enter 1/60 = 0.0167 in the *Hours/time*.

If a particular resource does not apply a unit of time for the unit of measure, you can select an alternative *Capacity unit* on the tab *Operation*. The field *Capacity* then contains the conversion factor to hours. In related route operations, select the option "Capacity" in the field *Formula* on the tab *Setup* then.

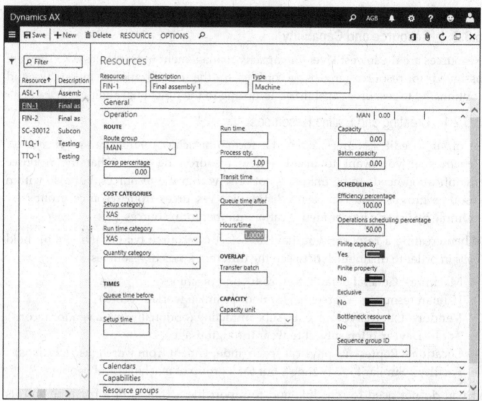

Figure 5-11: Managing capacity settings of a resource

The *Efficiency percentage* in the field group *Scheduling* provides the option to reduce or increase the scheduled time of a route. The default for the efficiency percentage is 100. If creating a resource, which is 25 percent faster than a standard resource for example, enter 125 in the efficiency percentage. Scheduling of an operation usually lasting 10 hours gives a scheduled time of 8 hours (= 10 * 100/125) on this resource.

The slider *Finite capacity* controls for the selected resource, whether capacity reservations from other production orders reduce the available capacity when scheduling an order. If the slider is set to "Yes", only one operation at a time is scheduled on this resource. Otherwise, scheduling calculates every production order separately regardless of other orders on the same resource. In most cases, finite capacity only applies to particular resources and resource groups which don't have the possibility to increase the capacity (e.g. by overtime hours).

In the master plan (for master planning) and in the update dialogs when scheduling a production order (for operations scheduling and job scheduling), you can choose to disregard the finite capacity setting of the resource.

The cost categories *Setup category* and *Run time category* determine the hourly rate of the resource, the *Quantity category* can specify a quantity-depending price. The other field groups on the tab *Operation* in the resource form contain fields providing a default value for route operations. These defaults apply when selecting the resource or resource group as costing resource in a route operation.

5.3.2.3 Resource Capabilities

Resource capabilities determine the kind of activities which a resource is able to do – for example welding or cutting. You can temporarily or permanently assign one or more capabilities to a resource. This capability assignment is only available on resources, not on resource groups. If you want to use capabilities in routes, assign resources to operations by specifying required capabilities in the resource requirements (see section 5.3.3 below).

In order to set up capabilities (shared across companies), open the form *Production control> Setup> Resources> Resource capabilities* and enter the identification and description of the capability. On the tab *Resources* of the capabilities form, assign resources to the particular capability.

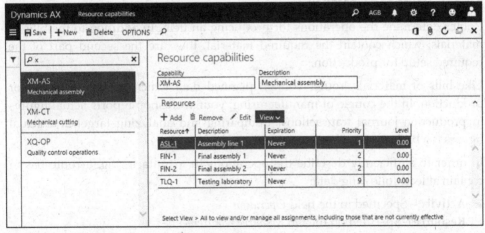

Figure 5-12: Managing the resource capability assignment in the capabilities form

As an alternative to the capability form, you can also assign capabilities to resources in the resource form. In the resource from you can select the capabilities of each resource by clicking the button *Add* in the toolbar on the tab *Capabilities* or the button *RESOURCE/Maintain/Add capability* in the action pane of the form.

Capability assignment is date effective, providing the option to record future changes of resource abilities. In addition, there is a *Priority* field in the assignment line. Depending on the scheduling parameters, Dynamics AX searches for the applicable resource with the highest priority (i.e. the lowest priority number – priority "1" is selected first) when executing job scheduling.

5.3.2.4 Settings for Ledger Integration

The tab *Ledger postings* in the resource form contains the main accounts which apply to route consumption. When posting a route card or job card journal in production, Dynamics AX in parallel posts the costs of the resource consumption (usually measured by the working time) to the main accounts specified in the field group *Accounts-Physical* of the resource form. When costing and ending a production order, ledger transactions are posted to the accounts in the field group *Accounts-Financial*.

The ledger settings in the resource only apply, if the option "Item and resource" is selected in the lookup field *Ledger posting* of the production order (see section 9.4.3). If the option "Item and category" is selected, applicable main accounts are derived from the cost categories.

5.3.2.5 New in Dynamics 'AX 7'

Items which are new in resource management include minor changes like the new resource type "Facility" and a separate tab for the calendar assignment in the resource form.

5.3.3   Route and Operation

Routes determine the operations for producing an item. In addition to the bills of materials, which contain the required material, they are the second part of the required setup for production.

Like bills of materials, routes contain planned data which provide a target for production. In the course of manufacturing, your workshop reports actual figures in production journal transactions. Comparing and analyzing target and actual figures is a basis for possible improvements.

In order to sufficiently describe the operations in manufacturing, a route has to contain at least following data:

➢ **Activity** – Specified in the field *Operation*
➢ **Resource** – Specified on the tab *Resource requirements*
➢ **Sequence of operations** – Specified by entering the next operation (field *Next*)
➢ **Time consumption** – Specified in the fields *Setup time* and *Run time*
➢ **Produced item** – Specified in the *Item number* of the route version
➢ **Required material** – Specified in the BOM of the produced item

If the workshop does not need all components of the bill of materials when starting the first operation, you can link BOM lines to the applicable route operation as shown in section 5.2.2.

5.3.3.1 Setup of Operations

Operations (*Production control> Setup> Routes> Operations*) are a prerequisite for setting up routes in Dynamics AX. After creating an operation, you can select it in as many routes as required.

An operation itself is independent from routes, containing only a unique identification and a name. Other details which are necessary to execute an operation – e.g. the provided time or the required resource – are not available in the operation record, but in the operation relations.

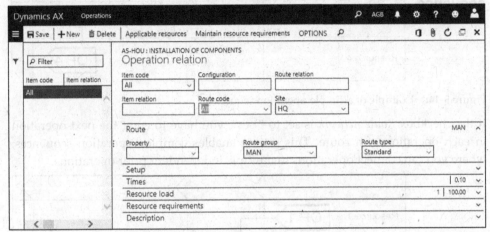

Figure 5-13: Managing general operation relations for an operation

In order to view and to edit operation details (operation relations), click the button *Relations* in the operations form. Depending on the requirements, enter operation relations at a general level or specific to a route:

➢ **General** – For operation details at a general level, select the option "All" in the field *Item code* and *Route code* of the operation relation (see Figure 5-13).
➢ **Route-specific** – Route-specific operation details contain the option "Route" in the *Route code* and the route number in the field *Route relation*.

After switching to the other tabs of the operation relations form, you can enter details of the particular operation relation including applicable resources and times. More information on this subject is available in the description of route operations further below in this section.

5.3.3.2 Operation Sequence

The sequence of operations is not specified in the operation record, but in the route. There are two types of operation sequences:

➢ **Simple sequence** – One operation after the other
➢ **Complex sequence** – Multiple predecessor for an operation possible

If the slider *Route network* on the tab *General* of the production control parameters is set to "No", simple operation sequences apply. Routes in this case only contain operations executed one after the other.

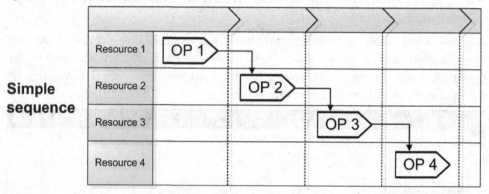

Figure 5-14:   Example of a simple operation sequence

If the checkbox *Route network* is set to "Yes", you have to enter the next operation in each operation of a route. This setting enables complex operation sequences, where you can connect operations to multiple independent prior operations.

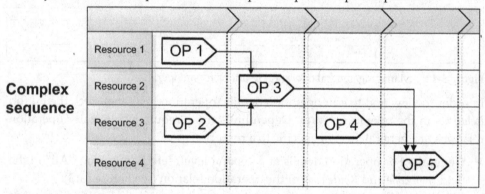

Figure 5-15:   Example of a complex operation sequence

Regardless of simple or complex operation sequences, you can specify to perform operations on multiple resources in parallel by entering a secondary operation in routes (selecting the *Priority* "Secondary" for the particular route operation).

If the available options in the route do not meet your specific requirements, you can set up an intermediate level of a virtual semi-finished item in the structure of the finished product. The line type of the BOM line, which contains the virtual item, should be "Pegged supply" for connecting the production order for the virtual semi-finished item directly to the production order of the finished item.

5.3.3.3 Creating Routes and Route Versions

Managing routes in Dynamics AX is similar to managing bills of materials, including the way to access the route form:

➤ **From the released product** (*Product information management> Products> Released products,* button *ENGINEER/View/Route*)

➤ **From the menu** (*Production control> All routes*)

The *Product readiness for discrete manufacturing* workspace is another place, from which you can access (link *All routes* in the pane on the very right) and create (button *NEW/ Route* in the action pane) routes. The functionality in the route page then is similar as if accessed from the menu.

Although the route form accessed from the menu and the route version form accessed from the released product are used to update the same route and route version records, the functionality and structure of these forms is different.

Like the assignment of bills of materials, the assignment of routes to finished items is called "Version", optionally specifying validity dates and a from-quantity. Unlike bills of materials, a route version always refers to a site.

If accessing the routes from the menu, Dynamics AX displays all routes in a list page. Clicking a route number shown as link in the grid of the list page opens the route form. This form shows the route header on the tab *General* and one or more assigned finished items ("Versions") on the tab *Versions*.

In order to create a new route, click the button *New* in the action pane of the route form or the list page. The route number derives from the appropriate number sequence or has to be entered manually. After entering a *Name* for the new route on the tab *General* of the route form, you can assign one or more finished items together with the applicable site on the tab *Versions*.

5.3.3.4 Route Operations

In order to access the route operations from the route form (or from the list page), click the button *ROUTE/Maintain/Route details* in the action pane.

The route operation details form then shows the route operations in the upper pane. In the lower pane of the route operation details form, you can view the operation relations (operation details) of the operation selected in the upper pane.

In order to insert a new operation, click the button *New* in the action pane. You can override the operation number in the column *Oper.No.* (if required) and enter the applicable operation in the column *Operation* next. If the production control parameters specify complex operation sequences , you have to enter the number of the next route operation (except for the last operation) in the column *Next* of the upper pane.

If the shop floor should execute operations in parallel, enter two operations with the same operation number, but a different *Priority*. In the example of Figure 5-16, the operation number 30 shows two parallel operations – one with priority "Primary" and the other with priority "Secondary 1".

If you want to specify additional time and material consumption to cover inevitable scrap caused by the operation, enter a *Scrap percentage*. Scrap in different route operations is multiplied. If you have a route containing two operations each with 10 percent scrap for example, the calculation of material and resource demand for the first operation shows a requirement of 123 % to receive 111 % output, which subsequently is reduced to an output of 100 % by the second operation.

Operation details (operation relations) are available in the lower pane of the form. If a general operation relation – indicated by the option "All" in the column *Route code* – is set up for the selected operation, it shows in the lower pane of the route form after saving the record in the upper pane. When changing data of a general operation relation in the route form, keep in mind that these changes apply to all routes referring to the particular general operation relation.

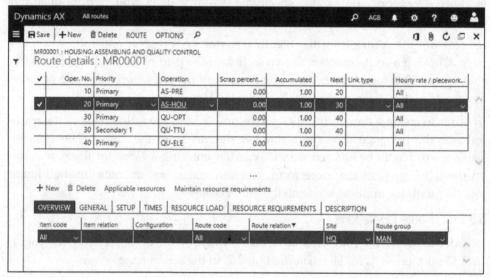

Figure 5-16:   Editing a route operation with a general operation relation (All/All)

If you want to record route-specific operation details, insert a line with a new operation relation in the lower pane of the route from. When inserting this operation relation, select the option "Route" in the column *Route code* and enter required data on the other tabs of the lower pane.

5.3.3.5 Route Groups

An essential setting for posting resource consumption related to an operation is the *Route group* on the tab *Overview* (and the tab *General*) in the lower pane of the route operation detail form. If you want to apply automatic posting of time consumption (actual = estimate), you have to select a route group with appropriate settings for automatic route consumption.

In order to access route group settings, choose the form *Production control> Setup> Routes> Route groups*. In route groups for automatic posting, set the sliders for *Setup time, Run time* and *Quantity* in the field group *Automatic route consumption* to "Yes". In addition, clear the checkboxes in the column *Job management* on the tab *Setup* for these route groups (automatic consumption is posted through route cards).

The sliders in the field group *Estimation and costing* control, whether to include assigned operations in estimation and cost calculation. For regular operations, you want to set the sliders for time based cost calculation or the slider for quantity based cost calculation to "Yes". If all sliders for costing are set to "No", Dynamics AX will only calculate the time but no costs for assigned operations.

5.3.3.6 Costing Resource and Cost Categories

The tab *Setup* in the lower pane of the route operation detail form contains the *Costing resource*, which specifies the resource used for the cost estimation of production orders. When – optionally – selecting a costing resource in an operation relation, data from this resource apply as default to the *Cost categories* and the fields on the tab *Times*.

Cost categories are a second setting for controlling cost estimation and cost calculation apart from the route group. You can assign different cost categories for setup time, run time and quantity. When assigning cost categories, make sure the appropriate sliders in the route group for including time or quantity in the cost calculation are set to "Yes".

Before creating a new cost category, you have to enter a related shared category in the form *Production control> Setup> Routes> Shared categories*. Shared categories ensure common category definitions across companies. For categories applicable to production, set the slider *Can be used in Production* in the shared category to "Yes".

Required cost categories in production control, are available in the form *Production control> Setup> Routes> Cost categories*. These categories contain three core settings:

> **Cost price** – Determining the hourly rate (for setup time and run time)
> **Cost group** – Classifying cost types in cost calculation (see section 7.3.3)
> **Ledger-Resources** – Determining main accounts similar to ledger integration settings of resources (see section 5.3.2 above) in case the production order shows the option "Item and category" in the lookup field *Ledger posting*

In order to specify a cost price for a category, click the button *CATEGORY SETUP/ Price* in the action pane of the cost categories to access the cost category price form. In the cost category price form, enter a cost price for the category per site or – if leaving the field *Site* empty – at company level with a costing version (costing versions are covered in section 7.3.3). In order to make the price effective, activate it by clicking the button *Activate*.

Cost estimation uses the cost price of the cost categories assigned to the route operation. The cost price for actual costs derives from the resource entered in the posted route consumption transaction.

5.3.3.7   Operation Times

The tab *Times* of the operations relations contains the provided time for the operation, split into setup time, run time, queue times and transit time. The field *Run time* contains the time, in which the workshop should process the quantity of the product entered in the field *Process qty*.

If the *Process qty.* is 1.00, the run time is the time in hours to produce one unit. You can apply other units of time, entering a conversion factor *Hours/time* in the route operation or selecting a capacity unit in the resource (see section 5.3.2).

The processing time of an operation calculates according to following formula:

$$PROCESSING \quad TIME \ = \ \frac{Setup \quad time \ + \left(Run \quad time \times Quantity \ \right)}{Efficiency \quad percentage \quad of \quad the \quad resource}$$

In addition to the processing time, queue and transit times are included in the total lead time.

5.3.3.8   Resource Requirements and Resource Load

On the tab *Resource load* of the operation relations, the field *Quantity* specifies the number of required resources (resources working in parallel). The calculation of required capacity then multiplies the operation time with the load quantity.

Applicable resources for the operation are specified on the tab *Resource requirements* (independently from the costing resource). If there are multiple requirement lines, applicable resources must meet all requirements.

By selecting the checkbox in the appropriate column you can specify requirements for *Operations scheduling* independently from requirements for *Job scheduling*. In the column *Requirement type*, you can select if a requirement is based on a resource group, resource, resource type, or capability. The options "Skill", "Courses", "Certificate" and "Title" apply to job scheduling for resources of the resource type "Human resource", referring to worker data in human resource management.

The button *Applicable resources* in the toolbar of the lower pane in the route operation detail form provides the option to check which resources meet the requirements entered for a route operation. Since the assignment of resources to resource groups and capabilities is date effective, you have to choose a date for displaying applicable resources. In addition, you have to choose whether you want to view applicable resources for operations scheduling or for job scheduling.

After closing the route operation detail form, you can click the button *Route feasibility* in the toolbar of the tab *Versions* in the route form to show an overview of the resource availability for all operations.

5.3.3.9   Approving and Activating Routes

Like bills of materials, routes and route versions have to be approved before they are available for production orders. You can approve a route by clicking the button

ROUTE/Maintain/Approve in the action pane of the route list page or the route form. In order to approve a route version, click the button *Approve* in the toolbar of the tab *Versions* in the route form. If approving the route version before approving the route, a slider to approve the route in parallel shows in the approval dialog.

If you want to apply a route as a default in production orders and in master planning, activate the route version by clicking the button *Activation* in the toolbar of the tab *Versions*. Active route versions show a checkmark in the column *Active* and have to be unique per date, quantity, and site.

Depending on settings in the production control parameters (sliders *Block editing* and *Block removal of approval* on the tab *General*, similar to the settings for BOMs), you can update an approved route at any time.

In order to remove the activation or the approval of a route, click the button for approval or activation again.

5.3.3.10 Routes in the Released Product

As an alternative to the menu item, you can access routes from the released product form. Clicking the button *ENGINEER/View/Route* in the action pane of the released product opens the route version form where you can view the routes assigned to the selected item.

The route version form accessed from the released product has got a different structure than to the route form accessed from the menu – it shows the route versions in the upper pane and the operations with operation number and operation relation details in the lower pane. If you want to enter a completely new route in this from, click the button *New/Route and route version* in the action pane. Click the button *New/Route version* for inserting a route version if you want to assign the item to an existing route.

If a general operation relation – indicated by the option "All" in the column *Route code* – exists for an operation, detail data from this relation apply to the route operation. Unlike the route form accessed from the menu, overriding data from the general operation relation in this form automatically creates a route-specific operation relation – indicated by the option "Route" in the column *Route code*.

In order to create a route-specific operation relation based on an applicable general operation relation, you can alternatively click the button *Copy and edit relation* in the toolbar of the lower pane (same result as simply overriding data). If you want to delete a route-specific operation relation and to apply an applicable general operation relation again, click the button *Delete relation* in the toolbar.

If no general operation relation exists for a route operation, you have to enter a new operation relation manually with all required data in the lower pane.

5.3.4   Case Study Exercises

Exercise 5.4 – Route Setup

In order to better understand the function of capabilities, route groups, and cost categories, you want to set up an example. As a start, create a capability C-## (## = your user ID) with the name "##-specific". Then enter a route group R-## for manual posting of working time consumption. Estimation and costing should only be based upon setup time and run time.

Finally, set up a new cost category G-## (together with a shared category applying to production). Select an appropriate cost group of your choice in the cost category and enter main accounts similar to the settings in existing cost categories. For the hourly rate, enter a cost price of USD 100 for a costing version of the costing type "Planned cost" and the main site. Then activate the cost price.

Exercise 5.5 – Resources and Resource Group

In order to produce the finished product of exercise 5.2, new resources are required. Enter a new resource group W-## with the name "##-assembly", referring to the main site and an appropriate production unit. The cost categories for setup time and for run time are the ones entered in exercise 5.4. Select a regular calendar of your choice as resource group calendar.

Then create two new resources, W-##-1 and W-##-2, of the type "Machine". For both resources, the route group and – for setup and for run time – the cost category of exercise 5.4 applies. Choose main accounts for the resources which are similar to the settings in existing resources. Assign both resources to the new resource group W-##, but only the resource W-##-2 to the capability entered in exercise 5.4. The resources use the same calendar as the resource group.

Exercise 5.6 – Operation

In order to produce your product, you need a new operation. Create the operation O-## (## = your user ID) with the name "##-processing". In general, the setup time for this operation is one hour and the run time two hours per unit. Select the resource W-##-1 of exercise 5.5 as costing resource, applying defaults for route group and cost categories. Resources applicable to the operation belong to the resource group W-## and show the capability C-## of exercise 5.4.

Exercise 5.7 – Route

Manufacturing your product also requires a new route, which you want to enter based on the elements in the previous exercises. After selecting your item I-##-F of exercise 5.2 in the released product form, open the route form by clicking the appropriate button. Create a new route, which contains the operation O-## of exercise 5.6 as the only route operation. There is no setup time, and the run time for the operation is one hour per unit. The other settings of route operation –

including costing resource, route group, cost categories and resource requirements – are the same as the applicable general operation relation entered in exercise 5.6.

Once you have entered the route details, approve and activate the route. Can you check applicable resources for executing the route operations? Finally, check all operation relations referring to the operation of exercise 5.6.

5.4 Production Order Management

A production order is a request to manufacture a particular product. Apart from the item number and quantity of the finished or semi-finished item, production orders contain data regarding required materials and resources.

The order status, which is updated with every step in the sequential flow of order processing displays, the progress of a production order.

5.4.1 Basics of Production Order Processing

Apart from manually entering a production order, there are following options for automatic creation:

> **Master planning** – Generating a planned production order which you can firm, or an actual production order (see section 6.3.4)
> **Pegged supply** – Automatically generating a production order from the BOM line of another production order (sub-production, see section 5.4.3)
> **Sales order** – Creating a production order by clicking the button *Product and supply/New/Production order* in the toolbar of a sales order line

If you create a production order manually, the first status is "Created". The status "Created" is the only status which allows deleting a production order. If you need to delete a production order in a later status, you have to reset the status first.

After creating a production order, it runs through the manufacturing cycle updating the order status in following steps:

> **Created** – Temporary status after creating a new order
> **Estimated** – Material and of resource demand is calculated
> **Scheduled** – Start and end dates are calculated
> **Released** – Order is transferred to the shop floor
> **Started** – Posting of actual consumption is possible
> **Reported as finished** – Finished item is received in inventory
> **Ended** – Order is finally closed

The order status changes whenever you update the production order by clicking a button for processing in the production order form or by executing a periodic activity in the folder *Periodic tasks* of the production control module. Depending on settings on the tab *Status* of the production control parameters, you can skip steps in the manufacturing cycle. Dynamics AX automatically executes the omitted steps when starting a subsequent step, applying standard parameter settings in this case.

You can also reset the status of an order depending on production control parameter settings. For this purpose, click the button *PRODUCTION ORDER/ Process/Reset status* in the action pane of the production order form. When resetting the status, keep in mind that Dynamics AX reverses all posted transactions related to the reversed status.

Unlike parameter settings in other areas, production control parameters are not only available at company level, but also at site level. The lookup field *Parameter usage* in the production control parameters at company level (*Production control> Setup> Production control parameters*) determines, if site-specific parameters apply to your company. Site-specific parameters are available in the form *Production control> Setup> Production control parameters by site*.

Scheduling parameters, initializing the update dialogs for scheduling production orders with default, are available in the form *Master planning> Setup> Scheduling> Scheduling parameters*. Like the production control parameters, they are available at company level and per site. Core scheduling parameters include the *Primary resource selection*, specifying if capability-based scheduling is based on the shortest duration or on the priority.

5.4.2   Production Order Registration

Creating a production order creates the header data, the production BOM lines, and the production route. Dynamics AX at this time creates an inventory transaction for the produced item with the status "Ordered" in the column *Receipt* (similar to a purchase order line).

The inventory transactions for the components of the production order (BOM lines) are not created until estimating the order. At this stage, master planning recognizes a supply of the produced item from the inventory transactions, but does not see the demand for components (inventory transactions are not created yet). For this reason, you should estimate a production order soon after creating it.

When automatically creating a production order from a planned order, settings in the applicable coverage group determine the initial status (usually "Scheduled").

5.4.2.1   Entering a New Production Order

Depending on how you want to proceed when manually creating a production order, you can start from the *Production floor management* workspace or from the production order form (*Production control> Production Orders> All production orders*).

Clicking the button *Create new/Production order* in the action pane of the workspace or the button *New production order* in the production order opens the *Create production order* dialog, where you have to choose the item number of the finished product. Depending on the selected item, several fields are initialized with default values which you can override as required (for example selecting a different BOM).

Clicking the button *Create* in the create order dialog then generates the production order. After creating, the order shows the status "Created" and switches to a subsequent status when updating the order. You can view a summary of executed status updates on the tab *Update* of the production order detail form.

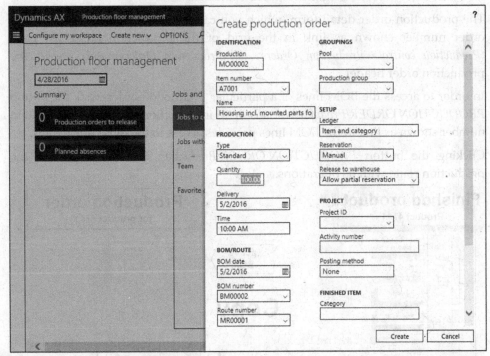

Figure 5-17: Creating a production order in the production floor management workspace

If required, you can change settings in a production order later (for example modifying the BOM lines or the route lines in the order). When changing an order which is estimated or scheduled already, run the estimation and/or scheduling after your changes again to ensure correct production data. If production papers have been printed already, you might need to reprint them with updated data.

Production orders, which have been created automatically, show a reference to their origin on the tab *References* of the production order detail form. If the production order refers to another order, this original order displays in the item reference type and number. If you have created the production order in a sales order line, the item reference type is "Sales order". In production orders generated as sub-production for the BOM line of another production order, the item reference type is "Production line".

5.4.2.2 Production BOM and Route

Like all documents, production orders contain a header with data common for the whole order – including the order number, the item number of the finished product, the order quantity, and the delivery date. But unlike sales orders or purchase orders, production orders include two different types of lines:

> **BOM lines** – Containing the required material
> **Route lines** – Containing the required operations

The production order detail form, which you can access by clicking a production order number shown as link in the grid of the production order list page (*Production control> Production Orders> All Production Orders*), only shows the production order header.

In order to access the BOM lines of a particular production order, click the button *PRODUCTION ORDER/Production details/BOM* in the action pane. Clicking an item number shown as link in the BOM lines provides access to the BOM line details.

Clicking the button *PRODUCTION ORDER/Production details/Route* shows the production route with its operations.

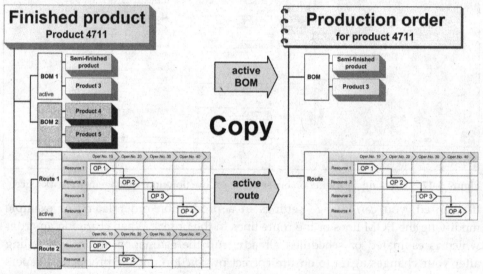

Figure 5-18:   Deriving BOM and route when creating a production order

When creating a production order, Dynamics AX copies the active BOM and route of the finished item into the production order. If multiple BOMs and routes are active for a finished item, the applicable version is determined based on site, date, and order quantity. For this purpose, the field *BOM date* – receiving its default from the delivery date – in the *Create production order* dialog determines the date applied for BOM selection.

If you do not want to apply the active BOM or route in a particular production order, you can select another approved BOM or route version – e.g. an alternative BOM and route for subcontracting – in the create order dialog.

5.4.2.3   New in Dynamics 'AX 7'

Items which are new in production order management refer to the browser-based user interface with dashboard and workspaces.

5.4.3   Processing Production Orders

After creating a production order, you want to update the status in order to prepare production order processing.

5.4.3.1   Default Values in Update Dialogs

When updating the status of a production order, an update dialog displays. In the update dialog, you can click the button *Default values* if you want to specify default values which are different from the standard defaults. Clicking the button *Make default for all users* in the default values dialog after entering appropriate settings applies the customized default values to all users.

5.4.3.2   Estimation

Estimation is the first step after creating a production order. The primary task of estimation is to calculate the required material and resources capacity for the production order. The basis for this calculation is the bill of materials and the route of the order.

In order to run the estimation, click the button *PRODUCTION ORDER/Process/ Estimate* in the action pane of the production order form. In the estimation dialog, the lookup field *Profit setting* determines the markup for sales price calculation.

In parallel to calculating required quantities and times, estimation determines projected costs based on the cost price of material components and route operations. The markup for the calculated sales price is specified in the cost groups of the items and route operations.

You can view the cost estimation by clicking the button *MANAGE COSTS/ Calculations/View calculation details* in the action pane of the production order form. The tab *Overview estimation* of the price calculation form shows the individual estimation lines. If you want to view a summary according to the costing sheet setup, switch to the tab *Costing sheet* in the price calculation form.

For the BOM lines of the production order, estimation creates inventory transactions which are similar to the inventory transactions of open sales order lines. You can view this transaction by clicking the button *Inventory/Transactions* in the BOM lines form of the production order.

Since there are no inventory transactions related to BOM lines before estimation, this status is the earliest order status for manual or automatic reservation (see section 7.4.5).

For BOM lines with the *Line type* is "Pegged supply", estimation creates an order:

> **Sub-production order** – Related sub-production order (regular production order linked to the main production order) for BOM lines with an item with the default order type "Production"
> **Purchase order** – Related purchase order for BOM lines with an item with the default order type "Purchase order"

For BOM lines with the line type "Phantom", estimation replaces the BOM line by the components of the phantom item (BOM and route).

5.4.3.3 Scheduling

Scheduling of a production order is necessary to calculate the exact dates/times of the material and resource demand and to reserve capacity on the applicable resource group or resource. In Dynamics AX, there are two types of scheduling:

> **Operations scheduling** – Resource group and day level
> **Job scheduling** – Resource and start/end time level

Depending on the setup and the requirements, you can execute either operations scheduling, or job scheduling, or both (first operations scheduling, then job scheduling).

Operations scheduling is a rough scheduling process, which calculates the required time per day. It reserves capacity on the resource group selected on the basis of the resource requirements in the route operation (capabilities, resource groups, resource types). If resource requirements for operations scheduling directly refer to a resource number, capacity reservation is on the particular resource instead of the group.

The operations scheduling calculation simultaneously includes the capacity of the resource group, the capacity per resource type, and the capacity per capability. The available capacity of a resource group is the total capacity of its resources.

Job scheduling at a later stage of production order processing calculates the capacity at resource level, reserving capacity with exact start and end times. Depending on scheduling parameters, the selected resource is the available resource with the shortest duration (throughput time) or with the highest priority (lowest priority number).

In addition to calculating exact start and end times, job scheduling generates jobs which split the route operations of a production order to individual tasks. These individual tasks show different job types, corresponding to the different time fields on the tab *Times* of the route operation (e.g. *Setup time* and *Run time*). Available job types for a particular operation are determined by the *Route group* of the operation (settings on the tab *Setup* in the route group form).

Job transactions (referring to job scheduling) are independent from route transactions (referring to operations scheduling). For this reason, you have to decide whether to schedule capacity and to post actual time consumption at operations level or at detailed job level. Jobs are not available in a production order, if you skip job scheduling.

If you want to view the route transactions, click the button *PRODUCTION ORDER/Production details/Route* in the production order. Jobs are recorded in a separate table, which you can access by clicking the button *PRODUCTION ORDER/Production details/All jobs* in the production order.

In a resource or resource group, you can view the capacity reservations in various inquiries – for example in the capacity load (button *RESOURCE/View/Capacity load* in the action pane of the resource form). Capacity reservations for operations scheduling and for job scheduling show separately and as a total.

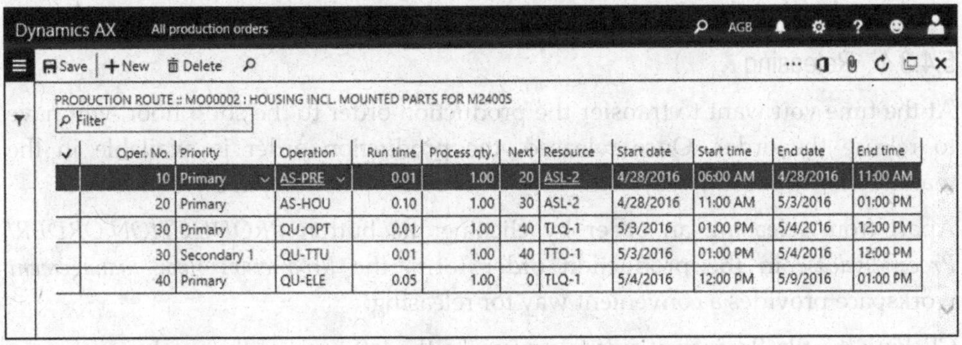

✓	Oper. No.	Priority	Operation	Run time	Process qty.	Next	Resource	Start date	Start time	End date	End time
	10	Primary	AS-PRE	0.01	1.00	20	ASL-2	4/28/2016	06:00 AM	4/28/2016	11:00 AM
	20	Primary	AS-HOU	0.10	1.00	30	ASL-2	4/28/2016	11:00 AM	5/3/2016	01:00 PM
	30	Primary	QU-OPT	0.01	1.00	40	TLQ-1	5/3/2016	01:00 PM	5/4/2016	12:00 PM
	30	Secondary 1	QU-TTU	0.01	1.00	40	TTO-1	5/3/2016	01:00 PM	5/4/2016	12:00 PM
	40	Primary	QU-ELE	0.05	1.00	0	TLQ-1	5/4/2016	12:00 PM	5/9/2016	01:00 PM

Figure 5-19: Production route transactions after job scheduling

In order to run scheduling, click the button *SCHEDULE/Production order/Schedule operations* or *SCHEDULE/Production order/Schedule jobs* in the action pane of the production order. If you want to schedule multiple orders together, execute the corresponding periodic activity in the menu folder *Production control> Periodic tasks> Scheduling*.

On the tab *Scheduling parameters* of the update dialog for scheduling, following parameters are available:

➢ **Scheduling direction** – Several variants of forward or backward scheduling ("Forward form today" applies if empty)

➢ **Finite capacity** and **Finite material** – Considering resource or item availability

➢ **Keep warehouse from resource** – Prevents selecting a resource assigned to a different input warehouse when re-scheduling a production order (applicable if the checkbox *Resource consumption* in BOM lines is selected)

➢ **Schedule references** – Scheduling sub-production orders in parallel

➢ **Primary resource selection** – Only for job scheduling, specifying whether capability-based resource selection should primarily search for the shortest duration (latest start date when scheduling backwards) or for the highest priority (i.e. the lowest priority number – priority "1" is selected first)

In addition, you can select to skip job types on the tab *Cancellation* if applicable. This applies for example, if you want to skip setup time when producing the same product again, or if you want to skip queue time for a particular production order of high importance.

If you do not execute operations or job scheduling as a separate task, scheduling runs automatically when updating to a later status (e.g. immediately releasing the order). In this case, the *Scheduling method* on the tab *Automatic update* of the production control parameters specifies whether Dynamics AX runs operations scheduling or job scheduling.

In order to take changes in orders and resource availability into account, you usually re-run scheduling in the course of time for orders which are not yet released. When rescheduling production orders, the related capacity reservations are deleted and replaced by new reservations.

5.4.3.4   Releasing

At the time you want to transfer the production order to the shop floor, you have to release the order. Once released, the production order is available in the manufacturing execution system (shop floor control module) in Dynamics AX.

Apart from releasing an order by clicking the button *PRODUCTION ORDER/ Process/Release* in the production order form, the *Production floor management* workspace provides a convenient way for releasing:

Clicking the tile *Production orders to release* in the left pane of the workspace opens the *Production orders to release* form, which shows orders not yet released in the upper pane and the related critical on-hand inventory in the lower pane. Taking the material availability into account, you can release an order by clicking the button *Release* in the toolbar of the upper pane there.

On the tab *General* of the update dialog for releasing, you can choose to print production papers like job cards or route cards. Selecting the checkbox *References* releases referenced sub-production orders in parallel.

5.4.3.5   Starting

Starting a production order (button *PRODUCTION ORDER/Process/Start*) is a required step before posting inventory and resource transactions. If you do not want to start the entire production quantity, you can enter a partial quantity on the tab *General* of the update dialog for starting. Entering a *From Oper.No.* and a *To Oper.No.* only starts the selected operations.

The automatic posting of resource consumption (working time consumption) is controlled by the field group *Route card journal* on the tab *General* of the update dialog. The field *Route card* there specifies the journal name for posting, initialized with a default from the production control parameters. In the lookup *Automatic route consumption*, the following options are available for automatic posting:

> **Route group dependent** – Automatic consumption depending on the route group of the operation (see section 5.3.3)
> **Always** – Automatic consumption of all route operations
> **Never** – No automatic consumption

The slider *Post route card now* controls whether to post the consumption journal immediately. If automatic route consumption is selected without setting this slider to "Yes", Dynamics AX generates a route card journal for manual editing (without posting it automatically). automatic consumption is posted through route cards

Controlling automatic BOM consumption in the field group *Picking list journal* of the update dialog works similar to the automatic route consumption. If you want to post automatic consumption depending on the settings in the BOM lines, choose the option "Flushing principle" (see section 5.2.1) in the lookup field *Automatic BOM consumption*. This option refers to the corresponding field on the tab *Setup* of the production BOM line details.

Setting the slider *Print picking list* in the update dialog to "Yes" prints the picking list in parallel to order starting. If you want to print a complete picking list, set the slider *Complete picking list journal* to "Yes". The picking list otherwise only contains items, which are included in the picking list journal generated for automatic consumption.

5.4.3.6 New in Dynamics 'AX 7'

Items which are new in order processing include the *Production floor management* workspace and the related release order page showing critical inventory.

5.4.4 Case Study Exercises

Exercise 5.8 – Production Order

There is a demand for five pieces of the finished item created in exercise 5.2. Enter a corresponding production order and check the BOM and the route in the order.

Exercise 5.9 – Change Status

You want to process the production order of exercise 5.8, starting with estimation. Once the estimation is finished, check the price calculation. Then execute operations scheduling and job scheduling one after the other. Once scheduling is finished, release the order from the *Production floor management* workspace.

Finally start the order, making sure to print a complete picking list as a print preview. You do not want to post the picking list. Is it possible to apply these settings as a default for all users?

5.5 Production Journal Transactions

Reporting of actual material and working time consumption is required to know the current inventory and to analyze production performance.

Basically, this reporting is done through production journals you can create and post in one of the following ways:

> **Manually** – Entering and posting journals (usually done in the office based on manual reports of the shop floor).
> **Automatically** – Creating journals based on route group and flushing principle.
> **Through terminals or devices** – Applying the manufacturing execution system (shop floor control module) in Dynamics AX, you can report consumption on touch-screen terminals or mobile devices in the shop floor.

In a warehouse applying advanced warehouse management, the consumption of material and the receipt of the finished item is registered through mobile device transactions (see section 8.1.3).

5.5.1   Journal Transaction and Ledger Integration

Production journals for posting consumption include following types:

> **Picking list** – Item consumption
> **Route card** – Resource consumption (working time) referring to operations
> **Job card** – Resource consumption (working time) referring to jobs

The journal type "Report as finished" does not refer to item consumption, but to the receipt of finished products in inventory.

If automatic resource and item consumption applies (route group, flushing principle), Dynamics AX creates production journals automatically (*Route card* for resource consumption and *Picking list* for item consumption) when starting a production order or when reporting as finished. Production journals are also generated automatically, if registrations are transferred from the manufacturing execution system.

For BOM lines or route operations which are not posted automatically, you have to create production journals and enter transactions manually as described below.

5.5.1.1 Journal Setup

As a prerequisite for posting transactions in manufacturing, you have to set up the required journals in the form *Production control> Setup> Production journal names*. Picking lists, route cards, job cards, and report as finished journals refer to different journal names, which you have to set up selecting the appropriate *Journal type*.

5.5.1.2 Ledger Integration

When posting production journal transactions, Dynamics AX posts the consumption to clearing accounts for WIP (work in progress). When ending and costing a production order, item and resource consumption are posted to the final ledger accounts.

As a prerequisite for posting item consumption to WIP accounts, the slider *Post picking list in ledger* on tab *General* of the production control parameters has to be set to "Yes" (not required for standard cost items). In addition, the checkbox *Post physical inventory* on the tab *Costing method & cost recognition* in the item model group of the picked item has to be selected.

Like ledger transactions referring to packing slips in purchasing and sales, general ledger transactions for route/job consumption journals and picking lists are reversed when ending and costing the production order.

5.5.2 Picking List

Picking list journals are there for posting item consumption. In order to access the picking list journals, click the button *VIEW/Journals/Picking list* in the action pane of the production order form or open the form *Production control> Adjustments> Picking list*.

Production journals are documents consisting of a journal header and journal lines. When accessing the picking list journals, the list page shows all open journal which are not posted yet. Applying an appropriate filter on the column *Posted* (you can use the filter pane, the grid column filter, or the advanced filter) provides the option to view also posted journals.

5.5.2.1 Creating Picking List Journals

If you want to create a new journal, click the button *New* in the action pane of the list page. After selecting an appropriate journal name in the *Create* dialog, Dynamics AX switches to the journal detail form in lines view.

In order to facilitate picking list registration, you can click the button *Picking list/ Create lines* in the journal list page instead of the button *New*. In the *Create lines* dialog, you can select which production BOM lines should be used as default for the proposal. Selecting "Remaining quantity" in the field *Proposal* applies the open BOM line quantity as default to the column *Proposal* of the picking list lines. If you set the slider *Consumption=Proposal* to "Yes", the column *Consumption* in the journal lines also receives the proposal quantity. In this case, you can immediately post the journal without manual data entry (consuming the estimated quantity).

5.5.2.2 Journal Lines

From the journal list page, you can access the journal detail form by clicking the journal ID shown as link in the grid of the journal page. Clicking the button *Header* below the action pane in the detail form switches to the header view, where you can view the complete journal header.

When manually entering a regular picking list line in the lines view, you have to select a *Lot ID* linking the consumption to a production BOM line before entering the *Consumption* quantity. Selecting the checkbox in the column *End* of the journal line sets the production BOM line to finished, no matter if consuming the total estimated quantity or less.

If you consume an item which is not included in the BOM lines of the production order, insert a picking list line entering the item number and leaving the lot ID empty. Dynamics AX in this case automatically creates a corresponding BOM line in the production order and applies the lot ID to the picking list line.

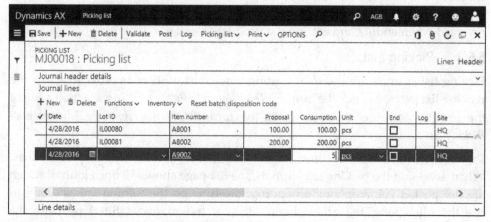

Figure 5-20:   Entering an additional picking list line in a picking list journal

Figure 5-20 shows an example of lines in a picking list journal, which are generated by a consumption proposal. The checkbox *Consumption=Proposal* has been selected in the consumption proposal dialog, which is why the column *Consumption* in the journal lines contains default values for the actual quantity. The last line in Figure 5-20 shows a manual entry for an item not included in the BOM. The columns *Proposal* and – only before saving the line – *Lot ID* are therefore empty in this line.

Once you have finished entering the picking list, post the journal by clicking the button *Post* in the journal list page or detail form. In inventory, the posted transactions reduce the quantity of the picked items similar to the packing slip transactions of sales orders.

Inventory valuation is applying a preliminary physical value to the picking list journal posting. Financial valuation is posted later when ending and costing the production order.

5.5.2.3 Inquiries and Reversal

If you want to view a posted journal, access the picking list journal form and apply an appropriate filter on the column *Posted*. The posted journal shows a checkmark in the column *Posted* and does not allow modifications.

Alternatively, you can view the posted transactions in the production posting form. In order to access this form, click the button *MANAGE COSTS/Production accounting/Production posting* in the production order form or access the menu item *Production control> Inquiries and reports> Production> Production posting*.

If you want to reverse a posted picking list journal, register and post a picking list journal with negative quantities. In order to facilitate registration, you can create an appropriate picking list proposal by clicking the button *Picking list/Create lines* and selecting the option "Full reversal" in the field *Proposal* of the proposal dialog.

5.5.3   Consumption of Resources

Depending on route group settings and on the way of scheduling the order, you have to use route cards or job cards to record resource consumption. Resource consumption is the usage of a resource, usually measured by the working time.

5.5.3.1   Route Card and Job Card

Route card journals are used to register resource consumption at operation level. You should use route cards if you only run operations scheduling but no job scheduling, or if the settings in the route group (checkboxes *Job management* on the tab *Setup* cleared) of an operation prevent using job cards.

Job card journals are used to register resource consumption at job level. Jobs are created when executing job scheduling. Depending on the route group settings, you should use job cards instead of route cards if there are jobs for an operation.

Automatic resource consumption when starting or reporting as finished is posted through route cards. Registrations transferred from the manufacturing execution system apply job card or route card journals depending on the setup (*Production control> Setup> Manufacturing execution> Production order defaults*, lookup *Job level* on the tab *Operations*).

5.5.3.2   Journal Registration

You can access the route card journals by clicking the button *VIEW/Journals/Route card* in the action pane of the production order form or through the menu item *Production control> Adjustments> Route card*. For job cards, click the button *VIEW/Journals/Job card* in the production order or access the menu item *Production control> Adjustments> Job card*.

Entering journal headers and lines for resource consumption works similar to entering picking list journals. But except for automatic consumption (option when starting an order or reporting as finished), there is no consumption proposal for route cards or job cards.

When inserting a journal line for resource consumption, select the operation number (or the job identification) first. Then enter the resource, the number of hours, the produced quantity (*Good quantity*), the task type (only in route cards, in job cards automatically from the job), and other data as applicable – e.g. the defective quantity (*Error quantity*) of the finished product. In a job card, you should additionally enter the start time, the end time, and the worker as applicable.

Once you have finished entering the journal lines, post the journal clicking the button *Post* in the journal list page or detail form.

If you want to view the posted journal afterwards, access the route card or job card journal form and apply an appropriate filter on the column *Posted*. In addition, you can view the posted transactions in the route transactions inquiry (button *MANAGE COSTS/Cost transactions/Route transactions* in the production order) or in the posting inquiry (*MANAGE COSTS/Production accounting/Production posting*).

5.5.3.3 Reporting as Finished

When registering the last operation or job in a journal line, you can select the checkbox in the column *Production report as finished* if you want to post a report as finished journal for the produced item in parallel to the route card or job card. The default for the report as finished setting in journal lines is specified in the production control parameters (tab *Journals*, slider *Automatic report as finished*).

5.5.4   Case Study Exercises

Exercise 5.10 – Purchasing Components

In order to process the production order of exercise 5.8, the required components have to be available in inventory.

Enter a purchase order, purchasing nine units of the first and five units of the second item of exercise 5.1 from your vendor of exercise 3.2. Once you have finished entering and confirming the purchase order, post the product receipt and the vendor invoice.

Exercise 5.11 – Picking List

You can pick the components required for the production order of exercise 5.8 now. Enter and post a picking list journal, picking nine units of the first and five units of the second item. You do not expect any additional consumption. Pick from the warehouse where you have received the items in exercise 5.10.

Exercise 5.12 – Job Card

Choosing a job card, you want to record the actual working time for executing the manufacturing operation. Enter and post a job card referring to the production order of exercise 5.8, producing five units in the time between 8:00 AM and 2:00 PM (6 hours). You do not want to post reporting as finished in parallel.

5.6   Reporting as Finished and Ending Production

In the cycle of production order processing, reporting as finished and ending are the last steps. Reporting as finished posts physical transactions and increases the inventory quantity of the finished product. Ending the order then performs costing and posts the financial transactions.

5.6.1   Reporting as Finished

Reporting as finished physically receives the finished item in inventory. In Dynamics AX, there are following options to report a production order as finished:

> ➢ **Order status update** – Updating the status of the production order
> ➢ **Production journal** – Posting a report as finished journal
> ➢ **Time registration** – Reporting as finished when posting the route card or job card for the last operation
> ➢ **Advanced warehouse management** – Transactions on the mobile device

The production input journal (*Inventory management> Journal entries> Item arrival> Production input*) provides the option to post an inventory registration before reporting as finished – similar to arrival journals in purchasing (see section 3.5.3).

5.6.1.1 Order Status Update

In order to report as finished by updating the order status, click the button *PRODUCTION ORDER/Process/Report as finished* in the action pane of the production order form or execute the periodic activity *Production control> Periodic tasks> Production order status update> Report as finished*. If you want to report only a part of the entire order quantity, adjust the *Good quantity* on the tab *Overview* or the tab *General* of the update dialog before clicking the button *OK*.

If you do not expect additional receipts for the current order to be reported as finished, set the slider *End job* to "Yes" (clearing any remaining open quantity).

If you are sure that the actual consumption of items and resources has been completely posted already and you do not want to receive messages concerning missing consumption (compared to the estimation), set the slider *Accept error* on the tab *General* to "Yes".

5.6.1.2 Production Journal

Apart from the status update, reporting as finished is also possible by posting a production journal. In order to access this journal, click the button *VIEW/Journals/Reported as finished* in the action pane of the production order form, or choose the menu item *Production control> Adjustments> Report as finished*.

The way to work in the report as finished journal is similar to the picking list journal (see section 5.5.2). But posting a report as finished journal generates transactions which are similar to product receipts in purchase orders: Inventory physically receives the item with a preliminary value and increases the on-hand quantity.

5.6.1.3 Automatic Consumption

Like when starting the production order, automatic item and resource consumption is also possible when reporting as finished. On the tab *General* in the dialog when reporting as finished, the field groups *Route card journal* and *Picking list journal* for this purpose control automatic consumption.

If you post automatic consumption when starting and when reporting as finished, select the flushing principle "Start" in the BOM line for consumption when starting the production order, and "Finish" for consumption when reporting as finished.

This setting allows consuming some items when starting and other items when finishing of a production order.

Route operations do not show this option. For all operations with automatic posting, you have to decide in common for the production order, whether automatic posting should apply when starting or when reporting as finished. In order to avoid duplicate posting, select the option "Route group dependent" in the lookup field *Automatic route consumption* only in the dialog for starting, or only for reporting as finished – not in both dialogs.

5.6.1.4 Ledger Integration

If you want to post the finished items to clearing accounts in the general ledger when reporting as finished, ledger integration has to be activated for reporting as finished. For this purpose, set the slider *Post report as finished in ledger* on tab *General* of the production control parameters to "Yes" (not required for standard cost items). In addition, the checkbox *Post physical inventory* on the tab *Costing method & cost recognition* in the item model group of the finished item has to be selected.

General ledger transactions for reporting as finished are reversed when ending and costing the production order.

5.6.1.5 Reporting Scrap

Scrap specified in the BOM or in the route is planned scrap, which is included in the estimated consumption of items and resources. The cost analysis therefore does not show it as deviation. A deviation only applies if you post excess resource (working time) or item consumption. In this context, data in the field group *Scrap* in the line details of the picking list journal are just for information purpose.

Scrapping a finished product in the course of production order processing is unplanned scrap. You can report this scrap by entering an *Error quantity* when reporting as finished. The default for the error quantity is the total of the reported error quantity of all operations.

From a financial perspective, you can allocate the costs for finished product scrap to the good quantity (which means that the good quantity carries all costs of the production order) or post scrap to a separate scrap account (default on the tab *Standard update* in the production control parameters). If you apply a scrap account, ending the production order posts an inventory receipt and an immediate issue (posting against the scrap account) for scrap when ending the order. Only when using a scrap account, you can completely scrap an order (no good quantity).

The scrap account option does not apply to finished products with standard costs.

5.6.2 Ending and Costing

Ending a production order is required for cost-accounting and closing the order. In parallel, WIP ledger transactions for production journals are reversed.

Consumption of items and resources and receipts of finished items post to the final ledger accounts.

You should end a production order in time. The finished item otherwise is still included in the WIP account balance instead of the stock account balance.

5.6.2.1 Ending

Ending an order closes it. Since it is not possible to post any transaction for a closed production order, you should not end the order until you are sure all transactions have been posted.

In order to end the production order, click the button *PRODUCTION ORDER/Process/End* in the action pane of the production order form. If you want to end multiple orders, execute the corresponding periodic activity in the menu item *Production control> Periodic tasks> Production order status update> End*.

After ending, the ending date of the production order shows in the field *Financial date* of the inventory transactions. The receipt status in inventory transactions of items reported as finished is "Purchased". For consumed items (BOM lines), the issue status is "Sold".

5.6.2.2 Costing

Costing a production order is the corresponding action to invoicing purchase and sales orders. When costing the order in the course of the ending routine, Dynamics AX calculates the actual costs for all item and resource consumption transactions. Based on these actual costs of the production order, the cost price of the finished item is calculated. If standard cost valuation applies to the finished item, costing posts the cost price differences to variance accounts.

✓ Type	Number	Level	Item/Res...	Dime...	Calc...	Unit	Estimated consumption	Realized...	Estimated cost amount	Realized...	Co
Production	MO00001	0	A7001	HQ/30	MAT	pcs	100.00	100.00	16,020.00	15,470.00	
Item	MO00001	1	A8001	HQ/10	MAT	pcs	100.00	100.00	10,000.00	10,000.00	
Item	MO00001	1	A8002	HQ/10	MAT	pcs	200.00	200.00	1,000.00	1,000.00	
Item	MO00001	1	A9001	HQ/10	MAT	pcs	100.00	100.00	3,000.00	3,000.00	
Process	MO00001	1	ASL			Hours	1.00		50.00		
Process	MO00001	1	ASL			Hours	10.00		500.00		
Setup	MO00001	1	TLQ			Hours	2.00	2.00	140.00	140.00	
Process	MO00001	1	TLQ	.		Hours	1.00	1.00	70.00	70.00	
Setup	MO00001	1	TTO			Hours	2.00	2.00	140.00	140.00	
Process	MO00001	1	TTO			Hours	1.00	1.00	70.00	70.00	
Process	MO00001	1	TLQ			Hours	5.00	5.00	350.00	350.00	
Surcharge	MO00001	1	MAT-OV			GBP	14,000.00	14,000.00	700.00	700.00	

Figure 5-21: Comparing estimation and costing in the calculation form

In order to compare the actual and the estimated consumption, click the button *MANAGE COSTS/Calculations/View calculation details* in the action pane of the production order form. The tab *Overview Costing* of the price calculation form then shows – at item and operation line level – a comparison of estimated and realized quantity consumption, and of estimated and realized costs. The tab *Costing sheet* contains a summary of estimation or costing according to the costing sheet setup.

5.6.2.3 Ledger Integration and Inquiries

Like when posting invoices in purchasing or sales, costing a production order posts financial transactions for the items consumed and reported as finished. First, costing reverses the WIP ledger transactions posted through picking list journals, route card journals, job card journals, and report as finished journals. In a second step, costing posts following ledger transactions to close the order financially:

➢ **Consumption of components** – To the stock accounts of the BOM line items
➢ **Consumption of resources** – To the costing accounts of the resources
➢ **Receiving the finished item** – To the stock account of the finished item
➢ **Indirect costs** – To the financial accounts as specified in the costing sheet

For the item transactions, applicable main accounts are specified in the inventory posting setup (*Inventory management> Setup> Posting> Posting*). For resource consumption, main accounts can derive from settings in the resource/resource group or in applicable cost categories. Apart from these settings, production groups are an alternative way to specify applicable main accounts for item and resource transactions.

Receiving a default from the production control parameters, the lookup *Ledger* on the tab *Setup* of the production order detail form determines which setting actually applies to retrieve appropriate main accounts (see section 9.4.3).

In order to view the transactions generated when ending and costing the order, click the button *MANAGE COSTS/Production accounting/Production posting* in the action pane of the production order form or access the menu item *Production control> Inquiries and reports> Production> Production posting*. In the production posting inquiry, the transactions posted when ending and costing the production order show the type "Costing". In order to view related ledger transactions, click the button *Voucher* in the action pane.

5.6.3   Case Study Exercise

Exercise 5.13 – Ending Production

By clicking the button *Process/Report as finished* in the production order form, report the entire quantity of the production order in exercise 5.8 as finished. On the tab *General* of the update dialog, set the slider *End job* to "Yes". Then end the production order and check the price calculation inquiry to compare estimation and costing afterwards.

5.7   Subcontracting

If a company cannot process a particular operation internally for technological reasons or because of the current capacity utilization, this operation is often subcontracted to an external vendor. BOM and/or route of the finished item then have to include the subcontracted service.

Some finished products are alternatively produced internally or at a subcontractor. In order to manage these alternatives, you have to work with two or more approved route and/or BOM versions for the item (like when using different resources for the same item depending on the production size).

In Dynamics AX, there are two basic options for subcontracting:

➢ **Outsourced operation** – Resource of the type "Vendor" in an operation
➢ **Purchased service** – Service item with the line type "Vendor" in a BOM line

Since a purchase order line needs to contain a physical item or a service item (procurement categories are not available for this purpose), only the second option includes creating a purchase order.

5.7.1   Outsourced Operation

You can use an outsourced operation, which is not linked to a BOM line with a service item, if you do not need to generate a purchase order – for example if there is a contract with a fixed capacity reservation and a fixed monthly fee.

In this case, create a separate resource group and resource per subcontractor. The resource is similar to a regular internal resource (see section 5.3.2), but applies the *Type* "Vendor" providing the option to enter the vendor number in the field *Vendor* on the tab *General* of the resource form. In addition, apply appropriate settings for the cost categories (depending on the contract, maybe only a *Quantity category*) and for the main accounts, making sure to post the right amount to the right accounts. Settings for the calendar and for finite capacity are depending on the contract.

In the related route operation, select the *Route type* "Vendor" on the tab *General* and enter the vendor resource as *Costing resource* together with appropriate resource requirements. Processing the outsourced operation in a production order works similar to processing a regular internal operation.

5.7.2   Purchased Service

If you need a purchase order for the outsourced operation, create a service item and include it in the BOM of the finished product. For scheduling purposes, you can link the BOM line with the service item to an outsourced operation.

5.7.2.1   Master Data for Purchasing Subcontracting Services

The required service item is a product with the *Product type* "Service", an *Item model group* generating inventory transactions ("Stocked product"), and the *Default order type* "Purchase order". In the *Cost group* on the tab *Manage costs* of the released product, you can select a cost group of the type "Direct outsourcing". The flushing principle should be "Finish". Other relevant settings in the released product include the item group, the cost price, the dimension groups, the units of measure, the purchase price, the main vendor, the default order settings, and the site-specific order settings.

In the BOM of the finished product, insert a BOM line with the service item and the *Line type* "Vendor", optionally including a *Vendor account* which overrides the main vendor from the released product.

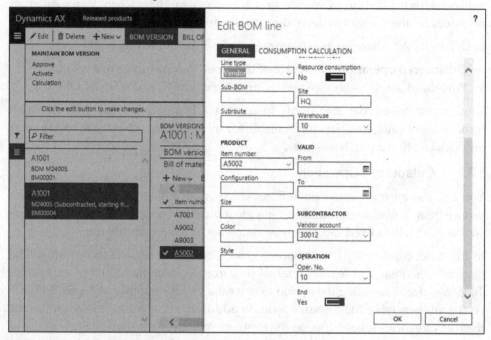

Figure 5-22: Settings in a BOM line for a subcontracted service

If you need an outsourced operation for scheduling purposes, you can set it up as described in the previous section. But unlike the settings for an outsourced operation which is not linked to a BOM line service item, the operation should contain a route group with settings for automatic consumption and – if all subcontracting costs are included in the service item – deactivated cost calculation (sliders in the field group *Estimation and costing* of the route group set to "No"). In order to link the BOM line with the service item (for purchasing the subcontracted activity) to the outsourced operation (for scheduling the subcontracted activity), select the appropriate operation number in the field *Oper.No.* on the tab *General* of the BOM line and make sure that the slider *End* there is set to "Yes" (you do not consume the service item before the operation is finished).

If material is supplied to the subcontractor, link the BOM lines of the appropriate components to the outsourced operation in the same way as linking BOM lines to an internal operation.

5.7.2.2 Production Order Processing with Purchased Services

You can manually or automatically create production orders including subcontracted service items in the same way as regular production orders (see section 5.4.2). When estimating the production order, a purchase order is created for the BOM line with the service item (triggered by the line type "Vendor" and the default order type "Purchase order"). The reference to the purchase order shows in the columns *Reference type* and *Number* of the production BOM lines (access by clicking the button *PRODUCTION ORDER/Production details/BOM* in the order). Like any other purchase order, the order has to be confirmed before receiving the service item.

Scheduling and releasing a production order with a subcontracted service is similar to any other production order.

Once you want to start the order, you can optionally use the list page *Production control> Subcontracted work* and click the button *Start* in the action pane after selecting the order there. On the tab *General* in the *Start* dialog, make sure to apply appropriate settings for automatic consumption (not consuming BOM items which are consumed when receiving the purchase order). In the *Print options* for the picking list (button in the *Start* dialog), you can set the slider *Use delivery note layout* for the picking list to "Yes" if you supply BOM items as components to the subcontractor.

When posting the product receipt for the purchase order afterwards, settings in the field group *Receive purchase order* on the tab *Automatic update* of the production control parameters determine if BOM and route consumption is posted in parallel to the product receipt. Choosing the option "Flushing principle" for the *Automatic BOM consumption* in the parameters provides the option to post the consumption only for particular BOM lines (included the service item).

Reporting the production order as finished and ending the order works as usual.

5.7.2.3 Item Transfer to Subcontractors

If you just enter an additional BOM line (with the service item) and an additional operation (with the vendor resource) in the regular BOM and route as described above, you can assign material to any operation (through the operation number in the BOM line) before or after the external operation (or to the external operation itself, if applicable). Depending on this assignment, consumption of components is before or after the external operation. There is no inventory transfer of a semi-finished item to or from the subcontractor.

In case you transfer a semi-finished item to the subcontractor after some internal operations, and you want to keep control of the material flow with the subcontractor, you have to apply additional BOM levels: Create a semi-finished item containing all items and operations before the external operation, and a second semi-finished item after the external operation. Both items got the default order type "Production". Components of the second semi-finished item are the first semi-finished item (line type "Pegged supply") and the subcontracting service item (and additional material directly supplied to the subcontractor if applicable). The BOM of the finished product contains the second semi-finished item (select the line type "Vendor") and the material required for later operations.

With this setup, there is a sub-production order for producing the first semi-finished item, which you receive in inventory by posting a report as finished transaction. You can transfer the item afterwards using a regular transfer order, and consume it when producing the upper-level production order (type "Vendor") of second semi-finished item. Processing the production order of the second semi-finished item works as described above for the simple scenario. When receiving the second semi-finished item from the subcontractor, report it as finished and consume it in the upper-level production order for the finished product.

5.8   Formula and Batch Production Order

Whereas discrete manufacturing is used to produce a distinct item assembled of several components, process manufacturing supports a continuous production process generating one or more batch-controlled formula items and co-products.

Production control in Dynamics AX supports the requirements of process industries by use of formulas (instead of discrete bills of materials). Resource and route management in process manufacturing uses the same functionality as discrete manufacturing.

If you are working in a discrete manufacturing environment, but have some requirements covered by process manufacturing features, you can use formulas. You can for example use a formula with co-products for a cutting operation, even if the items are not batch-controlled. The product configurator is not supported by formulas.

5.8.1   Formula Management

Formula management is based on bills of materials. Formulas, formula lines, and formula versions show the same concepts and functionality as bills of materials, BOM lines, and BOM versions. But in addition to the functionality in bills of materials, they include following core features:

➢ **Co-products and by-products** – Producing more than one product in parallel
➢ **Catch weight items** (see section 7.2.1) – As finished product and as component

In addition, there are features which help managing the quantity in formula lines (yield, percent controlled, scalable), and other options like the plan group supporting item substitutions.

5.8.1.1   Product Data for Formula Items

Formula items are finished items, which are produced using a formula. When creating such an item in the released product form, you can use similar settings to a BOM item (including the default order type "Production"). Although there are settings which are more common in process industry than in discrete manufacturing (e.g. weight as inventory unit), the only mandatory difference is the *Production type* on the tab *Engineer* with following options for process industry:

➢ **Formula** – Main item produced from the assigned formula
➢ **Co-product** – Item produced from a formula in parallel to a main item
➢ **By-product** – Like a co-product, but undesirable (causing costs instead of value)
➢ **Planning item** – Virtual main item, if a formula only produces co-products

Planning items are used, if there is no clear physical main item but equal co-products in a formula (e.g. in a refinery producing gasoline and diesel in parallel).

You can assign a formula only to an item with the production type "Formula" or "Planning item". Co-products and by-products are produced in a production order for the related formula or planning item. If there is a main formula or planning item for producing the co-product, you can enter the appropriate item number in the field *Planning formula* below the production type.

5.8.1.2   Working with Formulas

Managing formulas in Dynamics AX is similar to managing bills of materials, including the way to access the formula form:

➢ **From the released product** (*Product information management> Products> Released products*, button *ENGINEER/Formula/Formula versions*)
➢ **From the menu** (*Product information management> Bills of materials and formulas> Formulas*)

Like the assignment of BOMs, the assignment of formulas to finished items is called "Version", optionally specifying site, validity dates, and from-quantity.

Accessing the formula from the released product is only possible for items with the production type "Formula" or "Planning item". If you access the formula form from the menu, the list page shows all formulas. Clicking a formula ID shown as link in the grid of the list page opens the formula detail form in the lines view, where you can see the formula lines. Clicking the button *Header* below the action pane in the detail form switches to the header view, where you can view the formula versions (assignment of formula items or planning items to the formula).

The field *Formula size* in the formula version provides the default for the column *Per series* in the formula lines and is the default quantity when entering a production order for the particular product.

Co-products and by-products are optional. You can edit them in the formula detail form after clicking the button *Co-products* in the toolbar of the tab *Formula versions* (or the button *FORMULA VERSION/Maintain formula version/Co-products* in the action pane of the formula version form accessed from the released product). In the co-product form, you can add co-products and by-products with the respective quantity in the middle pane. For a co-product, you can select the *Co-product cost allocation* "Manual" and enter the *Cost allocation percent*. This percentage determines the inventory value of the co-product (specifying the percentage of the total production costs allocated to the co-product). For a by-product, you can specify the costs added to production (e.g. for disposal) by selecting the *By-product cost allocation*.

Like bills of materials, formulas and formula versions have to be approved before they are available for production orders.

5.8.2   Batch Production Order

Batch orders are production orders for formula items. There is no separate form for batch orders, they use the regular production order form. In the production control parameters, you can select a separate number sequence for batch orders or choose the same number sequence as for regular production orders.

The ways for creating a batch order are the same as for creating a regular discrete production order: Apart from manually entering it, you can create it automatically from master planning (including co-product demand in the calculation – select a *Planning formula* in the planned order if not specified in the released product), from an upper-level production order (line type "Pegged supply"), or from a sales order.

If you want to create a batch order manually, click the button *New/Batch order* in the *Production floor management* workspace or the button *New batch order* in the production order form and select the formula item in the *Create* dialog. It is not possible to select a co-product as order header item, but a related formula item or a planning item.

When creating a batch production order, Dynamics AX copies the active formula and route of the formula item into the order. In the order, you can access the formula lines (showing the components) by clicking the button *PRODUCTION ORDER/Production details/Formula* and the co-/by-products by clicking the button *PRODUCTION ORDER/Production details/Co-products*.

Processing the batch order – from estimation to ending – is not different from a regular production order except when reporting as finished: In addition to the receipt of the formula item, you can report co-products and by-products as finished.

When ending and costing a batch order with co-products or by-products, costs are allocated to the co-products according to the settings in the formula, and the additional costs caused by by-products are posted as route transaction with a burden cost category (specified in the production control parameters).

6 Operations Planning

The primary responsibility of operations planning is to make sure that items are available when needed while meeting the target of high economic efficiency at the same time. Operations planning accordingly has to solve the conflicting priorities of high supply readiness on the one hand and low inventory on the other.

6.1 Business Processes in Operations Planning

In Dynamics AX, long-term forecasting and short-term master planning are covered by the operations planning module ("Master planning").

6.1.1 Basic Approach

Operations planning includes forecasting to identify the item demand on a long-term basis. Master planning is used to calculate supply and demand on a short-term basis.

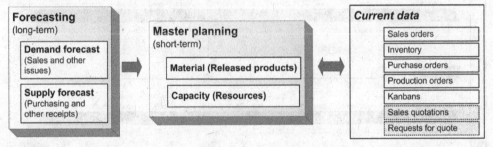

Figure 6-1: Operations planning in Dynamics AX (Forecasts and master planning)

6.1.1.1 Forecasting

Forecasting is a long-term prognosis for planning and budgeting purposes. It includes demand forecasts (sales and other issues) and supply forecasts (purchasing and other receipts). Different versions of forecasts provide the option to work with multiple parallel scenarios.

6.1.1.2 Master Planning

Master planning is the short-term planning for daily business. Based on current orders, on-hand inventory, sales quotations, and forecasts (as specified in the configuration), master planning calculates the item demand and supply. As a result, it generates actual and planned orders for purchasing, transfer, and production. Master planning, like forecasting, provides the option to use multiple scenarios in parallel. A core planning strategy supported by Dynamics AX is to maintain a static master plan for current master planning and a dynamic plan for simulation.

6.1.2   At a Glance: Master Planning

Before we start to go through the details of master planning, this section shows the basics on the example of the net requirements for a manufactured item.

As a basis for net requirements calculation, enter a sales order to be delivered today with a line containing a manufactured item (default order type "Production") which is out of stock. Clicking the button *Product and supply/Net requirements* in the toolbar of the sales order line provides access to the net requirements form, which shows the item availability. In order to update the net requirements with current data, execute local master planning by clicking the button *Update/Master planning* in the action pane of the net requirements form.

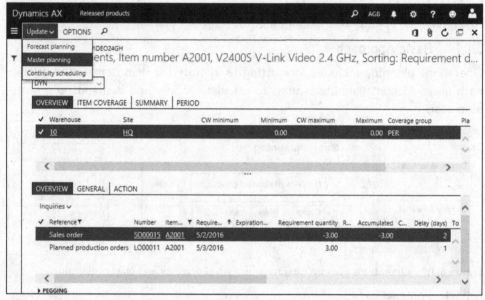

Figure 6-2:   The net requirements form after running local master planning

In the described scenario, master planning generates a planned production order to produce the manufactured item. Since the planned order needs to start in the past to meet the sales order delivery date, the requirement date in this line is adjusted to the earliest possible date (depending on the related setting for calculated delays in the master plan). The column *Delay (days)* in the sales order requirement shows the calculated delay.

Master planning supports multiple scenarios, distinguishing between a static and a dynamic plan. In the net requirements form, the dynamic plan (used for simulation and order promising purposes) is the default when executing master planning. The static plan is used in purchasing and production for scheduling and firming orders. In order to switch between the different plans, choose the appropriate option in the lookup field *Plan* at the top of the net requirements form.

6.2   Forecasting

Forecasting is a long-term prognosis, required to estimate and adjust future capacities of resources and material supply. In addition, you can use forecasting as a basis for budgeting in finance. In order to support planning of alternative scenarios for business development, you can maintain multiple forecasts in parallel.

Forecasting in Dynamics AX does not only include sales forecasts. Demand forecasts also include other sources of item issue – for example production, if you want to forecast at semi-finished product level. In addition, you can manage supply forecasts – for example as basis for long-term vendor contracts.

6.2.1   Basics of Forecasting

When entering or computing forecast figures in Dynamics AX, you have to select a forecast model (representing the planning scenario) which holds the forecast data. Forecast plans, which are the basis for calculating forecasts in forecast planning, then refer to particular forecast models. Forecast plans are also used in master planning as demand and supply source depending on the setup.

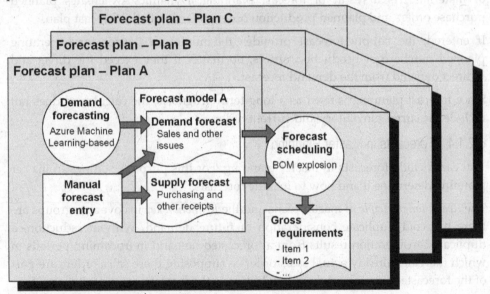

Figure 6-3:   Forecasting in Dynamics AX

6.2.1.1   Demand Forecast

Forecasting the future demand based on estimated sales figures is the starting point of the forecasting process. You can enter a demand forecast at different levels of the forecast dimension item, customer, and inventory (site/warehouse). Apart from direct sales (sales forecast), the demand forecast might also contain other demand – e.g. the demand for semi-finished items (instead of finished items) if it is not possible to specify reliable forecasts at the detail level of finished products.

Since forecast planning and master planning are based on released products, you have to use item allocation keys if you do not want to enter forecasts at the level of individual items. Item allocation keys are groups, specifying a percentage for each item in the group.

Apart from manually entering forecasts, Dynamics AX supports the automatic generation of demand forecasts through Azure Machine Learning.

6.2.1.2 Supply Forecasts

In parallel or after finishing demand forecasts, you can optionally manage separate supply forecasts (containing purchases and other types of item receipts). The inventory forecast then provides the option to align demand and supply forecasts.

6.2.1.3 Forecast Planning

Once you have finished recording forecast figures, you can execute forecast planning to calculate the gross requirements of finished items based on their bills of materials. As a result of forecast planning, Dynamics AX creates planned purchase orders and planned production orders referring to the forecast plan.

If entered, the supply forecast provides the minimum figures for generating planned purchase or production orders, no matter if they exceed the direct and indirect demand from the demand forecast.

Since forecast planning is used as a long-term prognosis, the calculation does not include the current inventory and current orders.

6.2.1.4 Forecasts in Master Planning

You can include forecasts in master planning. For this purpose, settings in master planning determine if and how to include forecasts.

The *Reduction principle* in master plans and the *Reduction key* in coverage groups are there to avoid duplicate consideration of future demand. Without reduction, a duplicate consideration results from a forecasted demand in upcoming periods in which there are already actual sales orders – supposing these sales orders are part of the forecasted quantity and not in addition to the forecast.

6.2.1.5 New in Dynamics 'AX 7'

As a result of the cloud-based architecture, Azure Machine Learning-based demand forecasting replaces the SQL Server Analysis Services-based demand forecasting introduced with Dynamics AX 2012 R3.

6.2.2 Forecast Settings

Before starting to register forecasts, you have to finish the required setup in Dynamics AX.

6.2.2.1 Forecast Models

Forecast models represent the different scenarios in forecasting. In order to use forecasts, you have to set up at least one forecast model in the form *Master planning> Setup> Demand forecasting> Forecast models*.

If you want to structure forecasts (e.g. grouping forecasts by region), you can set up two-stage forecasting through submodels. In this case you have to create the submodels like regular forecast models first. Then enter the main model and assign the submodels on the tab *Submodel* of the forecast model form.

If you want to protect forecasts against changes, set the slider *Stopped* in the forecast model to "Yes". You can use blocking for example if an annual forecast should not change once it is finished – use a separate forecast model for the next year in this case.

6.2.2.2 Forecast Plan

Whereas forecast models are used for entering and storing forecasts, forecast plans are the grouping element of separate forecast scenarios in master planning. In order to assign forecast models to forecast plans, open the form *Master planning> Setup> Plans> Forecast plans* and select a main model in the lookup field *Forecast model* of the forecast plans.

The forecast plan also contains settings on whether to include supply or demand forecasts. On the tab *Time fences in days*, enter the periods (starting from the day of calculation) which should be covered by forecast planning.

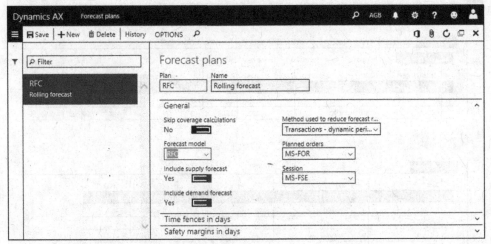

Figure 6-4:   Selecting a forecast model in the forecast plan

6.2.2.3 Parameters and Item Allocation Keys

In the master planning parameters (*Master planning> Setup> Master planning parameters*), the field *Current forecast plan* determines the default forecast plan for displaying forecast planning results.

Another important setting for item forecasts is the coverage group, which specifies how to summarize net requirements. The *Forecast plan time fence* on the tab *Other* in the coverage groups determines the applicable period for forecast planning. More information on coverage groups is available in section 6.3.3 later in this chapter.

If you do not want to enter forecasts at the level of individual items, use item allocation keys which provide the option to enter a forecast total for a group of items. In order to set up item allocation keys, open the form *Master planning> Setup> Demand forecasting> Item allocation keys*. The tab *Item allocation* in this form contains the assigned items with their percentage of the group total.

Setting up demand forecasting parameters (*Master planning> Setup> Demand forecasting> Demand forecasting parameters*) is required if you want to use Azure Machine Learning-based demand forecasting. Azure ML-based demand forecasts only include items which are assigned to item allocation keys. Prior to the setup in Dynamics AX, an Azure Machine Learning account is required if you want to generate forecasts using the Azure Machine Learning strategy.

6.2.3   Forecast and Forecast Planning

Apart from manually entering forecasts, for which you can use Excel integration, you can apply Azure ML-based demand forecasting for creating forecasts.

6.2.3.1   Manual Demand Forecast

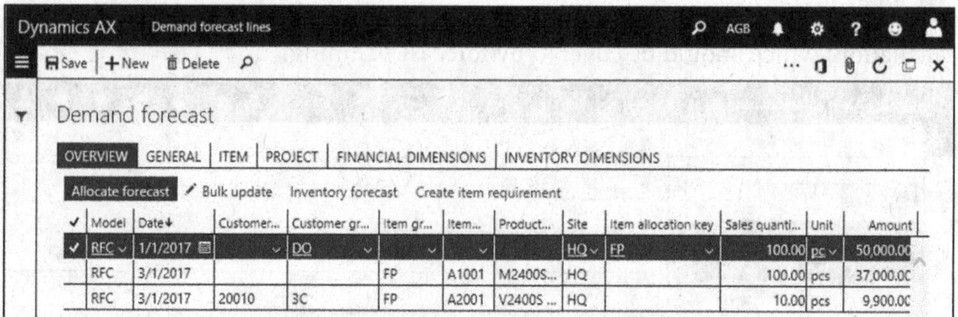

Figure 6-5:   Allocating a sales forecast line across periods

In order to enter demand forecasts manually, open the form *Master planning> Forecasting> Manual forecast entry> Demand forecast lines*. Alternatively, you can access demand forecasts by clicking the button *Demand forecast* or *Forecast* in the action pane of the respective master table form, for example in the released product (action pane tab *PLAN*) or in the customer (action pane tab *CUSTOMER*).

Once you are in the demand forecast lines, insert records selecting the appropriate (forecast) model. If you want to record different scenarios, enter different models in separate lines. In the date column, enter the start date of the individual forecast period – for example the first day of a month if entering a line per month. If you want to allocate a forecast line across periods, click the button *Allocate forecast* in the toolbar on the tab *Overview* and enter allocation details in the following dialog.

You can facilitate the manual forecast entry through bulk updates (button *Bulk update* on the tab *Overview*) or through Excel integration. In order to use Excel, click the button ▣ /*Edit demand forecast in Excel* in the action pane, change and add lines in Excel as appropriate, and publish the data back to Dynamics AX.

6.2.3.2 Azure Machine Learning-Based Demand Forecasting

As alternative to manually entering demand forecast lines, you can create them through Azure Machine Learning (Azure ML). The Azure ML-based demand forecasting calculates forecasts based on historical demand (originating from inventory transactions in Dynamics AX).

Once item allocation keys and demand forecasting parameters are set up, you can access the adjusted demand forecast form (*Master planning> Forecasting> Demand forecasting> Adjusted demand forecast*) and click the button *Generate statistical baseline forecast* to calculate the forecast using Azure ML with specified algorithm parameters (*Master planning> Setup> Demand forecasting> Forecasting algorithm parameters*, optionally override in demand forecasting parameters).

The forecast data in the adjusted demand forecast can be updated as required before creating the actual demand forecast lines by clicking the button *Authorize adjusted demand forecast*.

6.2.3.3 Supply Forecast and Inventory Forecast

If you want to maintain a supply forecast independently from the demand forecast, enter it in the form *Master planning> Forecasting> Supply forecast lines* or by clicking the button *Supply forecast* or *Forecast* in the action pane of the respective master table form (released product, vendor) similar to the demand forecast. Depending on the setup, forecast planning then includes the supply forecast in parallel to the demand forecast.

Inventory forecasts show the result of supply and demand forecasts at the level of item numbers and periods. You can access inventory forecasts in appropriate master table forms by clicking the button *Inventory forecast*.

6.2.3.4 Forecast Planning

The results of forecasts for trade items, finished items, and raw materials are a valuable basis to prepare production and purchasing for the future.

In order to determine forecast data on multiple BOM levels, you can perform forecast planning (*Master planning> Forecasting> Forecast planning*). The update dialog for forecast planning contains the lookup field *Forecast plan* for selecting the forecast plan to be calculated.

The results of forecast planning are available in the gross requirements form, which you can access by clicking the button *PLAN/Requirements/Gross requirement* in the action pane of the released product form. By default, the form shows the forecast plan set up as current forecast plan in the master planning parameters. The lookup field *Plan* at the top of the gross requirements form provides the option to select a different plan if applicable. Apart from the gross requirements form, also the planned order page *Master planning> Master planning> Planned orders* – after selecting the forecast plan in the lookup field *Plan* – shows planned orders generated by forecast planning.

6.2.3.5 Budget Transfer

If you want to use the results of demand or supply forecasting for financial budgets, transfer them to ledger budgets. For this purpose, execute the periodic activity *Budgeting> Periodic> Generate budget plan from demand forecast* (or *Generate budget plan from supply forecast*) filtering on the forecast *Model* and selecting the ledger budget model, which should receive forecast figures.

6.2.4   Case Study Exercises

Exercise 6.1 – Forecast Settings

You need a sales forecast for items, which you have set up in previous exercises – the merchandise item of exercise 3.5 and the finished item of exercise 5.2. Your forecast should be in a scenario which is separate from other forecasting scenarios.

In order to meet this requirement, create a new forecast model F-## (## = your user ID) without applying submodels. Then create a new forecast plan Y-##. Assign your forecast model to this forecast plan and make sure demand forecasts are included in this plan. The number sequences required can be similar to settings in existing forecast plans.

Exercise 6.2 – Demand Forecast

For the next quarter, you expect the customer of exercise 4.1 to order 200 units of the merchandise item and 100 units of the finished item on the first day of each month.

Enter these figures in a demand forecast using the forecast model of exercise 6.1. Once you have finished, run forecast planning for your forecast plan and check the results afterwards.

6.3 Master Planning

Master planning in Dynamics AX covers the short-term calculation of material and capacity requirements. It is the basis for the daily work in purchasing and production management.

The calculation in master planning includes data referring to released products and resources in all areas of Dynamics AX. Depending on the setup, these data include sales orders, purchase orders, production orders, on-hand inventory, forecast plans, and master data (released products, resources).

The result of master planning are planned orders for purchasing, production, Kanbans, and inventory transfer. Action messages and information on calculated delays support adjusting existing orders.

6.3.1 Basics of Master Planning

Item transactions, sales orders, purchase orders, production orders, and the on-hand quantity are an essential basis for master planning. In addition, master planning can include sales quotations, requests for quotation, approved purchase requisitions, and forecasts. You can adjust the demand resulting from forecasts and sales quotations by applying a probability percentage or a reduction principle.

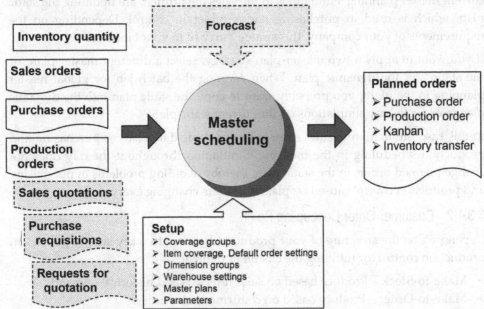

Figure 6-6: Elements of master planning

Like in forecasting, you can maintain multiple parallel scenarios in master planning. A scenario is represented by a master plan, which contains the particular settings for the scenario. These settings include the elements included in master planning and the calculation principles for planned orders.

6.3.1.1 Master Planning Strategies

Master planning usually is a batch job, which runs every night calculating the net requirements for all items. The result of this calculation is available in a scenario called "static master plan". The static plan is the master plan to be used in purchasing and production control for scheduling orders. It is the default plan when accessing planned order forms.

Apart from the master plan used for purchase and production scheduling, the sales department needs a plan to run simulations determining possible delivery dates in sales orders and quotations. This simulation requires executing master planning only for a particular item. The result of this simulation is available in a scenario called "dynamic master plan".

Based on both requirements, the master planning parameters provide the option to choose between two different strategies:

➢ **One plan strategy** – One common plan for scheduling and simulations
➢ **Two plan strategy** – Separate plans for scheduling and simulations

If selecting the same master plan for the static and the dynamic master plan in the master planning parameters, you run a one master plan strategy. Planned orders of current master planning simulations in the sales department are updating the static plan, which is used in purchasing and production control. Depending on the requirements of your company, this strategy may fit to your business.

If you want to apply a two master plan strategy, select a different master plan for the static and the dynamic plan. When running the batch job for global master planning in the night, you probably want to copy the static plan into the dynamic plan in order to base simulations on the current static plan.

In this case, simulation in sales starts with the same data basis as purchasing and production scheduling in the morning. Simulation throughout the day does not change planned orders in the static plan, thereby avoiding problems in purchasing and production control caused by planned orders changing every moment.

6.3.1.2 Customer Order Decoupling Point

Depending on the structure of your products, there are two key supply policies in production control for fulfilling the customer demand:

➢ **Make-to-Stock** – Produce based on sales forecasts and historical demand
➢ **Make-to-Order** – Produce based on confirmed sales orders

In addition, there are hybrid supply strategies applying a make-to-stock strategy for purchased or semi-finished items with a long lead time and a make-to-order strategy for finished products. If applying a hybrid strategy, the customer order decoupling point (push/pull point) determines the level in the product structure, to which the items are built to stock.

Dynamics AX supports all of these strategies by choosing appropriate coverage groups (see section 6.3.3). In case of a hybrid supply strategy, you can enter forecasts at semi-finished product level (which is the customer order decoupling point for these items). Reduction settings in master plans determine how master planning offsets forecasted demand with actual sales orders. Since forecasts on semi-finished products are not directly offset by sales orders, you should choose to include all inventory transactions – including BOM line demand from production orders – in the coverage groups of applicable semi-finished items in order to comply with this situation. In the coverage group form, the lookup field *Reduce forecast by* contains the required option for this purpose.

6.3.1.3 Master Planning and Planned Orders

Master planning generates planned purchase orders, planned production orders, planned Kanbans, and planned inventory transfer orders based on item demand and settings for master planning. Depending on the scheduling principle (see section 6.3.4), master planning deletes existing planned orders which are not in the status "Approved".

You can check and edit the planned orders in the planned orders form before transferring them to actual purchase orders, production orders, Kanbans, and inventory transfer orders.

6.3.2 Master Planning Setup

Before executing master planning, you have to finish the setup in Dynamics AX.

6.3.2.1 Master Plans

A master plan is a scenario, which contains the supply and demand calculation independently from the scenarios in other master plans. Depending on the planning strategy, one master plan or two master plans apply. If you need more simulation scenarios, set up additional master plans.

You can access the master plans in the menu item *Master planning> Setup> Plans> Master plans*. Sliders on the tab *General* determine whether to include following items in the particular master plan:

> **Current inventory** (on-hand inventory)
> **Inventory transactions** (open orders)
> **Sales quotations** (reduced by an optional probability percentage)
> **Approved purchase requisitions** (only for requisitions with the requisition purpose "Replenishment", which has to be enabled in the purchasing policy)
> **Shelf life dates** (for batch-controlled item)
> **Continuity plans** (from retail)
> **Requests for quotation** (entered in purchasing)
> **Forecasts** (supply and demand forecasts)

If you want to include forecasts in master planning, select the appropriate forecast plan in the lookup *Forecast model* of the master plan. In order to avoid excessive demand resulting from adding forecasts for a period to actual orders in the same period, you should offset the forecast by the current orders in this case. The lookup field *Reduction principle* in this case determines the way of reducing forecast data. If the selected principle refers to a *Reduction key*, you have to select a reduction key on the tab *Other* in the applicable coverage groups.

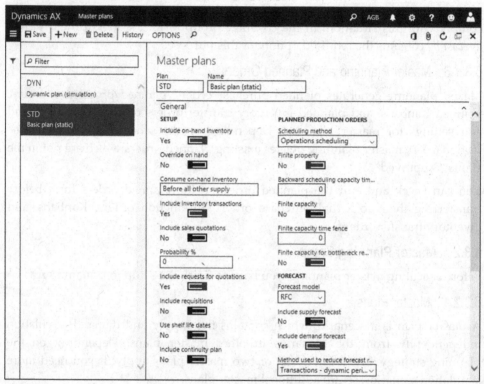

Figure 6-7:   Editing a master plan in the master plans form

The *Scheduling method* in the master plan controls whether to run operations scheduling or job scheduling (compare section 5.4.3) for planned production orders. Among other settings for scheduling planned production orders, there is the option to apply finite capacity.

The tab *Time fences in days* on the master plans form contains settings for overriding the time fences specified in the coverage group or in the item coverage.

On the tab *Calculated delays*, specify whether master planning may set the requirement date in the different types of planned orders to a date, which is after the actual requirement date, if it is not possible to meet the actual requirement date because of applicable lead times. This setting prevents impossible dates like a delivery date before today.

On the tab *Action message,* select for example if you want proposals to postpone planned purchase orders to a later date, if it is not necessary to receive the item as early as specified in the planned order date.

6.3.2.2 Master Planning Parameters

General parameters for master planning are specified in the form *Master planning> Setup> Master planning parameters.* A core setting controls the planning strategy: If applying a one master plan strategy, enter the same master plan in the field for the *Current static master plan* and the *Current dynamic master plan.*

If applying a two master plan strategy, select two different master plans. Optionally set the slider *Copy…* in this case to "Yes", which overrides the data in the dynamic plan with the static plan when executing master planning.

6.3.2.3 Warehouse Settings

If master planning should not include the on-hand quantity in specific warehouses – e.g. a consignment stock managed by the customer – set the slider *Manual* for the warehouse (*Inventory management> Setup> Inventory breakdown> Warehouses,* tab *Master planning*) to "Yes".

The warehouse form also contains a setting, whether the warehouse should be refilled from another warehouse (main warehouse). If selected, master planning generates item transfer proposals. As a prerequisite, the item has to contain a storage dimension group in which the checkbox *Coverage plan by dimension* is selected for the dimension "Warehouse".

6.3.3 Item Coverage and Item Settings

Coverage groups and settings on the released product control the calculation of lot sizes and delivery dates of planned orders generated by master planning.

6.3.3.1 Coverage Principle

The coverage principle, specified through the *Coverage code* in the coverage groups, is a main setting for item coverage. It controls, how requirements are summarized into a planned order.

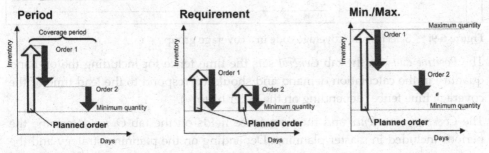

Figure 6-8:   Coverage principles in Dynamics AX

Dynamics AX includes four options for the coverage principle (see Figure 6-8):

> **Period** – Summarizing requirements within the coverage period (specified in the coverage group)
> **Requirement** – Planned order per requirement ("Make-to-Order")
> **Min./Max.** – Replenishing to the maximum quantity when inventory drops below the minimum quantity
> **Manual** – Planned orders are not generated in master planning

Master planning generates a planned order, if the calculated inventory at a date is below the minimum quantity (or below zero, if a minimum quantity is not entered in the item coverage of the released product).

6.3.3.2 Managing Coverage Groups

The coverage group (*Master planning> Setup> Coverage> Coverage groups*) determines the coverage principle and further settings for lot size and delivery date calculation. In order to access coverage group form, choose the menu item. The main setting in a coverage group is the *Coverage code*, which specifies the coverage principle. In case the *Coverage code* is "Period", the *Coverage period* below this field determines the number of days for combining demand in one planned order.

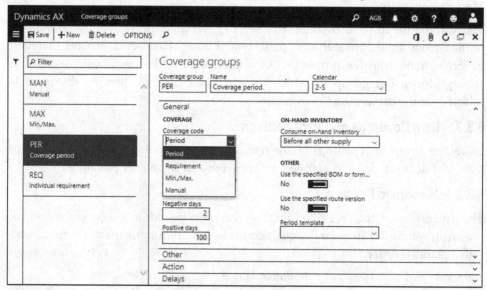

Figure 6-9:   Selecting the coverage code in a coverage group

The *Positive days* on the tab *General* sets the time fence for including the on-hand quantity in the calculation demand and should correspond to the lead time or the coverage time fence (depending on the order history).

The *Coverage time fence* and the time fence fields on the tab *Other* determine the periods included in master planning. Depending on the planning strategy and the lead time of the items, the number of days entered in the time fence fields should cover an applicable number of weeks or months.

The *Firming time fence* on the tab *Other* determines the period, for which master planning does not create a planned order but an actual purchase order or production order. If no main supplier is entered in the item record or specified through an applicable trade agreement for the purchased item, master planning still generates a planned purchase order (for selecting the vendor). As a prerequisite using vendors from trade agreements in master planning, the slider *Find trade agreement* in the master planning parameters has to be set to "Yes".

6.3.3.3 Forecast Plan Calculation and Reduction Keys

On tab *Other* of the coverage groups, the *Forecast plan time fence* and forecast reduction settings determine the calculation of forecast in master planning.

Reduction keys (*Master planning> Setup> Coverage> Reduction keys*) control the periods and percentages applied for reducing forecast figures in the course of time. As a prerequisite for applying the reduction key selected in the coverage group, the *Reduction principle* in the master plan has to refer to reduction keys.

The reduction principle in the master plan controls the way forecasted figures are reduced when considering them as demand. If entering forecasts for semi-finished items (hybrid supply strategy with customer order decoupling point, see section 6.3.1), reduction for the semi-finished product should not only include direct sales orders, but also demand derived from the finished product. Choosing the option "All transactions" in the lookup *Reduce forecast by* of the coverage group offsets forecasts by all issue transactions (including production BOM line demand).

6.3.3.4 Settings for Calculated Delays and Action Messages

Action messages, which are activated on the tab *Action* of the coverage group form, are messages from master planning to adjust actual or planned purchase and production orders. The aim of action messages is to support adjustments, which may not be done automatically (like postponing a purchase order, which is too early). They show proposals for optimizing quantities and dates of item receipt. Item availability is granted, no matter if you disregard action messages.

Unlike action messages, calculated delays show actual problems of item availability. A calculated delay is created, if the lead time of required items at all BOM levels results in a necessary supply before today, therefore causing delays in order fulfillment.

If activating both, calculated delays and action messages, usually select the option "Delayed date" in the lookup field *Basis date* on the tab *Action*. With this setting, action messages are based on the earliest possible date and not the original – impossible – requirement date.

6.3.3.5 Assigning Coverage Groups to Items

There are three levels for assigning a coverage group to an item:

> ➤ **Item coverage** – Button *PLAN/Coverage/Item coverage* in the released product
> ➤ **Released product** – Tab *Plan* in the released product
> ➤ **Master planning parameters** – *General coverage group* on the tab *General*

The coverage group specifies the method for calculating lot sizes. If there is a big difference in the lead time or in the cost price of your items, you want to group the items by entering different coverage groups in the released products based on the inventory value and the lead time.

6.3.3.6 Dimension Group Settings

Settings in the storage and tracking dimension groups control the inventory dimensions covered separately in coverage calculation. The dimension groups of an item therefore determine the available dimensions in the item coverage and the dimensions calculated separately in master planning (e.g. calculating supply and demand per warehouse).

You can edit dimension groups in the menu folder *Product information management> Setup> Dimension and variant groups* (see section 7.2.2). In the dimension groups, select the checkbox *Coverage plan by dimension* for storage and tracking dimensions which should be calculated separately in master planning. The dimension *Site* and the product dimensions are always calculated separately.

6.3.3.7 Item Coverage

Apart from the coverage group and the dimension groups, the item coverage is another important setting for master planning in the released product.

Clicking the button *PLAN/Coverage/Item coverage* on the action pane of the released product displays the item coverage form, where you can insert records specifying a minimum and – if applicable – a maximum quantity for the item. Depending on the dimension groups of the item and applicable dimension group settings (see above), you have to enter the item coverage per site, warehouse, or other dimensions like color or configuration.

The item coverage form contains settings for the item at dimension level, which may override settings from the item or the coverage group. You can, for example, select a *Coverage group* for a particular warehouse which is different from the coverage group in the released product. You can also select a specific main vendor and planned order type – for example purchasing an item from an external vendor in one specific warehouse, but producing it internally in the other warehouses.

If entering a minimum quantity, the lookup field *Minimum key* on the tab *General* provides the option to specify a seasonal trend for the minimum quantity. The results of the minimum key show on the tab *Min./Max.* of the item coverage form.

You can set up minimum keys in the form *Master planning> Setup> Coverage> Minimum/Maximum keys* with a percentage per period on the tab *Periods*.

6.3.4 Master Planning and Planned Orders

Based on item requirements and coverage settings, master planning generates planned orders for purchasing, production and inventory transfer. There are two different types of master planning:

> **Local master planning** – Availability check, e.g. in a sales order line
> **Global master planning** – Regular master planning for all items

6.3.4.1 Global Master Planning

Global master planning is the basis for creating orders in purchasing and production in daily business. Depending on the company size and the item structure, master planning involves extensive calculations which is why it usually runs as a batch job in the nighttime.

In order to start global master planning, access the menu item *Master planning> Run> Master planning*. In the *Master planning* dialog, select the applicable *Master plan* (for global master planning usually the current static master plan). It is not necessary to execute master planning separately with the dynamic master plan, if the slider *Automatic copy* in the master planning parameters is set to "Yes".

The lookup field *Planning method* in the master planning dialog determines the calculation principle showing following options:

> **Regeneration** – Complete calculation, deleting all not approved planned orders
> **Net change** – Generating action messages and calculated delays for all requirements, but planned orders only for new requirements
> **Net change minimized** – Like net change, limiting new messages to new requirements

If selecting the current static plan, "Regeneration" is the only available planning method. For dynamic plans you should also choose "Regeneration" if there are changes in coverage settings (like the minimum quantity for an item).

6.3.4.2 Local Master Planning

Unlike global master planning, local master planning aims to check the item availability and possible delivery dates limited to a particular item. You can execute local master planning in the net requirements form, which you can access by clicking the button *PLAN/Requirements/Net requirements* in the action pane of the released product form or by clicking the button *Product and supply/Net requirements* in the toolbar of order lines.

The net requirements form shows the result of the last master planning cycle for the dynamic master plan. If a one master plan strategy is in place, the lines in the net requirements are identical to those used in purchasing and production control.

Clicking the button *Update/Master planning* in the action pane of the net requirements form starts master planning. Local master planning updates the current dynamic master plan for the selected item and its components. When viewing the results, you have to take into account that not all dependencies of other items are covered by the calculation, in particular regarding resource capacity requirements.

6.3.4.3 Working with Action Messages and Calculated Delays

If calculated delays (showing availability problems) and action messages (for optimization requiring manual decisions) are activated in the applicable coverage groups, master planning generates corresponding messages. They show in the corresponding columns of the net requirements form.

In addition, the list page *Master planning> Master planning> Calculated delays* contains an overview of all calculated delays in the static or dynamic plan selected in the lookup field *Plan*. Clicking the button *CALCULATED DELAYS/Open/ Reference* in the action pane of the calculated delays form opens the related order, which you can adjust as applicable.

An overview of all action messages is available in the list page *Master planning> Master planning> Actions> Actions*. After selecting the appropriate plan in the lookup field *Plan* you can access related orders by clicking the order number shown as link in the column *Number*. The action pane of the actions form contains the button *Apply action* for immediately executing the action message of a particular line – e.g. deleting a purchase order. The button *Action graph* in the actions form provides access to a chart showing dependencies between action messages.

6.3.4.4 Planned Orders

Planned orders generated by master planning are shown in the list page *Master planning> Master planning> Planned orders* and in *Master planning* workspace (list *Urgent* and other lists). The lookup field *Plan* in the list page and the workspace provides the option to select the static, the dynamic, or any other master plan.

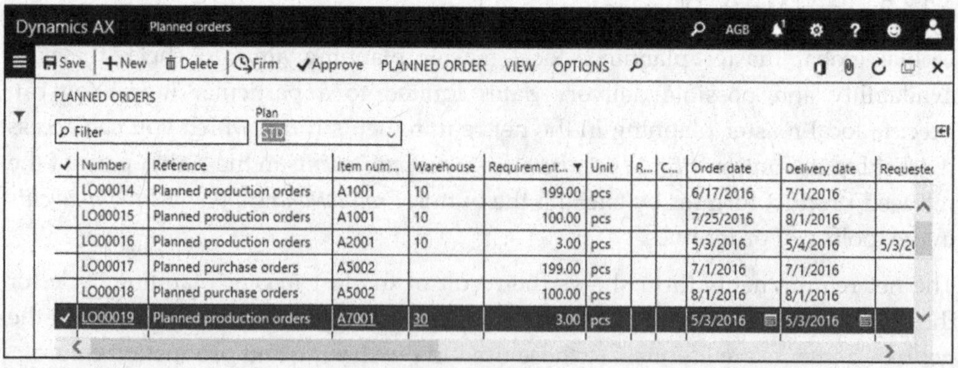
Dynamics AX
Planned orders
AGB
Save
New
Delete
Firm
Approve
PLANNED ORDER
VIEW
OPTIONS
PLANNED ORDERS
Plan
Filter
STD
Number
Reference
Item num...
Warehouse
Requirement...
Unit
R...
C...
Order date
Delivery date
Requestec
LO00014
Planned production orders
A1001
10
199.00
pcs
6/17/2016
7/1/2016
LO00015
Planned production orders
A1001
10
100.00
pcs
7/25/2016
8/1/2016
LO00016
Planned production orders
A2001
10
3.00
pcs
5/3/2016
5/4/2016
5/3/2
LO00017
Planned purchase orders
A5002
199.00
pcs
7/1/2016
7/1/2016
LO00018
Planned purchase orders
A5002
100.00
pcs
8/1/2016
8/1/2016
LO00019
Planned production orders
A7001
30
3.00
pcs
5/3/2016
5/3/2016

Figure 6-10: Working with planned orders

The planned order form in the master planning menu and the *Master planning* workspace show planned orders for purchasing, for production, and for inventory transfers (indicated by the column *Reference*). A filtered view of planned orders is available in the relevant modules – e.g. planned purchase orders in procurement and sourcing.

If the sliders *Add the calculated delay to the requirement date* on the tab *Calculated delays* in the selected master plan are set to "Yes", the *Delivery date* is adjusted to the earliest possible date and the required date shows in the column *Requested date*.

Apart from the delivery date and the requirement quantity, the planned orders page displays action messages and calculated delays in separate columns. The planned order detail form, which opens by clicking the order number shown as link in the column *Number*, shows details on action message and calculated delays on the tabs *Action* and *Delays*. The tab *Pegging* in the detail form shows the requirements covered by the particular planned order – e.g. sales orders, BOM lines of production orders, demand forecasts, or safety stock.

6.3.4.5 Firming an Order

You can edit the delivery date and the quantity on the tab *Planned supply* of the planned orders detail form. For planned purchase orders, make sure that a vendor number is entered in the lookup field *Vendor*.

If your company applies status management for planned orders, change the status to "Approved" (or to the status "Completed" if the planned order should not be firmed) by clicking the button *Approve* or *PLANNED ORDER/Process/Change status* in the action pane. Subsequent master planning does not change or delete approved planned orders.

After selecting one or more orders in the planned orders list page, click the button *Firm* in the action pane to generate corresponding purchase orders, production orders, or transfer orders. If you want to create a request for quotation (see section 3.8.3) instead of a purchase order, click the button *PLANNED ORDER/Maintain/Change to/Request for quotation*.

When firming a planned production order, the *Requested production status* on the tab *Other* of the applicable coverage group determines the initial status of the production order. When firming a planned purchase order, the purchase order always has the approval status "Approved" (independently from change management settings).

The firming history (*Master planning> Inquiries and reports> Master planning> Firming history*) displays a log of firming activities.

Apart from the planned order list page, the *Master planning* workspace also provides the option to edit and firm planned orders.

6.3.4.6 Net Requirements and Explosion

In order to get an overview of the net requirements related to a planned order, click the button *VIEW/Requirements/Requirement profile* in the action pane of the planned order form. The requirement profile shows the net requirements form, which you can also access from the released product form or from the order lines.

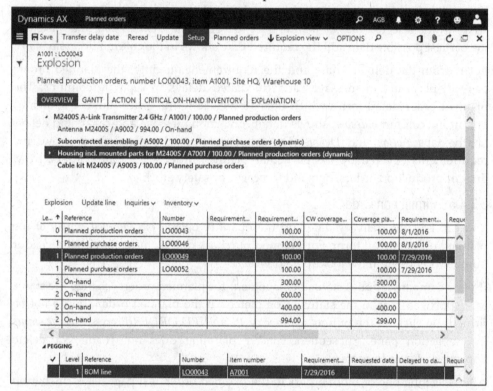

Figure 6-11: Analyzing the availability within the BOM structure in the explosion form

The button *VIEW/Requirements/Explosion* in the action pane of the planned order form provides access to another inquiry, the explosion form. This form, which you can also access from the released product or from the order lines in parallel to the net requirements, shows the item availability including components at all BOM levels. Clicking the button *Setup* in the action pane of the explosion form provides the option to change display settings.

The button *Explosion view* in the action pane determines the direction of explosion: If selecting "Down", the form shows semi-finished items and components of the selected item. If selecting "Up", the form shows a where-used analysis.

When updating the calculation by clicking the button *Update* in the explosion form, a dialog displays where you can set the slider *Enable trace* to "Yes". With this setting, Dynamics AX creates a log of the impacts and results of master planning, which you can view on the tab *Explanation* in the explosion form afterwards.

6.3.4.7   Supply schedule

The supply schedule form shows a comprehensive view of the future supply and demand – similar to the net requirements, but summarized per period and transaction type. As a prerequisite for using the supply schedule, you have to set up period types (*Organization administration> Setup> Calendars> Period templates*), which provide the option to flexibly set up the periods (configure periods on the tab *Periods* there).

When accessing the supply schedule from the master planning menu (*Master planning> Master planning> Supply schedule*), a dialog shows where you have to specify a filter on the *Plan* (for showing planned orders), *Period template, Item* or *Item allocation key*, and inventory dimensions (optional). Apart from this menu item, you can access the supply schedule from multiple pages by clicking a button in the action pane or toolbar (e.g. the button *PLAN/View/Supply schedule* in the released product or the button *Inquiries/Supply schedule* in the net requirements).

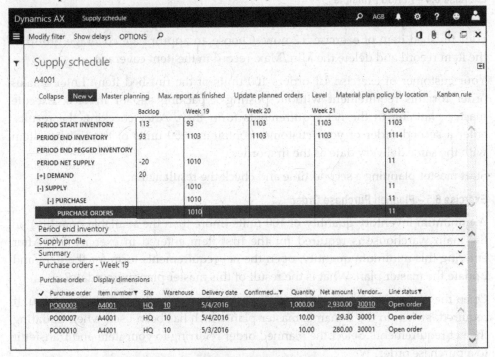

Figure 6-12:   Viewing supply details in the supply schedule

In the supply schedule form, you can view supply and demand details on a tab at the bottom after selecting a cell in a period column and clicking the button *Expand/ Collapse* in the toolbar. Clicking the button *Master planning* starts local master planning, and the button *New* provides the option to create planned or actual orders directly from the supply schedule.

6.3.4.8 New in Dynamics 'AX 7'

Apart from terminology changes ("calculated delays" replace "futures messages"), the *Master planning* workspace and the firming history are new in master planning.

6.3.5 Case Study Exercises

Exercise 6.3 – Min./Max. Principle

You want to apply a Min./Max. coverage principle to your finished item of exercise 5.2. Select an appropriate coverage group in the released product form and enter a minimum quantity of 500 units and a maximum quantity of 1000 units in the item coverage of the item.

Once you have finished, run master planning in the net requirements form and check the result. In a second step, change the minimum quantity to one unit. After executing master planning a second time, can you explain the result?

Exercise 6.4 – Period Principle

You want to apply a coverage principle summarizing requirements per period for your finished item of exercise 5.2 now. Choose an appropriate coverage group in the item record and delete the Min./Max. record in the item coverage.

Your customer of exercise 4.1 orders 100 units of the finished item. Enter a sales order for this requirement without posting a packing slip or invoice. Execute master planning in the net requirements form then. After checking the results, enter a second order of your customer containing 150 units of the finished item with the same delivery date as the first order.

Start master planning a second time and check the result again.

Exercise 6.5 – Planned Purchase Order

A minimum inventory quantity of 100 units (more than the available quantity) on the main warehouse is required for the first item entered in exercise 5.1. After entering this minimum quantity, open the net requirements form for the item and update the master plan. What is the result of this master planning update?

Open the planned purchase order form in the procurement and sourcing menu. If required, switch to the dynamic master plan which has been used when updating the net requirements. Select the planned order referring to your item and transfer it to a purchase order.

7 Inventory and Product Management

The primary responsibility of inventory management is to control the warehouse in terms of quantity and value. In order to perform this task in Dynamics AX, changes of the inventory quantity have to be registered and posted as transactions.

The current quantity in inventory always is the total of item issue and receipt transactions. Most of the transactions are not a result of business processes within inventory management, but created automatically from other areas. Dynamics AX for example posts a receipt transaction in inventory when posting a product receipt in procurement and sourcing.

7.1 Principles of Inventory Transactions

Before we start to go into details, the lines below show the principles of transactions in inventory management.

7.1.1 Basic Approach

The most important master data in inventory management are the product records of inventoried items. Inventory management then controls the inventory per product (item number). Depending on the dimension groups assigned to the particular product, the quantity and value of the item is controlled at the more detailed level of inventory dimensions. These dimensions include storage dimensions (e.g. warehouse or location), tracking dimensions (e.g. serial numbers), and product dimensions (e.g. configurations).

7.1.1.1 Types of Transactions

In order to change the on-hand quantity, you need to post an item transaction. Depending on the direction, the transaction belongs to one of the following types:

- ➤ **Item receipt** – Inbound transaction
- ➤ **Item issue** – Outbound transaction
- ➤ **Item transfer** – Between warehouses, locations, or tracking dimensions

Item receipts increase the on-hand quantity. They include product receipts in purchasing, customer returns in sales, product receipts in production (reported as finished), positive adjustments in counting, and manual journals in inventory.

Item issues on the other hand include vendor returns in purchasing, packing slips in sales, picking lists in production, negative adjustments in counting, and manual journals in inventory.

Inventory transfers include transfer orders and transfer journals. Transfer orders support the transfer of items from one warehouse to another, providing the option to post and print picking lists. Unlike transfer orders, transfer journals are not only available for transfers from one warehouse to another, but also for changing other dimension values (e.g. adjusting a serial number).

Although registering a transfer in a transfer journal only requires entering a single line, the posted transaction shows two lines. A transfer between warehouses for example creates one transaction line for the item issue from the shipping warehouse and one for the item receipt at the receiving warehouse.

7.1.1.2   Transactions from Other Areas

Most of the inventory transactions do not originate from inventory management, but derive from other areas in Dynamics AX. The transaction origin in the other module (e.g. a purchase order/product receipt) has to contain all data required for the inventory transaction – including warehouse, quantity, and cost price.

When viewing a posted inventory transaction, it shows the reference to the transaction origin including voucher number and date.

7.1.1.3   Inventory Quantity and Value

In order to grant an accurate inventory valuation, Dynamics AX distinguishes between the physical transaction (determining the on-hand quantity) and the financial transaction (determining the financial value).

For illustration purposes, Figure 7-1 shows the physical and the financial part of an inventory transaction related to a purchase order line.

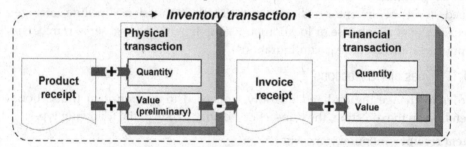

Figure 7-1:   Physical and financial transaction in inventory for a purchase order line

The physical transaction in Dynamics AX causes a change of the on-hand quantity in inventory. An example for posting a physical transaction is the product receipt in purchasing.

In terms of inventory quantity, the transaction is already completed when posting the product receipt. But inventory valuation only receives a preliminary cost price. The value of the product receipt shows in the field *Physical cost amount* separately from the field *Cost amount*, which contains the financial inventory value.

The second step in processing an inventory transaction is the financial transaction, which contains the cost amount referring to the invoiced quantity. An example for posting a financial transaction is the purchase order invoice.

Posting the vendor invoice reverses the related preliminary posting of the product receipt (physical amount) and posts the cost amount of the invoice. Quantity and amount of the invoice are subsequently included in the financial inventory value.

7.1.1.4 Posting Inventory Transactions

The differentiation between the physical and the financial transaction applies to every inventory transaction, no matter in which module it is generated. But the way of posting a transaction is depending on the origin.

For receipt transactions in purchase orders, posting the product receipt generates the physical transaction, and posting the vendor invoice the financial transaction. In production, reporting the produced item as finished posts the physical transaction. The financial transaction is posted by ending the production order.

For issue transactions in sales orders, the packing slip posts the physical and the invoice the financial transaction (similar to purchasing). In production, posting the picking list posts the physical transaction for BOM components. The financial transaction for BOM components is posted – in parallel to the financial transaction for receiving the finished item – by ending the production order.

Unlike the other transactions, journals in inventory management do not post the physical and the financial transaction in two separate steps, but in parallel.

7.1.1.5 Inventory Closing

The final financial value for receipt transactions is specified when posting the related invoice (apart from later manual adjustments). But for issue transactions, the financial inventory value often is not known and therefore not final when posting the invoice. You can, for example, receive the purchase invoice with the final cost price of an item after posting the sales invoice for the item. If the purchase invoice shows a price which is different from the preliminary amount posted with the product receipt, the final profitability shown in the sales transaction will change (except when using a standard cost price valuation).

Except for items referring to a standard cost price or a moving average valuation, you need to re-evaluate issue transactions through inventory closing. The main purpose of inventory closing, usually a month-end procedure, is to recalculate the financial value of issue transactions based on the final value of receipt transactions.

7.1.1.6 Ledger Integration

Inventory journals post to ledger accounts depending on applicable settings (see section 9.4) in the same way as inventory transactions generated in other modules.

7.1.2   At a Glance: Inventory Journal Transactions

Inventory journals are used to manually change the on-hand quantity of items, independently from orders in purchasing, sales, or production. The example below shows a manual item receipt in an inventory adjustment journal. In regular business, such transactions are an exception, since problems or missing end-to-end business processes in most cases are the reason for receiving an item not related to a purchase order, production order, or customer return order.

When accessing the menu item for inventory adjustment (*Inventory management> Journal entries> Items> Inventory adjustment*), the list page shows all open adjustment journals which are not posted yet. Applying an appropriate filter on the column *Posted* (you can use the filter pane, the grid column filter, and the advanced filter) provides the option to view also posted journals. The column *Lines* shows the number of lines in the journal. If somebody is currently working in a particular journal, the journal shows a user icon in the column *In use*. If you want to access the details of a journal, click the journal ID shown as link in the grid.

In order to register a new transaction, insert a record in the journal header list page by clicking the button *New* in the action pane or by pressing the shortcut *Alt+N*. In the *Create* dialog, select a journal name in the field *Name* and optionally enter a *Site* and *Warehouse* as default for the lines. If you want to support later analysis, enter a short text explaining the transaction in the field *Description*. The journal number in the field *Journal* derives from the applicable number sequence.

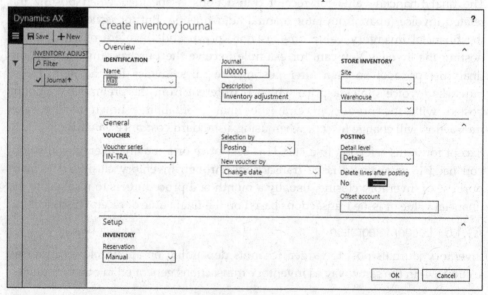

Figure 7-2:   Creating a new journal in the inventory adjustment journal form

After clicking the button *OK* in the dialog, Dynamics AX creates the journal header and switches to the journal detail form. Clicking the button *Header* below the action pane in the detail form switches to the header view, where you can view the complete journal header.

In the lines view, insert a line on the tab *Journal lines* and select the item number before entering site, warehouse, and other inventory dimensions as specified in the applicable dimension groups. In order to control the dimension columns displayed in the lines, click the button *Inventory/Display dimensions* in the toolbar of the *Journal lines* tab after saving a line. The *Line details* tab provides the option to enter further details.

If entering a positive quantity, the transaction is an item receipt. A negative quantity creates an item issue. Default values for warehouse, quantity, and cost price derive from the released product. The default for the quantity is 1.00, if the released product (default order settings or site-specific order settings) does not contain a default inventory quantity.

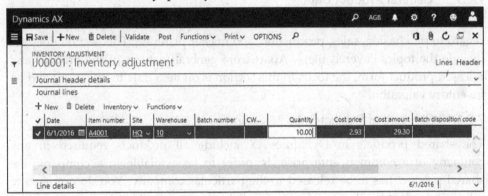

Figure 7-3: Registering a journal line

Unlike transactions in purchasing, inventory journal transactions are not split into a physical product receipt and a corresponding financial transaction from an invoice. Inventory journals post the physical and the financial transaction at the same time, which is why you should make sure that journal lines with a positive quantity (item receipts) contain a correct cost price when posting the journal.

In order to post the journal after entering the last journal line, click the button *Post* in the action pane of the journal list page or detail form.

Before posting, you can optionally click the button *Validate* for checking potential problems. But validation does not check all possible problems, which is why you might sometimes receive an error message when posting a journal, even if the validation does not show a problem.

7.2   Product Information Management

Since all business processes related to inventory require inventoried products, product data are the core element of master data in supply chain management.

The data structure of products in Dynamics AX includes two levels – the shared products with basic item data common to all companies, and the released products with company-specific item data.

The product table contains all physical items – raw materials, components, semi-finished products, and finished products. In addition, product records also include non-inventoried items like service or phantom items. These items do not exist physically, but you can use them in order management or in bills of materials.

In some areas of the application, the label "Item" refers to released products.

7.2.1   General Product Data

Product data have already been discussed in section 3.3, 4.3, 5.2.1 and 6.3.3 with regard to purchasing, sales, production, and master planning. This section does not include the topics covered there. Apart from general features of the product and released product form, the focus in this section is on item data in inventory and on inventory valuation.

7.2.1.1   Structure of Product Data

The shared products in Dynamics AX include all products required in any company of a common enterprise. In order to be available in a company, the shared product has to be released to the particular company. You do not need to release a product to all companies in parallel, it is also possible to release a product to some companies earlier and to other companies later.

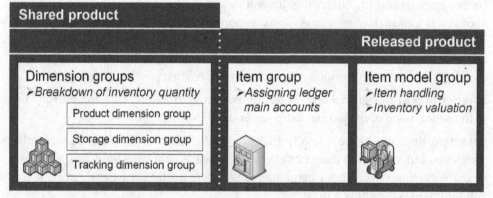

Figure 7-4:   Main control groups of a product

Data in the shared products are common to all companies to which a product has been released. These data include the product number, the product type and subtype (non-inventoried, inventoried, or configurable item), and the dimension groups. If applicable, you can leave the dimension groups in the shared product empty and enter them at company level in the released products.

Most product details are specified at company level in the released product form. Required fields there include the dimension groups (if not specified in the shared product), the item group, the item model group, and the unit of measure.

7.2.1.2 Creating a Shared Product

Depending on the requirements, there are two ways for creating a new product (compare section 3.3.2):

> **Start with the shared product** – Create a shared product and release it
> **Start with the released product** – Create a product in the released product form, automatically generating a shared product in the background

In order to view the list of all existing shared products, open the form *Product information management> Products> All products and product masters*. The list pages *Products* (for items without configurations or variants) and *Product masters* (for configurable items) show a filtered view of all shared products.

If you want to create an item in the shared product form, click the button *New* in the action pane. You can subsequently release the product to one or more companies by clicking the button *Release products* in the action pane and selecting applicable companies in the *Release products* wizard.

The menu item *Product information management> Products> Released products* provides access to the released products. Alternatively, you can access a released product directly from the shared product by clicking the link in the *Item number* field on the right-hand side of the FactBox *Released to companies* and then clicking the link in the field *Item number* of the product information dialog.

The *Released product maintenance* workspace is another place, from which you can to access released products. In the tabbed list pane there, the list *Recently released* shows the items released within the last days (specify the date range by clicking the button *Configure my workspace*) and the validation result (missing field values).

Instead of creating a new product in the shared product form, you can also create a product in the released product form by clicking the button *New* in the action pane. The *New released product* dialog then includes data for the shared and for the corresponding released product (containing all mandatory fields of the released product). If there are templates for released products, the additional field *Apply template* for selecting an appropriate template shows in the dialog.

You can also apply templates (see section 2.3.2) for released products at a later time. In order to apply a template later, click the button *PRODUCT/Maintain/Apply template* in the action pane of the released product. The template then overrides data in the released product with data from the template. If you want to create a template in the released product form, click the button *PRODUCT/New/Template*.

7.2.1.3   Product Number and Name

The *Product number*, which identifies the shared product, has to be unique across companies. It is assigned automatically to new products, if the number sequence for products numbers (*Product information management> Setup> Product information management parameters*, tab *Number sequences*) does not specify a manual assignment.

The *Item number* identifying items at released product level is identical to the shared product number, if there is no other setting in the number sequence for item numbers (*Inventory management> Setup> Inventory and warehouse management parameters*, tab *Number sequences*) of the particular company.

When creating a shared product, the default for the *Search name* derives from the *Product name*. You can update the search name in the shared product and enter a longer product description in the field *Description*. If there are different product names and descriptions in foreign languages, enter them after clicking the button *PRODUCT/Languages/Translations* in the action pane of the shared product form.

Product name and description are only editable at shared product level. The *Search name* in the shared product is a default for the released products, which you can override at released product level.

7.2.1.4   Product Type and Subtype

The *Product type* controls, if a product is an inventoried item. Whereas the product type "Item" characterizes a regular item, the product type "Service" specifies an item without inventory control in any company.

The *Product subtype* controls item configuration. Whereas the product subtype "Product" applies to a regular standard item, the product subtype "Product master" characterizes a base item for assigned product variants.

7.2.1.5   Product Master

If a product refers to the product subtype "Product master", the product number alone does not uniquely identify the item in inventory. In transactions with this item, you have to enter the product variant which distinguishes the different sizes, colors, styles, or configurations of the product.

When creating a product master (selecting the product subtype "Product master"), the *Product dimension group* – one of the three dimension groups described in section 7.2.2 below – shows in the *Create product* dialog. The product dimension group is selected at shared product level, determining which of the dimensions *Configuration, Size, Color* and/or *Style* apply.

The *Configuration technology*, which is the second mandatory field when creating a product master, determines the way of creating product variants.

If selecting the configuration technology "Predefined variant", you can enter dimension values for product variants after clicking the button *Product dimensions* in the action pane of the shared product. The left pane of the *Product dimensions* form then shows the dimensions, which are applicable to the product according to the selected product dimension group.

After entering product dimension values for applicable dimensions in the product dimensions form, you have to specify available variants (dimension value combinations) after clicking the button *Product variants* in the shared product. The button *Variant suggestions* in the product variants form facilitates creating new variants. In general, you want to create variants manually if the particular product is – for example – not available in all colors for each size. If a product only includes one active product dimension or if all dimension combinations are available, set the slider *Generate variants automatically* in the shared product detail form to "Yes" before starting to enter product dimension values.

Before you can select a product variant in a transaction, you have to release it by clicking the button *Release products* in the action pane of the shared product. In the *Release product* wizard, you can choose the variants which should be released. Apart from releasing product variants in parallel to releasing the product master, you can also release variants separately at a later time. An alternative way for releasing variants is to create released product variants (based on shared product variants) manually in the released product variants form (access from the released product by clicking the button *PRODUCT/Product master/Released product variants*).

If there are common variants for multiple products, you can use variant groups to populate the product dimensions. After creating a new variant group for sizes (*Product information management> Setup> Dimensions and variant groups> Size groups*), colors, or styles with the related dimension values, you can select the color group, size group, or style group as applicable in the shared product detail form. The dimension values of the variant group then are a default in the product dimensions of the shared product.

7.2.1.6 Core Settings in Released Products

Whereas the shared product form only contains a limited number of fields, the released product form includes a wide range of detail data for characterizing the particular item.

Only a few fields in the released product are mandatory, including the unit of measure, the item group, the item model group (see section 7.2.3), and – either at shared product level or at released product level – the dimension groups (see section 7.2.2). The button *PRODUCT/Maintain/Validate* in the action pane of the released product provides the option to check if a released product contains all mandatory data.

Other data in the released product like the item sales tax groups and the cost price (see section 7.3.3) are not mandatory, but depending on the specific requirements nevertheless of high importance.

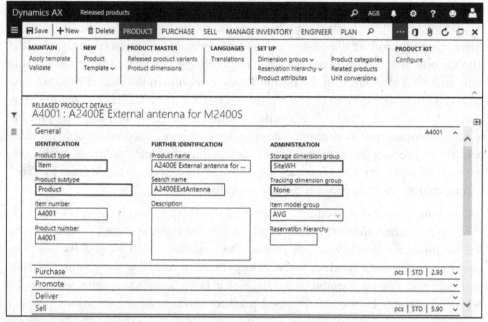

Figure 7-5: Managing an item in the released product form

7.2.1.7 Units of Measure

When releasing a new product, Dynamics AX applies the default unit of measure as specified in the inventory management parameters (field *Unit* on the tab *General* of the parameters). As long as there is no transaction for the item, it is possible to change the inventory unit of a released product.

If an item requires different units of measure in purchasing, sales, and inventory, enter the appropriate units on the tabs *Purchase*, *Sell* and *Manage inventory* of the released product form. The unit in the released product is the default in transactions entered for the item, e.g. in a sales order line. In the transaction, you can override the unit if necessary. When choosing a different unit, there needs to be a unit conversion between the selected unit and the inventory unit.

Units of measure are shared across companies. If you require a new unit of measure, you have to set it up in the *Units* form (*Organization administration> Setup> Units> Units*) before assigning it to a released product. The *Unit class* (e.g. "Quantity" or "Mass") determines the area to which a unit of measure applies. In one unit per unit class, you can select the checkbox *System unit* which applies this unit to quantity fields without a related unit of measure. The net weight field in the released products is an example for such a quantity field, whereas order lines for example contain a field for the quantity and a field for the unit.

Clicking the button *Unit conversions* in the *Units* form provides access to the unit conversions. Conversion factors between units entered on the tab *Standard conversion* apply to all products. The tab *Intra-class conversions* provides the option to enter conversions per item number within a *Unit class*, the tab *Inter-class conversions* across unit classes (e.g. between the length and the quantity in pieces).

7.2.1.8 Item Group

The main purpose of item groups is to collect products, which post to a common main account in the general ledger. For this reason, you need to set up at least as many item groups as there are different stock and revenue accounts for inventory items in finance. You can find more details on the inventory posting setup in section 9.4.2.

When releasing a product, you have to keep in mind that you should not change the item group on tab *Manage costs* of the released product after registering the first transaction. Dynamics AX displays a warning on possible issues with inventory reconciliation in finance if you do not carefully check the consequences of changing the group. But the warning does not prevent changing the item group, if necessary.

Item groups do not only control ledger integration, they also are a filtering and sorting criteria in many reports.

7.2.1.9 Non Inventoried Items and Services

Apart from regular products, which you want to track in inventory, there are items – e.g. services or office supplies – which are not included in inventory.

Dynamics AX provides two separate options to specify whether inventory control applies to a product:

> **Product type** – Option "Item" or "Service"
> **Item model group** – Checkbox *Stocked product*

Depending on the combination of both settings, inventory control works different (see Table 7-1).

Table 7-1:   Options for the inventory control of products

Product type Item model group	Item	Service
Stocked product	Inventory transactions, inventory quantity	Inventory transactions, no quantity
Non-stocked product	No transactions	No transactions

The product type "Service" is used for products, which do not apply inventory control in any company. But if assigned to an item model group for stocked products, products of this type generate inventory transactions. This setting is required for intangible items and services which are part of a BOM.

When setting up items of the product type "Service", you have to assign a specific item group and item model group for granting correct inventory valuation and ledger postings.

Linking a released product to an item model group, which shows a cleared checkbox *Stocked product*, does not only avoid an inventory quantity but also prevents inventory transactions. Since the item model group is assigned to the released product, this setting makes it possible to deactivate inventory control for an item at company level.

7.2.1.10 Number Groups

When entering a batch or serial number in a transaction, the batches or serial numbers table (*Inventory management> Inquiries and reports> Tracking dimensions*) has to include this number.

If you are in control of specifying the batch or serial numbers – for example if you produce the item – you can set up Dynamics AX to generate batch or serial numbers automatically through tracking number groups (*Inventory management> Setup> Dimensions> Tracking number groups*). On the tab *General* of the tracking number groups, specify the structure of the related numbers and select a *Number sequence code* if included in the structure (*Number sequence No.* set to "Yes"). Settings on the tab *Activation* determine which transactions actually generate numbers.

In the released product form, the *Tracking dimension group* (see section 7.2.2 below) controls, if batch or serial numbers apply to an item. If this is the case, you can select a batch or serial number group on the tab *Manage inventory* of the released product to generate batch or serial numbers for the item automatically.

7.2.1.11 Catch Weight Products

A catch weight product (*CW product*) is an item with weight as primary unit of measure, and a secondary unit (catch weight unit) for a countable number (e.g. pieces) in parallel. The weight per unit varies, and as a result there is no fixed unit conversion between the weight unit and the catch weight unit. In the order lines of purchase orders, sales orders, or batch production orders, only the catch weight quantity (the number of pieces) is editable. When registering inventory transactions, both weight and catch weight quantity have to be entered in parallel.

The catch weight functionality originates from process industries. Examples of catch weight products are animals (or parts of animals) in food industry requiring to show the counted number and the weight in parallel. Usually, catch weight only applies to items with batch and/or serial number control.

In Dynamics AX, the catch weight functionality is generally available in inventory, purchasing and sales, where all applicable forms contain additional fields for the catch weight. Usage in production is limited to batch production orders, since only formulas – not regular bills of materials – can include catch weight items. Because of its complexity, you should only use catch weight if you actually need to track weight and catch weight quantity independently from each other.

In order to set up a catch weight item, set the slider *Catch weight (CW product)* to "Yes" when creating the shared product. Then click the button *PRODUCT/Set up/ Unit conversions* in the shared product and enter an *Inter-class conversion* between the inventory unit (weight) and the catch weight unit (pieces). The catch weight unit has to be a unit without decimals (*Decimal precision* zero in the unit).

When releasing the product, the inventory unit of the item has to be a weight unit (the default unit in the inventory parameters usually is a weight unit in applicable companies). On the tab *Manage inventory* in the released product form, select the catch weight unit in the field *CW unit* and enter the *Minimum quantity* and the *Maximum quantity* in the fields below, determining the range for the allowed conversion factor (weight per unit). Like for other products, enter further required data including item model group, item group, and dimension groups as applicable.

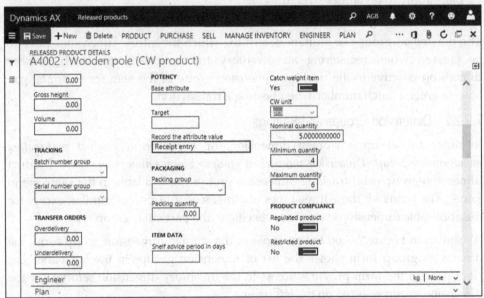

Figure 7-6: Entering catch weight settings in the released product

When registering a purchase order line, enter the catch weight quantity (number of pieces) in the column *CW quantity*. The column *Quantity*, which is not editable for a catch weight item, shows the quantity according to the regular unit conversion. When receiving the item in the inventory registration form or in an item arrival journal (see section 3.5.3), you have to enter the CW quantity and the inventory quantity (default from the unit conversion) independently in parallel.

CW quantity and the quantity in inventory unit have to be entered independently in all inventory transactions, including sales order picking and inventory journals. Inquiries of the current inventory show both, weight and catch weight quantity.

7.2.1.12 New in Dynamics 'AX 7'

New items which in product management refer to the browser-based interface including changes like a separate tab for variant settings in the released product.

7.2.2   Inventory Dimension Group

Inventory dimensions control the breakdown of inventory quantity within released products. Through the use of dimensions, you can split the inventory quantity and the transactions to a more detailed level than the item number.

7.2.2.1   Available Dimensions

Inventory dimensions in Dynamics AX are divided into following groups:

➤ **Product dimensions** – Configuration, size, color and style provide the option to subdivide an item based on product characteristics (only for product masters)
➤ **Storage dimensions** – Site, warehouse, location, inventory status, and license plate apply to inventory structures
➤ **Tracking dimensions** – Batch and serial number control tracking options

The dimension groups of an item determine which inventory dimensions have to be entered when registering an inventory transaction. If the batch number dimension is active in the tracking dimension group of the item for example, you have to enter a batch number when posting a transaction.

7.2.2.2   Dimension Groups and Settings

In order to set up a storage dimension, open the form *Product information management> Setup> Dimension and variant groups> Storage dimension groups*. Product dimension groups and tracking dimension groups are available in the same menu folder. The forms for these three types of dimension groups look similar, except for the applicable dimensions which are specific to the particular group type.

As shown in Figure 7-7 on the example of the storage dimension group form, the dimension group form shows the list of dimension groups in the left pane. The right pane of the form provides access to the inventory dimension settings for the dimension group selected on the left pane.

If you need an additional dimension group, insert a new record by clicking the button *New* in the action pane and specify the inventory dimension settings of the new dimension group by selecting the checkboxes as explained in Table 7-2.

In storage dimension groups, the dimension *Site* (see section 10.1.5) is always active, which is why a site has to be entered in every inventory transaction. For the dimension *Warehouse*, setting the additional parameter *Mandatory* to "Yes" requires registering a warehouse already when entering an order line or other transaction (if not selected, the warehouse may remain empty until posting).

Table 7-2: Available settings for inventory dimensions in a dimension group

Parameter	Explanation
Active	Dimension available for transactions of the item
Active in sales process	Simplified sales serial numbers (tracking dimension group)
Primary stocking	Mandatory dimension for reservation; Displays as default dimension in the on-hand inquiry
Blank receipt allowed	Dimension value not required for receipt transactions
Blank issue allowed	Dimension value not required for issue transactions
Physical inventory	Item availability per dimension value (depending on the item model group, no negative inventory e.g. per batch number)
Financial inventory	Inventory value per dimension value (necessary for calculating value and cost price e.g. per batch number)
Coverage plan by dimension	Separate item coverage in master planning per dimension value (see section 6.3.3)
For purchase prices	Dimension available for purchase price agreements (see section 3.3.3)
For sales prices	Dimension available for sales price agreements

In product dimension groups, only the parameters *Active, For purchase prices* and *For sales prices* are available.

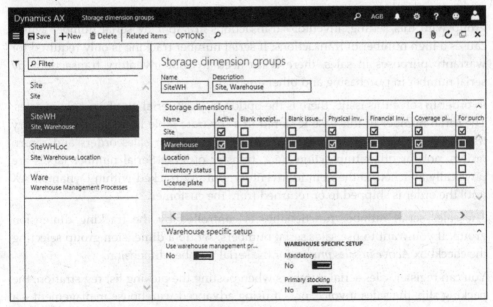

Figure 7-7: Managing storage dimension groups

When creating a product, you have to select dimension groups with active dimensions according to your requirements. You can for example only view the on-hand quantity per location, if the dimension *Location* is active for the particular item. If you need a particular dimension for some, but not all transactions of an item, the best way is to use a pseudo-value for transactions where the dimension is not suitable. If locations for example are only used in some warehouses, use pseudo-locations as default in all warehouses without locations.

7.2.2.3 Dimension Groups in the Released Product

In order to assign applicable inventory dimensions to a released product, click the button *PRODUCT/Set up/Dimension groups* in the action pane of the released product. If a dimension group is already specified on the corresponding shared product, it is not editable in the released product.

In order to avoid invalid dimension values in posted transactions, it is not possible to change inventory-related settings of a dimension group once a transaction refers to the dimension group. For the same reason, it is not possible to change the dimension group of an item, if there is an open transaction or an on-hand quantity in inventory.

If you need to change dimension settings for an item, post transactions completely issuing the stock physically and financially. After inventory closing, assign the new group and then post counting transactions to match the actual on-hand quantity.

7.2.2.4 Simplified Serial Numbers in Sales Processes

If you need to track serial numbers along the whole supply chain, the tracking dimension *Serial number* has to be active. For items linked to a tracking dimension group with this setting, inventory transactions are split by serial number which causes a high number of transactions. If serial number tracking is only required for warranty purposes in sales, there is no need to split inventory transactions by serial number in purchasing and other areas.

In order to solve this issue, there is the option to track serial numbers only in sales. The serial number in this case is stored in a separate table linked to the inventory transactions. Sales serial numbers are only available for sales orders and return orders, not for other transactions (e.g. transfer orders). Serial number labels are physically attached to the item in inventory, but not tracked within Dynamics AX until the order is shipped to or returned from the customer.

The sales serial number functionality is controlled by the tracking dimension group. If you want to use sales serial numbers, set up a dimension group selecting the checkbox *Active in sales process* for the serial number dimension.

You can register sales serial numbers when posting the picking list registration, the packing slip, the sales invoice, or – if using advanced warehouse management – a sales transaction on the mobile device.

After entering a sales order including one or more lines with items linked to sales serial number control, open – in the example of a packing slip – the packing slip posting dialog by clicking the button *PICK AND PACK/Generate/Packing slip* in the action pane of the sales order. On the tab *Lines* of the posting dialog, click the button *Update line/ Register serial numbers* to access to the sales serial number registration form.

In the serial number registration form, which supports using a scanner, enter or scan the serial numbers one after another. If a serial number label is missing or not readable on the physical item, click the button *Not readable* for the particular item. After closing the serial number registration, you can post the packing slip.

For return orders, registration of sales serial numbers is also required in the packing slip posting dialog or on the mobile device. If you do not post a packing slip, but ship the item with the sales invoice (or receive it with the credit note), you can access the serial number registration from the invoice posting dialog.

If you want to know which serial numbers have been shipped, open the serial number inquiry in the related journal inquiry. In case of a packing slip, click the button *Inquiries/Serial numbers* in the toolbar on the *Lines* tab of the packing slip journal. Tracking of sales serial numbers is also possible in the item tracing form (*Inventory management> Inquiries and reports> Tracking dimensions> Item tracing*).

7.2.2.5 Dimension Display Settings

The default for displaying dimension columns in detail forms is specified on the tab *Inventory dimensions* in the parameter form of all relevant modules. The inventory dimensions in the sales order lines for example are controlled in the accounts receivable parameters (*Accounts receivable> Setup> Accounts receivable parameters*, tab *Inventory dimensions*).

Forms which show inventory dimension columns provide the option to change the display settings by clicking the appropriate button in the toolbar – e.g. *Sales order line/Display/Dimensions* in the toolbar of the sales order lines or *Inventory/Display dimensions* in inventory journal lines.

When selecting inventory dimensions to display in a report or in an inquiry of inventory quantity and inventory value, you have to take into account that only these queries show a reliable result, which comply with the dimension setup. It is for example not useful to show the inventory value and cost price per warehouse, if the checkbox *Financial inventory* is not selected in the applicable storage dimension group. The reason is, that inventory valuation according to this setting does not link item issue transactions with item receipt transactions on warehouse level, causing a result which is different from your expectation.

7.2.2.6 New in Dynamics 'AX 7'

Since the old "Warehouse Management II" module is not supported in the new release, the dimension pallet which refers to this functionality has been removed. And as a result of the cloud-based architecture, renaming of product dimensions is not available in the user interface.

7.2.3   Item Model Group

Item model groups contain settings on the valuation method and on item handling. The number of required item model groups are depending on the requirements for processing items. In a usual Dynamics AX implementation, there are at least two groups – one for inventoried items and one for service items. The item model group for service items should allow negative physical and negative financial quantity and deactivate ledger integration.

If you change the *Inventory model* or *Ledger integration* settings of an item model group after posting related item transactions, reconciliation of inventory and finance might become difficult. Before changing any of these settings, you should carefully consider the consequences.

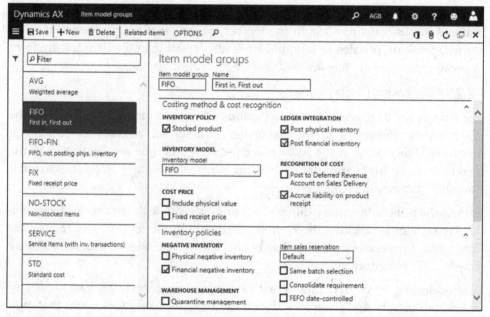

Figure 7-8:   Available settings in the item model group

In order to edit an item model group, open the form *Inventory management> Setup> Inventory> Item model groups*. The left pane of the item model group form displays a list of available groups. The right pane of the form then provides access to the settings of the group selected on the left pane.

7.2.3.1 Settings on Item Handling

In item model groups for inventoried items, the checkbox *Stocked product* needs to be selected. If this checkbox is cleared, products assigned to the group do not generate inventory transactions. This is the right choice for non-inventoried products like service items (except subcontracted production services).

The checkbox *Quarantine management* controls the automatic generation of a quarantine order (see section 7.4.6) when posting an item receipt.

The checkbox *Registration requirements* controls, if you have to post an inventory registration (registration form, item arrival journal, mobile device transaction), before you can post the product receipt in purchasing (see section 3.5.3). The checkbox *Picking requirements* in a similar way controls posting the pick transaction before posting the packing slip in sales.

The checkboxes *Receiving requirements* and *Deduction requirements* control, if you have to post a packing slip in sales or a product receipt in purchasing before posting the invoice.

7.2.3.2 Negative Inventory

In most cases you do not allow a negative physical inventory for inventoried items, but you do accept a negative financial inventory. A negative financial inventory results from posting a sales invoice before posting the purchase invoice (supposing no other stock is available for the item).

Settings on negative inventory in the item model group are depending on dimension group settings: Dynamics AX controls negative physical (or financial) inventory only at the level of the inventory dimensions, for which the checkbox *Physical inventory* (or *Financial inventory*) is selected.

7.2.3.3 Inventory Model

Selecting an inventory model (FIFO, LIFO, weighted average, moving average, or standard cost) on the tab *Inventory model* determines the inventory valuation method. The valuation method is the way Dynamics AX assigns issue transactions to receipt transactions in terms of valuation.

Details on inventory valuation methods are available in section 7.3 of this book, details on ledger integration in section 9.4.2.

7.2.4   Transactions and Inventory Quantity

The transactions and the inventory quantity of an item are directly accessible from the released product form. Both inquiries, the transaction inquiry and the on-hand inquiry, are also available (in a filtered view on the current record) by clicking the button *Inventory* in the toolbar of order and journal lines (e.g. the sales order lines).

The list page *Inventory management> Inquiries and reports> On-hand inventory* shows an overview of the on-hand quantity for multiple items selected in a filter dialog.

7.2.4.1 Inventory Transactions Inquiry

If you want to access the inventory transactions from the released product form, click the button *MANAGE INVENTORY/View/Transactions* in the action pane of the released product. The inventory transaction inquiry then shows all transactions of the selected item. The columns *Reference* and *Number* display the original voucher.

In order to view the details of a transaction, click the button *Transaction details* in the action pane.

In addition to posted transactions, the transactions form also shows future transactions not posted yet. These transactions include quotation and order lines in sales, purchasing, and production, for which no packing slip/product receipt or invoice has been posted. You can recognize such lines by the empty physical and financial date and the receipt status "Ordered" or the issue status "On order" ("Reserved physical" in case there is a reservation).

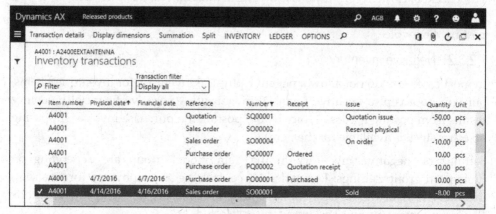

Figure 7-9:   Inventory transactions of an item in the transactions form

The cost transactions of an item show a cost-oriented view of inventory transaction data. You can access the cost transactions by clicking the button *MANAGE COSTS/ Cost transactions/Transactions* in the released product.

7.2.4.2 Physical and Financial Transaction

When posting a product receipt in purchasing, a packing slip in sales, a picking list in production, or a report as finished journal, Dynamics AX inserts the posting date into the *Physical date* of the inventory transaction. In parallel, the status of the transaction changes to "Received" or "Deducted". In the transaction detail form, the field *Physical cost amount* on the tab *Updates* shows the preliminary inventory value of the transaction.

The *Financial date* in an inventory transaction is updated when posting the invoice in purchasing or sales, or when ending the production order. The status of the transaction then changes to "Purchased" or "Sold", and the inventory value of the transaction displays in the column *Cost amount*.

Dynamics AX does not change the posted financial cost amount any more. If you post an adjustment of the inventory value in the course of inventory closing or through a manual adjustment, the posted difference shows separately in the field *Adjustment* on the tab *Updates* of the transaction detail form.

7.2.4.3 Inventory Picking and Registration

Inventory picking in sales (see section 4.5.2) and registration in purchasing (see section 3.5.3) are special steps when processing an inventory transaction. Posting a picking or registration transaction updates the on-hand quantity of the item and the status of the inventory transaction. But unlike product receipt and packing slip transactions, picking and registration do not generate an unchanging voucher.

After posting the packing slip in sales (or the product receipt in purchasing), the date of picking (or registration) shows in the field *Inventory date* on the tab *General* in the transaction detail form. If you do not proceed the regular way – posting a packing slip after picking, or posting a product receipt after registration – but cancel the registration, it is not possible to view the original picking or registration transaction in the inventory transactions any more.

7.2.4.4 Transaction Details and Ledger Integration

In addition to the data in the inventory transaction list page, the tab *Update* of the transaction detail form contains core information on the inventory transaction. The fields on this tab are split into the field groups *Physical*, *Financial*, and *Settlement*.

The field group *Physical* contains the date, number and preliminary value of the product receipt or packing slip. Invoice data show in the field group *Financial*.

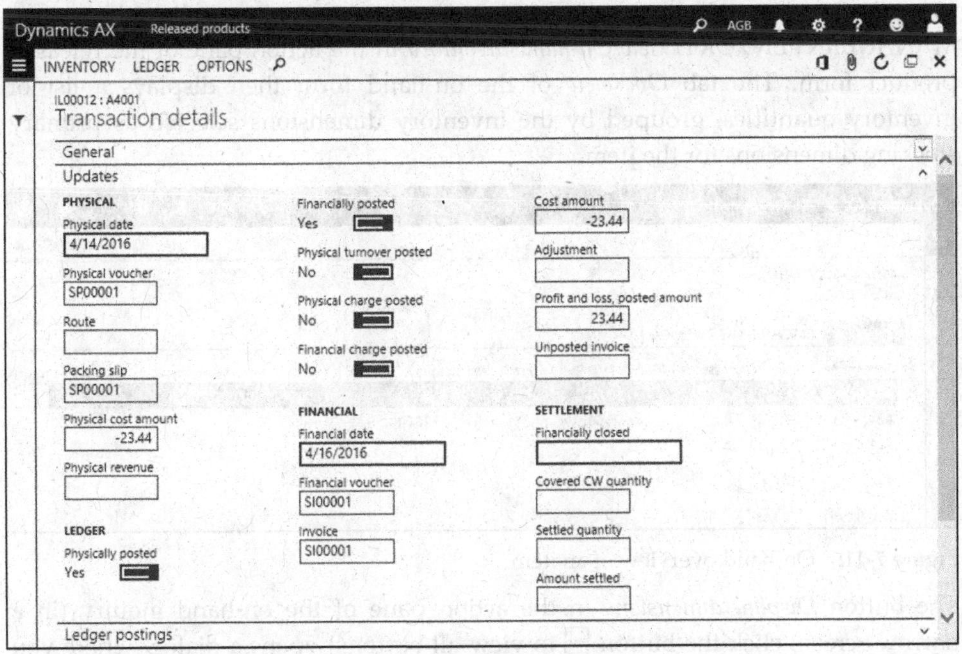

Figure 7-10: Physical and financial data in an inventory transaction

If the value of a transaction changes after posting the invoice (through inventory closing according to the valuation method, or through manual adjustments), the value difference shows in the field *Adjustment*. The original financial *Cost amount* does not change any more, all later adjustments add in the field *Adjustment*.

The field group *Settlement* shows if an inventory transaction is already settled by inventory closing. If the quantity of a transaction completely settles offsetting item issues or receipts, inventory closing records the closing date in the field *Financially closed* and closes the transaction (the field *Value open* on the tab *General* then shows "No"). Registering a manual adjustment of a closed transaction reopens it again.

The slider *Physically posted* on the tab *Updates* of the transaction details shows if the product receipt or packing slip has been posted to the general ledger. As a prerequisite, ledger integration for physical transactions has to be activated in the item model group of the particular item.

If ledger integration for financial transactions is activated, the option "Yes" in the slider *Financially posted* indicates that the invoice related to the inventory transaction has been posted. For purchase invoices, the slider is set to "Yes" after invoice posting even if ledger integration is not active for an item. The reason is that a purchase invoice for items always posts a ledger transaction: To a stock account for the receipt transaction if ledger integration is active, or to an expense account for immediate financial consumption otherwise.

7.2.4.5 On-Hand Inventory Inquiry

In order to view the current inventory quantity of an item, click the button *MANAGE INVENTORY/View/On-hand inventory* in the action pane of the released product form. The tab *Overview* of the on-hand form then displays a list of inventory quantities, grouped by the inventory dimensions selected as primary stocking dimensions for the item.

Figure 7-11:   On-hand overview of an item

The button *Display dimensions* in the action pane of the on-hand inquiry (in a narrow screen, click the button ⋯ to view all buttons) opens a dialog, where you can select which dimension columns to display in the inquiry. If choosing to show an additional column with the batch number for example, the on-hand inquiry lines display the quantity per batch number. In order to view the total quantity of an item, clear all dimension checkboxes in the display dialog.

7.2.4.6 On-Hand Inventory Details

In order to view the details of a line in the on-hand inquiry, switch to the tab *On-hand*. Apart from the *Physical inventory*, which is the current quantity in inventory, the form shows availability data and the current cost price (average cost price, except for items with a standard cost price or a fixed receipt price).

The physical inventory is the total of the transactions with following status:

> **Posted quantity** – Invoiced quantity (purchase invoices minus sales invoices)
> **Received** – Product receipts in purchasing, added to the posted quantity
> **Deducted** – Packing slips in sales, deducted from the posted quantity
> **Registered** – Registration and item arrival, added to the posted quantity
> **Picked** – Picking in sales, deducted from the posted quantity

Apart from purchasing and sales, the same status and calculation applies to transactions in production.

All data shown in the on-hand form refer to the selected dimensions. The dimensions for example selected in Figure 7-11 are the site "HQ" and the warehouse "10". According to this selection, Dynamics AX applies a filter showing the quantity and cost amount for this site and warehouse after switching to the tab *On-hand*. When viewing the cost price and cost amount, you have to take into account that data on costs are only reliable for dimensions with separate financial inventory (according to the dimension group settings).

7.2.4.7   On Hand Inventory in the Past

If you want to view the physical inventory on a date in the past, print or view the report *Inventory management> Inquiries and reports> Physical inventory reports> Physical inventory by inventory dimension*.

7.2.5   Case Study Exercises

Exercise 7.1 – Dimension Groups

In order to investigate the functionality of dimension groups, create a new storage dimension group DS-## and a tracking dimension group DT-## (## = your user ID). Set up the dimension groups in a way that the dimensions *Site, Warehouse* and *Batch number* are required in every transaction. For the warehouse dimension, separate financial inventory valuation should apply.

Exercise 7.2 – Item Model Group

As preparation for the next exercise, create a new item model group T-## (## = your user ID) with FIFO valuation (inventory model "FIFO"). The ledger integration for physical and financial inventory should be active. The item model group applies to stocked products and a negative financial inventory is allowed. All other checkboxes remain cleared, approved vendors are not required.

Then set up a second item model group S-## for standard cost valuation, which got the same settings as the first group, except that the inventory model is "Standard cost" and a negative physical inventory is possible.

7.3   Inventory Valuation and Cost Management

Based on the deep integration of the entire application, Dynamics AX provides a very accurate calculation of inventory values. In addition to the valuation methods for moving average and standard costs, there is the option to use an end-to-end FIFO or LIFO valuation.

Apart from the inventory management module, which contains all data on inventory quantity and value, the module "Cost management" collects all forms and features related to inventory costing and valuation.

7.3.1   Valuation and Cost Flow

Inventory transactions update the physical inventory quantity and the financial inventory value. In addition to the inventory transaction, which contains the complete physical and financial information, there is a cost transaction which only contains the cost-related information. Cost transactions are not generated for inventory transfers with no impact on the inventory value.

7.3.1.1 Basics of Inventory Valuation

The basis for inventory valuation is a simple principle:

> **Receipt costs** – The value of receipts is specified in the receipt transaction
> **Issue costs** – The value of issues is calculated according to the valuation model

The receipt transactions determine the cost price and cost amount of related consumption (issue transactions). The principle for linking issue and receipt transactions is given by the valuation model (FIFO, LIFO, average). It is not possible to enter the cost price or the cost amount in an issue transaction.

The standard cost price, which specifies the inventory value independently from the actual costs, is an exception to this principle. In Dynamics AX, there are two options for standard cost valuation:

> **Standard cost** – Inventory value according to a pre-defined item cost price
> **Fixed receipt price** – Similar to standard cost, but determining the receipt price

The option "Fixed receipt price" is available in combination with the valuation methods FIFO, LIFO and average cost. Applying this option fixes the receipt cost price in advance, preventing to change it when recording a transaction.

Unlike the fixed receipt price, the inventory model "Standard cost" provides true standard costs, immediately applying the standard cost price of an item to all issue and receipt transactions.

The difference between the methods "Standard cost" and "Fixed receipt price" is obvious when changing the standard cost price of an item. Whereas the standard cost method immediately posts an adjustment of inventory value, the fixed receipt price method does not adjust the value of on-hand stock but applies the new price only to new receipts – existing inventory will be issued with the old price until it is completely consumed.

Including the standard cost valuation, there are seven valuation methods (selected in the field *Inventory model* of the item model group) for calculating the cost price and cost amount of issue transactions in Dynamics AX:

> **FIFO** – First in, first out
> **LIFO** – Last in, first out
> **LIFO date** – LIFO, applying only receipts with a posting date before the issue
> **Weighted average** – Average of receipts
> **Weighted average date** – Average, but limited to receipts before the issue
> **Standard cost** – Pre-defined standard cost price
> **Moving average** – Keeping the average cost price

7.3.1.2   Valuation of Item Receipts

The final value of a physical receipt is set by the related financial transaction (invoice). Except for the standard cost valuation, which uses a pre-defined fixed price, the cost price and the cost amount in the different receipt transactions is calculated as follows:

> **Purchase order receipt** – Amount of the invoice line including related item charges, adding indirect costs from the costing sheet as applicable
> **Production receipt** – Cost amount of the production order (total cost of BOM item consumption and resource utilization, including applicable indirect costs)
> **Sales return** – Original value of the returned item if assigned to an original sales order; Otherwise return cost price entered in the return order
> **Other receipt** – Cost amount entered in the journal line

7.3.1.3   Valuation of Item Issues

At the time when you post an item issue (e.g. a sales packing slip), the cost price and amount is determined by the current average cost price (except for items using a standard cost price). Depending on the checkbox *Include physical value* in the item model group, this average cost price is only based on financial transactions (invoices) or includes the preliminary value of item receipts not yet invoiced.

The valuation method is used when closing inventory.

Inventory closing calculates the exact cost price and amount of an issue transaction based on assigned receipts. The inventory model (FIFO, LIFO, or average) is determining this assignment. The issue price and amount therefore is not final until you have posted the financial transaction (invoice) of all assigned receipts and inventory closing is finished.

Assigning issue transactions to receipt transactions through inventory closing is required for all transaction except for items with following valuation methods:

➢ **Standard cost price** – The standard cost price ("Standard cost" or "Fixed receipt price") immediately applies to issue and receipt transactions

➢ **Moving average** – Keeps the posted cost price of issue transactions and does not require inventory closing

7.3.1.4 Standard Cost Price

Items with the inventory model "Standard cost" do not require inventory closing because all receipt and issue transactions immediately apply the standard cost price specified in the item price form (see section 7.3.3).

When activating a new standard cost price, Dynamics AX immediately posts an adjustment of the current stock value in inventory and in the general ledger. The new standard cost price therefore applies to issues of existing stock right away.

7.3.1.5 Fixed Receipt Price

The checkbox "Fixed receipt price" in the item model group applies in combination with the valuation methods FIFO, LIFO, or average cost. When selecting this option, the cost price entered in the released product form or in the item price form specifies a fixed cost price for receipt transactions.

The cost price and cost amount are calculated according to the valuation method and – as long as you do not change the item cost price – always comply with the fixed receipt price of the item.

When changing the item cost price, consumption transactions immediately apply the new cost price. Since there is no posting of revaluation when changing a fixed receipt price, the financial value of existing stock however still complies with the old price. As a result, inventory closing is required for the option "Fixed receipt price" in order to adjust the cost amount of issue transactions to the old price according to the valuation method (until all inventory received with the old price has been consumed).

7.3.1.6 Moving Average Price

For items with the inventory model "Moving average", receipt transactions are posted with the price provided by the transaction (e.g. through a vendor invoice). When posting the vendor invoice, the financial transaction is depending on whether the quantity covered by the invoice is still on hand:

➢ **Complete quantity still on hand** – The total amount in the purchase invoice – including possible differences – is posted as financial cost value in inventory.

➢ **Part of the quantity already consumed** – For the quantity not on stock, the difference between the physical cost amount and the financial cost amount is posted as an adjustment to a price difference account.

When posting an issue transaction (e.g. a sales packing slip), the average cost price at the time of posting applies. This cost price does not change any more, which is why inventory closing is not required.

7.3.1.7 Inventory Value Calculation

The following table shows an overview of available valuation methods:

Table 7-3: Inventory models controlling the valuation methods in Dynamics AX

Inventory model	Explanation
FIFO (*First In First Out*)	Item issues are assigned to the oldest item receipt still on stock
LIFO (*Last In First Out*)	Item issues are assigned to the newest item receipt on stock available when closing inventory
LIFO date	Like LIFO, limiting the assignment of issues to receipts before the particular issue
Weighted average	The cost price of item issues in a period is the average cost price of all receipts (including the beginning balance) in this period (inventory closing period)
Weighted average date	The cost price of item issues is the average cost price calculated separately for each day
Standard cost	The cost price of item issues and receipts is equal to the active standard cost price of the item
Moving average	The cost price of item issues is the average cost price of the inventory quantity at the time of posting the issue

Table 7-4 shows a short example of the cost price calculation for the different valuation methods. Basis of the example are three receipt transactions with different cost prices and an issue transaction in between:

Table 7-4: Posted transactions for comparing valuation methods

Date	Transaction	Quantity	Cost amount
July 1	Receipt	10	100
July 2	Receipt	10	200
July 3	Issue	10	(to be calculated)
July 4	Receipt	10	300

After inventory closing, the cost amount of the issue shows following value depending on the valuation method:

Table 7-5: Valuation of the item issue in Table 7-4

Inventory Model	Amount	Explanation
FIFO	100	From the receipt on July 1
LIFO	300	From the receipt on July 4
LIFO date	200	From the receipt on July 2
Weighted average	200	Average of all receipts
Weighted average date	150	From the receipts on July 1 and July 2
Moving average	150	Current average when posting the issue

7.3.1.8 Financial Inventory Dimensions and Inventory Marking

In addition to the inventory model, the inventory dimension settings have got an impact on calculating the cost amount of an item issue. An assignment of issues and receipts is not possible across dimensions with a separate financial inventory according to the dimension group settings.

If separate financial inventory is for example activated for the dimension *Warehouse*, issues of a warehouse "20" only assign receipts to the warehouse "20" (including transfers). If separate financial inventory is not active for the dimension *Warehouse*, assignments comply with the date sequence independently from the warehouse in the transactions.

Marking is another option with an impact on the automatic assignment according to the inventory model. Markings work like lots for inventory valuation, assigning the cost amount of a particular receipt to a specific issue – e.g. used in vendor returns (see section 3.7.1). If you want to mark a transaction, click the button *Inventory/Marking* in transactions inquiries, order lines, or journal lines.

7.3.1.9 Inventory Value Report

The inventory value report is a configurable report with the option to set up multiple report versions for showing relevant inventory valuation data.

As a prerequisite to run the inventory value report, you have to set up at least one value report layout (*Cost management> Inventory accounting policies setup> Inventory value reports*) specifying the inventory value data you want to show. When printing the inventory value report (*Cost management> Inquiries and reports> Inventory accounting - status reports> Inventory value*), select the report layout in the field *ID* of the print dialog.

7.3.1.10 New in Dynamics 'AX 7'

Items which are new in inventory valuation include the cost transactions and the new module "Cost management".

7.3.2   Inventory Closing and Adjustment

At the time of posting an issue transaction, Dynamics AX always applies the average cost price (except for items using standard cost a price). In order to calculate the final cost price and amount according to the valuation method (*Inventor model*) of the item, you have to close inventory. Only items assigned to the inventory model "Standard cost" or "Moving average" are not included in inventory closing.

You need to close inventory periodically – usually as part of the month closing procedure in finance – in order to show correct item costs in finance and to close inventory transactions. After closing inventory, it is not possible to post inventory transactions in the closed period any more. If you have to post a transaction in a closed period, the only option is to cancel inventory closing.

7.3.2.1 Inventory Closing

In order to close inventory, open the form *Inventory management> Periodic tasks> Closing and adjustment* which shows a list of previous closings. If you want to close a period there, click the button *Close procedure.*

The first and second option in the close procedure, checking open quantities and cost prices, generate reports which help assessing inventory transactions. You can run these reports to take corrective actions – e.g. in case of missing or wrong transactions – before actually closing a period. But it is not required to perform these steps.

In order to finally close an inventory period, click the button *Close procedure/Close inventory* in the inventory closing form. Depending on the number of transactions, it might be useful to run closing as a batch job not within regular business hours.

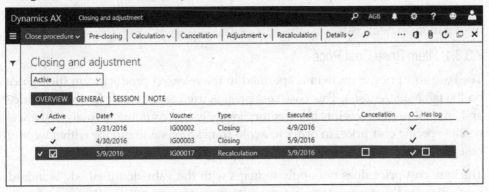

Figure 7-12:   The inventory closing and adjustment form

As a prerequisite for closing a period in inventory, the accounting period in the ledger calendar has to be open. As far as possible, you should post all vendor invoices related to item receipts in purchasing, and end all production orders which are reported as finished. The corresponding product receipts in purchasing and production then show the financial cost amount (instead of the physical cost amount which shows before invoicing) which minimizes the number of open transactions.

After closing inventory, you can access the posted adjustment transactions by clicking the button *Details/Settlements* in the inventory closing form. If you have to cancel inventory closing, click the button *Cancellation.* The button *Recalculation* calculates and posts adjustment transactions similar to closing, but does not actually close a period.

7.3.2.2 Manual Adjustment of Inventory Value

If you want to manually adjust the inventory value of an item, use the *Adjustment* feature in the inventory closing form.

The button *Adjustment/On-hand* provides the option to adjust the cost price and cost amount of the current inventory quantity at the level of inventory dimensions (e.g. on warehouse level). The button *Adjustment/Transactions* in the closing form provides the option to adjust the cost amount of individual receipt transactions.

In the adjustment form, click the button *Select* for choosing applicable items or transactions. In the selected records, enter a positive or negative adjustment amount in the column *Edit now* or retrieve a proposal for the adjustment selecting an appropriate option in the button *Adjustment*. Clicking the button *Post* in the adjustment form finally posts the adjustment.

7.3.3   Product Cost Management

The financial value of inventory is a result of the quantity and the cost price of products. In order to support inventory cost management, the cost management module with the workspaces *Cost administration* and *Cost analysis* collects relevant information on item costs.

7.3.3.1   Item Base Cost Price

The base cost price of an item is specified in the released product form (field *Price* on the tab *Manage costs*). This base cost price is used as a default for the cost price and amount of item receipts in inventory journals and counting journals, if there is no site-specific cost price. In order to avoid transactions without (or with a wrong) cost price, make sure the base cost price is correct.

The base cost price does not apply to items with the valuation method "Standard cost". Standard cost price items require entering a cost price in the item price form.

7.3.3.2   Costing Versions and Item Price Form

Before entering a record in the item price form, an appropriate costing version (*Cost management> Inventory accounting> Costing versions*) has to be available. Costing versions contain separate versions of prices used for simulation and activation, providing the option to set up different calculation principles. Items with standard cost valuation use a costing version with the *Costing type* "Standard cost", the costing type "Planned cost" refers to the other valuation methods.

The cost price per site (in parallel to the purchase price and the sales price per site) is available in the item price form, which you can access by clicking the button *MANAGE COSTS/Set up/Item price* in the action pane of the released product form.

In order to enter a new cost price in the item price form, switch to the tab *Pending prices* there. For a cost price, choose the *Price type* "Cost" and select the costing version in the column *Version*. Select the applicable *Site* in case there is no default value from the costing version. Apart from the *Price* itself, the item price form contains additional price details like the *Price unit* or the price charges (similar to corresponding settings in the released product form, see section 3.3.3).

Once you have finished entering (or calculating) the pending price, activate it by clicking the button *Activate pending price(s)* in the action pane of the item price form. Active prices then show on the tab *Active prices* of the form.

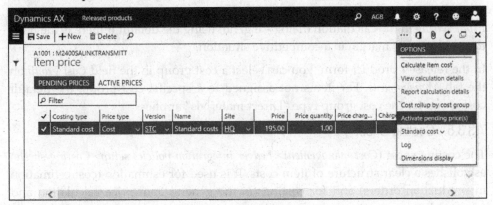

Figure 7-13:   Activating a pending price in the item price form

For product master records, cost prices are available at product variant level if the slider *Use cost price by variant* on the tab *Manage costs* in the released product is set to "Yes".

7.3.3.3 Calculation Group

Calculation groups determine the basis for calculating cost prices and sales prices.

You can set up calculation groups in the form *Cost management> Predetermined cost policies setup> Calculation groups*. The default calculation group is specified in the inventory management parameters (*Inventory management> Setup> Inventory and warehouse management parameters*, tab *Inventory accounting*). At item level, you can select a different *Calculation group* on the tab *Engineer* in the released product form.

7.3.3.4 Cost Groups

Cost groups classify and group different types of costs in cost calculation on the one hand, and specify different margins for sales price calculation on the other hand. You can access cost groups in the form *Cost management> Inventory accounting policies setup> Cost groups*. The *Cost group type*, which determines the basic costing structure, contains following options:

> **Direct materials** – Material consumption
> **Direct manufacturing** – Resource operations
> **Direct outsourcing** – Purchased subcontracting services
> **Indirect** – Overhead margins
> **Undefined** – Unspecific cost classification

In one cost group per *Cost group type* you should set the checkbox *Default* to "Yes", making the selected cost group a default for the cost group type.

In order to specify margins for sales price calculation, expand the tab *Profit* in the cost group form. You can register up to four lines with a different *Profit-setting* on this tab, entering an appropriate *Profit percentage* per profit-setting level. When executing a cost calculation or estimating production orders, choose an appropriate *Profit-setting* in the calculation dialog – e.g. not using the default if there is the need to apply a lower margin in a competitive situation.

In the released product form, you can select a cost group in the field *Cost group* on the tab *Manage costs*. For items not assigned to a specific cost group, the default cost group for the cost group type "Direct materials" applies.

7.3.3.5 Costing Sheet

The costing sheet (*Cost management> Ledger integration policies setup> Costing sheets*) establishes a clear structure of item costs. It is used for estimation (cost estimation in production orders) and for costing (in the general item price calculation and when ending production orders), and has got two different purposes:

➢ **Cost classification** – Classification by cost groups
➢ **Overhead costs** – Specifying rules for calculating overhead costs of manufactured and purchased items

For classification purposes, the costing sheet constitutes a multi-level structure of the different costs. Apart from the cost groups, which are the bottom level in the structure, the costing sheet can contain nodes for totals at multiple levels.

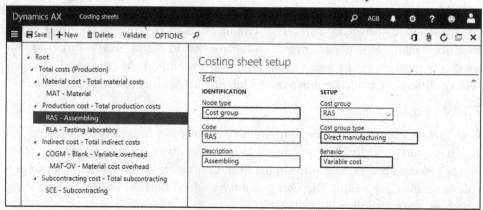

Figure 7-14: Setting up a simple costing sheet

Directly below the *Root* node, you can set up two primary nodes with the *Node type* "Price" and a different *Type* (field group *Setup*). The *Type* groups following items:

➢ **Manufactured items** – Node with the *Type* "Cost of goods manufactured"
➢ **Purchased items** – Node with the *Type* "Costs of purchase" (optional structure, if you want to apply indirect costs from the costing sheet instead of indirect costs through charges in purchase orders)

If you want to enter a new node in the costing sheet, select the higher-level node and click the button *New* in the action pane. In case you want to create a node for a cost group, choose the option "Cost group" in the field *Select node type* of the *Create* dialog. Then select the appropriate *Cost group* on the tab *Edit* in the new node.

If you want to define overhead costs, select a node in the costing sheet with a *Cost group* referring to the *Cost group type* "Indirect". Sub-nodes of such a node specify the calculation rules for overhead costs. When creating a sub-node for overhead cost calculation, select the option "Surcharge" or "Rate" in the field *Node type* of the sub-node. On the tab *Absorption basis* of the sub-node, select a *Code* specifying the basis for the calculation. Then you can enter a percentage or rate per costing version on the tab *Surcharge* (or *Rate*) before activating the indirect costs by clicking the button *Activate* in the toolbar of the tab. Main accounts for posting indirect costs to the ledger have to be entered on the tab *Ledger postings*.

Before closing the costing sheet, save your changes by clicking the button *Save*.

7.3.3.6 Item Price Calculation

For finished or semi-finished items, you can run a price calculation based on the bill of materials and the route. For this purpose, there are two different options:

➢ **For a particular item** – Calculating from the item price form, for example when creating a new item
➢ **For all items** – Calculating from the costing version, for example if you want to calculate a new price for all items once a year

If you want to execute the price calculation for a particular item, open the item price form (button *MANAGE COSTS/Set up/Item price* in the released product) and click the button *Calculate item cost* after switching to the tab *Pending prices*. The calculation works the same way as the calculation for all items in the costing version form (*Cost management> Inventory accounting> Costing versions*), where you can click the button *Calculation* after selecting a costing version.

In the calculation dialog, select the *Site* and the *Calculation date* which determine the applicable active BOM and route from the released product. If starting the calculation from the item price form, you can override the default *Quantity*, or select a particular *BOM* and *Route number* in the dialog. If starting from the costing versions, you can enter an item filter on the tab *Records to include* of the calculation dialog. On the tab *Price recordings in version* of the dialog, you can specify whether to calculate the cost price and/or the sales price.

Clicking the button *OK* in the dialog starts the calculation. Once finished, you can view the result in the pending prices (in the costing versions form, click the button *Price/Item price* for access). If you want to check the calculation, click the button *View calculation details* in the item price form to show all price components. After selecting one or more pending prices in the item price form you can activate them by clicking the button *Activate pending price(s)*.

7.3.4   Case Study Exercises

Exercise 7.3 – Product Record

Enter two new items in the released product form as a preparation for examining the effects of the settings in the dimension groups and the item model groups:

> ➢ Item I-##-S with standard costs (item model group S-## from exercise 7.2)
> ➢ Item I-##-T with FIFO valuation (item model group T-## from exercise 7.2)

For both items, the product subtype is "Product" and the storage and the tracking dimension group are the groups you have set up in exercise 7.1. Select an item group for merchandise and the unit of measure "Pieces". The item sales tax groups for purchasing and sales should refer to the standard tax rate. The base purchase price and the base cost price is USD 50. The base sales price is USD 100. For purchasing, inventory and sales, enter the main site in the *Default order settings* and the main warehouse of the main site in the *Site specific order settings*.

For the item I-##-S, you have to enter and to activate a standard cost price. Specify a standard cost price of USD 50 for the main site in the item price form.

Exercise 7.4 – Inventory Value of Transactions

Create a purchase order selecting your vendor of exercise 3.2. The order contains a line of 100 units of the first and 100 units of the second item entered in exercise 7.3. Enter a purchase price of 60 USD in both order lines and confirm the order.

Try to find out, if you can post a product receipt without a batch number. Choosing the option *View details* in the batch number column, create the batch number B001 for both items in the batch table afterwards. Then insert this batch number in the purchase order lines.

In the next step, post the product receipt and the invoice receipt for the complete quantity. If you look at the item transactions and the quantity on hand, can you explain the difference of the cost amount and the cost price for the two items?

Exercise 7.5 – Valuation of Purchase Orders

You want to order 100 units of the first and 100 units of the second item of exercise 7.3 from your vendor of exercise 3.2. Enter an appropriate purchase order choosing the batch number B001 and a purchase price of 80 USD in both order lines.

Once you have finished entering the order, confirm it and post the product receipt and the vendor invoice for the entire quantity. In the *Product receipt date* (on the tab *Setup* of the product receipt posting dialog) and in the *Posting date* (in the vendor invoice), enter the day after the posting date of exercise 7.4 (e.g. July 2, if exercise 7.4 has been on July 1).

After posting the invoice, check the inventory transactions, the inventory quantity, and the inventory value (cost amount) of the two items.

Exercise 7.6 – Valuation of Sales Order

Your customer of exercise 4.1 orders 150 units of the first and 150 units of the second item of exercise 7.3. Enter an appropriate sales order choosing the batch number B001 in both order lines. Then post the sales invoice for the entire order quantity. In the *Invoice date* on the tab *Setup* of the posting dialog, enter the day after the posting date of exercise 7.5 (e.g. July 3, if exercise 7.5 has been on July 2).

After posting the invoice, check the inventory transactions, the inventory quantity. and the inventory value (cost amount) of the two items again.

Exercise 7.7 – Closing Inventory

Run a *Recalculation* in the inventory closing form in order to calculate the correct inventory value according to the valuation method. In the recalculation form, set the recalculation date to the posting date of exercise 7.6 (e.g. July 3) and enter an appropriate filter which restricts the calculation to the items used in this exercise.

For these two items, check the cost price and the inventory value (cost amount) in the inventory transactions and in the inventory on-hand quantity. Which changes are a caused by recalculation, can you explain the result?

7.4 Business Processes in Inventory

The only way to change the inventory quantity of an item is to post an inventory transaction. Business processes, which change the inventory quantity and do not originate in inventory management but in other functional areas like purchasing, sales, or production, generate these transactions automatically in the background.

A description of the processes in other areas is available in the corresponding chapter of this book. The lines below cover the business processes within inventory management itself.

7.4.1 Inventory Structures and Parameters

As a prerequisite for inventory transactions, the setup in inventory management and in product management has to be finished.

7.4.1.1 Warehouse Management

Dynamics AX includes three storage dimensions which group the inventory within a company according to the physical warehouse structure: *Site*, *Warehouse*, and *Location*. Depending on the applicable dimension group, you need to record these dimensions in every inventory transaction.

In order to set up a new warehouse, open the form *Inventory management> Setup> Inventory breakdown> Warehouses* and click the button *New*. In the new record, enter the warehouse ID, the *Name* and the *Site*. The site (see section 10.1.5) is a mandatory field which groups the warehouses within a company from a geographical and financial point of view.

The lookup field *Type* determines whether the warehouse is a regular warehouse ("Default"), or a quarantine warehouse, or a transit warehouse. Quarantine warehouses are used for quarantine orders (see section 7.4.6), and transit warehouses for transfer orders (see section 7.4.4).

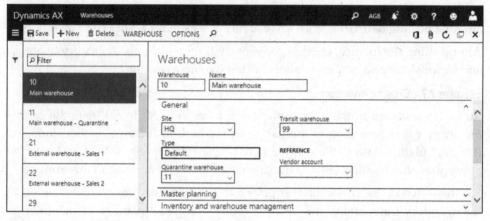

Figure 7-15:   Managing warehouses in the warehouse form

A further structuring of warehouses including aisles and locations is required in the advanced warehouse management (see chapter 8.1.1).

7.4.1.2 Storage Dimensions

When setting up the warehouse structures, be aware that the storage dimension groups of the released products control the inventory dimensions, which are required in an inventory transaction. If you need locations in a particular warehouse, the storage dimension groups of all involved items have to contain an active dimension *Location*. Since this setting activates locations for all warehouses, you need to set up at least one (pseudo-)location for each warehouse in this case.

7.4.1.3 Inventory Parameters and Journal Setup

If you want to enter a manual transaction in inventory, you have to register it in a journal. Apart from sites and warehouses, inventory journals are another required setup. You can split the journals in inventory to two different groups:

➢ **Inventory journals** – General transactions
➢ **Warehouse management journals** – Receipts related to orders

Inventory journals are used to register general transactions like item receipts, item issues, item transfers, and inventory counting. In order to configure inventory journals, open the form *Inventory management> Setup> Journal names> Inventory*. You have to set up at least one journal name for the *Journal type* "Movement", "Inventory adjustment", "Transfer", "BOM", and "Counting" before you can enter and post corresponding transactions. Assigning a number sequence in the lookup *Voucher series* provides the option to use a separate number sequence per journal.

Warehouse management journals are used for order-related item receipts and include two journal types: Item arrival journals (for purchase order receipts and customer returns), and production input journals (for finished goods receipts in production). In order to set up warehouse management journals, open the form *Inventory management> Setup> Journal names> Warehouse management*.

Inventory parameters (*Inventory management> Setup> Inventory and warehouse management parameters*) contain settings for number sequences, the default unit of measure, the default calculation group, and defaults for journal names. On the tab *Inventory dimensions*, you can choose the dimensions which display as default in the inventory journals.

7.4.2 Inventory Journal

You have to use an inventory journal, if you want to record a transaction independently from other functional areas like purchasing, sales, or production.

7.4.2.1 Journal Structure

Inventory journals in Dynamics AX show a common structure with following journal types for the different types of transactions:

> **Inventory adjustment** – Manually changing the on-hand quantity
> **Movement** – Like inventory adjustment, but with a user-defined offset account
> **Transfer** – Between warehouses or other inventory dimension
> **Bills of materials** – Consuming components and receiving a finished item
> **Counting** – Registering the actual on-hand quantity and posting adjustments
> **Tag counting** – Using tags as preparation for counting
> **Item arrival** – Receipt related to a purchase order or sales return order
> **Production input** – Finished goods receipt related to a production order

Since inventory transactions have an impact on finance, the voucher principle applies: A journal has to be entered, before it is possible to post it in a second step.

When accessing an inventory journal, Dynamics AX displays the related list page with the open journals which are not posted yet. If you want to view posted journals, apply an appropriate filter on the column *Posted*. You can access the journal detail form, which includes a header view and a lines view, by clicking the journal ID shown as link in the grid.

7.4.2.2 Movement Journals and Inventory Adjustment Journals

If you want to record manual changes of the item quantity in inventory, you can either use a journal of the type "Movement" or "Inventory adjustment".

The difference between movement journals and inventory adjustment journals is, that movement journals show the field *Offset account* where you can enter the expense account for item consumption (or the revenue account for item receipt). In inventory adjustment journals, the offset account derives from the inventory posting setup and does not show in the journal lines. For this reason, you want to use a movement journal for example when posting the item consumption of a department referring to a specific expense account.

Section 7.1.2 at the beginning of the current chapter explains how to register and to post an inventory adjustment journal.

In order to register a movement journal, click the button *New* in the list page *Inventory management> Journal entries> Items> Movement* and select a *Name* (journal name) in the *Create* dialog. In the field *Offset account* on the tab *General* of the dialog, you can optionally enter a default for the offset account in the journal lines. After switching to the detail form, enter one or more journal lines with posting date, item number, appropriate inventory dimension values, and quantity (negative for item issues). For item receipts, the cost price is editable (receiving its default value from the item). Finally post the movement by clicking the button *Post* in the action pane after making sure to apply the right main accounts in the column *Offset account* and appropriate financial dimension values on the sub-tab *Financial dimensions* of the *Line details* tab.

7.4.2.3 Transfer Journals

Unlike movement journals and inventory adjustment journals, which record issues and receipts, transfer journals are used to register a transfer of item inventory from one dimension-combination to another. In most cases, this is the transfer from one warehouse or location to another. But you can also use a transfer journal to change the batch or serial number.

In order to register an item transfer, open the form *Inventory management> Journal entries> Items> Transfer* and enter a line similar to an adjustment journal line. But in addition to the data entered in inventory adjustment journal lines, you have to enter the applicable inventory dimensions to which the item should be transferred.

Entering the *Quantity* with a negative sign issues the item from the "from-dimensions" and receives it at the "to-dimensions".

Once you are finished with entering the lines, post the journal by clicking the button *Post* in the action pane of the journal list page or detail form.

7.4.2.4 BOM Journals

Bill of materials journals (*Inventory management> Journal entries> Items> Bills of materials*) provide the option to post the receipt of a finished item while consuming the components at the same time. In addition, you can – by entering a negative quantity – also disassemble a finished item.

Unlike the way you work in the other journals, you do not need to enter journal lines manually in a bill of materials journal. In order to create journal lines, click the button *Functions/Report as finished* in action pane of the BOM journal detail form.

In the report as finished dialog, insert a line and select the finished item which you want to receive in inventory. If you select the checkbox in the column *Post now*, the bill of materials journal will immediately post once you close the report as finished form by clicking the button *OK*. If the checkbox *Post now* is cleared, the finished item and its component show in the bill of materials journal lines, where you can edit them before posting the journal by clicking the button *Post* in the action pane.

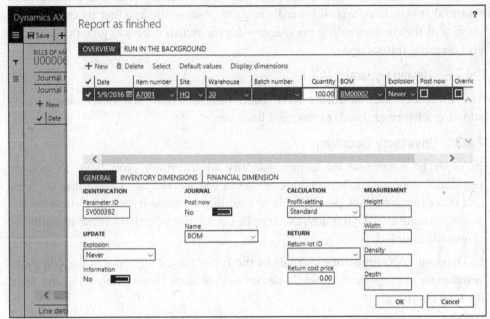

Figure 7-16:   Report as finished dialog, opened from the bill of materials journal

7.4.2.5 Item Arrival Journals

Item arrival journals (*Inventory management> Journal entries> Item arrival> Item arrival*) provide the option to post item receipts referring to purchase orders (see section 3.5.3) or customer returns (see section 4.7.1). Production input journals (*Inventory management> Journal entries> Item arrival> Production input*), which work similar to item arrival journals, can be used to receive finished products in a production order.

Entering an item arrival journal is similar to entering an inventory adjustment journal. In order to specify the reference to a purchase order, switch to the tab *Default values* in the *Create* dialog (or in the header view of the detail form), and select the option "Purchase order" in the lookup field *Reference* before entering the order number in the field *Number*. For customer returns, select the *Reference* "Sales order" and enter the *RMA number*. If you want to use quarantine management, make sure that the appropriate slider in the field group *Mode of handling* is set to "Yes".

After creating the journal, you can optionally click the button *Functions/Create lines* in the action pane of the list page or detail form to retrieve default values for the item numbers, the inventory dimensions, and the open quantity from the purchase order lines (or the return order lines).

In order to post the arrival journal, click the button *Post* once all lines are entered correctly. Unlike inventory journals, which immediately post the physical and financial transaction, arrival journals require posting the product receipt and the invoice of the corresponding purchase order (or return order) to generate physical and financial transactions.

7.4.2.6 New in Dynamics 'AX 7'

The inventory journal forms have been redesigned in the new release (now showing a list page, header view, and lines view).

7.4.3   Inventory Counting

In order to determine the actual quantity in inventory, you have to execute physical inventory counting (stocktaking) in the warehouse. Depending on legal and other requirements, periodical item counting is necessary to make sure that the posted quantity in Dynamics AX complies with the actual on-hand quantity as physically counted.

In Dynamics AX, inventory journals of the type "Counting" or – in the advanced warehouse management – mobile device transactions (see section 8.1.4) are used for item counting.

When posting an item counting journal, the difference between the counted quantity and the quantity in Dynamics AX is posted as item issue or receipt – similar to the transactions in an inventory adjustment journal. Since the counting difference is calculated as of the counting date, you do not need to stop other transactions in inventory while counting. But if required for organizational reasons, you can lock inventory (slider *Lock items during count* on the tab *General* of the inventory parameters).

7.4.3.1 Counting Journal

In order to register a counting journal, click the button *New* in the list page *Inventory management> Journal entries> Item counting> Counting*. In the *Create* dialog, you have to choose the inventory dimensions which are the basis for the counting journal. After creating the journal, there are two options for registering inventory counting:

➢ **Manual** – Entering counting journal lines
➢ **Automatic** – Creating counting journal lines from a proposal

If you want to execute a completely manual registration, enter a journal line with counting date, item number, warehouse, and applicable dimensions like in any other inventory journal. The counted quantity has to be entered in the column

Counted. The column *On-hand* shows the corresponding inventory quantity in Dynamics AX as of the counting date. The difference between the counted and the on-hand quantity shows in the column *Quantity*. This quantity applies to the issue or receipt transaction when posting the counting journal.

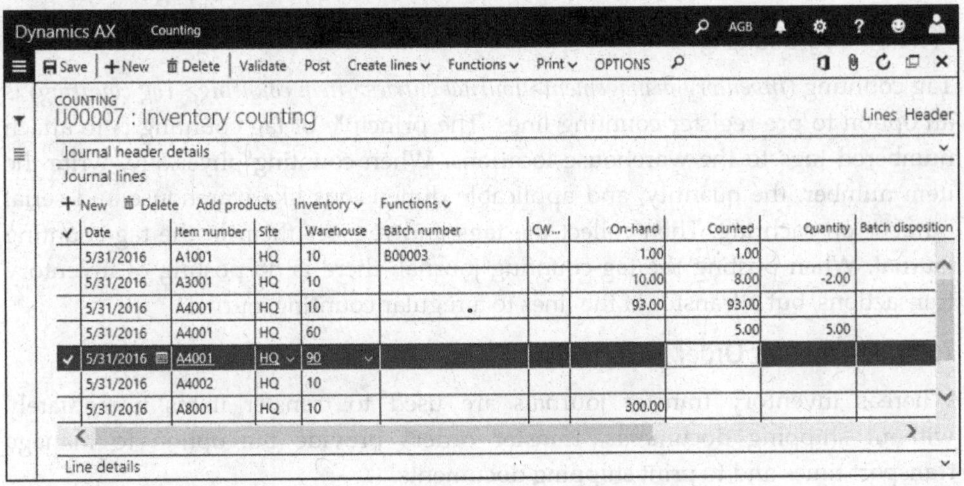

Figure 7-17: Entering the counted quantity in a counting journal line

If you want to create counting lines automatically, click the button *Create lines/On-hand* (creating lines for items and related inventory dimension values which are, or have been, on hand) or the button *Create lines/Items* (creating lines for all items) in the action pane of the counting journal. In the *Create counting journal* dialog, select a filter on the tab *Records to include* – e.g. for counting a particular warehouse. Additional parameters in the dialog provide the option to restrict counting for example on items and inventory dimensions, which show an inventory transaction after the last inventory counting.

After creating the counting journal lines manually or automatically, you can optionally print a counting list by clicking the button *Print/Counting list* in the action pane of the counting journal (before, after, or before and after entering the counted quantity).

Once you are finished with registering and checking the counting journal, post it by clicking the button *Post* in the action pane of the journal list page or detail form.

7.4.3.2 Counting Groups

In order to support the selection of items when automatically creating counting lines, you can filter on counting groups in the *Create counting journal* dialog. Counting groups (*Inventory management> Setup> Inventory> Counting groups*) are not only used for grouping and sorting purposes, they also contain specific settings for counting. A core setting is the *Counting code*, which controls when to execute counting (periodically, when equal or below minimum stock, or when reaching zero stock). You can assign a counting group to an item in the released product form (tab *Manage inventory*) or in the warehouse items form (button *MANAGE INVENTORY/ Warehouse/Warehouse items* in the released product form).

If you want to apply the counting code when automatically creating counting lines, set the slider *Activate counting code* in the *Create counting journal* dialog to "Yes".

7.4.3.3 Tag Counting

Tag counting (*Inventory management> Journal entries> Item counting> Tag counting*) is an option to pre-register counting lines. The principle of tag counting is to attach numbered tags to the warehouse locations. When counting physically, write the item number, the quantity, and applicable dimensions like warehouse and serial number on each tag. Then collect the tags and register them in the tag-counting journal. When posting the tag-counting journal, there is no posting of inventory transactions, but a transfer of the lines to a.regular counting journal.

7.4.4   Transfer Order

Whereas inventory transfer journals are used to transfer items immediately without shipping documents, transfer orders provide the option to manage transport times and to print shipping documents.

7.4.4.1 Setup for Transfer Orders

As a prerequisite for working with transfer orders, you have to set up at least one warehouse of the type "Transit" in the warehouse form. This transit warehouse receives the items for the time of the transport. In addition, you have to assign a transit warehouse to each regular warehouse from which you issue transfer orders. If items apply the storage dimension *Location*, you should specify a *Default receipt location* and a *Default issue location* for the transit warehouse in the warehouse form.

Delivery date control optionally applies to transfer orders (similar to sales orders, see section 4.4.3).

7.4.4.2 Processing Transfer Orders

In order to create a transfer order, open the form *Inventory management> Inbound orders> Transfer order* and click the button *New* in the action pane. The transfer order consists of a header, where you have to enter the *From warehouse* and the *To warehouse*, and transfer order lines, which contain the items to be transferred.

After selecting the *From warehouse* in the header, the transfer order retrieves the related transit warehouse (shown on the tab *General* in the header view). In the transfer order lines, enter one or more records with item number, transfer quantity, and inventory dimensions as applicable.

Similar to sales order processing, you can execute picking using basic warehouse processes (see section 4.5.2) or advanced warehouse processes (see section 8.1.3). Depending on the setup, you can also post the shipment immediately without prior picking.

In order to post the shipment, click the button *SHIP/Operations/Ship transfer order*. In the upper pane of the *Shipment* posting dialog, select the option "All" in the column *Update* for shipping the complete quantity (depending on the previous steps, you can alternatively select the picked or the ship-now quantity). The checkbox *Print transfer shipment* provides the option to print a shipping document. Clicking the button *OK* in the dialog posts a transfer to the transit warehouse.

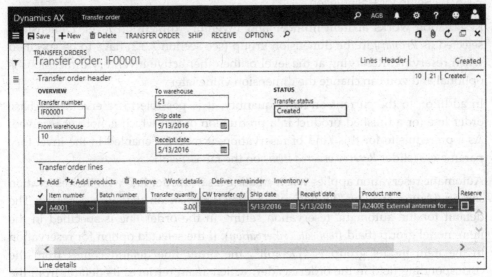

Figure 7-18:   Entering a line in a transfer order

When receiving the item at the destination warehouse, process the receipt – optionally posting a prior inventory registration or item arrival similar to the options in a purchase order (see section 3.5.3).

In order to post the final transfer receipt (similar to the product receipt in purchasing), click the button *RECEIVE/Operations/Receive* in the transfer order form. In the *Receive* posting dialog, choose the option "All" in the column *Update* (depending on the previous steps, you can alternatively select the registered or the receive-now quantity). Clicking the button *OK* in the posting dialog then posts a transfer from the transit warehouse to the destination warehouse.

7.4.5   Item Reservation

Master planning is used to ensure that a sufficient quantity is available to cover the future demand from sales orders, production orders, and other issue transactions. But in some cases, the supply provided through master planning is not sufficient to cover a changing demand. This situation can occur for example, if a short-term sales order picks inventory originally allocated to another order.

In order to prevent that a later demand picks inventory already assigned to a particular order, you can use reservations. Reservations are primarily used for sales orders lines and BOM components in production orders, but you can also use them for any other issue (e.g. vendor returns, or transfer orders). Apart from manual reservation, Dynamics AX also supports automatic reservation.

Reservation, which makes sure an item is available for a future consumption, works separately and independently from marking (see section 3.7.1), which links posted transactions for valuation purposes.

7.4.5.1 Setup for Reservation

Reservation works at item number and inventory dimension level. Dimensions selected as *Primary* in the dimension group (see section 7.2.2) have to be specified when reserving. Reserving at the level of the other active inventory dimensions is optional and you can change the dimension value later.

In addition to the current on-hand quantity, it is possible to reserve a purchase order line (or a finished product in a production order) which is not yet received. As a prerequisite for this kind of reservation, it must be enabled in the inventory parameters (slider *Reserve ordered items* on the tab *General*).

Automatic reservation applies when creating a sales order line with the reservation setting "Automatic" or "Explosion" (field *Reservation* on the sub-tab *Setup*). The default for the automatic reservation setting in the order line is specified in the item model group (field *Item sales reservation*). If the selected option for reservation in the item model group is "Default", the order line default comes from the corresponding field in the order header, which again retrieves its default from the accounts receivable parameters (lookup field *Reservation* on the tab *General*).

Automatic reservation of BOM lines in a production order is controlled by the lookup field *Reservation* on the tab *Setup* in the production order header, receiving a default from the production control parameters. Unlike the automatic reservation of sales orders, automatic reservation of production BOM lines does not apply when creating the order but when estimating, scheduling, releasing, or starting (depending on the option selected in the order header).

7.4.5.2 Working with Reservations

If you want to execute a manual reservation in a sales order, click the button *Inventory/Reservation* in the toolbar of the sales order lines.

In the reservation form, you can manually enter the reserved quantity in the column *Reservation*, or click the button *Reserve lot* in the action pane. Clicking the button *Display dimensions* in the toolbar of the tab *On-hand quantities* provides the option to show applicable inventory dimensions if needed for a more detailed control of reservation at dimension level. If required, you can change or delete the quantity in the column *Reservation* and enter a quantity in another reservation line. Depending on the related inventory parameter setting, you can reserve only current inventory or also ordered items.

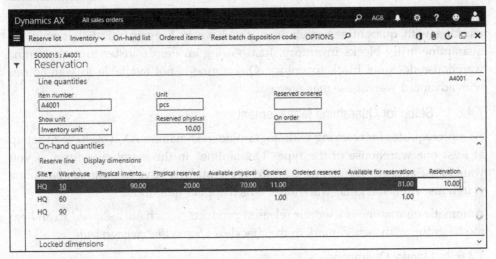

Figure 7-19: Reserving current inventory for a sales order line

If automatic reservation applies, the reservation is done in the background and you can edit the reservation in the reservation form the same way as a manual reservation. In case there is not sufficient quantity available to cover the automatic reservation, the *Autoreservation* dialog immediately shows the problem.

After reservation, the reserved quantity shows as *Physical reserved* (*Ordered reserved* if reserving a future receipt) in the inventory transaction and the on-hand inquiry. The reserved quantity is not available for any other transaction.

7.4.5.3 Removing Reservations

If you view the on-hand inquiry and it shows a reserved quantity which you need for another purpose, you can remove the reservation. From the on-hand inquiry, you can access the inventory transactions by clicking the button *Transactions* in the action pane. Select the appropriate inventory transaction with the issue status "Reserved physical" and click the button *INVENTORY/View/Reservation* to show the reservation form, where you can update the reservation as required.

7.4.6 Quarantine and Inventory Blocking

If you want to exclude a particular quantity of an item from the available stock – for example because of the test results in quality control – you can alternatively use following functionality in Dynamics AX:

➢ **Inventory Blocking** – Short-term temporary blocking
➢ **Quarantine Management** – Transfer to a quarantine warehouse

Inventory blocking, which is primarily used for quality inspection, generates a temporary inventory transaction for blocking.

Quarantine management in comparison is based upon quarantine orders, which post a transfer to a quarantine warehouse. You can create quarantine orders manually whenever necessary, or automatically with every item receipt. When working with quarantine warehouses you have to keep in mind that only the quarantine order blocks inventory. Just posting an item transfer to a quarantine warehouse does not block inventory. Quarantine is not available in warehouses with advanced warehouse management.

7.4.6.1 Setup for Quarantine Management

As a prerequisite for working with quarantine in Dynamics AX, you have to set up at least one warehouse of the type "Quarantine" in the warehouse form. If you want to use automatic quarantine for item receipts, you have to assign a quarantine warehouse to each regular warehouse which applies quarantine.

Automatic quarantine is used for released products, which are assigned to an item model group with a checkmark in the checkbox *Quarantine management*.

7.4.6.2 Manual Quarantine

The quarantine order page (*Inventory management> Periodic tasks> Quality management> Quarantine orders*) shows the list of open quarantine orders. After selecting the checkbox *View ended* you can also view ended quarantine orders.

	Quarantine... ↑	Item number	Site	Warehouse	Batch number	Quarantine warehouse	CW quantity	Quantity	Status	Disposition co
	IQ00001	A7001	HQ	30	B00001	11		20.00	Started	
	IQ00002	A1001	HQ	10	B00003	11		1.00	Ended	
	IQ00003	A4001	HQ	10		11		5.00	Created	

Figure 7-20:   Managing quarantine in the quarantine order form

In order to create a new quarantine order manually, click the button *New* in the action pane and enter the item number, quantity, warehouse, and applicable inventory dimensions. The default for the quarantine warehouse on the tab *Quarantine inventory dimensions* derives from the quarantine warehouse of the original warehouse in the quarantine order. The default for all other quarantine inventory dimensions are the initial dimension values of the quarantine order.

After closing the quarantine order detail form, you can access it again by clicking the *Quarantine number* shown as link in the grid of the quarantine order list page.

Clicking the button *Start* in the quarantine order form transfers the quantity to quarantine. Transfer to quarantine includes moving the item to the quarantine warehouse and reserving it for quarantine in order to block issue transactions. In parallel to the quarantine transaction, Dynamics AX generates a second inventory transaction for the future re-transfer to the original warehouse without date.

If you want to partly or completely scrap an item in quarantine, click the button *Functions/Scrap*.

In order to end quarantine with or without prior scrapping of a partial quantity, click the button *End* in the quarantine order form. Ending quarantine posts the re-transfer to the original warehouse and makes the quantity available again.

Clicking the button *Report as finished* in the quarantine order posts the completion of inspections as an intermediate step. The item is not available in inventory before ending the quarantine order, which is why you want to apply this step only if you want to post the transfer back to the original warehouse separately.

7.4.6.3 Automatic Quarantine

When posting item arrival journals, production input journals, or product receipts, Dynamics AX automatically creates and starts a quarantine order for items, which are assigned to an item model group with selected *Quarantine management*. The further proceeding of quarantine works similar to manual quarantine.

7.4.6.4 Inventory Blocking

Inventory blocking usually applies in combination with quality orders (see section 7.4.7). But you can also execute manual inventory blocking without using the quality management functionality.

In order to block inventory of an item manually, open the form *Inventory management> Periodic tasks> Inventory blocking* and click the button *New* in the action pane. In the blocking record, enter the item number, the quantity and – on the tab *Inventory dimensions* – applicable dimensions. If you expect the item to become available again (like in a quarantine order), set the slider *Expected receipts* to "Yes". Depending on the expected receipts setting, Dynamics AX generates one or two inventory transactions showing "Inventory blocking" in the column *Reference*. If you want to end inventory blocking, simply delete the line in the inventory blocking form.

7.4.7   Quality Management

Quality management in Dynamics AX is integrated in the supply chain and helps to manage quality processes and issues. It consists of two components:

> **Quality control** – Managing quality orders with quality tests
> **Non-conformance** – Managing items which do not meet the quality standards

Since quality issue processing is also possible by use of the case management (see section 10.5.2), which offers a much more flexible solution than the non-conformance features in quality management (*Inventory management> Periodic tasks> Quality management> Non conformances*), the focus in the section is on quality control functionality.

7.4.7.1 Setup for Quality Control

As a prerequisite for using quality control, quality management has to be enabled in the inventory management parameters (slider *Use quality management* on the tab *Quality management*). The required setup for executing tests in quality control further includes:

> **Tests** – Measuring individual characteristics of the tested quantity
> **Test variables** – Only for tests with results from a list of values
> **Test groups** – Sequence of tests to be executed in a quality order

In order to set up a test, open the menu item *Inventory management> Setup> Quality control> Tests* and insert a line with test ID, *Description*, *Type* ("Fraction" for numbers with decimals, "Integer" for whole numbers, "Option" for distinct values), and *Unit* (for *Type* "Fraction" or "Integer"). For tests with the *Type* "Option", you have to create a test variable (*Inventory management> Setup> Quality control> Test variables*) with the list of possible result values (button *Outcomes* in the test variable form).

Once tests and applicable test variables are defined, you can create a test group (*Inventory management> Setup> Quality control> Test groups*). After inserting a test group in the upper pane of the form, assign the individual tests in the lower pane. For tests with the type "Option", you have to select the *Test variable* and the *Default outcome* on the tab *Test*. For the other test types, the tab *Test* contains the field group *Test measurement values* for specifying the standard value and tolerances. If it is not possible to utilize the tested quantity after the test, select the checkbox *Destructive test* in the upper pane.

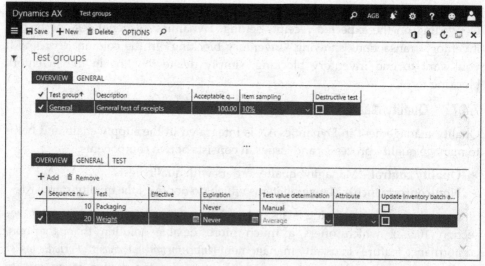

Figure 7-21: Setting up a test group

If you want to generate quality orders automatically, you have to set up item sampling and quality associations.

Item sampling (*Inventory management> Setup> Quality control> Item sampling*) determines the test quantity when automatically generating a quality order. In the field *Quantity specification*, you can select to test a percentage or a fixed quantity. As long as a quality order is not finished, the tested quantity is always blocked through inventory blocking (see section 7.4.6). If you set the slider *Full blocking* to "Yes", blocking applies to the complete transaction quantity no matter which percentage is tested. After setting up item sampling, you can select it as default in the test group.

Quality associations (*Inventory management> Setup> Quality control> Quality associations*) are used to assign items to test groups. When setting up a quality association, select the *Reference type* (e.g. "Purchase" for purchase receipts, or "Sales" if you want to execute tests before sales shipping), the item (with the options "Table"/ "Group"/ "All"), and the *Test group* (on the tab *Specifications*). The fields *Event type* and *Execution* on the tab *Process* determine the trigger for quality order generation. If you want to assign items at group level, you have to set up quality groups (*Inventory management> Setup> Quality control> Quality groups*) and – through *Item quality groups* – assign each relevant item to one or more quality groups. On the tab *Conditions* in the quality association, you can restrict the association to vendors, customers, or other applicable characteristics.

7.4.7.2 Processing Quality Orders

If you want to create a quality order manually, open the menu item *Inventory management> Periodic tasks> Quality management> Quality orders* and click the button *New* in the action pane. After selecting the *Reference type* (default "Inventory") and further reference data as applicable, enter *Item number*, *Test group*, *Quantity* and required inventory dimensions in the *Create* dialog. The quality order header then shows in the upper pane of the form, the tests as specified in the test group show in the lower pane. The tested quantity is blocked through inventory blocking.

After performing a test, click the button *Results* in the toolbar of the lower pane and enter the result (*Outcome* for the test type "Option", otherwise the *Test result* value) with the *Result quantity* in one or more lines. Depending on the results and the *Acceptable quality level* specified on the tab *Test* of the quality order, the column *Test result* in the lower pane of the quality order shows whether the test is passed or not. Once the last test is finished, click the button *Validate* in the action pane of the quality order. Depending on the results, the column *Status* in the quality order header then shows "Pass" or "Fail". Inventory blocking is removed and the quantity is available again (in case the test is non-destructive).

In order to further block the quantity in case of a failed test, you can select to generate a related quarantine order when validating the quality order.

Automatic quality order generation applies, if there is an applicable quality association when posting an event like a product receipt. The *Item sampling* in the quality association determines the quality order quantity. Depending on the *Full blocking* setting, the complete quantity or only the quality order quantity is blocked. Processing the quality order then works similar to a manual quality order.

7.4.8   Case Study Exercises

Exercise 7.8 – Journal Transaction

In the main warehouse, you find 100 units of the item I-## (created in exercise 3.5). Post an appropriate transaction in an inventory adjustment journal.

Exercise 7.9 – Transfer Journal

You want to transfer the quantity received in exercise 7.8 to another warehouse. Register an appropriate inventory transfer journal and post it. After posting, check the transactions and the quantity of your item in the selected warehouse.

Exercise 7.10 – Inventory Counting

You want to execute inventory counting for the item I-## (created in exercise 3.5) in the main warehouse. The counted quantity is 51 units. You can create a counting journal line either registering it manually, or generating it automatically with a filter on your item and the main warehouse. After entering the counted quantity, post the journal and check the quantity on hand.

Exercise 7.11 – Transfer Order

You want to move 60 units of the item, which you have transferred in exercise 7.9, back to the main warehouse by processing a transfer order. Before entering the transfer order, make sure a transit warehouse is assigned to the warehouse from where the item ships. Then register an appropriate transfer order and post the shipment. After posting, check the inventory transactions and the inventory quantity of your item in all warehouses. Finally, receive the item transfer in the main warehouse.

Exercise 7.12 – Manual Quarantine

Because of reported quality issues, you want to block the quantity you have transferred in exercise 7.11. Enter a manual quarantine order, choosing an appropriate quarantine warehouse. Check the quantity on hand of your item and start the quarantine order. After making sure that there is no problem with the item, end the quarantine and check the inventory quantity before and after ending.

Exercise 7.13 – Manual Quality Order

In order to prevent further quality issues, you want to set up and perform quality tests. Create a new test for measuring the length of an item in centimeters (including decimals). Then create a test group which only includes this test. The standard length is 100 cm with a tolerance of 10 percent above and below.

Enter and process a quality order applying this test to 10 units of the item I-## (from exercise 3.5) in the main warehouse. The length of all tested items is 105 cm.

8 Warehouse and Transportation Management

Depending on the particular requirements, you may need to manage pallets and to track detailed transactions within the warehouse. In Dynamics AX, the advanced warehouse management provides the necessary functionality for this purpose.

Transportation management supports managing carriers and external transports. It is linked to the advanced warehouse management, but can be used independently.

8.1 Advanced Warehouse Management

The advanced warehouse management (WHS) in Dynamics AX, which provides the option to register transactions through mobile devices on a HTML-based portal, is an enhancement of the basic warehouse functionality. Compared to the basic warehouse management, the advanced warehouse management adds following features:

➢ **Mobile device support** – HTML-based portal for small-screen devices
➢ **Detailed tracking** – Full visibility by generating regular inventory transactions
➢ **Flexible setup** – Through location directives and work templates
➢ **Picking waves** – Combining warehouse work for shipments
➢ **Simplified reservation** – Through reservation hierarchies
➢ **Inventory status** – Storage dimension for the status of units (e.g. damaged)
➢ **License plate** – Storage dimension for handling units (e.g. pallets)

Transactions covered by the advanced warehouse management are inventory registration in purchasing, picking in sales, and comparable transactions in production and transfer orders. In inventory, these transactions are preliminary steps before posting the physical transaction (e.g. product receipt, packing slip).

8.1.1 Core Setup for Warehouse Management

Before you can start to execute advanced warehouse management processes, you have to complete the specific warehouse management setup in addition to the setup for inventory management.

Advanced warehouse management only applies if both conditions are met: The item has a storage dimension group enabling advanced warehouse management processes, and the warehouse is enabled for advanced warehouse management processes.

8.1.1.1 Parameters and Mobile Devices Portal Installation

In order to use mobile devices, the mobile devices portal has to be installed. After downloading the stand-alone installer through the menu item *Warehouse management> Setup> Mobile device> Download Warehouse Mobile Devices Portal,* you can install and configure the mobile devices portal locally with a connection to the cloud-based Dynamics AX system.

If the mobile devices portal is not installed, you can simulate the portal and execute warehouse transactions using the form *WHSWorkExecute*. You can access this form through the web address *https://XX.com/?f=WHSWorkExecute&cmp=YY* (XX.com = Dynamics AX URL, YY = Company), in this case signing in with a Dynamics AX user before you can access the login form for the warehouse user.

The warehouse management parameters (*Warehouse management> Setup> Warehouse management parameters*) contain basic settings for the warehouse management module, including the number sequences in warehouse management.

8.1.1.2 Inventory Status

The storage dimension "Inventory status" indicates the status or condition of inventory – for example good, damaged, or used. It only applies to items with a storage dimension group which has the advanced warehouse management processes enabled. In warehouses, which have the advanced warehouse management processes enabled, the inventory status is also used to block inventory (quarantine management is not available for these warehouses).

Create at least one status for available inventory in the inventory status form (*Warehouse management> Setup> Inventory> Inventory statuses*). This status is required even if there is no need to block inventory through the inventory status. Optionally you can set up further status values. The checkbox *Inventory blocking* in the inventory status form controls whether a status blocks inventory.

The default for the inventory status of transactions can be specified at multiple levels: At company level (warehouse management parameters), at site level (site form), at warehouse level (warehouse form), and in the default item status form (*Warehouse management> Setup> Inventory> Default item status*).

Blocking through the inventory status applies the regular blocking feature in inventory (see section 7.4.6). Section 8.1.4 describes how to change the inventory status for blocking or unblocking an item.

8.1.1.3 Warehouse-Related Settings

In order to set up a warehouse applying advanced warehouse management, following configuration is required:

➤ **Location formats** – Specify the structure of location IDs
➤ **Location types** – Indicate the purpose of a location
➤ **Location profiles** – Control available options in a location
➤ **Warehouses, locations** – Show the physical structure of the warehouses

Location formats provide a flexible setup for the structure of location IDs. Since it is a required setup, create at least one format with its segments in the location formats (*Warehouse management> Setup> Warehouse> Location formats*).

Location types (*Warehouse management> Setup> Warehouse> Location types*) are used for filtering and grouping purposes. You have to create at least one location type for shipping and – if you use staging – one location type for staging. After setting up the location types, enter the location type for staging and the location type for shipping in the warehouse management parameters. Putting an item to the shipping location is the last step in processing a picking wave (see section 8.1.2), setting the status of the inventory transaction to "Picked".

Location profiles (*Warehouse management> Setup> Warehouse> Location profiles*) group locations with common characteristics, for example determining location format, license-plate tracking, mixed items, mixed inventory status, and cycle counting. On the tab *Dimensions*, you can specify the capacity of the locations in terms of weight and physical dimensions (depth, width, height). The location capacity and the required storage capacity (weight, volume) of released products are a basis for calculating if there is capacity left for storing a product on a location.

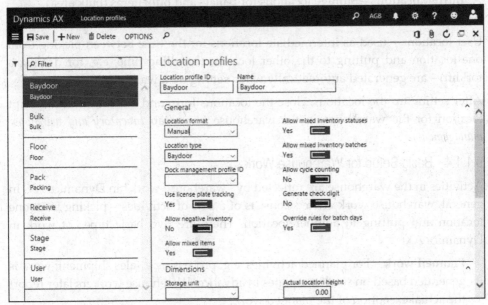

Figure 8-1:   Setting up a location profile

When setting up a location profile, select the appropriate *Location format*. In location profiles for regular locations, the slider *Allow cycle counting* should be set to "Yes" to make counting possible. In the location profiles for shipping and for staging locations, select the proper *Location type* for shipping or for staging. After creating a location profile for user locations, you have to assign it in the warehouse management parameters (tab *General*).

Warehouses (*Warehouse management> Setup> Warehouse> Warehouses*) have to be entered as described in section 7.4.1. In addition to the general settings, the tab *Warehouse management* contains settings for advanced warehouse management. If you want to create a warehouse applying advanced warehouse management, insert a new record in the warehouse form and set the slider *Use warehouse management processes* immediately to "Yes". In order to access the warehouse locations, click the button *WAREHOUSE/View/Inventory locations* in the warehouse.

In the locations form, optionally click the button *Location setup wizard* which provides a convenient way to set up multiple locations. For each location, the assigned location profile controls the characteristics of the location (e.g. the location ID format, the location type, or settings whether to allow different items in one location).

In a typical warehouse, you can find at least following types of locations:

> **Receiving location** – Intermediate location for purchase receipts
> **Shipping location** – Intermediate location for sales shipping (bay door)
> **Staging location** – Intermediate location for preparing shipments
> **Buffer locations** – Storage locations for pallets and bulk items (bulk area)
> **Floor locations** – Storage locations for single items (picking area)

User locations – used as intermediate locations for the time between picking from one location and putting to the other location (handling time, e.g. for driving a forklift) – are generated automatically when setting up a warehouse user.

After setting up the locations, close the locations form and select a default receipt location for the warehouse in the warehouse form (tab *Inventory and warehouse management*).

8.1.1.4 Basic Setup for Warehouse Work

Activities in the warehouse are reflected by "warehouse work" in Dynamics AX. In general, warehouse work always consists of a pair of activities – picking from one location and putting to another location. There are two basic types of work in Dynamics AX:

> **Planned work** – For planned activities, e.g. processing a sales shipment, work is generated based on work templates in advance. Warehouse workers later report the actual execution of the planned work.
> **Unplanned work** – Unplanned work, e.g. a manual quantity adjustment, is at the same time created and reported when executing such an activity.

Unplanned work does not require a specific setup. For planned work, following setup is necessary:

> **Work classes** – Group and to characterize work
> **Work templates** – Determine what to do (e.g. "Pick" or "Put")
> **Location directives** – Determine where to pick or put (e.g. location "01-001")

Work classes (*Warehouse management> Setup> Work> Work classes*) for planned work represent the different types of work which are processed on mobile devices. In mobile device menu items, the work class determines which work you can execute through the particular menu item. In work templates for planned work, the work class is a mandatory field which links the work template to one or more mobile device menu items.

Work templates (*Warehouse management> Setup> Work> Work templates*) are grouped by source document type ("Work order type"). If you want to edit the work templates related to a particular source document type, e.g. "Purchase orders", select the appropriate option in the lookup field *Work order type*. In the work template lines, enter one line with the *Work type* "Pick" and a second line with the *Work type* "Put". If required, you can enter additional lines – for example with the *Work type* "Print". The button *Edit query* provides access to filtering criteria which control the selection of a work template when automatically creating warehouse work. Since Dynamics AX searches the appropriate template in the order of the *Sequence number*, templates with more specific criteria should be first in sequence.

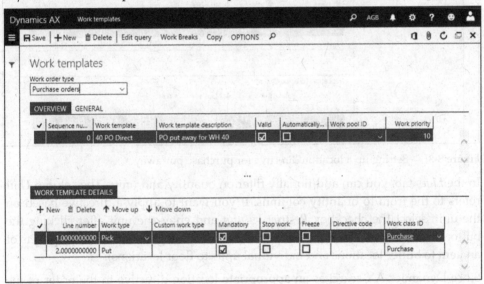

Figure 8-2: Setting up a work template for purchase put-away

Location directives (*Warehouse management> Setup> Location directives*) control the physical place where to execute work per *Work order type*. The location directives for the *Work order type* "Purchase orders" and the *Work type* "Put" for example determine to which location to put an item after receiving a purchase order in the warehouse.

You can set up multiple location directives per work order type (similar to setting up multiple work templates per work order type). After selecting the *Work order type* in the left pane of the location directives form, the tab *Location directives* on the upper right-hand side contains filter criteria on the source document generating warehouse work (e.g. a purchase order line with its warehouse and item). The button *Edit query* in the action pane provides access to filtering criteria based on item details and other relevant data. The *Warehouse* is a mandatory field in the location directive and therefore always applies as a filter.

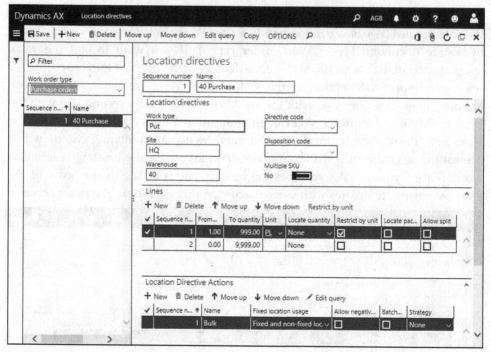

Figure 8-3:   Setting up a location directive for purchase put-away

In the *Lines* tab, you can additionally filter on quantity and units. The column *Unit* refers to the from/to quantity columns. If you want to apply a directive based on the unit, select the checkbox *Restrict by unit* and enter the unit after clicking the button *Restrict by unit* in the toolbar of the tab *Lines* (e.g. for moving full pallets of an item to buffer locations and individual units to floor locations).

Since Dynamics AX searches an appropriate location directive in the order of the *Sequence number*, directives (and directive lines within a directive) with more specific filter criteria should be first in sequence.

The *Location Directive Actions* tab specifies the location or location range to which to put (if the *Work type* selected on the tab *Location directive* is "Put") or from which to pick (if the *Work type* selected on the tab *Location directive* is "Pick"). Enter appropriate filter criteria for this location after clicking the button *Edit query* in the toolbar of this tab. In the filter dialog, you can switch to the tab *Sorting* in order to specify sorting criteria (e.g. referring to the column *Sort code* in the warehouse locations).

If there are products with batch numbers, select the checkbox *Batch enabled* in the location directive action for the work type "Pick" (as additional line if you got some items with and other items without batch control).

8.1.1.5 Basic Setup for Shipments

Load templates (*Warehouse management> Setup> Load> Load templates*) represent the different inbound and outbound transportation units (e.g. different truck sizes or different standard containers). They are based on the different options for the physical dimensions of load. When generating a load for an outbound shipment (see section 8.1.2), the load refers to a load template. In transportation management, loads are the basis for planning and executing transports (see section 8.2.2).

Wave process methods (*Warehouse management> Setup> Waves> Wave process methods*) are predefined steps for wave processing. If the methods are not initialized, click the button *Regenerate methods* for initializing.

Wave templates (*Warehouse management> Setup> Waves> Wave templates*) control the picking work with regard to characteristics like the grouping of work, automated steps, and applicable methods.

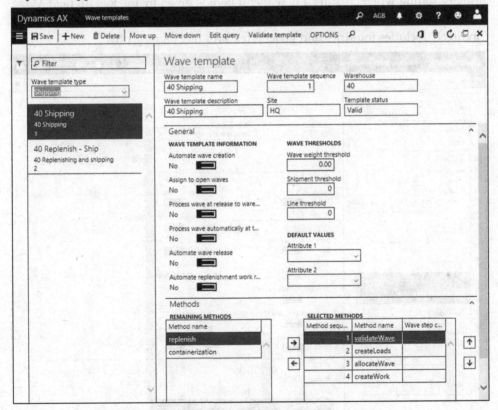

Figure 8-4:   Setting up a wave template for manual wave creation

In wave templates applying automatic wave creation, you can click the button *Edit query* in order to specify filter criteria.

8.1.1.6 Setup for Mobile Devices

In the advanced warehouse management, you can flexibly set up multiple menu structures and menu items according to your requirements. After setting up one or more menus, assign each warehouse worker to the appropriate menu.

The required mobile device setup in Dynamics AX includes the following items:

> ➤ **Mobile device display settings** – Specifying the screen layout
> ➤ **Mobile device menu items** – Determining the forms on mobile devices
> ➤ **Mobile device menus** – Determining menu structures

Mobile device display settings (*Warehouse management> Setup> Mobile device> Mobile device display settings*) define the display settings for mobile devices and refer to a style sheet on the Internet Information Server.

Mobile device menu items (*Warehouse management> Setup> Mobile device> Mobile device menu items*) determine the forms which are available on mobile devices. The primary setting when creating a new menu item is given by the lookup field *Mode*: The mode "Work" refers to warehouse work (executing transactions), the mode "Indirect" includes inquiries and general features like logging off.

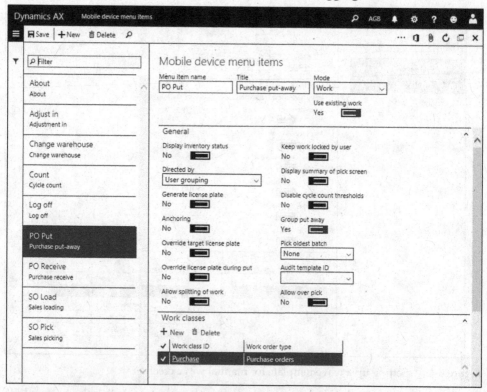

Figure 8-5:   Setting up a mobile device menu item for purchase put-away

For menu items with the mode "Work", the slider *Use existing work* controls if the menu item refers to work previously generated through a work template.

In a menu item for creating work (required to execute unplanned work), set the slider *Use existing work* to "No" and select the applicable work item – e.g. "Adjustment in" – in the field *Work creation process*.

In menu items for existing work (required to execute planned work), set the slider *Use existing work* to "Yes". The lookup field *Directed by* in this case controls whether the system ("System-directed") or the user ("User-directed") chooses which work to execute. For *User-directed* work, the warehouse user has to enter or scan the work ID of the work which he wants to execute, whereas Dynamics AX shows which work to do next in case of *System-directed* work. In case the option "User grouping" or "System grouping" is selected in the field *Directed by*, the worker can register multiple pick-work lines on the mobile device, then press the button *Done*, and finally register one common or multiple separate put-transactions (controlled by slider *Group put away*).

The tab *Work classes* in menu items for existing work determines the work which is available in the particular menu item. If there is for example only one line with a work class "Purchase" in this tab, you can only execute work generated from a work template line with the work class "Purchase" (and not a "Sales" work).

Mobile device menus (*Warehouse management> Setup> Mobile device> Mobile device menu*) control the menu structure of the mobile device menu items. You can set up multiple menus and submenus.

8.1.1.7 Work User Settings

The workers using mobile devices are workers in the human resources module. In order to set up a new worker, open the form *Human resources> Workers> Workers* and create a new record (see section 10.2.2).

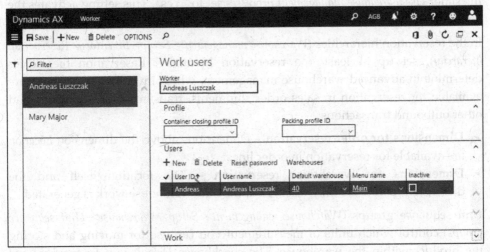

Figure 8-6:   Setting up a warehouse worker

Based on the worker record in human resources, you can create the company-specific warehouse workers in the form *Warehouse management> Setup> Worker*. For each worker, you can enter one or more work users on the tab *Users*. User ID and password for the work users are used for logging on to the mobile device.

Multiple work users for one worker provide the option to display different menus for one worker depending on the warehouse. If a work user may switch between warehouses, click the button *Warehouses* in the toolbar of the tab *Users* and enter applicable warehouses.

Creating a work user automatically creates a related location which is used as intermediate location while executing warehouse work.

Note: If you do not want to set up warehouse workers as workers in human resources, you can create one "dummy" worker in human resources and enter multiple warehouse workers related to this "dummy" worker record.

8.1.1.8   Product-Related Settings

Related to products, following setup is required for using the advanced warehouse management functionality:

➢ **Storage dimension groups** – Enable advanced warehouse management
➢ **Reservation hierarchies** – Control the inventory dimensions for reservation
➢ **Unit sequence groups** – Control the available units of measurement

The storage dimension group as core setting controls whether the advanced warehouse management functionality applies to a released product. In the storage dimension groups (*Product information management> Setup> Dimension and variant groups> Storage dimension groups*), set up at least one storage dimension group with the slider *Use warehouse management processes* set to "Yes". This setting activates the inventory dimensions *Inventory status* and *License plate*.

In the reservation hierarchies (*Warehouse management> Setup> Inventory> Reservation hierarchy*), set up at least one reservation hierarchy. Reservation hierarchies determine in advanced warehouse management, which inventory dimensions are available for reservation in sales order shipments, transfer order shipments, and other outbound transactions:

➢ **Dimensions for order reservation** – Dimensions above the dimension *Location* are available for reservation in order lines
➢ **Dimensions for warehouse reservation** – The location itself and the dimensions below are only reserved at the time warehouse work is generated

Unit sequence groups (*Warehouse management> Setup> Warehouse> Unit sequence groups*) control which units of measurement you can use for moving and storing the product within the warehouse. The checkboxes *Default unit for purchase and transfer* and *Default unit for production* in the unit sequence group determine which unit applies as default for receiving assigned items (e.g. pallets for purchase receipts). The checkbox *License plate grouping* controls whether Dynamics AX generates a separate license plate per unit (e.g. pallet), or one license plate for the whole quantity in the selected unit, when receiving an item (grouping also requires selecting the checkbox *LP grouping* in the applicable mobile device menu item).

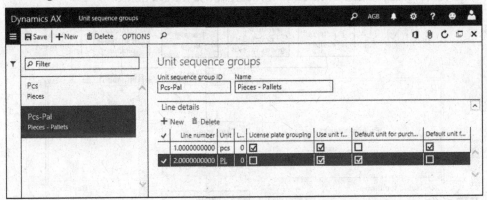

Figure 8-7:   Setting up a unit sequence group with pieces and pallets

When creating a released product (*Product information management> Products> Released products*) for advanced warehouse management, you have to select an appropriate storage dimension group (for advanced warehouse management), a reservation hierarchy, and a unit sequence group in addition to the general settings as described in section 7.2. Apart from the weight and physical dimensions (depth, width, height) on the tab *Manage inventory*, you can enter the dimensions for the different warehouse units of an item (specified in the unit sequence group) after clicking the button *MANAGE INVENTORY/Warehouse/Physical dimensions* in the action pane of the released product. Weight and physical dimensions can be used to calculate the utilization of location capacity and transportation loads.

In order to assign a reservation hierarchy to an item, click the button *PRODUCT/ Set up/Reservation hierarchy* in the action pane of the released product. The inventory dimensions in the reservation hierarchy have to match the active dimensions in the dimension groups of the item.

The *Unit sequence group* of an item is specified on the tab *Warehouse* of the released product form. Depending on the units in the selected unit sequence group, enter appropriate unit conversions for the item.

8.1.1.9   New in Dynamics 'AX 7'

As a result of the cloud-based architecture, a stand-alone installer for the portal replaces the setup option in the Dynamics AX installation process.

8.1.2   Basic Warehouse Processes

Core warehouse transactions include inbound processes – e.g. purchase order receipts, transfer order receipts, or finished goods receipts in production – and outbound processes – e.g. sales order shipments, transfer order shipments, or raw material picking in production.

The figure below gives an overview of the warehouse layout and the structure of warehouse work, which is the basis for warehouse transactions.

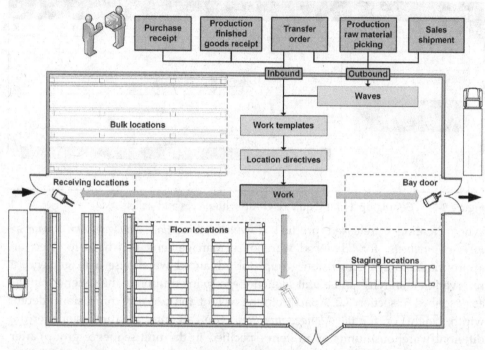

Figure 8-8:   Warehouse layout and the structure of warehouse work

In the overall order process, the mobile device transactions are another way for recording the inventory registration in purchasing (see section 3.5.3), the picking list in sales (see section 4.5.2), and comparable transactions in production orders and transfer orders.

8.1.2.1 Purchase Order Receipt

Starting point for a purchase order receipt in the warehouse is a purchase order line with a product and a warehouse which both are enabled for advanced warehouse management. The basic receipt process then includes following steps:

➤ **Initial receipt** – Receive the item in the default receipt location
➤ **Put away** – Move the item from the receipt location to the final location
➤ **Product receipt** – Post the product receipt in the Dynamics AX client

Section 8.1.3 describes further options for purchase receipts on the mobile device.

The initial receipt of a purchased item is not based on work created upfront, but "unplanned work" generated when posting the receipt. Applicable mobile device menu items show the setting *Mode* "Work", *Use existing work* "No", *Work creation process* "Purchase order line receiving" (or "Purchase order item receiving").

In order to register the initial warehouse receipt on the mobile device, open the applicable menu item in the warehouse portal and enter or scan the purchase order number and the line number (or the item number). The default *Unit* for the receipt is specified in the unit sequence group, but you can select other units specified in the unit sequence group and split the quantity. Depending on mobile device menu item settings (slider *Generate license plate*), the license plate for identifying the handling unit (e.g. a pallet, a box, or an individual piece) has to be entered/scanned manually in the field *LP* (from a pre-printed tag) or is generated from a number sequence (which requires to print the tag when receiving). Dynamics AX then receives the item on the default receipt location of the warehouse.

Posting the initial receipt generates warehouse work for executing the second step, the put-away work (picking the item from the receipt location and putting to the final bulk or floor location). Dynamics AX creates this work based on the applicable work template and related location directives in pairs of two or more pick/put steps (work lines), which are to be processed on a mobile device. You can view this work in the list page *Warehouse management> Work> All work*.

In order to register the put-away work on the mobile device, open an appropriate menu item on the mobile device (with the setting *Use existing work* "Yes", including the *Work class* specified in the applicable work template for purchase orders). Depending on the setting in the field *Directed by* of the menu item, Dynamics AX shows the next work ("System-directed") or you have to enter/scan the work ID or license plate ("User-directed") identifying the put-away work. After picking from the receipt location, Dynamics AX shows the put location (based on the location directive). Depending on work user settings, you can override the put-location.

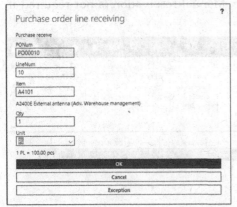

Figure 8-9:   Registering the initial receipt and the put transaction on the mobile device

After finishing the registration of the inbound transactions on the mobile device, the next step is posting the product receipt in the Dynamics AX client (see section 3.5.4). Whereas inventory registration (including mobile device transactions) does not require a purchase order confirmation, the order has to be confirmed before posting the product receipt.

When posting the product receipt in the purchase order or the summary update dialog, select the option "Registered quantity" (or "Registered quantity and services") in the lookup *Quantity* of the posting dialog to make sure that the product receipt refers to the quantity registered on the mobile device. In case the product receipt refers to an inbound load (see section 8.2.2), you can also use the load planning workbench or the load form (*Warehouse management> Loads> All loads*, button *SHIP AND RECEIVE/Receive/Product receipt*) to start posting the product receipt.

8.1.2.2 Sales Order Shipment

Starting point for a sales order shipment in the warehouse is a sales order line with a product and a warehouse which both are enabled for advanced warehouse management. The basic shipment process then includes the following steps:

> **Reservation** – Reserve the item before shipment
> **Shipment** – Create the shipment and include the item
> **Load** – Create a load for external transportation (before or after the shipment)
> **Wave** – Create and release a picking wave with the shipment
> **Warehouse work** – Execute the picking work on the mobile device
> **Confirm shipment** – Close the shipment
> **Packing slip** – Post the packing slip in the Dynamics AX client

Before you can start processing a shipment in the advanced warehouse management, you have to make sure that the item is reserved. Reservation in the warehouse management applies reservation hierarchies. In order to manually reserve an item, open the item reservation form by clicking the button *Inventory/Reservation* in the sales order line. Manual reservation is not required if automatic reservation applies.

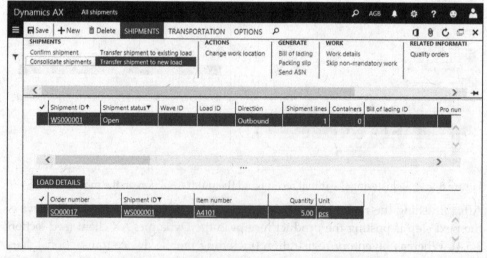

Figure 8-10: Creating a load in the shipment form

Shipments (*Warehouse management> Shipments> All shipments*) represent separate deliveries. If you want to ship a complete sales order, you can create the shipment by clicking the button *WAREHOUSE/Actions/Release to warehouse* in the sales order form. Alternatively, you can create shipments automatically through the batch job *Warehouse management> Release to warehouse> Automatic release of sales orders*. This batch job applies related settings in the accounts receivable parameters (tab *Warehouse management*) and in the customer form as minimum criteria for releasing. After creating the shipment, the order header shows the status "Released" (column *Release status* in the sales order list page).

If there is a load already before the shipment (e.g. for transportation planning purposes), you have to generate the shipment from the load in the load planning workbench (see section 8.2.2).

A load (*Warehouse management> Loads> All loads*) represents an inbound or outbound transportation unit (e.g. a truck). One load contains one or more shipments. One sales order line can be split into multiple shipments and loads, for example if the transportation unit is too small to cover the complete order line quantity. In this case, reduce the quantity when creating the first load and then create a second load.

You can create the load before creating the shipment (in the load planning workbench), or after creating the shipment (in the shipment form), or skip manually creating the load. If you want to create a load from the shipment, click the button *SHIPMENTS/Shipments/Transfer shipment to new load* in the shipment form. If you want to ship multiple orders together, add them to one common load (button *Transfer the shipment to an existing load*). If the load is not created before processing the wave, it is generated automatically at this step. Depending on warehouse management parameter settings, loads are already created automatically at order entry.

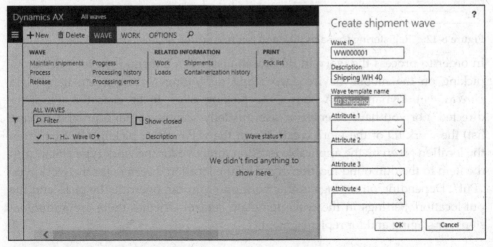

Figure 8-11:   Manually creating a wave

A wave (*Warehouse management> Outbound waves> Shipment waves> All waves*) is a group of shipments to be processed together in the warehouse. Depending on settings in the *Wave template*, waves are created and processed automatically. If automatic wave processing applies, settings in the warehouse management parameters determine whether wave processing runs online or in a batch job.

In order to create a wave manually, click the button *New* in the wave form and select a wave template in the *Create* dialog. Then add one or more shipments in the *Maintain shipments* form, which you can access by clicking the button *WAVE/Wave/ Maintain shipments* in the wave.

Alternatively, create a wave in the workspace *Outbound work planning* by selecting the shipment in the tabbed list pane and clicking the button *Add to new wave* in the toolbar of the list.

The next step is to process the wave by clicking the button *WAVE/Wave/Process* in the wave form. Processing a wave generates the warehouse work. You can view this work by clicking the button *WAVE/Related information/Work* in the action pane of the wave form, or through the menu item *Warehouse management> Work> All work*. At this stage, the wave has the status "Held" and the work is blocked. Before you can actually start executing the warehouse work, you have to release the wave (button *WAVE/Wave/Release* in the wave form).

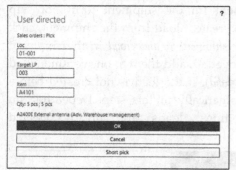 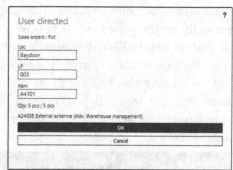

Figure 8-12: Registering the sales pick and put transaction on the mobile device

In order to process the wave in the warehouse, open a menu item for sales order picking on the mobile device. Depending on settings in the menu item (field *Directed by*), Dynamics AX shows the picking work to be executed ("System-directed") or you have to enter or scan (usually scanning from a printed picking list) the work ID of the work created from the wave. After picking the item from the location given by the applicable location directive for the work type "Pick", put the item to the outbound location given by the location directive for the work type "Put". Depending on settings in the work user you can override the pick- and the put-location. Settings in the wave template control whether there are additional steps for staging and for replenishment.

As last step in the outbound warehouse process, confirming closes the shipment and the load. Apart from automatically confirming through appropriate work audit templates, there are following options for manually confirming a shipment:

> **In the shipment form** – Button *SHIPMENTS/Shipments/Confirm shipment* (only available if the load does not contain multiple shipments)
> **In the load form** – Button *SHIP AND RECEIVE/Confirm/Outbound shipment*
> **In the load planning workbench** – Button *Ship and receive/Outbound shipment* on the tab *Loads*

After confirming the shipment, you can post the packing slip by clicking the button *SHIPMENT/Generate/Packing slip* in the shipment form (select the checkbox *Display closed shipments* if the shipment does not show). Alternatively, you can post the packing slip in the load form (button *SHIP AND RECEIVE/Generate/Packing slip*), or in the load planning workbench (button *Generate/Packing slip* in the toolbar on the tab *Loads*), or in the sales order form (see section 4.5.4).

8.1.2.3 New in Dynamics 'AX 7'

Items which are new in processing advanced warehouse management transactions include the workspaces *Outbound work planning* and *Outbound work monitoring*.

8.1.3   Advanced Options for Inbound and Outbound Processes

In addition to the basic process for purchase order receipts and sales order shipments, there are variants of these processes including the option to automatize steps or to apply staging. Transfer orders and production orders are further variants of the inbound and outbound processes.

8.1.3.1 Task Automation

Apart from manually executing activities, there is the option to automatically perform particular tasks. Depending on the setup, Dynamics AX provides following options:

> **Work execution** – Automatically executing warehouse work
> o **Automatically process** – Checkbox in work templates (*Warehouse management> Setup> Work> Work templates*) for automatically executing the work when releasing a wave (e.g. for bulk items not tracked in detail)
> o **Work confirmation setup** – Button in the action pane of mobile device menu items (*Warehouse management> Setup> Mobile device> Mobile device menu items*), providing the option to *Auto confirm* the *Work type* "Put" for example (you only need to register the pick work on the mobile device in this case)
> **Picking process** – Automatically creating/releasing shipments/loads/waves
> o **Release to warehouse** – Automatically creating shipments through the batch job *Warehouse management> Release to warehouse> Automatic release of sales orders* (applies customer and accounts receivable parameter settings)

o **Automate wave creation** – Slider in the wave template (*Warehouse management> Setup> Waves> Wave templates*), controlling automatic wave creation when releasing to warehouse

o **Automatically process waves** – Sliders in the wave template for processing the wave when releasing to warehouse or when reaching the threshold in the wave template (in batch or online, depending on warehouse parameters)

o **Automate wave release** – Slider in the wave template for releasing waves

o **Automatically create loads** – Setting in the warehouse parameters; In addition, loads are always created automatically when processing a wave if there is no load

General options for automatic reservation when entering a sales order line (see section 7.4.5) also apply to the advanced warehouse management. In addition, the tab *Warehouse* in the warehouse form contains the sliders *Reserve inventory at load posting* (reserving when releasing to warehouse from the load planning workbench) and *Reserve when orders are released by a batch job* (reserving when running the *Release to warehouse* batch job mentioned above) providing further options for automatic reservation in the advanced warehouse management.

Work audit templates (*Warehouse management> Setup> Work> Work audit template*) provide the option to assign additional actions to a mobile device menu item. You can for example create an audit template with a line (on the tab *Lines*) containing the *Function* "Event" and the *Event* "Shipping confirmed" and select this audit template in an applicable mobile device menu item, if you want to automatically confirm the shipment after executing the warehouse work for sales picking. Other features in the audit template lines include the option to display and print data.

8.1.3.2 Options for Purchase Receipts

The advanced warehouse management in Dynamics AX supports following options for purchase order receipts:

➢ **Two-step order receipt** – Receiving with reference to the purchase order number and separately putting away (described in section 8.1.2)

➢ **Load item receipt** – Receiving with reference to the load (instead of the order)

➢ **One-step receipt** – Receiving and putting away in one step

A load item receipt is based on an inbound load, which includes one or more purchase orders. As a prerequisite for load item receipts, you have to set up a mobile device menu item with the *Work creation process* "Load item receiving". After entering a purchase order and creating a related load in the load planning workbench (see section 8.2.2), you can execute the receipt selecting the *Load ID* instead of the purchase order number on the mobile device. Receiving generates put away work, which is to be executed like purchase order receipts.

Apart from the two-step receipt, which preliminarily receives the items on the default receipt location, you can execute a one-step receipt immediately moving the items to the final location. As a prerequisite for one-step receipts, you have to create a mobile device menu item with the *Work creation process* "Purchase order item receiving and put away", or "Purchase order line receiving and put away", or "Load item receiving and put away". Using one of these menu items, receiving and putting away is done in one common transaction.

8.1.3.3 Directive Codes

When generating warehouse work, Dynamics AX independently searches for the appropriate work template and location directive. If you want to link a work template with a location directive, you can use directive codes. Following setup is required for this purpose:

> **Directive code** – Create a code (*Warehouse management> Setup> Directive codes*)
> **Work template** – Select the *Directive code* in applicable work template lines (only in "Put" work template lines of outbound processes)
> **Location directive** – Select the directive code in location directives as needed

When creating work based on a work template with an assigned directive code, Dynamics AX does not independently search the location directive but applies the location directive with the same directive code.

8.1.3.4 Staging

Staging is used to collect and prepare picked items on a special location for staging before loading (e.g. a truck).

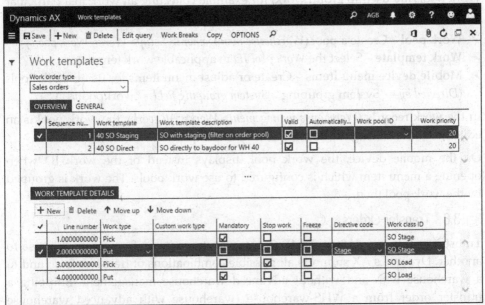

Figure 8-13: Work template for staging (without a directive code for the final put work)

In addition to the basic setup for sales order shipments, following setup is required if you want to use staging:

> **Directive code** – Additional directive code for staging
> **Work template** – Contains work lines for staging and for loading
> **Location directive** – Location directive to put to the staging location
> **Mobile device menu items** – Contain the *Work class* of the work template lines

In order to link the "Put" work template line for staging with the related location directive, enter a directive code in this work template line. Then set up a particular location directive (with this directive code) for putting to the staging location. If there is no general default location directive for putting to the final shipping location which you can use also after staging, you have to set up a separate directive code and location directive for this final put work.

In a similar way to the sales order picking process without staging, you can execute the outbound process if you use staging. Create the shipment, the load, and the wave, and release the wave (applying the work template for staging).

The work created from the wave includes four steps in case of staging: Picking from the original location, putting to the staging location, picking from the staging location, and putting to the final shipping location. On the mobile device, the warehouse work for staging (pick and then put to the staging location) and for loading (pick and then put to the final shipping location) has to be registered in separate steps.

8.1.3.5 Work Pools

Work pools are used to group work, for example collecting all work in a particular warehouse zone. In order to use work pools, following setup is required:

> **Work pool** – Create a pool (*Warehouse management> Setup> Work> Work pools*)
> **Work template** – Select the *Work pool ID* in applicable work templates
> **Mobile device menu items** – Create or adjust menu items for using work pools (*Directed by* = "System grouping", *System grouping field* = "workpoolid")

In the work records (*Warehouse management> Work> All work*), the work pool is an editable field receiving the default from work template.

On the mobile device, the work pool displays instead of the work ID when opening a menu item which is configured to use work pools. The work is grouped by the work pool then.

8.1.3.6 Transfer Orders

Transfer orders (see section 7.4.4) are used to move items from on warehouse to another. Dynamics AX supports all possible combinations of transfers from and to a warehouse with and without advanced warehouse management. Shipping a transfer order from a WHS-warehouse (warehouse with advanced warehouse management) works similar to shipping a sales order, and receiving a transfer order on a WHS-warehouse works similar to receiving a purchase order.

As a prerequisite for processing transfer orders in a shipping or receiving warehouse with advanced warehouse management, following setup is required (similar to the setup for purchase order receipts and sales order shipments):

➤ **Item, warehouse(s)** – Enabled for advanced warehouse management (a transfer between two WHS-warehouses requires a WHS-enabled transit warehouse)

➤ **Work classes, work templates, location directives** – For the work order types "Transfer issue" and "Transfer receipt"

➤ **Mobile device menu items**
  o **For transfer issue** – *Use existing work* = "Yes", work class for transfer issue
  o **For transfer receipt** – *Use existing work* = "No", *Work creation process* = "License plate receiving" or "License plate receiving and put away" (or "Transfer order line receiving" if the from-warehouse is not WHS-enabled)
  o **For transfer receipt put-away** – *Use existing work* = "Yes", work class for transfer receipt (only required for two-step receipts)

➤ **Wave template** – Only if you don't want to use the template for sales shipments

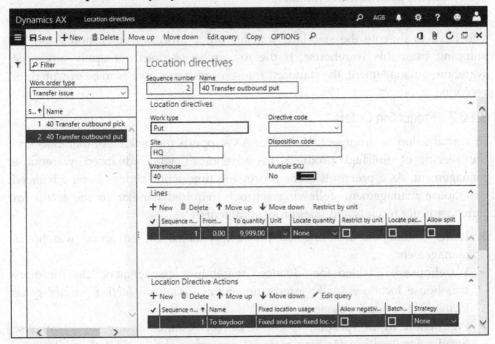

Figure 8-14:   Location directive for transfer issues ("Put" work to the shipping location)

In order to use the advanced warehouse management in transfer processing, create a transfer order (*Inventory management> Inbound orders> Transfer order*) which ships from and/or to a warehouse with advanced warehouse management.

If the from-warehouse is WHS-enabled, the first step is to reserve the item (automatically or manually). Then create a shipment (similar to sales order shipments) by releasing the transfer order manually or automatically to the warehouse, e.g. by clicking the button *SHIP/Operations/Release to warehouse* in the transfer order form. Then create the load and the wave, assign the transfer order, process the wave, and release the wave (depending on settings in the wave template, the steps are executed automatically or manually). On the mobile device, you can execute the picking work including putting to the final shipping location in the from-warehouse afterwards.

Confirming the shipment then posts a transfer to the transit warehouse.

In order to receive the item in the to-warehouse, make sure the warehouse worker is signed in to the appropriate warehouse in the warehouse portal and execute the receipt work on the mobile device similar to receiving a purchase order. When receiving a transfer from a WHS-enabled warehouse, you have to use a menu item for "License plate receiving" requiring to enter/scan the license plate(s) assigned to the item in the prior shipping process. If the from-warehouse is not WHS-enabled, you have to use a menu item for "Transfer order line receiving" requiring to enter/scan the transfer order number.

In case the from-warehouse does not apply advanced warehouse management, you have to execute the standard transfer order process (see section 7.4.4) for shipping from this warehouse. If the to-warehouse does not apply advanced warehouse management, the standard transfer order process has to be executed for receiving.

8.1.3.7 Production Orders

In a production environment, Dynamics AX supports the picking of materials and the receipt of finished products in warehouses with advanced warehouse management. As a prerequisite for processing production orders using advanced warehouse management, following setup is required (similar to the setup for purchase order receipts and sales order shipments):

➤ **Items** – Materials and finished products enabled for advanced warehouse management
➤ **Warehouse** – Enabled for advanced warehouse management; One or more warehouse locations in the production area; *Default production finished goods location* in the warehouse form
➤ **Production input location** – On resource, resource group, or warehouse (production location for raw material consumption, thus "Put" location for warehouse work)
➤ **Work classes, work templates, location directives** – For the work order types "Raw material picking" and "Finished goods put away"
➤ **Wave template** – Separately from sales shipment templates, select "Production orders" in the left pane of the wave template form

> **Mobile device menu items**
>   o **For materials** – *Use existing work* = "Yes", work class for raw material picking
>   o **For finished product receipt** – *Use existing work* = "No", *Work creation process* = "Report as finished" (or "Report as finished and put away")
>   o **For finished product put-away** – *Use existing work* = "Yes", work class for finished product receipt (only required for two-step receipts)

In order to use the advanced warehouse management in manufacturing, create and process a production order (*Production control> Production Orders> All production orders*) as described in section 5.4.2. Depending on settings for automatic reservation (field *Reservation* on the tab *Setup* of the production order detail form), you may have to reserve the raw materials manually after estimation or releasing.

Once the production order is released, create a production wave (*Warehouse management> Outbound waves> Production waves> All waves*), assign the production order (button *Maintain productions*), process the wave, and release the wave (depending on settings in the production wave template, the steps are executed automatically or manually). Processing the wave creates warehouse work for raw material picking, which you can view by clicking the button *WAVE/Related information/Work* in the action pane of the wave form.

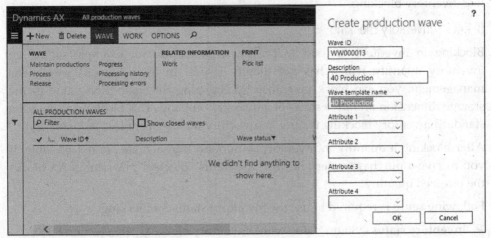

Figure 8-15: Manually creating a production wave

On the mobile device, you can execute the warehouse work then. After putting the item to the production input location, the material is immediately consumed (inventory status "Picked") or only reserved (inventory status "Reserved physical") depending on the setting for the *Issue status after raw material picking* (field on the tab *Inventory and warehouse management* in the warehouse form). In the Dynamics AX client, you can start the production order and post the picking list related to the registered warehouse work afterwards.

In order to receive the finished product, open the menu item for "Report as finished" or "Report as finished and put away" on the mobile device (working similar to a purchase order receipt). The mobile device transaction posts a report as finished journal in production and receives the product on the *Default production finished goods location* of the warehouse (or directly on the final floor or bulk location in case of a one-step receipt). In case of a two-step receipt, the mobile device receipt generates warehouse work for the put-away to the final bulk or floor location to be executed in a separate menu item on the mobile device.

In order to update the production order status to "Reported as finished", click the button *PRODUCTION ORDER/Process/Report as finished* in the action pane of the production order form as usual.

Instead of reporting as finished by receiving the finished product on the mobile device, you can first report a production order as finished in the Dynamics AX client. In this case, reporting as finished in the production order initially receives the item and – based on the work template for "Finished goods put away" – creates warehouse work for the put-away to the final bulk or floor location.

8.1.4   Tasks within the Warehouse

Apart from inbound and outbound transactions, warehouse operations include internal transactions like counting and movements between locations and tasks like inventory blocking.

8.1.4.1   Inventory Blocking

Blocking in inventory is used to prevent transactions, for example selling an inventory quantity which has got quality issues. In the advanced warehouse management, you can block inventory by changing the dimension value in the storage dimension *Inventory status* of a quantity on-hand. This blocking applies the standard inventory blocking feature in inventory management (see section 7.4.6).

After blocking a quantity in inventory, outbound transactions are not possible. If you receive a purchase order line with the status "Blocked", Dynamics AX blocks the received quantity.

Following setup is required to use the inventory status for blocking:

➢ **Inventory status** – Status value with "Inventory blocking" (see section 8.1.1)
➢ **Disposition codes** – Required for changing the status on mobile devices
➢ **Mobile device menu items** – Setting to show the disposition code

Forms for blocking inventory on the mobile device do not directly show the inventory status, but the disposition code. Each disposition code (*Warehouse management> Setup> Mobile device> Disposition codes*) is linked to an inventory status.

If you want to be able to change the inventory status through the disposition code in a separate transaction on the mobile device, create a mobile device menu item with the required settings (*Mode* = "Work", *Use existing work* = "No", and *Work creation process* = "Inventory status change") and include it in the mobile device menu.

If you want to be able to change the status when registering an inbound arrival or a put-away movement, set the slider *Display disposition code* in applicable mobile device menu items to "Yes". If the location selected for the put away of the received items is depending on the disposition code, you can additionally create a location directive with the applicable disposition code.

Changing the inventory status for blocking or unblocking inventory generates an inventory transaction. You can execute inventory status changes on the mobile devices portal or in the Dynamics AX client.

On the mobile device, you have got following options to change the status:

➢ **Separate transaction** – Execute a menu item for "Inventory status change"
➢ **Together with a movement** – Register an arrival or a put-away in an appropriate menu item (*Display disposition code* = "Yes") and select the required code in the *Disposition code* field which displays then.

In the Dynamics AX client, you got following options

➢ **Inventory status change** – Menu item *Warehouse management> Periodic tasks> Inventory status change* with flexible filtering options
➢ **Warehouse status change** – Menu item *Warehouse management> Periodic tasks> Warehouse status change* for blocking/unblocking on warehouse level
➢ **On-hand inquiry** – Button *Inventory status change* in the on-hand inquiry by location (*Warehouse management> Inquiries and reports> On hand by location*)
➢ **Quality order** – Automatically changing the inventory status from a quality order if specified in the test group (*Inventory management> Setup> Quality control> Test groups*, slider *Update inventory status* on the tab *General*)

On a license plate, a mixed inventory status with inventory partly blocked and partly unblocked is not possible. If you want to block a partial quantity of a license plate, move the required quantity to another license plate and block it there. For locations, you can specify in the location profile whether a mixed inventory status is allowed.

8.1.4.2 Movements and Adjustments

Movements and adjustments are manual transaction in inventory. Apart from registering these transactions on a mobile device as shown in this section, you can use regular inventory journals (see section 7.4.2) entering all required inventory dimensions manually.

Movements are used for manual transfers between locations. As a prerequisite for registering movements on a mobile device, set up a mobile device menu item with the required settings (*Mode* = "Work", *Use existing work* = "No", and *Work creation process* = "Movement") and include it in the mobile device menu. On the mobile device, you can execute movements using this menu item afterwards.

You can use location directives to suggest the put location in a movement. In this case, following setup is required:

> **Mobile device menu item for creating work** – *Use existing work* = "No", *Work creation process* = "Movement by template", *Create movement* = "Yes"
> **Work template and location directives** – For the work order type "Inventory movement"
> **Mobile device menu item for executing work** – *Use existing work* = "Yes", work class for inventory movement

Whereas movements are used for transfers, adjustments are used for manually increasing or reducing the quantity on hand. They generate inventory transactions through inventory counting journals. The journal name used for this transaction is specified in the adjustment type (*Warehouse management> Setup> Inventory> Adjustment types*).

Following setup is required for registering adjustments on the mobile device:

> **Adjustment types** – For grouping purposes, specify the inventory journal name
> **Mobile device menu item** – *Use existing work* = "No", *Work creation process* = "Adjustment in" (or "Adjustment out")

In order to record an adjustment on the mobile device, select the menu item for "Adjustment in" or "Adjustment out" and enter the transaction quantity by which you want to change inventory. The quantity is always a positive number, for increasing the inventory quantity select "Adjustment in" and for reducing "Adjustment out".

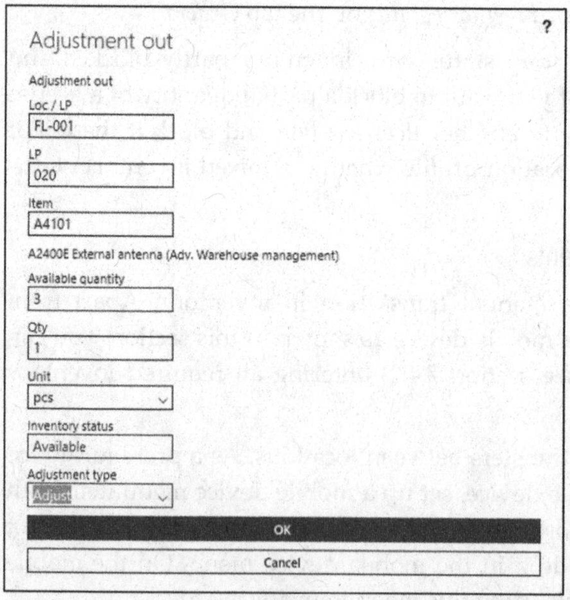

Figure 8-16: Adjustment on the mobile device (reducing the quantity by one piece)

8.1.4.3 Inventory Counting

Counting is used to audit the on-hand quantity of items, generating inventory transactions for discrepancies. The advanced warehouse management supports following strategies for counting:

> **Planned counting** – Periodical counting (e.g. annual stocktaking)
> **Threshold counting** – Counting when inventory reaches the threshold limit
> **Spot counting** – Ad-hoc counting on the mobile device

Following setup is required for executing inventory counting on mobile devices:

> **Location profile** – In the location profile of all locations included in counting, set the slider *Allow cycle counting* to "Yes"
> **Parameters** – Enter a default adjustment type and a default work class on the tab *Cycle counting* in the warehouse management parameters. If the checkbox *Remove reservations* is selected in the settings of the default adjustment type, reservations in sales orders (and other issue transactions) do not block counting.
> **Unit sequence group** – Controls the available units for counting

Planned counting is used to create and execute counting work periodically. In addition to the general setup for counting on the mobile device, following setup is required for planned counting:

> **Mobile device menu item for cycle counting** – *Use existing work* = "Yes", work class for cycle counting; Button *Cycle counting* in the action pane for additional settings (e.g. how often to re-count if there is a discrepancy).
> **Warehouse worker** – In the work user, select if the worker is a supervisor or which counting discrepancy does not require approval.
> **Cycle count plan** – Basis for planned cycle counting, with filter on items and locations (*Warehouse management> Setup> Cycle counting> Cycle count plans*).

In order to execute planned counting, you have to generate counting work first. You can create work based on cycle count plans through the menu item *Warehouse management> Cycle counting> Cycle count scheduling* or by clicking the button *Process cycle counting plan* in the cycle count plan form. If you want to create counting work independently from cycle count plans, choose the periodic activity *Warehouse management> Cycle counting> Cycle count work by location* or *Warehouse management> Cycle counting> Cycle count work by item*.

Once the planned counting work is created, you can execute counting on the mobile device using the menu item which is set up for cycle counting. After entering the quantity (including "0") in all counting units for an item and location, you have to confirm the quantity in case of discrepancies (depending on the settings for the menu item). Depending on settings in the work user, discrepancies between the counted quantity and the current quantity in Dynamics AX are posted immediately to adjust inventory. The work form (*Warehouse management> Work> Warehouse> Cycle count work pending review*) shows discrepancies which are not posted immediately. Click the button *WORK/WORK/Cycle counting* to access the cycle counting review form and click the button *Accept count* there to post the inventory adjustment if applicable.

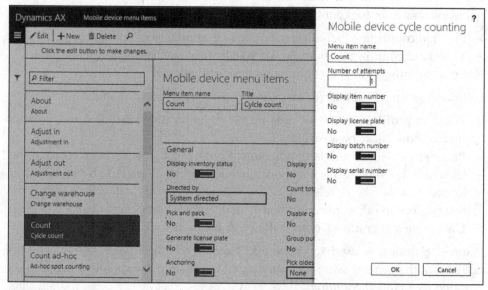

Figure 8-17:   Cycle counting settings in the mobile device menu item

Unlike planned counting, threshold counting is a strategy to execute counting automatically when inventory reaches the threshold limit. As a prerequisite for threshold counting, you have to set up a cycle counting threshold (*Warehouse management> Setup> Cycle counting> Cycle count threshold*). The buttons *Select items* and *Select locations* provide the option to specify filter criteria for the threshold. Registering an outbound transaction on the mobile device (e.g. picking) then triggers threshold counting if the quantity on the location reaches the cycle counting threshold. If the slider *Process cycle counting immediately* in the cycle counting threshold is set to "No", Dynamics AX generates cycle counting work which has to be executed later on the mobile device like regular planned counting work. If this slider is set to "Yes", a counting dialog displays immediately when registering the outbound transaction.

Spot counting is an ad-hoc counting on the mobile device. As a prerequisite for spot counting, create a mobile device menu item with the required settings (*Mode* = "Work", *Use existing work* = "No", and *Work creation process* = "Spot cycle counting"). The button *Cycle counting* in the mobile device menu item provides access to the additional counting parameters. After finishing the setup, you can execute spot counting using the menu item for spot counting (similar to periodic cycle counting, but you are free to choose the location). Posting and resolving discrepancies works like for periodic counting.

8.1.4.4 Replenishment

The target of replenishment within the warehouse is to move required items from buffer locations to picking locations in order to achieve short ways in the picking process. Dynamics AX supports two basic strategies for replenishing locations:

> **Based on minimum/maximum quantities** – Using minimum and maximum stocking limits on location level
> **Based on demand** – Replenishment of missing quantity on picking locations, triggered by the picking process for outbound orders

Minimum/maximum replenishment applies if you want to fill a location to the maximum once the current quantity is below minimum. For using minimum/ maximum replenishment, following setup is required:

> **Replenishment template** – *Replenishment type* "Minimum or maximum", template details lines with the min/max quantity, filter on items and locations (*Warehouse management> Setup> Replenishment> Replenishment templates*)
> **Work template and location directives** – For the work order type "Replenishment"
> **Fixed locations for items** – required if you want to refill empty locations (*Warehouse management> Setup> Warehouse> Fixed locations*)
> **Mobile device menu item for replenishment** – *Use existing work* = "Yes", work class for replenishment

In order to process minimum/maximum replenishment, run the replenishment batch job (*Warehouse management> Replenishment> Replenishments*) which generates the replenishment work. In the warehouse, execute the replenishment on the mobile device using the menu item for replenishment.

Whereas minimum/maximum replenishment refills locations independently from current picking processes, wave demand replenishment applies if you want to refill a location when processing a wave. Replenishment is only created if there is no quantity available on the location selected by the location directive for picking.

If you want to use wave demand replenishment, following setup is required:

> **Replenishment template** – With the *Replenishment type* "Wave demand" and a *Wave step code*
> **Wave template** – With the additional method "replenish" and the wave step code of the replenishment template
> **Work template and location directives for replenishment** – For the work order type "Replenishment" (Match "Put" locations in the replenishment location directive with "Pick" locations in the sales order picking location directive)

➢ **Work template and location directives for picking** – For the work order type "Sales orders" (only if you want settings different from regular picking)

➢ **Mobile device menu item for replenishment** – *Use existing work* = "Yes", work class for replenishment (often the same menu item as for minimum/maximum replenishment)

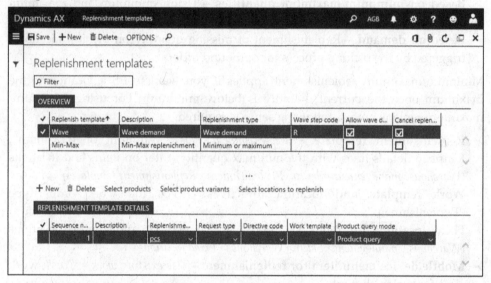

Figure 8-18:   Setting up a wave demand replenishment template

If the wave template for the sales order shipments is set to automatically release waves, set the slider *Automate replenishment work release* in the wave template to "Yes" (replenishment has to be released and executed before sales picking).

In order to execute wave replenishment, create the shipment, the load, and the wave for sales order picking (applying the wave template for replenishment), assign the sales order, process the wave, and release the wave (depending on settings in the wave template, the steps are executed automatically or manually). If no quantity is available on the picking location, a replenishment wave with replenishment work is created when processing the sales order wave. On the mobile device in the warehouse, execute the replenishment work before picking and loading.

Apart from the wave demand replenishment, the load demand replenishment is another type of demand replenishment. The difference between these two types is that wave demand is processed automatically through the wave template whereas load demand replenishment has to be calculated through a batch job.

8.1.4.5 Warehouse Inquiries

You can use inquiries on the mobile devices portal to show the current quantity in inventory. In order to set up an inquiry for mobile devices, create a menu item with the *Mode* "Indirect". In an inquiry on the item quantity for example, select the

Activity code "Item inquiry" in the mobile device menu item. On the mobile device, you can access the inquiry in the appropriate menu item. In case of an item inquiry, enter/scan the item number to view the quantity on the different locations.

In the Dynamics AX client, the on-hand inquiry by location (*Warehouse management> Inquiries and reports> On hand by location*) is one of the main pages for viewing the current inventory in the advanced warehouse management. After selecting a warehouse and refreshing the page, the inquiry shows the locations with the item quantities. The button *Inventory status change* provides the option to change the inventory status.

8.1.5 Case Study Exercises

Exercise 8.1 – Warehouse Setup

In order to investigate the options for warehouse setup, create a new location format L-## (## = your user ID) with two segments: A segment with a length of one digit, followed by the separator "-" and a 3-digit segment.

Then set up a location profile F-## for floor locations and a location profile B-## for bulk locations. Both location profiles refer to the new location format L-## and allow cycle counting, but only floor locations use license plate tracking. Accept the default settings in the other fields of the location profile form.

After the basic setup is done, create a new warehouse WH-## which applies advanced warehouse management processes. This warehouse has got the receiving location "RECV", the shipping location "SHIP", three floor locations ("F-001" to "F-003"), and six bulk locations ("1-001" to "2-003). Floor locations and bulk locations refer to the appropriate location profiles created before. The location "RECV" is the *Default receipt location* in your warehouse.

Exercise 8.2 – Work Template, Location Directive and Wave Template

You want to process the purchase put-away work for your new warehouse WH-## separately. Create a new work class PO-## (## = your user ID) for this purpose.

Then create a new work template for purchase orders, which only refers to your warehouse and this work class. In addition, enter a sales order work template which only applies to your warehouse and only includes one pair of pick and put work (no staging). This work template refers to an existing sales order work class.

In order to use the warehouse in purchasing and sales, related location directives are required. Create a location directive for your warehouse WH-##, which specifies to put purchase order receipts to bulk locations in case of full pallets and to floor locations otherwise. Then enter another location directive for sales picking which should pick full pallets from bulk locations. Other units should be picked from floor locations first, and in second line from bulk locations (if all floor locations are empty). The sales order put location directive should direct to the location "SHIP".

Finally set up a wave template "T-##" for your warehouse WH-## which does not apply any automatic action.

Exercise 8.3 – Mobile Device Menu and Work User

A new mobile device menu for executing warehouse work in the following exercises is required. Create following mobile device menu items for this purpose (select to generate license plates automatically):

➢ Menu item ##-PO-Receive with the *Work creation process* "Purchase order line receiving"

➢ Menu item ##-PO-Put (referring to the work class created in exercise 8.2 and *Directed by* = "User directed") for putting the purchase receipt from the default receipt location to floor or bulk locations

➢ Menu item ##-SO-Direct (referring to the sales order work class selected in exercise 8.2, and *Directed by* = "User grouping") for sales order picking

Then set up a new mobile device menu "##-Main" containing these menu items. In addition, the menu should include a menu item "About" and a menu item for logging off.

In the warehouse worker form, create a new worker record who is linked to any worker employed in the current company. On the tab *Work users* of the warehouse worker form, enter a user with the *User ID* U##. Select the *Menu name* created before and the warehouse WH-## (created in exercise 8.1) for this user.

Exercise 8.4 – Released Product for Advanced Warehouse Management

In order to apply the advanced warehouse management for a product, you need an appropriate storage dimension group, reservation hierarchy, and unit sequence group. You can use an existing storage dimension group, but you want to create a new reservation hierarchy R-##, which does not contain tracking dimensions, and a unit sequence group U-##, which includes pieces and pallets (pallets as default unit for purchasing).

Create an item I-##-W with the name "##-AdvWarehouseMgmt" in the released product form. It is a regular stocked product without variants or batch numbers, but you want to use the advanced warehouse processes. Select an item group which is appropriate for merchandise, and an item model group related to FIFO-valuation. The item does not require approved vendors. The item sales tax groups for sales and for purchasing refers to the standard tax rate. The base purchase price and the base cost price is USD 50. The base sales price is USD 100. The unit of measure for the item is "Pieces" in all areas except purchasing. For purchasing, you want to apply pallets (1 pallet = 10 pieces) as default. Make sure to choose the same units of measurement which you have selected when creating the unit sequence before. Then assign the new item to the unit sequence group U-## and the reservation hierarchy R## created before.

Exercise 8.5 – Advanced Warehouse Management in Purchasing Processes

You want to order 34 units of the item I-##-W (created in exercise 8.4) from any vendor (e.g. the vendor of exercise 3.2) to be received on your warehouse WH-## (created in exercise 8.1). Enter an appropriate purchase order and confirm it. Check the inventory transaction related to the purchase order line afterwards.

Log on to the mobile devices portal using the credentials of the work user U-## (created in exercise 8.3) next. Access the menu item for receiving the purchase order and post the receipt for the complete quantity of your purchase order. Which status do the inventory transactions of your item show? Access the inquiry "On hand by location" in the warehouse management menu, filter on your warehouse WH-## and take a note of the license plate shown for the posted quantity.

Then open the mobile device menu item for the put-away of the purchase receipt. Post the transaction there (refer to the license plate shown in the previous inquiry). Review the inventory transactions and the inquiry "On hand by location" for your warehouse WH-## again. What is different now? Finally post the product receipt for the purchase order based on the mobile device transactions registered before.

Exercise 8.6 – Advanced Warehouse Management in Sales and Distribution

A customer (e.g. your customer of exercise 4.1) orders 12 units of your item I-##-W, which you have purchased in the previous exercise. Enter an appropriate sales order to be shipped from your warehouse WH-##, reserve the quantity, and create the shipment. Which status do the inventory transactions of your item show?

Then create a load for the shipment, and a wave choosing the wave template T-## created in exercise 8.2. Take a note of the *Work ID* generated when processing the wave, and release the wave. Check the inventory transactions of your item. What is different now? Review the inquiry "On hand by location" for your warehouse WH-## and take a note of the license plate shown for the floor location.

In the next step, open the mobile device menu item for sales order picking (logged on as the work user U-## created in exercise 8.3). Post the picking transaction entering the work ID and – if picking from the floor location – the license plate noted before.

Check the inventory transactions and the inquiry "On hand by location" for your warehouse WH-## again. What is different now? Finally, post the packing slip for the sales order based on the mobile device transactions registered before.

8.2 Transportation Management

Transportation management in Dynamics AX is based on the advanced warehouse management. It is primarily used to select external freight carriers for inbound and outbound shipments, and to manage these inbound and outbound shipments.

Based on the load (e.g. a truck load), the origin address, and the destination address, Dynamics AX calculates possible transportation routes with their costs. After creating a route based on the rate calculation (or manually, independent from calculated rates), you can record the agreement as transportation tender. Managing dock appointments for loading the truck and reconciling the freight invoice with the route are additional options in the transportation management.

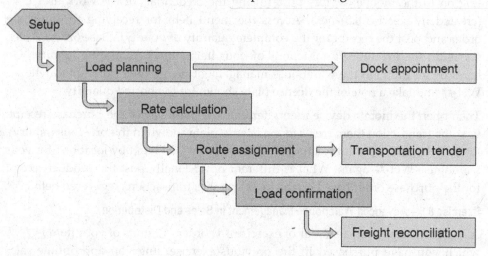

Figure 8-19:   Overview of the transportation management functionality in Dynamics AX

8.2.1   Core Setup for Transportation Management

Before starting to use transportation management processes, you have to complete the setup for transportation management.

8.2.1.1   Transportation Management Parameters

Transportation management parameters (*Transportation management> Setup> Transportation management parameters*) contain basic settings like the number sequences in the transportation management module. The button *Initialize base engine data* in the toolbar of the sub-tab *Engines* on the tab *General* in the parameters provides the option to initialize engine setup data for the available base engines.

8.2.1.2   Transportation Methods and Shipping Carriers

Transportation methods (*Transportation management> Setup> Carriers> Transportation methods*) represent the different kinds of transport. The transportation method is a required field in the shipping carrier service.

In order to set up an active shipping carrier, open the form *Transportation management> Setup> Carriers> Shipping carriers* and insert a carrier with the sliders *Activate shipping carrier* and *Activate carrier rating* set to "Yes". On the tab *Services* in the shipping carrier form, enter the carrier service.

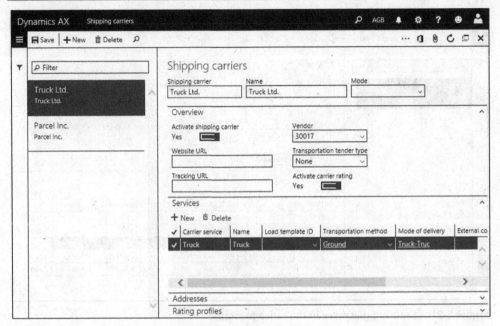

Figure 8-20: Entering a carrier with his service

8.2.1.3 Rate Base Types and Rate Engines

Rate base types (*Transportation management> Setup> General> Rate base type*) determine the lookup criteria for calculating the rates of a shipping carrier. These lookup criteria are fields which are relevant for the transport – for example the postal code of the destination address. They are used as parameters for the rate engines and have to match the internal requirements of rate engines. Primary rate base types are generated when initializing the base engine data in the parameters.

Engines provide the calculation routines for transportation routes in Dynamics AX. Rate engines (*Transportation management> Setup> Engines> Rate engine*) are the basic engines for calculating transportation costs. They can refer to sub-engines like the mileage engines.

Mileage engines (*Transportation management> Setup> Engines> Mileage engine*) determine the distance between origin and destination addresses, usually based on postal codes. You can enter the distance between the postal codes of the relevant origin and destination locations on the tab *Details* of the mileage engines. The button *Metadata* provides access to the definition of available and mandatory fields for entering distances. By adding or removing fields you can control the columns shown in the mileage engines. The field selection has to match the requirements of the engine.

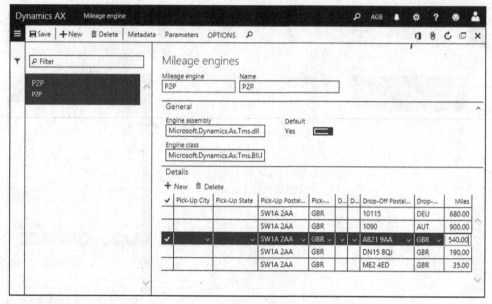

Figure 8-21:   Entering distances in the mileage engine

Transit time engines (*Transportation management> Setup> Engines> Transit time engine*) determine the time required for the transport between addresses. The setup is similar to the mileage engine, except that you have to enter days (instead of miles in the mileage engine) and that the transit time is depending on the carrier service.

8.2.1.4   Break Masters, Rate Masters and Rating Profiles

Break masters, rate masters and rating profiles are the basis for calculating the price of a transport.

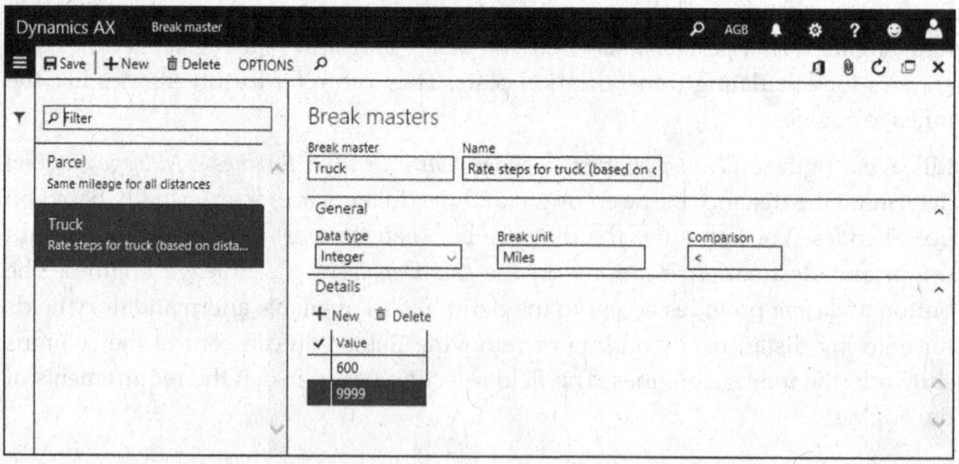

Figure 8-22:   Setting up a break master

Break masters (*Transportation management> Setup> Rating> Break master*) determine the steps (intervals) and the unit (e.g. miles) for different rate prices.

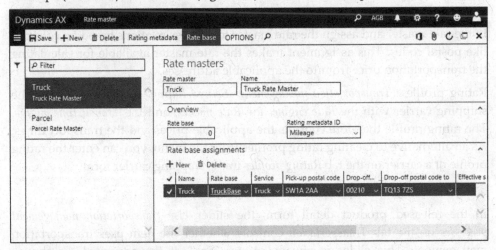

Figure 8-23: Setting up a rate master

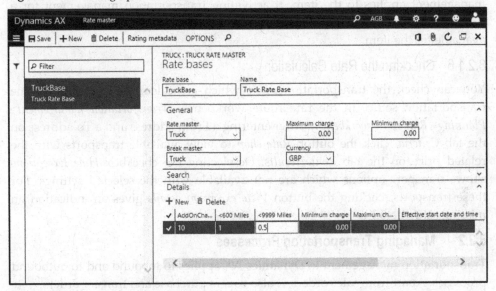

Figure 8-24: Setting up a rate base

Rate masters (*Transportation management> Setup> Rating> Rate master*) give the pricing structure of the carriers. When creating a rate master, select the *Rating metadata ID* (determining the columns on the tab *Rate base assignment*) on the tab *Overview*. The tab *Rate base assignment* contains the assignment of *Rate bases* to addresses.

Before entering a rate base assignment, click the button *Rate base* and enter rate bases. Rate bases contain the pricing of the rate master applying the steps (intervals) for prices as specified in the *Break master* selected on the tab *General*. After creating a new rate base, you can enter the prices on the tab *Details*.

Once you have finished the setup of the rate base, open the tab *Rate base assignment* in the rate master and assign the rate master to address relations based on columns like postal codes. This assignment makes the rate master available for calculating the transportation price from/to the applicable addresses.

Rating profiles (*Transportation management> Setup> Rating> Rating profile*) link the shipping carrier with the *Rate engine*, the *Rate master*, and the *Transit time engine*. The rating profile therefore controls the applicable prices and the transport times. As an alternative to creating rating profiles from the menu, you can enter the rating profile of a carrier on the tab *Rating profiles* in the shipping carrier form.

8.2.1.5 Settings in the Released Products

In the released product detail form, the slider *Use transportation management processes* on the tab *Transportation* controls whether the item uses transportation management. This slider is always set to "Yes", if the advanced warehouse management applies to the item. If activating transportation management for a product not applying the advanced warehouse management, loads are not available for the item.

8.2.1.6 Checking the Rate Calculation

You can check the transportation rates, which are calculated according to the transportation setup, in the rate route workbench (*Transportation management> Planning> Rate route workbench*). After entering a From-address and a To-address on the tab *Criteria*, click the button *Rate shop* to view available transports with the related price on the tab *Route results*. Deselecting the checkbox *Hide Exceptions* shows transport options which are not available with the selected settings. For these transports, clicking the button *View exception details* gives an indication on missing setup details.

8.2.2   Managing Transportation Processes

Transportation management in Dynamics AX applies to inbound and to outbound processes. Apart from sales orders, it also covers purchase and transfer orders.

8.2.2.1 Core Transportation Process

Starting point for the transportation process is a sales order (or purchase/transfer order) with a product which is enabled for transportation management.

The next step is planning the transport. For this purpose, open the load planning workbench from the menu (*Transportation management> Planning> Load planning workbench*) or by clicking the button *WAREHOUSE/Loads/Load planning workbench* in the action pane of the sales order. In the load planning workbench, select the appropriate order line on the tab *Sales lines* and add it to a new load (button

SUPPLY AND DEMAND/Add/To new load in the action pane) or to an existing load. The load then shows on the tab *Loads* of the load planning workbench.

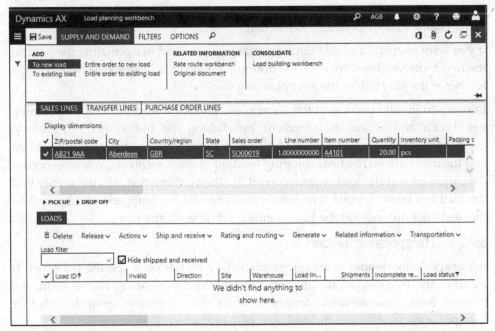

Figure 8-25: Adding a sales order line to a new load in the load planning workbench

In order to calculate the transportation price, select the appropriate load in the load planning workbench and click the button *Rating and routing/Rate route workbench* in the toolbar of the tab *Loads* providing access to the rate route workbench.

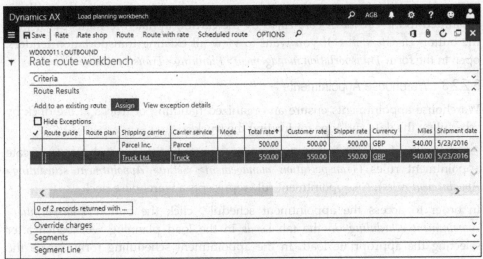

Figure 8-26: Selecting a route in the rate route workbench

In the rate route workbench, click the button *Rate shop* to calculate available options and prices for the transport (clicking the button *Rate* just shows the least expensive transport). Once you have decided on the transport, select the appropriate line and click the button *Assign* on the tab *Route results*. Assigning creates a route and links this route, which you can view in the form *Transportation Management> Planning> Routes*, to the load.

If you want to create a route with a manual price (instead of calculating the price in the rate route workbench), click the button *Rating and routing/Manual rating* in the toolbar of the tab *Loads* in the load planning workbench.

In order to initiate picking in the warehouse, select the load in the load planning workbench and create the shipment by clicking the button *Release/Release to warehouse* in the toolbar of the tab *Loads*. Once all warehouse processes are finished and the items are on the final shipping location of the warehouse, you can confirm the shipment and the load (see section 8.1.2). The confirmation tells the carrier that the load has been shipped. The load status changes to "Shipped" and by default the load does not show in the load planning workbench any more.

8.2.2.2 Transportation Tenders

A transportation tender is an agreement with a carrier on a specific transport. It includes the transportation date and the rate. In the shipping carrier form, the lookup field *Transportation tenders* on the tab *Overview* controls whether transportation tenders are updated manually or through EDI.

In order to access the transportation tenders, click the button *Transportation tenders* after selecting the appropriate route in the route form (*Transportation Management> Planning> Routes*), or the button *TRANSPORTATION/Transportation tenders* in the load form (*Transportation Management> Planning> Loads> All loads*). Clicking the button *New* in the transportation tenders creates a new tender. Once the tender is submitted to the carrier or confirmed by the carrier, update the status by clicking the button *Update status*. If you want to view all existing transportation tenders, open in the form *Transportation management> Planning> Transportation tenders*.

8.2.2.3 Warehouse Appointments

Warehouse appointments ensure an organized handling of trucks at the dock by scheduling the date and time for loading the truck.

As a prerequisite for using warehouse appointments, you have to create appointment rules (*Transportation management> Setup> Appointment scheduling> Appointment rules*). An appointment rule represents a warehouse dock.

In order to access the appointment schedule, click the button *Transportation/ Appointment scheduling* on the tab *Loads* in the load planning workbench after selecting the appropriate load. In the appointment scheduling form, create the appointment (assigned to an *Appointment rule*) with start/end time and confirm it by clicking the button *Update status/Firm*. Existing appointments show in the form *Transportation management> Dock appointment scheduling> Appointment scheduling*.

When the truck arrives, register the driver check-in and check-out in the form *Transportation management> Dock appointment scheduling> Driver check-in and check-out*. Alternatively, you can register the check-in/check-out in the appointment form or on a warehouse mobile device (select an appropriate mobile device menu item).

8.2.2.4 Transportation Constraints

Transportation constraints restrict available options for transportation, for example preventing that a particular carrier transports a particular item number.

In order to set up constraints based on items or carriers, open the menu item *Transportation management> Setup> Routing> Constraints* and enter the disallowed combinations of items, shipments, and carriers. The field *Constraint action* controls whether to create a warning or an error.

When calculating routes in the rate route workbench, a constraint which is applicable to a transport generates an exception (shown in the column *Constraints*).

8.2.2.5 Segmented Transports

Segmented transports apply if you want to change the carrier within a transport. Hub masters for this purpose represent the hubs where you can switch carrier.

As a prerequisite to use segmented transports, following setup is required:

> **Hub types** – Different types of hubs, e.g. harbors, airports (*Transportation management> Setup> Routing> Hub types*)
> **Hub masters** – Places with address (e.g. different harbors) for switching between carriers (*Transportation management> Setup> Routing> Hub masters*)
> **Route plans** – Sequence of transports from the origin to the first destination hub, from the first hub to the next hub, and between all following hubs (*Transportation management> Setup> Routing> Route plans*); Enter the rate per segment on the tab *Details* in spot rates if applicable (button *Spot rates*)
> **Route guide** – With *Origin* and *Destination* address selection; Enter the route plan on the tab *Result* (*Transportation management> Setup> Routing> Route guides*)

In order to calculate the rates using segmented transports, click the button *Route with rate* in the rate route workbench. After selecting a route on the tab *Route results*, switch to the tab *Segments* to view the transport segments with their rate.

8.2.2.6 Freight Discounts

Rate engines calculate the base rate for transportation as described above. Freight discounts (*Transportation management> Setup> Rating> Discounts*) allow adjusting this base rate. They available in both directions, the rate paid to the carrier (*Discount type* "Shipper") and the rate charged to the customer (*Discount type* "Customer"). When setting up a freight discount, select the *Discount type* and the start/end date (on the tab *Dates*). Additional fields in the discounts form are available to restrict the discount, e.g. for a particular *Shipper carrier*. In order to enter the discount value, switch to the tab *Discount*, select the *Result type*

("Percentage" or "Amount") and enter the percentage or rate. Positive discounts reduce the freight rate, and negative discounts increase the rate.

When calculating a rate in the rate route workbench, the amounts in the columns *Customer rate* and *Shipper rate* deduct the discount from the base rate shown in the column *Total rate*.

8.2.2.7 Charging Freight to the Customer

If you want to charge the customer a freight rate which is different from the actual base rate calculated by the rate engine, there are following options:

> **Freight discount** – For the *Discount type* "Customer" (as described before)
> **Override charges** – Customer rate independent from the actual transport

Override charges (*Transportation management> Setup> Rating> Override charges*) provide the option to enter a fixed price or to apply the charges of a fixed carrier, independently from the selected route. For a fixed price, set the slider *Manual* on the tab *Charge* of the override charges form to "Yes" and enter the price on the tab *Charge manual rates* which shows then. If the charges of a fixed carrier always apply, no matter which carrier does the actual transport (e.g. the customer pays only truck charges), select the *Shipping carrier* on the tab *Charge*. When calculating the freight rate for the customer in the rate route workbench then, the *Customer rate* shows the rate as specified in the override charges.

If you want to include transportation costs in the sales order, following setup is required:

> **Charges code** – Set up a charges code (*Accounts receivable> Charges setup> Charges code*) with the posting type combination *Customer – Ledger* (for adding charges to the order total) or *Ledger – Ledger* (for internal posting).
> **Charges assignment** – Create a miscellaneous charges assignment (*Transportation management> Setup> Rating> Miscellaneous charges*) with a start date, linking the charges code in accounts receivable to freight charges in transportation management.
> **Delivery terms** – Create delivery terms (*Sales and marketing> Setup> Distribution> Terms of delivery*) with the slider *Add transportation charges to orders* set to "Yes".

In order to generate charges in the sales order with this setup, enter a sales order, create the load, calculate the rate, and create/assign the route. Then create the shipment ("Release to warehouse") and execute the warehouse processes. When confirming the shipment, the freight charges are added as miscellaneous charges to the sales order line.

9 Financial Management

The primary responsibility of finance administration is to control and to analyze all value-based transactions of an enterprise. These transactions occur in business processes all over the organization, including transactions within the enterprise and transactions with external parties.

Finance management therefore is the core area of business management solutions. In Dynamics AX, a deep integration of business processes in all areas with finance grants accurate financial figures which are immediately available.

9.1 Principles of Ledger Transactions

Before we start to go into details, the lines below show the principles of ledger transactions.

9.1.1 Basic Approach

The core task of finance is to manage accounts in the general ledger as basis for the balance sheet and the income statement (profit and loss statement). In addition to the general ledger, accounting keeps subledgers like accounts receivable, accounts payables, fixed assets, projects, and inventory. These subledgers contain detailed data which support particular parts of the general ledger. Inventory management for example includes inventory transactions, which contain the details of changes in stock account balances.

Whenever reporting a value-based transaction in a subledger, for example an invoice in sales or a counting difference in inventory, there is a transaction in the general ledger. If you post a sales order invoice, it has includes following areas:

➢ **Inventory** – Financial value (in the transaction and the on-hand quantity)
➢ **Accounts receivable** – Customer debt (customer transaction)
➢ **General ledger** – Stock account, revenue account, COGS account (cost of goods sold), customer summary account

Ledger integration, which is a core characteristic of Dynamics AX, provides traceability of all financial vouchers back to the origin in other modules. Depending on settings for subledger batch transfer, subledger transactions are immediately posted to the general ledger.

The voucher principle is the general principle for processing transactions in Dynamics AX: Throughout the whole application, you have to register a voucher before you can post it. After posting, it is not possible to modify a voucher any more. If you want to cancel a transaction, you have to post a reversing transaction.

9.1.2   At a Glance: Ledger Journal Transactions

In order to record a manual ledger transaction in Dynamics AX, you have to register a journal. The lines below show how to post a single-line transaction.

After accessing the form *General ledger> Journal entries> General journals*, create a journal header by clicking the button *New* (or pressing the shortcut key *Alt+N*). Alternatively, you can access the *General journal processing* workspace and create a journal header by clicking the tile *New journal* there. In the journal list page, select a journal name for the new journal in the column *Name* and optionally enter a text explaining the transaction in the column *Description*. If sales tax (VAT) applies, the slider *Amounts include sales tax* on the tab *Setup* of the journal header controls whether the debit (or credit) amount in the journal lines includes tax.

In order to switch to the journal lines, click the *Journal batch number* shown as link in the grid of the journal list page or click the button *Lines* in the action pane. When registering a simple ledger transaction in the journal lines, leave the default option "Ledger" in the column *Account type* and select the account number including financial dimensions in the column *Account* (using segmented entry control). If you want to post to a subledger, choose a different account type and enter the related account number – for example "Vendor" in the *Account type* and the vendor number in the *Account* for accounts payable.

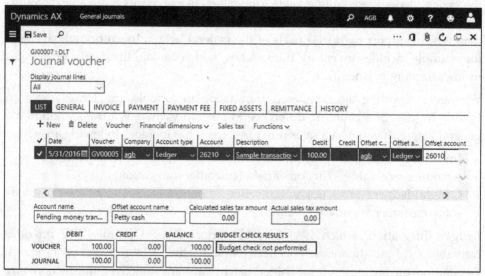

Figure 9-1:   Registering a journal line (related to an account structure without dimensions)

In a single-line transaction, you can enter the account and the offset account (including applicable financial dimensions) in the one common journal line. Once you have finished registering the line, post the journal by clicking the button *Post* in the action pane of the journal header or lines (in a narrow screen, click the button ⋯ to view all buttons of the action pane).

9.2   Core Setup for Finance

Since finance management in Dynamics AX contains core settings of the application, you have to complete the basic finance configuration before setting up other modules and before posting a transaction in any part of the application.

This basic configuration includes the following elements:

➢ **Fiscal and ledger calendar** – Specifying financial periods
➢ **Currencies and exchange rates** – Specifying monetary units
➢ **Chart of accounts** – Specifying ledger accounts

Charts of accounts, fiscal calendars, and currencies/exchange rates are shared across companies in Dynamics AX. In order to use a shared calendar or chart of accounts in a company, select the appropriate chart of accounts and fiscal calendar in the ledger form. But if applicable, you can keep a separate chart of accounts or fiscal calendar at company level by choosing a different assignment per company.

9.2.1   Fiscal and Ledger Calendar

The primary purpose of fiscal calendars is to determine the fiscal year, specifying the start date and the end date of financial periods within the fiscal year. The ledger calendar, which is based on the fiscal calendar, then controls at company level which financial periods are open for transactions.

9.2.1.1   Fiscal Calendar

Fiscal calendars are shared across all companies within a common Dynamics AX database. The field *Fiscal calendar* in the ledger form (*General ledger> Ledger setup> Ledger*) then determines the applicable fiscal calendar for a company. You have to select it during the initial company setup.

Within the fiscal years of a fiscal calendar, the accounting periods are defined with their start date and end date. The length of the individual periods is depending on the reporting requirements of the company.

In order to edit the fiscal calendars, open the form *General ledger> Calendars> Fiscal calendars*. If you want to create a new fiscal calendar, click the button *New calendar* and enter the calendar identification and applicable settings for the first fiscal year (start date, end date, name, period length, and unit – be sure to select the unit "Months" in case of monthly periods).

If you want to add a fiscal year to an existing fiscal calendar, select the particular calendar in the left pane of the form before clicking the button *New year* in the action pane. A drop-down window then provides the option to simply copy the settings from the last year (slider *Copy from last fiscal year* set to "Yes") or to edit the end date, period length, and unit for the new year. Clicking the button *Create* then creates the new year with its accounting periods.

9.2.1.2 Closing and Opening Periods

Apart from regular operating periods showing the *Type* "Operating", there are two particular period types which you can't use when posting a regular transaction: *Closing periods* and *Opening periods*. Dynamics AX provides the option to attach multiple closing periods to each regular operating period.

Closing periods contain period-end or year-end transactions. Registration and posting of these transactions is only possible through closing sheets (*General ledger> Period close> Closing sheet*).

Opening periods contain the opening transactions for a fiscal year. After closing the previous year, you can create these transactions in the form *General ledger> Period close> Year end close* based on the closing transactions.

9.2.1.3 Ledger Calendar

As a prerequisite for posting a transaction in Dynamics AX, the posting date of the transaction has to be included in an applicable ledger period with the period status "Open". The required period status is controlled at company level in the ledger calendar, not in the shared fiscal calendar.

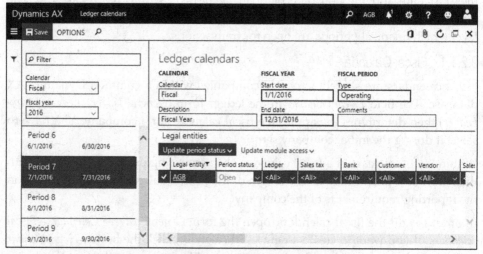

Figure 9-2:   Managing the period status in the ledger calendar

The ledger calendar (*General ledger> Period close> Ledger calendar*) is based on the periods of the fiscal calendar, which is assigned to the particular company (selected in the ledger form).

After selecting a fiscal year and a period in the left pane of the ledger calendar form, the *Legal entities* pane on the right-hand side shows all assigned companies with the period status. You can open or close periods for companies individually in the column *Period status*, or in common by clicking the button *Update period status* after selecting the appropriate companies.

The period status "Open" enables posting of transactions in the period, whereas the period status "On hold" blocks posting. The status "Closed" also blocks posting – but unlike periods on hold, closed periods do not provide the option for reopening. For this reason, use the status "Closed" only if a period is definitely closed in accounting (i.e. after reporting to the authorities).

The button *Update module access* and the related columns provide the option of a module-specific blocking of transactions and to exclude user groups from blocking.

In order to support period closing, the *Financial period close* workspace shows a list of tasks which you can set up in the form *General ledger> Period close> Financial period close configuration*.

9.2.1.4 New in Dynamics 'AX 7'

Apart from the browser-based user interface, items which are new in financial calendar administration include the period close workspace, the access to ledger calendars, and the option to close periods in multiple companies in parallel.

9.2.2   Currency and Exchange Rate

All value-based transactions refer to currencies – general ledger transactions as well as subledger transactions like inventory or customer transactions. A transaction is always recorded in the accounting currency of the company, and sometimes additionally in a foreign currency. Currencies therefore are a main requirement before you can post any transaction in Dynamics AX.

9.2.2.1 Currencies

In order to facilitate currency management in multi-company organizations, the currency table is shared across all companies within a common Dynamics AX database. The currencies form (*General ledger> Currencies> Currencies*) shows all available currencies with currency code and name. After selecting a currency in the left pane, the tabs on the right-hand side show the related settings of the currency including the definition of the rounding precision on the tab *Rounding rules*.

9.2.2.2 Exchange Rates

Exchange rate types (*General ledger> Currencies> Exchange rate types*) in Dynamics AX provide the option to manage multiple exchange rates per currency in parallel. Different exchange rates are required for example, if you want to use other rates for budget entries than for current transactions.

In order to access the *Currency exchange rates* form, choose the menu item *General ledger> Currencies> Currency exchange rates* or click the button *Exchange rates* in the *Exchange rate types* form. After selecting an *Exchange rate type* in the upper area of the left pane in the currency exchange rates form (see Figure 9-3), you can view the applicable currency relations in the lower left pane. If you need an additional relation (e.g. if working with a currency not used before), click the button *New* in the action pane provides and enter the details in the upper area of the right pane. The *Conversion factor* specifies the applicable factor for exchange rate calculation.

The tab *Add or remove exchange rates* in the right pane shows the exchange rates for the currency relation selected in the left pane. The filter *From date* and *To date* determines the date range for which valid exchange rates are displayed. In order to enter an exchange rate for a new date, click the button *Add* in the toolbar of the tab. The column *Exchange value* then shows the conversion result, providing the option to check if the exchange rates are entered the right way. In daily business, you should enter or import new exchange rates continuously (usually at least once a month) in order to apply a correct conversion in foreign currency transactions.

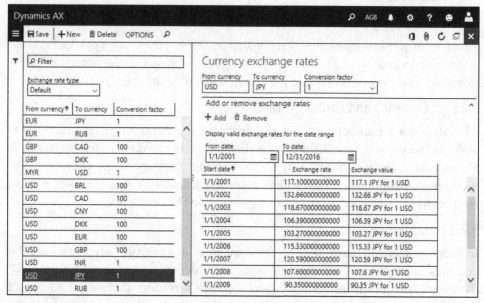

Figure 9-3:   Managing exchange rates in the currency exchange rates form

Currency exchange rates and exchange rate types are shared across all companies. If required, you can keep exchange rates at company level by choosing a different exchange rate type per company in the ledger form.

9.2.2.3 Currency Settings in the Ledger Form

The *Accounting currency* on tab *Currency* in the ledger form (*General ledger> Ledger setup> Ledger*) determines the home currency of the current company. This currency is used in all financial transactions. It is not possible to change the accounting currency selection of a company once transactions are registered. If you need to change the home currency later (e.g. converting to a new currency in your country), specific conversion tools are required.

The *Exchange rate type* on the tab *Currency* in the ledger form determines the default exchange rate type for regular transactions. In addition, a separate default for budget transactions is available.

The main accounts for exchange rate gains and losses in the current company are specified on the tab *Accounts for currency revaluation* in the ledger form.

9.2.3 Financial Dimensions

In addition to the main accounts specified in the chart of accounts, financial dimensions (like cost center or department) provide further levels for structuring financial transactions. The financial dimensions which you have to enter in a transaction are depending on the account structures assigned to the current company.

Based on the posted dimension values, financial analysis and reports are not only available at company level, but also at the level of financial dimensions. This is important in conjunction with the multisite functionality: Assigning a financial dimension to the inventory dimension "Site" (see section 10.1.5) for example makes it possible to report the income statement per subsidiary within a legal entity.

9.2.3.1 Managing Financial Dimensions

In Dynamics AX, financial dimensions and dimension values are shared across all companies within a common Dynamics AX database.

Financial dimensions are not limited to standard dimensions like department, cost center and purpose. You can easily set up as many financial dimensions as required. But if you consider the impact on the structural clearness, the probability of wrong entries, and the effort for registration, do not set up more dimensions than really required.

In order to set up a new financial dimension, open the form *General ledger> Chart of accounts> Dimensions> Financial dimensions* and insert a record by clicking the button *New*. The lookup field *Use values from* then specifies the origin of related financial dimension values:

> **<Custom dimension>** – Creating a dimension not referring to other tables
> **One of the other options** – Linking the dimension to other entities in the application (e.g. customers, item groups, or cost centers)

If you select for example the option "Departments" in the lookup field *Use values from*, the financial dimension is linked to operating units of the type "Department". In this case, all departments entered in the organization management (*Organization administration> Organizations> Operating units*) at the same time automatically apply as financial dimension values for the dimension.

If you select the option "<Custom dimension>" in the lookup field *Use values from*, the financial dimension values have to be entered manually.

After creating a new dimension, a system administrator (or a user with appropriate privilege) has to activate it by clicking the button *Activate* in the action pane.

9.2.3.2 Financial Dimension Values

You can access the dimension values of a financial dimension by clicking the button *Financial dimension values* in the financial dimensions. For custom dimensions, you have to create the *Dimension values* with *Description* manually. For other financial dimensions, you can edit dimension value details but you cannot create records (since the dimension values derive from other areas).

After selecting a dimension value in the left pane of the form, you can edit the dimension value details in the right pane. The tab *General* in the right pane contains shared settings applicable to all companies using the dimension. The slider *Suspended* and the date fields *Active from* or *Active to* for example provide the option to block future transactions referring to the selected dimension value. On the tab *Legal entity overrides*, you can enter further blocking on company level.

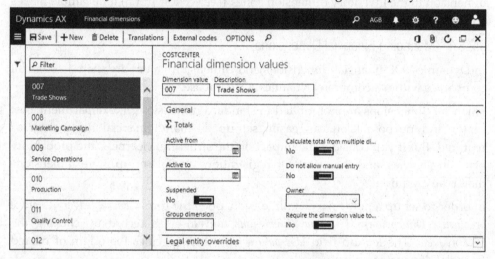

Figure 9-4:   Managing dimension values for a financial dimension

9.2.3.3 Applying Financial Dimensions

After creating a financial dimension, it has to be included in account structures or in advanced rule structures which apply to the particular company, before you can use it in transactions and inquiries. Settings in the applicable account structure and advanced rule structure in addition specify, if and which dimension value is optional or required when posting to a particular account.

In master data forms (for example the customer form or the released product form), the tab *Financial dimensions* shows all financial dimensions included in account structures and advanced rule structures which apply to the current company. Dimension values entered on this tab are used as default dimension values when registering an order or a journal line.

When registering a transaction in a ledger journal line or in any other form containing a ledger account field, financial dimensions are not shown as separate fields. Using segmented entry control (see section 9.3.2), you have to enter financial dimensions together with the main account in one – segmented – field.

9.2.3.4 Balancing Financial Dimension and Interunit Accounting

Interunit accounting, an optional feature in Dynamics AX, ensures a balanced balance sheet for a selected financial dimension – the balancing dimension. Following settings are required as a prerequisite for interunit accounting:

> **Accounts for automatic transactions** – Enter appropriate main accounts for the *Posting type* "Interunit-debit" and "Interunit-credit" in the accounts for automatic transactions (see section 9.2.4)
> **Balancing financial dimension** – Selection in the ledger form

If the field *Balancing financial dimension* in the ledger form is not empty, you have to provide a dimension value for this dimension when posting any transaction. If the from-value and the to-value for the balancing dimension are different in a transaction, Dynamics AX posts additional balancing transactions to the main accounts "Interunit-debit" and "Interunit-credit". This applies for example in a transaction from one department to another, if departments are the balancing dimension.

9.2.3.5 New in Dynamics 'AX 7'

Apart from the browser-based user interface, items which are new in financial dimension management include the dimension activation and changes in the way to edit company-specific dimension value details.

9.2.4 Account Structure and Chart of Accounts

Account structures and charts of accounts determine the basic structure in finance. Account structures, charts of accounts, and main accounts are shared across companies in Dynamics AX. In a company, the chart of accounts selected in the ledger form determines the applicable main accounts. The assignment of account structures controls the applicable financial dimensions.

9.2.4.1 Ledger Account and Main Account

When entering a financial transaction, the ledger account field contains the main account and applicable financial dimensions. The account structure assigned at company and main account level controls the financial dimensions which are included in the ledger account.

9.2.4.2 Charts of Accounts

In order to access all charts of accounts in your enterprise, open the menu item *General ledger> Chart of Accounts> Accounts> Chart of Accounts*. Depending on the structure of your organization and the number of legal entities, the left pane in the chart of accounts form shows one or more charts of accounts. The right pane of the form contains the main accounts of the chart of accounts selected in the left pane. If you display the FactBox pane, it shows the ledgers and legal entities which use the selected chart of accounts.

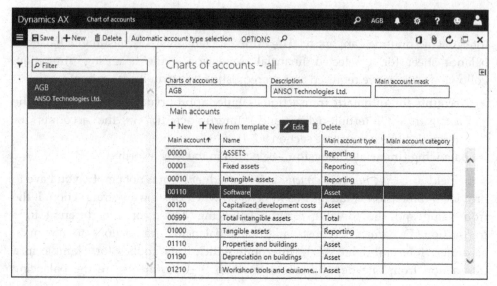

Figure 9-5: Managing charts of accounts (FactBox pane not shown)

If you want to create a completely new chart of accounts, click the button *New* in the action pane. Clicking the button *New* or *Edit* in the toolbar of the tab *Main accounts* form opens the main accounts form, where you can insert or modify the main accounts of the selected chart of accounts as described further below.

9.2.4.3 Settings in the Ledger Form

Settings in the ledger form (*General ledger> Ledger setup> Ledger*) determine the chart of accounts and the account structures which are assigned to the current company. These settings are required before registering the first transaction.

You can share a chart of accounts, assigning multiple companies to one common chart of accounts. After posting the first transaction in a company, it is not possible to change the chart of accounts assignment any more.

The tab *Account structures* in the ledger form contains the account structures linked to the current company. In order to add an account structure, click the button *Add* in the toolbar of this tab. Since account structures determine the available financial dimensions when posting to a main account, each main account included in the chart of accounts has to be uniquely assigned to one account structure without overlapping or missing assignments.

If you use interunit accounting, select the balancing financial dimension of the company in the ledger form. If selected, this dimension has to be included in all account structures of the company.

9.2.4.4 Account Structures

You can access the account structures list page through the menu item *General ledger> Chart of Accounts> Structures> Configure account structures*. If you want to access the related detail form, click the *Name* field of the appropriate account structure shown as link in the grid of the list page. Alternatively, you can access the account structure detail form from the ledger form (button *Configure account structures* on the tab *Account structures*).

If you want to define a completely new segment combination consisting of main account and applicable financial dimensions, create a new account structure by clicking the button *New* in the action pane. In the *Create* drop-down window, the slider *Add main account* usually remains set to "Yes" in order to include the main account as the first segment. You can set this slider to "No" if you want to use a financial dimension, and not the main account, as first segment – e.g. if divisions apply and should be the first segment when entering transactions. After clicking the button *Create*, Dynamics AX shows the account structure detail form.

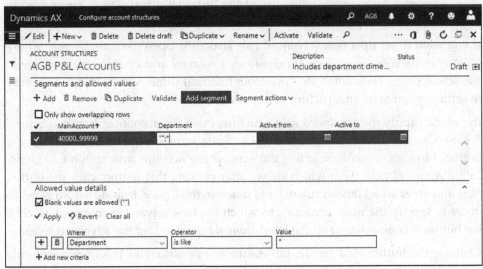

Figure 9-6: Configuring an account structure in the detail form

When creating a new account structure or editing an existing structure, it has got the status "Draft". You can add dimensions to the account structure by clicking the button *Add segment* in the toolbar of the upper pane in the detail form. After selecting a segment field in the appropriate column of the upper pane, you can enter a filter expression in this field or on the tab *Allowed value details*. If you select the checkbox *Blank values are allowed* for a financial dimension, entering a dimension value is optional and you are not required to select a dimension value when registering a transaction for a main account referring to the account structure.

The example in Figure 9-6 shows a simple account structure applying to main accounts starting with account 40000, containing the financial dimension "Department" without restricting available dimension values on this dimension.

If applicable to your account structure, you can add one or more lines for a segment – including the main account – with appropriate filters which prevent overlapping definitions. This way you can specify multiple allowed dimension value combinations.

Once you have finished the setup of account structure segments, click the button *Activate* to make the account structure available. If you want to edit an existing account structure later, click the button *Edit* in the action pane. The account structure status then changes to "Draft", which also allows it to be deleted.

9.2.4.5 Advanced Rule Structures

Advanced rule structures are an optional setup which you can use, if you want to apply an additional financial dimension only when posting to one or a few specific main accounts. An example is the use of the financial dimension "Campaigns" in combination with a specific marketing main account in order to track campaigns.

If you want to set up a new advanced rule structure, open the form *General ledger> Chart of Accounts> Structures> Advanced rule structures* and click the button *New* in the action pane. Then enter the applicable financial dimension(s) in a similar way to setting up an account structure as described above.

In order to apply the advanced rule structure, open the account structures (*General ledger> Chart of Accounts> Structures> Configure account structures*) and click the button *Advanced rule* after selecting the appropriate account structure in *Edit* mode. In the *Advanced rules* form which shows after clicking this button, click the button *New* and enter an advanced rule ID and name in the *Create* drop-down window. In order to specify the main accounts, to which the new advanced rule applies, click the button *Add new creteria* on the tab *Advanced rule criteria* of the advanced rules.

Clicking the button *Add* on the tab *Advanced rule structures* links advanced rule structures to the advanced rule. Activating the account structure, to which the advanced rule applies, activates the advanced rule in parallel.

9.2.4.6 Main Accounts

The structure and the format of the main accounts in the chart of accounts are only depending on the internal requirements of the company. In order to comply with the different reporting structures for balance sheet, income statement and other reports in finance, there are financial reports which you can set up in the Management Reporter independently from the structure of the chart of account.

If you want to edit the main accounts, open the form *General ledger> Chart of accounts> Accounts> Main accounts* and click the button *Edit* there. Alternatively, you can access the main accounts from the chart of accounts form (button *Edit* in the toolbar of the tab *Main accounts*).

The main accounts form shows the chart of accounts assigned to the current company. The name of this chart of accounts in shown in the header of the right pane. In case other companies are also assigned to this chart of accounts, you have to keep in mind that changes on main accounts also affect the other companies.

If you want to enter a new account, click the button *New* in the action pane and enter a unique *Main account* number, a *Name* and a *Main account type*. In case a translation of the account name is required, click the button *Name Translations*.

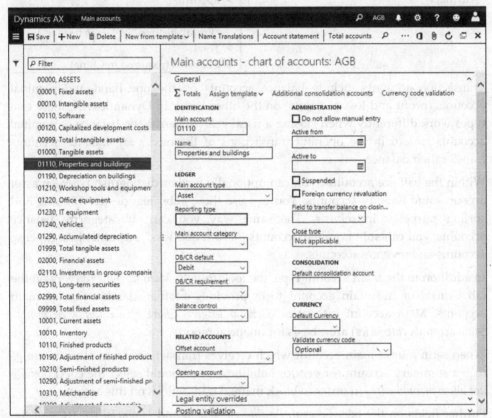

Figure 9-7: Editing a main account

In the structure of the main accounts, you have to distinguish between transaction accounts and auxiliary accounts. The core difference between transaction accounts and auxiliary accounts is that you can only select a transaction account when registering a financial transaction. Auxiliary accounts support a clear structure of the chart of accounts, but they are not necessarily required.

The *Main account type*, a lookup field in the main accounts form, groups accounts to transaction accounts and auxiliary accounts as shown in table 8-1 below.

Table 9-1:   Structure of main accounts

Type		Main account type in Dynamics AX
Transaction accounts	Balance accounts	➢ Balance sheet ➢ Asset ➢ Liability ➢ Equity
	Nominal accounts	➢ Profit and loss ➢ Expense ➢ Revenue
Auxiliary accounts		➢ Reporting (*Reporting type* options "Header", "Empty header", or "Page header") ➢ Total ➢ Common (required in China)

Transaction accounts include balance accounts on the one hand and nominal accounts (profit and loss accounts) on the other hand. In Dynamics AX, these two types work differently when closing a fiscal year: Whereas the balance of nominal accounts is zero in the opening transactions of the next year, balance accounts transfer their balance.

Within the balance accounts, you can optionally further distinguish between asset accounts and liability accounts. You can use these subcategories for filtering and sorting purposes in reports. The same way you can subcategorize balance accounts, you can split nominal accounts ("Profit and loss" accounts) into expense accounts and revenue accounts.

In addition to the main account type, the lookup field *Main account category* on the tab *General* of the main account form provides another classification of main accounts. Main account categories (*General ledger> Chart of accounts> Accounts> Main accounts categories*) are a basis for financial reports.

When setting up a main account which receives transactions from other modules (e.g. a summary account for vendor liabilities), you should select the checkbox *Do not allow manual entry* in order to block manual transactions on this account.

Further fields on the tabs *General*, *Posting validation*, and *Financial reporting* of the main accounts form provide the option to specify default value data and to enter restrictions for allowed transactions. On the tab *Legal entity overrides*, you can block a main account or enter default values for financial dimensions on company level.

9.2.4.7 Trial Balance

If you want to view the balances of main accounts, open the trial balance form (*General ledger> Inquiries and reports> Trial balance*). The button *Parameters* in the action pane of the trial balances provides the option to select the period used for calculating the account balances.

In order to view the transactions of an account, click the button *All transactions* in the trial balance after selecting the appropriate main account. The transaction form contains following buttons which provide access to further details:

➤ **Voucher** – Shows all general ledger transactions posted with selected voucher
➤ **Transaction origin** – Shows the related transactions in all modules
➤ **Original document** – Provides the option to reprint the document

9.2.4.8 Accounts for Automatic Transactions

Settings in the *Accounts for automatic transactions* apply to ledger transactions, which are posted automatically through ledger integration and for which there is no other setting (e.g. for invoice discounts).

If you want to enter a new setting for automatic transactions, open the form *General ledger> Posting setup> Accounts for automatic transactions* and insert a record selecting the posting type and the assigned main account. Clicking the button *Create default types* generates a basic set of posting types, for which you can enter default accounts. Core settings in the accounts for automatic transactions include:

➤ **Error account** – Applying in case of missing account settings
➤ **Penny difference in accounting currency** – For small payment differences
➤ **Year-end result** – Account for profit/loss when closing the fiscal year
➤ **Sales tax rounding**
➤ **Order invoice rounding** – Sales invoice rounding
➤ **Purchase invoice rounding-off** – Purchase invoice rounding
➤ **Vendor invoice discount** – Main account for purchase order total discounts
➤ **Customer invoice discount** – Main account for sales order total discounts

If the slider *Interrupt in case or error account* in the general ledger parameters is set to "Yes", Dynamics AX displays an error message instead of posting to the error account when trying to post a transaction for which no main account is specified in the integration settings.

9.2.4.9 Default Descriptions

Default descriptions (*General ledger> Journal setup> Default descriptions*) determine a default text in transactions which are posted automatically through ledger integration. After selecting the transaction type in the field *Description*, you can enter the *Language* ("user" for a generic description) and the *Text*, which can include fixed variables (shown in the lower area of the right pane).

9.2.4.10 New in Dynamics 'AX 7'

Items which are new in main account management refer to the browser-based user interface, for example the main accounts form not showing account balances (use the trail balance) and the Management Reporter for financial statements.

9.2.5   Customer, Vendor, and Bank Account

When entering a ledger journal line, you can – apart from a ledger account – select a customer, a vendor, a project, a bank account, or a fixed asset for the account and the offset account.

9.2.5.1   Bank Accounts

Before selecting a particular bank account in a transaction, you have to set it up in the form *Cash and bank management> Bank accounts*. When creating a new bank account by clicking the button *New*, enter the bank account ID, the *Routing number* identifying the bank, your *Bank account number* as specified by the bank, and a *Name* for the bank account.

The field *Main account*, where you have to enter the main account assigned to the particular bank account, is another important setting on the tab *General* of the bank account form. The *Currency* field specifies the currency of the bank account. If you want to enable transactions in additional currencies, set the slider *Allow transactions in additional currencies* to "Yes". The tab *Additional identification* contains the fields for SWIFT/BIC and IBAN.

If a company has got multiple bank accounts at a particular bank, you can create a bank group (*Cash and bank management> Setup> Bank groups*) which contains general bank data like routing number, address, and contact information. Selecting the bank group in the related field on the tab *General* of bank accounts then applies these data as default for the bank account.

9.2.5.2   Vendors

As shown in section 3.2.1, you can manage vendor records in the list page *Accounts payable> Vendors> All vendors*. If you want to view vendor transactions (invoices and payments) there, click the button *VENDOR/Transactions/Transactions* in the action pane after selecting the particular vendor. Apart from the invoice or payment amount, the vendor transaction form shows the open, not yet settled amount in the column *Balance*.

9.2.5.3   Settlement of Vendor Transactions

If you want to apply a posted payment to an invoice, access the open vendor transactions by clicking the button *INVOICE/Settle/Settle transactions* in the action pane of the vendor form.

In the *Settle transactions* dialog, select the checkbox *Mark* in the transaction lines which you want to clear. You can settle one or multiple invoices with one or multiple payments or credit notes. If there are transactions in foreign currencies, you can choose the settlement date (for calculating exchange rate gains or losses) in the lookup field *Settlement posting date* in the upper pane of the dialog. The lookup field *Date used for calculating discounts* determines the date for cash discount calculation with following options:

➢ **Transaction date** – Select the transaction line containing the date for discount calculation and click the button *Mark as primary payment* in the toolbar.

➢ **Selected date** – Enter the discount calculation date in the date field on the right.

You can check the balance of the marked transactions in the *Settlement balance* fields at the bottom of the dialog. Clicking the button *Post* posts the settlement.

If you do not want to post the settlements as a separate step, you can register the settlement already when entering a payment (see section 9.3.4).

In case you have to cancel a posted settlement, access the closed transaction form by clicking the button *INVOICE/Settle/Undo settlement* in the action pane of the vendor form and reverse the settlement there.

9.2.5.4 Customers

A description of the core elements in the customer record (*Accounts receivable> Customers> All Customers*) is available in section 4.2.1 of this book. The way to execute transaction inquiries and to settle transactions (on the action pane tab *COLLECT*) for customers is similar to the procedures in vendor management.

9.2.6   Sales Tax / VAT Settings

The sales tax/VAT functionality in Dynamics AX supports various tax regulations – e.g. the sales tax in the United States or the value added tax in Europe.

Sales tax codes, which determine the tax rate, are the basis for sales tax calculation. In an invoice line, the applicable sales tax code is depending on both, the item sales tax group of the item and the sales tax group of the customer or vendor.

9.2.6.1 Parameters on Sales Tax

A primary setting for tax calculation is whether sales tax applies: If it does, set the slider *Apply sales tax taxation rules* on the tab *Sales tax* of the general ledger parameters to "Yes". With this setting, sales tax jurisdictions are an additional grouping in the tax calculation.

9.2.6.2 Sales Tax Authorities

The first step in the setup of sales tax calculation is to enter the competent authorities (*Tax> Indirect taxes> Sales tax> Sales tax authorities*) with their authority ID, name, and report layout for tax reporting.

9.2.6.3 Sales Tax Settlement Periods

Applicable periods for tax reporting (usually monthly periods) are specified in the form *Tax> Indirect taxes> Sales tax> Sales tax settlement periods*.

When creating a settlement period definition with ID and description, you have to assign the applicable *Authority* and the period length (*Period interval unit* and *Period interval duration*) on the tab *General*. Then switch to the tab *Period intervals* and click the button *Add* in the toolbar to enter the first period manually (e.g. Jan 1 – Jan 31).

In order to create further periods automatically, click the button *New period interval* in the toolbar of the tab.

9.2.6.4 Ledger Posting Groups

Sales tax ledger posting groups control the main accounts for sales tax transactions (depending on the sales tax code of the invoice transaction).

In order to create a sales tax ledger posting group, open the form *Sales tax> Setup> Sales tax> Ledger posting groups*. After entering the group ID and description, select the main account for *Sales tax payable* (tax for purchasing), or for *Sales tax receivable* (tax for sales), or for *Use tax expense* and *Use tax payable* as applicable. The *Settlement account* specifies the balance account for the amount to be paid to the authorities.

9.2.6.5 Sales Tax Codes

Sales tax codes control the tax rate and the calculation base. In order to create a sales tax code, open the form *Tax> Indirect taxes> Sales tax> Sales tax codes* and insert a record with code and name. On the tab *General*, assign the *Settlement period* and the *Ledger posting group*. Detailed calculation parameters are available on the tab *Calculation*. In order to specifying the tax rate, click the button *SALES TAX CODE/ Sales tax code/Values* in the action pane of the sales tax code form and enter the applicable rate in the column *Value* of the *Sales tax code values* form.

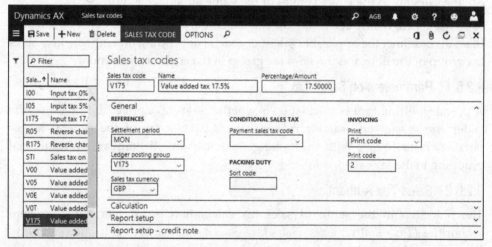

Figure 9-8:   Managing sales tax codes

After creating a sales tax code, assign it to applicable sales tax groups and item sales tax groups. Dynamics AX determines the sales tax code of an invoice line from the sales tax code, which is included in the settings of both – the item sales tax group of the item and the sales tax group of the customer (or vendor).

In order to apply a tax code "V175" in a sales invoice line for example, the line has to comply with both following conditions:

> **Item sales tax group** – The item sales tax group (e.g. "STD" for a standard rate) of the item contains the sales tax code "V175"

> **Sales tax group** – The sales tax group of the customer (e.g. "CDO" for domestic customers) contains the sales tax code "V175"

9.2.6.6 Sales Tax Groups and Item Sales Tax Groups

If you want to set up a sales tax group, open the form *Tax> Indirect taxes> Sales tax> Sales tax groups*. After entering the tax group identification and description on the tab *Overview*, switch to the tab *Setup* and enter all sales tax codes which apply to the customers or vendors belonging to the group.

In order to assign the sales tax groups to customers and vendors, open the customer or vendor form and select the *Item sales tax group* on the tab *Invoice and delivery* in the detail form (usually when creating a customer or vendor).

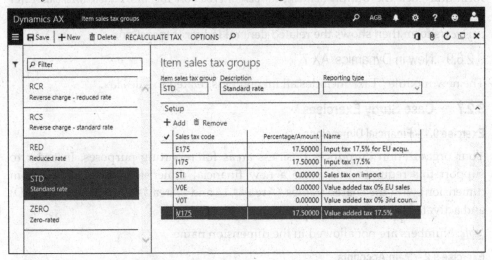

Figure 9-9: Managing item sales tax groups

The menu item *Tax> Indirect taxes> Sales tax> Item sales tax groups* provides access to the items sales tax groups, which apply to the released products. Setting up an item sales tax groups works similar to setting up a sales tax group.

In order to assign item sales tax groups to items, open the released product form (*Product information management> Products> Released products*) and select the *Item sales tax group* for sales (on the tab *Sell*) and for purchasing (on the tab *Purchase*) in the detail form. If you are using product categories in order lines, you can assign item sales tax groups to categories in the procurement categories form (*Procurement and sourcing> Procurement categories*) and in the sales categories form (*Sales and marketing> Setup> Categories> Sales categories*).

9.2.6.7 Sales Tax Transactions

When entering a transaction in a journal line or an order line, Dynamics AX initializes the sales tax code based on the combination of item and customer or vendor. In order to view the calculated tax before posting, click the button *Sales tax* in the action pane or toolbar of journal lines, sales and purchase order headers or lines, or in the posting dialog when posting a transaction (e.g. a sales invoice).

If necessary, you can change the sales tax groups or the sales tax code in a journal line or order line before posting. When posting an invoice, Dynamics AX generates a transaction for the sales tax in the general ledger (according to the ledger posting group assigned to the sales tax code) and a sales tax transaction in the tax ledger.

9.2.6.8 Sales Tax Payment

In order to calculate and post the sales tax payable to the authorities in a period, execute the periodic activity *Tax> Declarations> Sales tax> Settle and post sales tax*.

If you want to view the posted settlements, open the sales tax settlement periods form and click the button *Settlements per interval* on the tab *Period intervals* after selecting the appropriate period. Clicking the button *Voucher* in the *Sales tax payments* form then shows the related general ledger transactions.

9.2.6.9 New in Dynamics 'AX 7'

The new module "Tax" includes all menu items related to sales tax.

9.2.7   Case Study Exercises

Exercise 9.1 – Financial Dimensions

Your organization introduces business areas for reporting purposes. In order to support this requirement, create a new financial dimension "##Areas" (custom dimension) with the shared values "Area ## 1" and "Area ## 2" (## = your user ID) and activate it.

Note: Numbers are not allowed in the dimension name.

Exercise 9.2 – Main Accounts

Following new main accounts are required in your company (## = your user ID):
➢ Main account "111C-##", Name "Petty cash", account type "Balance Sheet"
➢ Main account "111B-##", Name "##-Bank", account type "Balance Sheet"
➢ Main account "6060##", Name "## - Consulting", account type "Expense"
➢ Main account "ZZ##", Name "## account structure test", account type "Balance Sheet"

Create these accounts making sure to apply the right chart of accounts.

Exercise 9.3 – Account structures

Unlike the other main accounts created in Exercise 9.2, your main account "ZZ##" is not included in an account number range covered by existing account structures. For this reason, set up a new account structure only applying to this main account.

Create and activate a new account structure "ZS##", with the main accounts and the financial dimension "##Areas" (and additionally the balancing dimension, if interunit accounting applies) as segments. Your main account "ZZ##" is the only applicable main account in this account structure. Then assign the account structure to your test company.

Note: If you are sharing the Dynamics AX training database, remove your account structure once you have finished all exercises in order to avoid confusing other people with too many applicable financial dimensions.

Exercise 9.4 – Bank Accounts

Your company opens a new bank account at your preferred bank. Create an appropriate bank account "B-##" with any routing number and bank account number. Assign the main account "111B-##" from exercise 9.2 to this bank account.

9.3   Business Processes in Finance

Every business process in connection with financial values generates general ledger transactions in Dynamics AX.

Most of the ledger transactions do not origin in accounting, but derive from transactions in other areas like purchasing, sales, or production. Transactions in these areas automatically generate ledger transactions in the background.

Some ledger transactions originate from activities in accounting. In order to record these transactions, you have to post a journal in the general ledger module.

9.3.1   Basic Setup for Journal Transactions

In addition to the basic finance setup of described in the previous section, you have to configure journal names before you can register a journal transaction in the general ledger.

9.3.1.1   Journal Names

Journal names (*General ledger> Journals setup> Journal names*) classify transactions by subject matters. The lookup field *Journal type* in this form controls in which journals you can use the selected journal name. The most common journal types are:

> **Daily** – General journal
> **Periodic** – Periodic journal
> **Vendor invoice recording** – Invoice journal in accounts payable
> **Vendor disbursement** – Vendor payment
> **Customer payment** – Payment of customers

If you want to use the invoice register and the invoice approval journals in accounts payable, you need the journal types "Invoice register" and "Approval".

Ledger journals show a common structure, which is independent from the journal type. The difference between the journal types is that different fields show in the different journals. In addition, some journals contain additional functionality – e.g. the payment proposal feature in the vendor payment journal.

Selecting different number sequences in the *Voucher series* field of journal names makes it possible to distinguish different journals by the voucher numbers. The default for the offset account in journal lines is specified in the fields *Account type* and *Offset account* of the journal names. The example in Figure 9-10 shows the bank account "E001" provided as default for the offset account in journal lines which use the journal name "GEB".

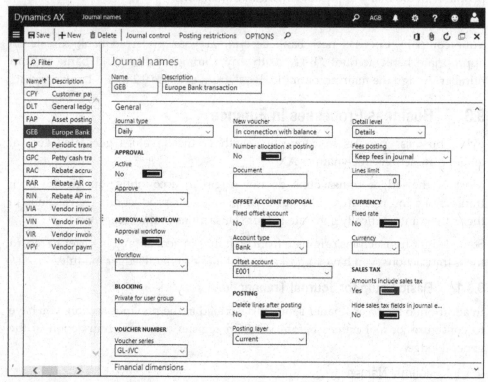

Figure 9-10:   Managing journal names

Another important setting on journal names is the slider *Amounts include sales tax*. If this slider is set to "Yes", amounts entered in the journal lines include sales tax (or input tax) if applicable. Otherwise, the entered line amount is a net amount to which Dynamics AX adds the sales tax.

9.3.1.2   Journal Approval

There are two options in the journal name setup, which define that a registered journal has to be approved before posting:

> **Journal approval system** – Enabled in the field group *Approval*
> **Approval workflow** – Enabled in the field group *Approval workflow*

If you want to activate the journal approval system for a journal name, set the slider *Active* in the field group *Approval* to "Yes". Then choose the user group, which is responsible for approval, in the corresponding lookup field *Approve*.

If you want to apply the approval workflow, an appropriate general ledger workflow has to be specified in the form *General ledger> Journal setup> General ledger workflows*. The workflow type "Ledger daily journal workflow" determines approval workflows for daily journals. More information on workflows is available in section 10.4.

9.3.1.3 Posting Layer

The *Posting layer* specified in journal names and used for transactions usually is "Current". If you need to cut off particular ledger transaction (for example because of local tax regulations), you can create separate journal names with the posting layer "Operations", "Tax", or one of the custom layers.

Selecting the appropriate posting layer in the closing sheet (when executing the fiscal year closing) or by selecting an appropriate journal name (when posting a journal transaction) provides the option to post transactions, which are not included in regular reports based on the layer "Current". In order to analyze and report the transactions in other layers, set up separate versions of financial reports which include the transactions in these layers.

9.3.1.4 General Ledger Parameters

The general ledger parameters form (*General ledger> Ledger setup> General ledger parameters*) contains further basic settings for journal transactions. As an example, you should reject duplicate vouchers in order to avoid confusion when looking at posted documents.

9.3.2 General Journal

If you want to post a manual transaction in the general ledger, register a general journal. The *General journal processing* workspace provides the option to view, to create, and to edit general journals. Alternatively, you can access the general journals from the menu (*General ledger> Journal entries> General journals*). Global general journals (*General ledger> Journal entries> Global general journals*) work the same way as regular general journals, except that you have to select the company when creating a journal (regular journals use the current company).

General journals refer to the journal type "Daily". Depending on the particular transaction, you can choose a journal related to another journal type instead of a general journal – for example an invoice journal in the accounts payable menu, or a payment journal in the accounts payable or the accounts receivable menu. If you do not need the advanced functionality available in the specific journals (e.g. payment proposals in payment journals), it does not matter if you register a transaction in the specific journal or in the general journal.

9.3.2.1 Journal Header

Journals are vouchers and therefore consist of a header and at least one line. The header contains common settings and defaults for the corresponding lines.

You can override the default values from the header in each line, for example entering a different offset account. Before you can post a journal, the balance of the individual vouchers (lines with the same voucher number) and the balance of the complete journal (shown at the bottom of the lines form) have to be zero.

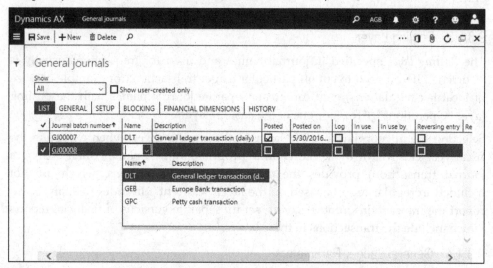

Figure 9-11:   Selecting a journal name when inserting a general journal header

The option selected in the lookup field *Show* at the top of the general journal list page determines whether open or posted journals display. In order to register a new journal, click the button *New* and select a journal name. In a general journal, only journal names with the journal type "Daily" are available.

On the tab *Setup* of the journal header, you can override the default values which derive from the journal name (e.g. the offset account or the currency). If somebody works in the lines of a particular journal while you are viewing the journal header, it is displayed in the columns *In use* and *In use by*.

9.3.2.2 Journal Lines

In order to switch to the journal lines, click the *Journal batch number* shown as link in the grid of the journal list page or click the button *Lines* in the action pane. The default for the posting date when entering a new line is the current session date. Dynamics AX retrieves the voucher number from the number sequence of the journal name which you have selected in the header. Depending on the option selected in the column *Account type* of the lines, you have to enter a ledger account, a vendor, a customer, a bank account or a fixed asset in the column *Account*.

If entering a ledger account in the *Account* field, segmented entry control applies (see below). The main account usually has to be entered in the first segment of the ledger account field in this case. If and which financial dimension segments are available and need to be entered is depending on the applicable account structure for the selected main account. Depending on the currently active segment in the ledger account field, the value lookup shows available values for that segment.

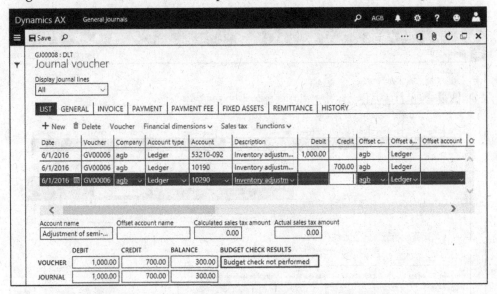

Figure 9-12: Registering a voucher with multiple offset transaction lines

After selecting the account, you can enter the applicable amount in the column *Debit* or *Credit*. In a single-line transaction, which shows the same amount for the debit and the credit account, enter the *Offset account type* and the *Offset account* (including segments for financial dimensions as applicable) in the appropriate columns of the journal line.

The columns *Company* and *Offset company* provide the option to register intercompany transactions. As a prerequisite, set up intercompany accounting (*General ledger> Posting setup> Intercompany accounting*) for these companies.

If a transaction has to be split to more than one offset account, you have to record the voucher in multiple lines. In this case, do not enter an offset account in the first line, but in one or more separate journal lines for the offset transactions. As long as the balance of the voucher is not zero, Dynamics AX retrieves the same voucher number as in the previous line. Once the voucher balance is zero, the next line shows a new voucher number (as prerequisite, the option "In connection with balance" has to be selected in the field *New voucher* of the journal name).

In order to support registration, a separate pane at the bottom of the lines form shows the balance of the voucher related to the selected line and the balance of the complete journal.

9.3.2.3 Segmented Entry Control

Segmented entry control supports entering the ledger account in account fields across all areas of the application. Since the main account and all applicable financial dimensions are merged into one single ledger account field, entering this field – by selecting main account and financial dimension values one after the other – provides the complete posting information according to the account structure.

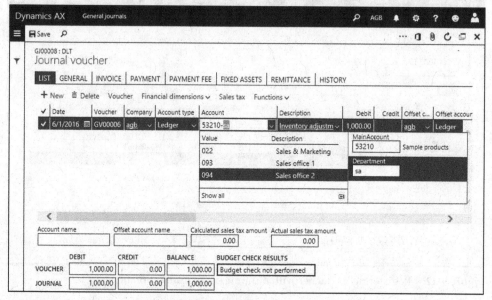

Figure 9-13:   Segmented entry for main account and financial dimensions

When entering the ledger account, the value lookup refers to the currently active segment of the account field. In order to search a segment value, enter the search content – the first characters of the identification or the name – in the appropriate segment of the account field before or after opening the value lookup by clicking the lookup button ⌄ or pressing the shortcut key *Alt + Down*.

The example in Figure 9-13 shows the segment lookup after entering "SA" in the second segment of the ledger account field. This lookup contains the department list filtered on departments beginning with "SA" in the ID or the name.

The sequence and the number of segments are depending on the account structure applicable to the selected main account (see section 9.2.4). If the account structure does not apply financial dimensions or allows blanks for a particular segment, it is not required to enter a corresponding segment value.

9.3.2.4   Posting Financial Journals

Once you have finished entering the journal lines, you can post the journal by clicking the button *Post/Post* or *Post* in the action pane of the journal header or lines (in a narrow screen, click the button ⋯ to view all buttons). In case of incorrect data, Dynamics AX shows an error message and does not post the transaction.

Clicking the button *Post/Post and transfer* (instead of *Post/Post*) in the journal header only posts vouchers, which contain correct data. Vouchers in the journal with incorrect data are transferred to a new journal where you can correct them.

9.3.2.5 Using the Journal Approval System

If journal approval – applying either the journal approval system or the approval workflow – is activated for the applicable journal name, you can't post the journal before receiving the required approval.

In case of the journal approval system, you can request the approval by clicking the button *Approval/Report as ready* in the journal header. The responsible for approval then clicks the button *Approval/Approve* to release the journal for posting.

9.3.2.6 Periodic Journals and Voucher Templates

If a particular transaction has to be registered and posted repeatedly, you can use one of the two options which support recurring registration:

> **Periodic journals** – Recurring on a regular basis
> **Voucher templates** – Used as copy template

Periodic journals support registering transactions which are repeated on a regular basis (e.g. office rent or monthly installments). In order to create a periodic journal, access the form *General ledger> Journal entries> Periodic journals* and enter a journal header and journal lines (similar to registering a general journal). An alternative way for creating a periodic journal is to copy a general journal to a periodic journal by clicking the button *Period journal/Save journal* in the lines of a general journal. The column *Date* in the periodic journal lines specifies the start date for the periodic transactions. The frequency of the transaction (e.g. monthly) has to be specified in the columns *Units* and *Number of units* (also shown on the tab *Periodic*).

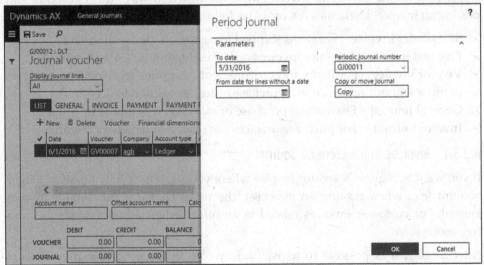

Figure 9-14: Retrieving a periodic journal for posting

In order to post a periodic journal, you have to create a general journal in each period. In the lines of this general journal, retrieve the periodic journal by clicking the button *Period journal/Retrieve journal*. Once the journal has received the periodic journal lines, you can edit and post the general journal lines as required. Apart from general journal, you can also use invoice journals in accounts payable to retrieve a periodic journal.

After retrieving journal lines, the column *Date* in the lines of the periodic journal shows the next date for posting the journal. This date is calculated by adding the frequency period to the date shown before retrieving the periodic journal. The column *Last date* shows when the periodic journal has been retrieved the last time.

Unlike periodic journals, voucher templates are templates for copying journals without managing a periodic interval. In order to create a voucher template, click the button *Functions/Save voucher template* in the toolbar of the journal lines in a general journal or in the action pane of invoice journal lines. In the dialog when saving the template, select the option "Percent" in the *Template type* if you want to apply a proportional distribution of line amounts

If you select this voucher template in a journal at a later time by clicking the button *Functions/Select voucher template*, a dialog shows where you can enter the amount to be distributed to the lines according to the proportion in the template.

9.3.2.7   New in Dynamics 'AX 7'

Items which are new in general journal processing include the *General journal processing* workspace and the global journals.

9.3.3   Invoice Journal

Depending on the particular invoice, there are different ways for registering and posting an invoice. Dynamics AX provides following options for this purpose:

> **Sales order invoice** – For items shipped to customers (see section 4.6.1)
> **Free text invoice** – For sales invoices not related to items (see section 4.6.3)
> **Vendor invoice** – For items and procurement categories received from vendors (with or without reference to a purchase order, see section 3.6.2)
> **General journal** – For manual purchase or sales invoices (not to be printed)
> **Invoice journal** – For purchase invoices not related to items or categories

9.3.3.1   Invoices in the General Journal

If you want to register a vendor invoice where you have to specify an offset ledger account (e.g. when posting an expense), the usual choice is the vendor invoice journal. For customer invoices related to an offset ledger account, you can use a free text invoice.

Alternatively, it is possible to register an invoice in the general journal. This is useful for example, if you want to record sales invoices which are not printed in Dynamics AX (e.g. invoices from a separate application like a POS solution).

When entering a sales invoice in a general journal, select the *Account type* "Customer" and enter the customer number in the column *Account* of the journal lines. In the column *Offset account*, enter an appropriate revenue account. On the tab *Invoice*, you have to enter the invoice number and the terms of payment or the applicable cash discount. Before posting, you should check on the tab *General* if correct sales tax groups are used. You can additionally check the sales tax calculation by clicking the button *Sales tax* in the toolbar of the tab *List*.

Registering a vendor invoice in a general journal works similar to the sales invoice (for a vendor invoice, choose the *Account type* "Vendor").

9.3.3.2 Accounts Payable Invoices

Whereas there is a specific form, the free text invoice, for registering a sales invoice with an offset ledger account in accounts receivable, there is no such form in purchasing or accounts payables.

You can register a vendor invoice – with or without reference to a purchase order – in the vendor invoice form (*Accounts payable> Invoices> Pending vendor invoices*, see section 3.6.2), but this form requires entering item numbers or procurement categories and does not contain a field for entering offset ledger accounts.

In order to register a vendor invoice not referring to an item number or a procurement category, but directly to a ledger account (e.g. for office rent), you have to enter a journal transaction. In accounts payable, following journals are available for registering and approving invoices:

➢ **Invoice journal** – Main form for vendor invoices in accounts payable
➢ **Invoice register** – In conjunction with the *Invoice approval journal*
➢ **General journal** – As described above

If you want to apply an approval workflow to invoice journals, set up an appropriate workflow with a template referring to the particular journal type in the form *Accounts payable> Setup> Accounts payable workflows* and assign it to the particular journal name.

The open vendor invoices page (*Accounts payable> Invoices> Open vendor invoices*) shows all invoices not yet paid, irrespective of the way of posting the invoice. The button *New/Invoice* in the action pane of this list page provides an alternative access to the different vendor invoice journals and the vendor invoice form. Similar options are available in the *Vendor invoice entry* workspace and in the vendor form (action pane tab *INVOICE*).

9.3.3.3 Invoice Journal

The invoice journal, which you can access through the menu item *Accounts payable> Invoices> Invoice journal* or through the *Vendor invoice entry* workspace, is the main form for registering invoices in accounts payable.

Like in every voucher, you have to create a header record in the invoice journal before you can switch to the lines. Once you have finished registering the invoice lines including vendor number (*Account*), vendor invoice number (*Invoice*), transaction text, amount, offset account, terms of payment, approver (*Approved by* on the tab *Invoice*) and other data like sales tax and cash discount as applicable, post the invoice by clicking the button *Post* in the action pane of the header or lines.

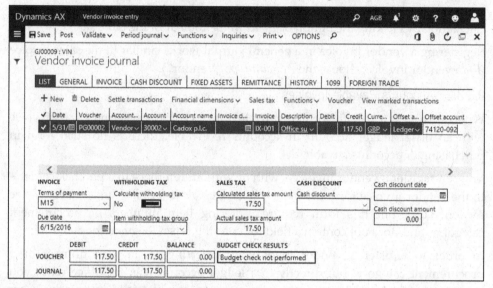

Figure 9-15:   Registering an invoice journal line

9.3.3.4 Invoice Register

The invoice register, which you can access through the menu item *Accounts payable> Invoices> Invoice register* or through the *Vendor invoice entry* workspace, provides the option to pre-register vendor invoices. The invoice register already posts the vendor transaction, applicable sales tax transactions (depending accounts payable parameter settings), and ledger transactions (to interim accounts). Depending on prior procedures, you can assign a purchase order to the invoice in the invoice register.

The structure of the invoice register with journal header and lines is similar to the structure of the general journals, but restricting the account type to "Vendor". In the journal lines, enter the employee responsible for approval (*Approved by* in the lower pane of the journal lines), the terms of payment, the cash discount, and sales tax groups as applicable. If the invoice refers to a purchase order, select the purchase order number in the appropriate column of the journal lines to facilitate later approval. In order to post a journal in the invoice register, click the button *Post* in the toolbar of the header or lines.

Posting a journal in the invoice register creates a regular vendor transaction, which you can access from the vendor form by clicking the button *VENDOR/Transactions/ Transactions* in the action pane after selecting the particular vendor. The slider *Approved* on the tab *General* of this transaction is set to "No", which is why the invoice is not included in payment proposals.

The ledger transactions of the invoice register are posted to interim accounts. These interim accounts are specified in the posting profile (*Accounts payable> Setup> Vendor posting profiles*, columns *Arrival* and *Offset account* on the tab *Setup*).

Sales tax posting of invoice register transactions is controlled by the accounts payable parameters, where the lookup field *Time of sales tax posting* on the tab *Ledger and sales tax* determines if sales tax is already posted with the invoice register or later with the invoice approval.

9.3.3.5 Invoice Approval Journal

After posting a journal in the invoice register, the employee who is responsible for approval can approve it in the invoice approval journal.

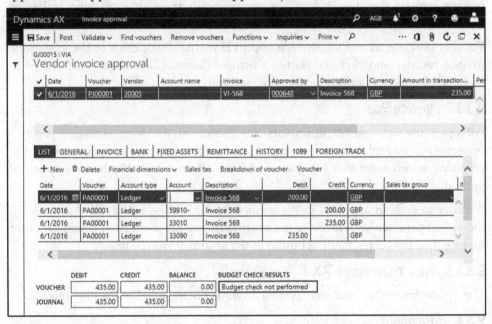

Figure 9-16: The invoice approval journal lines after fetching an invoice register

Invoice approval starts with creating a new header in the invoice approval journal (*Accounts payable> Invoices> Invoice approval*). After switching to the journal lines, click the button *Find vouchers* in order to retrieve the posted invoice register. The *Find vouchers* dialog shows all available invoice registers in the upper pane. Click the button *Select* there to choose one or more invoices for approval. Closing the *Find vouchers* dialog by clicking the button *OK* transfers the selected invoice(s) to the approval journal lines.

If you want to remove a selected invoice from the approval journal lines before posting, click the button *Remove vouchers* in the action pane of the invoice approval.

The next steps are depending on whether the invoice refers to a purchase order:

➢ **Not related to a purchase order** – In this case, select a ledger account – e.g. an expense account – in the lower pane of the invoice approval journal lines (first line in the lower pane of Figure 9-16). The expense amount does not include sales tax. If multiple expense accounts apply, enter multiple lines sharing the total amount. In order to post the approval finally, click the button *Post*.

➢ **Related to a purchase order** – In this case, click the button *Functions/Purchase order* in order to access the posting dialog for the related purchase order invoice. In the posting dialog, post the invoice as described in section 3.6.2.

9.3.3.6 Rejecting Invoice Approval

If you do not want to approve a vendor invoice, which has been posted in the invoice register (because it does not comply with applicable purchase orders or because of other reasons), you have to post a cancellation.

For this purpose, access the invoice approval journal lines, retrieve the applicable invoice register and click the button *Functions/Cancel*. Clicking the button *Post* in the invoice approval journal posts the cancellation.

9.3.3.7 Invoice Pool

All open invoice register approvals are shown in the form *Accounts payable> Invoices> Invoice pool*. You can use the invoice pool to post the approval for invoice registers, which refer to a purchase order (as alternative to the invoice approval journal).

In order to post an approval in the invoice pool, click the button *Purchase order* in the action pane which will show the posting dialog for the related purchase order invoice (like the corresponding button in the approval journal lines).

9.3.3.8 New in Dynamics 'AX 7'

The *Vendor invoice pool excluding posting details* is not included in the new release.

9.3.4 Payment

Posting an invoice creates an open transaction for the vendor liability or the customer debt.

9.3.4.1 Open Transactions

In order to view the open transactions, click the button *COLLECT/Settle/Settle transactions* in the customer form or the button *INVOICE/Settle/Settle transactions* in the vendor form. The button *CUSTOMER/Transactions/Transactions* in the customer form or *VENDOR/Transactions/Transactions* in the vendor form opens the transactions form which shows all transactions. Selecting the checkbox *Show open only* there applies a filter showing only open transactions.

In order to print the open transactions, choose the report *Accounts receivable> Inquiries and reports> Open transactions report* for customers and the report *Accounts payable> Inquiries and reports> Invoice> Vendor invoice transactions report* for vendors.

9.3.4.2 Customer Payment

If you want to register a customer payment, open the customer payment journal (*Accounts receivable> Payments> Payment journal*) or the general journal.

If you work in the customer payment journal, create a record in the journal header there and switch to the lines. In the journal lines, enter the payment with customer number, transaction text, payment amount, and offset account. If the customer has paid to your bank account, choose "Bank" for the offset account type.

If you want to settle a paid invoice when entering a payment line, select the invoice number in the column *Invoice* of the journal line (automatically inserting the invoice amount for payment). Alternatively, you can apply one or multiple invoices to a payment line by clicking the button *Settle transactions* in the toolbar of the lines. In the settlement dialog, select the paid invoices by selecting the checkbox in the column *Mark*. After clicking the button *OK* in the dialog, the marking applies to the payment journal line.

Apart from entering a payment in the payment journal lines, you can click the button *Enter customer payment* in the payment journal header in order to create and to settle payment lines by selecting paid invoices. Another option for creating payment lines, which you can use for direct debiting (withdrawing from the customer bank account), is the customer payment proposal in the payment journal lines (similar to the vendor payment proposal, see below).

Once you have finished entering payment lines, post the customer payment journal by clicking the button *Post* in the journal header or lines.

9.3.4.3 Vendor Payment

In a similar way to customer payments, payments to vendors can be entered in a specific payment journal or in a general journal. The menu item of the payment journal for vendors is *Accounts payable> Payments> Payment journal*.

Manually registering a vendor payment works like registering a customer payment (including the options for settlement). But in most cases, you need additional support and control for outgoing payments. In Dynamics AX, the payment proposal and the payment status are available for this purpose.

If you want to prevent paying a particular invoice, open the vendor transaction and switch to the tab *General*, where you can set the slider *Approved* to "No" or enter an *Invoice payment release date*. The payment proposal does not include the invoice until you set the approval in the transaction to "Yes" again or until the release date has passed.

9.3.4.4 Method of Payment

Methods of payment (*Accounts payable> Payment setup> Methods of payment*) are an important setting for processing vendor payments. Usually there are at least two methods of payment: One for manual transfers and one for electronic banking.

In payment methods related to electronic payment, you should select the *Payment status* "Sent" or "Approved" in order to prevent posting a payment before generating a related payment export file. Further settings for electronic payments (e.g. file formats) are available on the other tabs.

The field *Period* specifies if you want to collect all invoices in the selected period option to one payment or if you want to generate a separate payment per invoice.

In the field group *Posting* on the tab *General* of the methods of payment, you can enter a bank (or ledger) account from which you want to pay. This account is the default for the offset account when using the method in a payment. If you want to support bank reconciliation by posting to a bridging account (see below), set the slider *Bridging posting* to "Yes" and enter the bridging account number.

On the tab *Payment* in the vendor form, you can assign a *Method of payment* to a vendor. The payment method selected in the vendor record is the default for purchase orders, vendor transactions, and payment journals.

9.3.4.5 Vendor Payment Proposal

The payment proposal supports selecting vendor invoices for payment. In order to run a payment proposal, click the button *Payment proposal/Create payment proposal* in the action pane of the journal lines in a vendor payment journal.

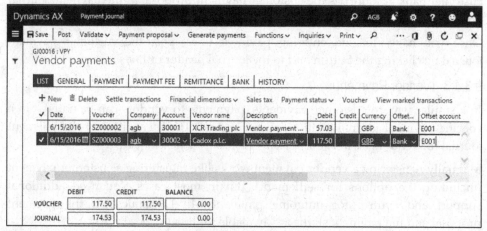

Figure 9-17: Registering lines in a vendor payment journal

In the *Vendor payment proposal* dialog, you can enter the proposal type (*Select invoices by* "Due date", or "Cash discount date", or both) and a date range for this date (*From date* and *To date*). If you select the option "Cash discount date" in the parameter *Select invoices by*, invoices without cash discount are not included in the proposal. On the tab *Records to include* of the dialog, you can enter a filter on vendor and transaction data.

Depending on the proposal type, the proposal for the *Date to pay* is the invoice due date or the cash discount date. If the due date (or cash discount date) is in the past,

Dynamics AX applies today as the *Date to pay*. If you have entered a future date in the field *Minimum date* of the dialog (e.g. tomorrow's date if preparing the payment for the next day), the *Minimum date* is used instead of today's date. The *Payment date* in the dialog is used if the method of payment refers to the *Period* "Total".

After closing the dialog by clicking the button *OK*, the payment proposal displays another dialog where you can check and edit the payment proposal. After removing invoices or changing *Date to pay* (by editing the *Due date* on the tab *Invoices* or the *Cash discount date* on the tab *Cash discount*) as applicable, you can click the button *Create payments* to transfer the proposal to the payment journal.

The payment proposal applies a settlement for the selected invoices. Depending on the method of payment in the particular invoices, there is one payment line for multiple invoices or a separate payment line per invoice.

Before posting the vendor payment, you can still edit the transferred proposal by clicking the button *Payment proposal/Edit invoices for selected payment*.

9.3.4.6 Generating and Posting Payments

In order to check the payment before generating and posting it, you can optionally print the payment journal by clicking the button *Print/Journal* in the header or lines.

If you require an export file for electronic payment, click the button *Generate payments* in the payment journal lines once you have finished entering the payment lines. Make sure to generate an export file before posting the payment, if you need the file. When generating the payment, Dynamics AX sets the payment status of the journal lines to "Sent". If required, you can change the payment status manually in the appropriate column or by clicking the button *Payment status* in the toolbar of the lines.

Finally click the button *Post* in the payment journal to post the payment from the selected bank or ledger account.

9.3.4.7 Applying Bridging Accounts

Bridging transactions are used, if you want to keep the payment on a separate account for the time from posting the payment until recognizing the transaction on the bank account (e.g. if you send a check).

In this case, the payment does not directly post to a bank account but to a bridging account as specified in the payment method. When recognizing the transaction on the bank account (e.g. when checking the bank statement), you have to post a transfer from the bridging account to the bank account.

In order to register and post this transfer, create a new journal in the general journals (*General ledger> Journal entries> General journals*). In the action pane of the general journal lines, click the button *Functions/Select bridged transactions* in order to access the form for selecting and accepting the transaction.

9.3.4.8   Centralized Payment

The functionality of centralized payments supports a company structure with a central company processing payments of an affiliated group. As a prerequisite for using centralized payments, you have to set up intercompany accounting (*General ledger> Posting setup> Intercompany accounting*) for the respective legal entities. In addition, appropriate permission settings applying an organization hierarchy with the purpose "Centralized payment" are required.

Payment journals and payment proposals show the company in the column *Company accounts*. When posting a payment applying centralized payments, you can settle invoices in other companies as applicable.

9.3.5   Reversing Transactions

In Dynamics AX, there are two different types of transaction reversals: Manually entered reversals (for corrections) and automatic reversals (for accruals).

9.3.5.1   Transaction Reversal

The transaction reversal, which is available for ledger transactions, vendor transactions, and customer transactions (including free text invoices), provides a simple way for correcting wrong vouchers in finance.

The transaction reversal is not available for transactions which refer to inventory, purchase orders, or sales orders. In order to reverse these transactions, register an appropriate document in the original menu – for example a customer return order in the *Sales and marketing* menu.

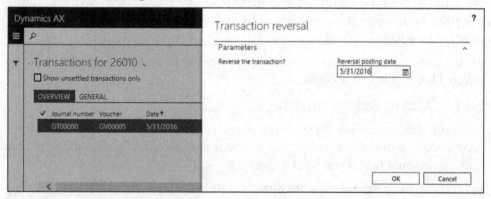

Figure 9-18:   Reversing a ledger transaction

In order to reverse a financial transaction using the transaction reversal, open the transaction inquiry by clicking the button *CUSTOMER/Transactions/Transactions* in the customer form or the button *VENDOR/Transactions/Transactions* in the vendor form. For ledger transactions, click the button *All transactions* in the trial balance (*General ledger> Inquiries and reports> Trial balance*) after selecting a main account.

After selecting a transaction, click the button *Reverse transaction* in the action pane which shows a dialog for entering the *Reversal posting date*. If you want to reverse a settled vendor or customer transaction (e.g. a paid invoice), you have to cancel the settlement (see section 9.2.5) before you can reverse the transaction.

Transaction reversal posts a new transaction, offsetting the original transaction. If required, you can reverse a reversal.

9.3.5.2 Automatic Reversal with Reversing Entries

Unlike manual transaction reversals, which are used to correct wrong transactions, reversing entries are transactions generated automatically in order to reverse accruals in a later period.

Reversing entries are available in the general journals (*General ledger> Journal entries> General journal*). In order to generate a reversing entry, select the checkbox *Reversing entry* and enter a *Reversing date* in the rightmost columns of the journal lines when entering the original transaction. In the general journal header, the checkbox *Reversing entry* and the *Reversing date* provide a default for the lines.

When posting a general journal with automatic reversal, Dynamics AX in parallel posts a second transaction reversing the original transaction.

9.3.6 Case Study Exercises

Exercise 9.5 – Journal Names

You want to register the transactions of the next exercises in your own journals. For this purpose, create a journal name "G-##" (## = your user ID) with the type "Daily", a journal name "I-##" with the type "Vendor invoice recording", and a journal name "P-##" with the type "Vendor disbursement". Choose an existing number sequence in all these journal names.

Exercise 9.6 – Segmented Entry in General Journals

You want to transfer USD 50.00 from your main account "ZZ##" in "Area ## 1" to your petty cash account "111C-##" (both accounts entered in Exercise 9.2). Register this transaction in a general journal using your journal name "G-##".

Which segments apply to your main account "ZZ##"? Check the value lookup for the main account and the financial dimension. Then post the journal. Finally check the balance and transactions of both accounts entered in the journal line.

Exercise 9.7 – General Journal

You want to withdraw USD 100.00 from the bank account "B-##" entered in Exercise 9.4 and put it to your petty cash account "111C-##" entered in Exercise 9.2. Register this transaction in a general journal using your journal name "G-##".

Before posting, check the balance and transactions for the bank account and the petty cash account. Then post the journal and check the balances and transactions again.

Exercise 9.8 – Purchase Invoice

The vendor, which you have entered in exercise 3.2, submits the invoice "VI908" showing a total of USD 50.00 to your company. The invoice shows expenses which refer to the main account "6060##" entered in Exercise 9.2.

Record this invoice in an invoice journal with your journal name "I-##". The terms of payment and the cash discount entered in exercise 3.1 apply to this invoice.

Before posting, check the vendor transactions and balance for the vendor and the ledger transactions and balance for the expense account. Then post the invoice and check the balances and the transactions again.

Exercise 9.9 – Vendor Payment

You want to pay the invoice "VI908" which you have posted in the previous exercise. Register the payment in a vendor payment journal applying your journal name "P-##". Pay from your bank account "B-##" entered in Exercise 9.4 and withdraw applicable cash discount.

Before posting, check the vendor balance and the bank account balance. Then post the payment and check the balances, the voucher transactions, and the transaction origin for the payment.

Exercise 9.10 – Transaction Reversal

Your vendor of exercise 3.2 now submits the invoice "VI910" with a total of USD 30.00 to your company. Register and post the invoice like you did in Exercise 9.8.

Afterwards you notice that the invoice is incorrect, which is why you want to reverse it. Before reversing, check the vendor transactions and balance for the vendor and the ledger transactions and balance for the expense account. Then reverse the invoice and check the balances and transactions again.

9.4   Ledger Integration

One of the main advantages of an integrated business solution like Dynamics AX is, that business transactions registered anywhere in the application are also available in all other areas. For example, posting a sales order invoice does not only generate the required document, it also affects other areas generating following transactions:

➢ **Inventory transactions** – Reducing inventory value
➢ **General ledger transactions** – Revenue, COGS, stock, and customer accounts
➢ **Customer transaction** – Open invoice in accounts receivable
➢ **Sales tax transactions** – As applicable

Depending on the particular transaction, the invoice may for example also post transactions for commission, discount, or cash payment.

9.4.1 Basics of Ledger Integration

Ledger integration – the integration of the general ledger in finance with the other areas of the application – is one of the core characteristics of an integrated business solution (ERP solution). In Dynamics AX, transactions in all areas relevant to finance (e.g. sales, purchasing, inventory, or production) automatically post transactions to the general ledger.

9.4.1.1 Basic Settings

A number of settings control, whether and which main accounts apply to the different transactions in business. For the areas of purchasing, sales, inventory, and production covered in this book, following settings are relevant:

> **Summary accounts for vendor liabilities and customer debts** – In the posting profiles for accounts payable/receivable
> **Main accounts for inventory transactions** – In the inventory posting setup
> **Main accounts for production resource consumption** – In resources, cost categories, and production groups

In addition, specific settings are available for particular transactions like sales tax, cash discount, indirect costs, or miscellaneous charges.

9.4.1.2 Vendors and Customers

Vendor posting profiles control the assignment of vendor transactions to summary accounts in the general ledger. Customer posting profiles for customer transactions work similar. More details on posting profiles are available in section 3.2.3.

9.4.1.3 Subledger Accounting

Subledger accounting in Dynamics AX decouples subledger posting (e.g. in accounts receivable) from general ledger posting. The subledger journal entry functionality for this purpose provides the option to execute the transfer to the general ledger either synchronous or asynchronous, and either detailed or summarized. Subledger accounting does not apply to all subledger transactions, but to some particular document types including:

> **Free text invoice** – See section 4.6.3
> **Product receipt** – Purchase order receipt, see section 3.5.4
> **Vendor invoice** – Purchase order invoice, see section 3.6.2

In the general ledger parameters, settings on the tab *Batch transfer rules* controls the subledger transfer per company and per document type. The *Transfer mode* specifies, when a subledger transaction is posted to the general ledger:

> **Synchronous** – Immediately posting to the general ledger
> **Asynchronous** – Posting as soon as sever capacity is available
> **Scheduled batch** – In a separate batch job (e.g. in the nighttime), providing the option to view subledger transactions before transferring to the general ledger

For documents applying the scheduled batch transfer, posted subledger transactions are shown in the form *General ledger> Periodic tasks> Subledger journal entries not yet transferred* before transfer. Clicking the button *Transfer now* (for an immediate transfer) or *Transfer in batch* (for a scheduled transfer) in this form posts the subledger transaction to the general ledger.

The button *View accounting* in the subledger journal entries form and in applicable source documents (e.g. free text invoices) provides access to the complete accounting information including all applicable financial segments.

9.4.2   Ledger Integration in Inventory

When posting inventory receipts and issues to the general ledger, Dynamics AX distinguished two different types of transactions (see section 7.1.1):

➢ **Physical transaction** – Packing slip
➢ **Financial transaction** – Invoice

Physical and financial transactions refer to different main accounts.

9.4.2.1   Physical Transaction

Posting of physical transactions to the general ledger is optional, not compulsory. Relevant settings on this subject include following checkboxes and sliders:

➢ **Post physical inventory** (in the item model group)
➢ **Post product receipt in ledger** (Accounts payable parameters, tab *General*) or **Post packing slip in ledger** (Accounts receivable parameters, tab *Updates*).

For transactions in production control, relevant settings are available on tab *General* of the production control parameters. Physical transactions in production are picking list and report as finished transactions.

Independently from the parameter settings, physical transactions of items with the inventory model "Standard costs" are always posted to the ledger.

9.4.2.2   Financial Transaction

For financial transactions, the checkbox *Post financial value* in the item model group determines whether inventory transactions post to the general ledger. If this checkbox is cleared in an item model group, ledger integration is not active for the assigned items. This is the appropriate setting for service items. Posting a purchase invoice in this case directly posts to the expense account for consumption. Inventory issues do not post ledger transactions.

9.4.2.3   Assignment of Main Accounts

In order to check the main accounts applying in an inventory transaction, open the inventory posting setup (*Inventory management> Setup> Posting> Posting*). The inventory posting setup form includes account settings for following transactions:

> **Sales order tab** – Packing slips and invoices in sales
> **Purchase order tab** – Product receipts and invoices in purchasing
> **Inventory tab** – Journal transactions in inventory
> **Production tab** – Picking lists, reporting as finished, and costing in production
> **Standard cost variance tab** – Standard cost variances

Each of these tabs shows a list of available transaction types in the left pane. After selecting a transaction type in the left pane, the right pane shows the main accounts for this transaction type.

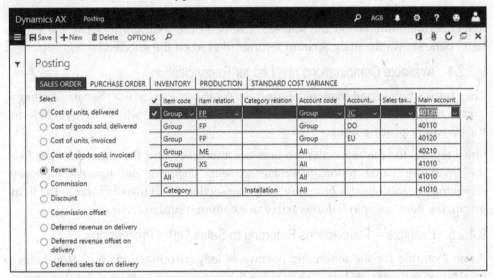

Figure 9-19:   The inventory posting setup, showing account settings for revenue

The inventory posting setup is primarily depending on the combination of two dimensions:

> **Item dimension** – Items or categories
> **Account dimension** – Customers or vendors

In addition, main account settings optionally include the sales tax group and – for standard cost variance transactions – the cost group as applicable dimensions.

For the item dimension and the account dimension (customer on the tab *Sales order*, vendor on the tab *Purchase order*), there are three levels for main account settings:

> **Table** – Individual item, customer, or vendor
> **Group** – Item group, customer group, or vendor group
> **All**– All items, customers, or vendors

The *Item code* "Category" – an additional option for the item dimension in sales and purchasing – provides the option to enter settings at product category level. The last line of the revenue settings in Figure 9-19 shows an example for such a setting.

When posting a transaction, Dynamics AX always searches for the specific setting ("Table") first, then for the group setting, and finally for the general setting ("All").

Settings for the customer and item number for example have the highest priority in a sales invoice transaction, followed by group settings. Settings on the tab *Ledger and sales tax* of the accounts receivable parameters control, whether the search should prioritize the item or the customer dimension. A similar setting for purchasing is available in the accounts payable parameters.

Main account assignment is not only available in the inventory posting setup form. You can alternatively access these settings by clicking the button *Posting* in the item group form, or the button *Setup/Item posting* in the customer group or vendor group form. When accessing the posting setup from a group form, it shows the ledger settings filtered on the selected group. In the item group form, the right-hand pane shows the main account settings filtered on the selected item group.

9.4.2.4 Available Combinations and Ledger Reconciliation

The transaction combinations form (*Inventory management> Setup> Posting> Transaction combinations*) determines the dimension levels, which are available in the inventory posting setup.

Since reports for the reconciliation between inventory and the general ledger like the inventory value report (*Cost management> Inquiries and reports> Inventory accounting - status reports> Inventory value*, see section 7.3.1) usually refer to the item group, the item group relation is active in a common setup scenario.

9.4.2.5 Example – Transactions Referring to Sales Order Processing

As an example for the automatic posting of ledger transactions based on ledger integration settings, the lines below show the transactions in sales order processing with activated ledger integration for packing slip and invoice posting (physical and financial transactions).

When posting the packing slip for the sales order, Dynamics AX posts a ledger transaction to the main accounts specified for *Cost of units, delivers* and *Cost of goods sold, delivered* in the inventory posting setup. When posting the invoice, Dynamics AX reverses the ledger transactions of packing slip posting, and posts a ledger transaction from the account *Cost of units, invoiced* to the account *Cost of goods sold, invoiced*. In parallel, a customer debt to the summary account (specified in the posting profile) is posted against the account *Revenue* and – if applicable – the sales tax account.

If the inventory posting setup includes a setting in the option *Discount* for the line discount, the discount is posted to this account. Otherwise, the discount is not posted separately but reduces the revenue amount.

9.4.2.6 Standard Cost Price and Moving Average

For items assigned to an inventory model "Standard cost" (see section 7.3.1), there are essential settings on the tab *Standard cost variance* of the inventory posting setup. This tab contains the main accounts which are used for posting differences between the actual cost price of the purchase order invoice (or of production order costing) and the standard cost price, split by posting type (e.g. *Purchase price variance*).

For items assigned to an inventory model with a fixed receipt price, settings for posting the price difference are available on the tabs *Purchase order* and *Inventory*.

For items assigned to an inventory model "Moving average", settings for posting the price difference (for quantities not on stock any more when receiving the invoice) and for revaluation are available on the tab *Inventory*.

9.4.2.7 Service Items and Non-Stocked Items

Items not tracked in inventory (e.g. office supplies or consumables) can be linked to the product type "Service" and a specific item group and item model group for service items. In the item model group, ledger integration for physical and financial transactions should be deselected.

When posting a purchase order invoice for such an item, there is a transaction against the expense account for consumption (instead of a stock account transaction). When posting a sales order invoice, there is only a ledger transaction from the customer summary account to the revenue account (and no transaction from the account *Cost of units, invoiced* to *Cost of goods sold, invoiced*).

If a non-stocked items is not included in a bill of materials, you can use an item model group with a cleared checkbox *Stocked product* (see section 7.2.1). This setting prevents inventory transactions and ensures that ledger integration for physical and financial transactions is deselected.

9.4.2.8 Change of Settings

In order to avoid issues when reconciling inventory and general ledger, you should not change integration settings in the item model group, in parameters and in the inventory posting setup for items, which are on stock or show open inventory transactions. This includes both, changing the setup itself, and changing the assignment of active items to item groups.

9.4.3 Ledger Integration in Production

Unlike ledger transactions referring to purchasing, sales, or inventory, ledger transactions referring to production have to include the cost of resource operations in the inventory value of manufactured items.

9.4.3.1 Production Control Parameters

In order to comply with this requirement, the production control parameters include the lookup field *Ledger posting* with following options:

➢ **Item and resource**
➢ **Item and category**
➢ **Production groups**

The setting in the production control parameters, which is not available in the production parameters by site, is the default for production orders. It is possible to override this default in the particular production orders, for example if applying specific settings for prototype production.

The option "Item and resource" in the *Ledger posting* parameter applies the main accounts specified in the inventory posting setup to item transactions. For resource operations, the main account settings in the resource (*Production control> Setup> Resources> Resources*, tab *Ledger postings*) apply.

The option "Item and category" in the *Ledger posting* parameter also applies the main accounts specified in the inventory posting setup to item transactions. But for resource operations, settings of the applicable cost category (*Production control> Setup> Routes> Cost categories*, tab *Ledger postings*) apply.

The option "Production group" in the *Ledger posting* parameter applies settings in the posting group (*Production control> Setup> Production> Production groups*). Production orders show the applicable production group on the tab *General* in the detail form (default from the tab *Engineer* in the released product).

9.4.3.2 Ledger Transactions in Production

When processing a production order, following ledger transactions are posted to the main accounts as specified in the *Ledger posting* parameter:

➢ **Picking list** – Account *Estimated cost of materials consumed* against *Estimated cost of materials consumed, WIP* (WIP = "Work In Process")
➢ **Resource operation** – Account *Estimated manufacturing cost absorbed* against *Estimated manufacturing cost consumed, WIP*
➢ **Report as finished** – Account *Estimated manufactured cost* against *Estimated manufactured cost, WIP*
➢ **Indirect costs** – Settings in the costing sheet: *Estimated indirect costs absorbed* against *Estimated cost of indirect cost consumed, WIP*

Costing the production order reverses all these transactions and posts the final finished product receipt, component issue, resource issue, and indirect cost transactions to the main accounts as specified in the *Ledger posting* parameter.

10 Core Setup and Essential Features

The organization of an enterprise determines the setup of the ERP system. Before starting to work in Dynamics AX, there needs to be an implementation project which includes the setup of the enterprise organization and other core parameters.

10.1 Organizational Structures

If you want to set up an independent installation of Dynamics AX, which contains its own database and application, you have got to access the Microsoft Dynamics Lifecycle Services. After creating or opening a project and accessing the *Cloud-hosted environments*, you can add an environment and deploy it on Azure (or locally on a virtual hard disk for development and demo purposes). Usually there is at least one environment for development and for tests, which is separate from the operational environment.

Within one Dynamics AX environment with its database, the organization model represents the structure of the enterprise and its business processes. The organization model has to be configured according the operational and statutory structure of the enterprise. Depending on the type and size of the organization, there are different organizational structures which you can classify into following groups:

➢ **Statutory organization structures for legal reporting** – Hierarchies according to the regulations of public authorities (e.g. for tax purposes)
➢ **Operational organization structures for management reporting** – Hierarchies according to the requirements of the management (e.g. divisional structures, for controlling purposes and for improving business processes)
➢ **Informal structures** – Not showing organizational hierarchies

In order to comply with the different reporting requirements, large enterprises can show different organizational structures and hierarchies in parallel. You can for example set up one hierarchy matching the structure and purpose of legal entities, another hierarchy supporting the divisional structure, and a third hierarchy complying with regional structures.

For other enterprises, one simple hierarchy without the need for different organizational structures may be adequate.

10.1.1 Organization Model Architecture

The organization model in Microsoft Dynamics AX supports the requirements of different organization types. Depending on the requirements, the organization setup alternatively includes multiple organization hierarchies in parallel, decoupling the operational organization from the statutory organization, or only one simple hierarchy used for all purposes at the same time.

10.1.1.1 Organization Types

Following organization types are included in the organization model:

➤ **Legal entities** – Showing the statutory organization
➤ **Operating units** – Showing the operational organization
➤ **Teams** – Showing informal structures

Only organization units of the type "Legal entity" and "Operating unit" are applicable elements for setting up organization hierarchies in Dynamics AX.

Since organization units of the type "Team" are an informal type of organizations, they are not included in hierarchies. Teams are used in various areas of the application, for example as a basis for restricting access to the global address book.

10.1.1.2 Using the Organization Model within Dynamics AX

Following areas apply the organization model within Dynamics AX:

➤ **Company structure** – Legal entities are linked to companies in Dynamics AX, which is why you have to set up legal entities for creating companies.
➤ **Financial dimensions** – Since legal entities and operating units are available as basis for financial dimensions, they can be used for financial reporting.
➤ **Data security** – Based on the organization hierarchy purpose *Security*, access of users to organizations may be configured independently from the structure of legal entities.
➤ **Business policies** – Business rules for areas like approval processes and centralized payments can apply a structure which is different from the hierarchy of legal entities.

Legal entities and operating units are not only part of the organization hierarchies, but they are also included in the global address book (see section 2.4). For this reason, features of the global address book like address and contact administration are available for legal entities and operating units.

10.1.1.3 New in Dynamics 'AX 7'

Virtual company accounts (supporting shared data across companies in former releases) are not supported in the new version, but starting with the May 2016 update you can use cross-company data replication.

Data partitions, which have provided the option to separate data of organizations working in a common Dynamics AX 2012 R2/R3 database, are not officially supported in the new version. In the initial release of Dynamics 'AX 7', data partitions are still included as key field in each relevant table and you can use the parameter "&prt" to select a partition when accessing Dynamics AX (e.g. *https://XXX.com/?&prt=ps* for the data partition "ps"), but it is not possible to manage partitions within the Dynamics AX client. It is recommended to set up separate databases instead of partitions.

10.1.2 Organization Unit

The organization model includes organization units of the type "Legal entity", "Operating unit" and "Team". Legal entities and operating units are the basic elements in the organizational hierarchies of an enterprise.

The list page *Organization administration> Organizations> Internal organizations* shows an overview of all organizations with their type. Forms tailored to the specific requirements of the different organization types are available in the other menu items of the folder *Organization administration> Organizations*.

Internal Organization		
Legal Entities	**Operating Units**	**Teams**
Statutory organization (Companies)	*Operational organization* ➢ Departments ➢ Cost centers ➢ Business units ➢ Value streams ➢ Retail organization types	*Informal organization*

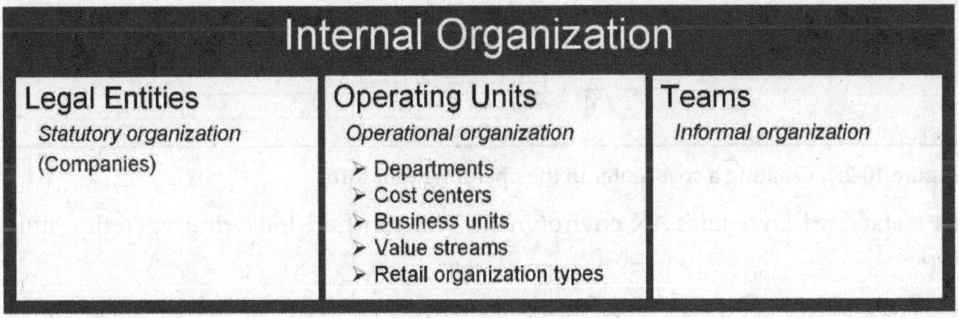

Figure 10-1: Organization units in the organization model

10.1.2.1 Legal Entities

Legal entities (*Organization administration> Organizations> Legal entities*) are company accounts in Dynamics AX (see section 10.1.4 below), constituting the basic level for legal reporting. Tax reports and financial statements like balance sheets and income statements are based on legal entities.

If a Dynamics AX database contains multiple legal entities, you can manage the relations between these legal entities. Depending on the requirements, following features are available:

➢ **Financial consolidation** – Managing financial consolidation of companies in an affiliated group

➢ **Intercompany** – Automating business processes between the legal entities of a multi-company organization

➢ **Organization hierarchies** – Applying legal entities in the organization model (e.g. for setting up data security or approval processes)

10.1.2.2 Operating Units

Operating units (*Organization administration> Organizations> Operating units*) are used for reporting and the internal control of business processes. Depending on the enterprise, operating units include different types like divisions or regions.

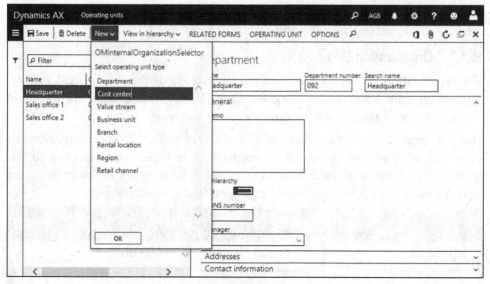

Figure 10-2:   Creating a cost center in the operating unit form

In a standard Dynamics AX environment, you can find following operating unit types:

➢ **Department** – Representing functional categories, also used in human resources
➢ **Cost center** – For budgeting and expenditure control
➢ **Value stream** – Referring to production flows (lean manufacturing)
➢ **Business unit** – Controlling strategic business objectives (e.g. divisions)
➢ **Other types for retail** – Referring to retail management

When setting up a new operating unit by clicking the button *New* in the action pane of the operating units form, select the *Operating unit type* first. Then enter additional data like name, addresses and contact data in the detail form.

Once an operating unit is assigned to one or more hierarchies, you can click the button *View in hierarchy* to check the allocation within organizational structures. Linking operating units to financial dimensions (see section 9.2.3) provides the option to report on their performance.

10.1.2.3 Teams

Teams (*Organization administration> Organizations> Teams*) represent the informal organization of an enterprise. A team is a group of people, without a hierarchical organization structure between different teams.

Team types, which you can access by clicking the button *Team types* in the action pane of the *Teams* form, restrict the team membership to different kinds of people – e.g. Dynamics AX users, employees, or sales contacts.

When creating a new team, you have to select the team type. On the tab *Team members*, you can subsequently assign people to the team by clicking the button

Add team members in the toolbar. Depending on the team type, available members are for example Dynamics AX users, vendors, or employees.

Teams are used in various areas of the application, for example in collections (select the responsible team in the accounts receivable parameters).

10.1.3 Organization Hierarchy Structures

An organization hierarchy shows the relationship between the different organization units according to the particular purpose of the hierarchy. An organizational hierarchy of legal entities for example shows the legal structure.

Depending on the requirements of your enterprise, there are multiple hierarchies in parallel. The purposes of a hierarchy determine its functional areas. Hierarchies of the type *Security* for example apply to data security.

10.1.3.1 Organization Hierarchies

In order to view the organization hierarchies in your enterprise, open the form *Organization administration> Organizations> Organization hierarchies*. If you want to create a new hierarchy, click the button *New* and enter the hierarchy name. Then click the button *Assign purpose* on the tab *Purposes* to assign one or more hierarchy purposes to the hierarchy.

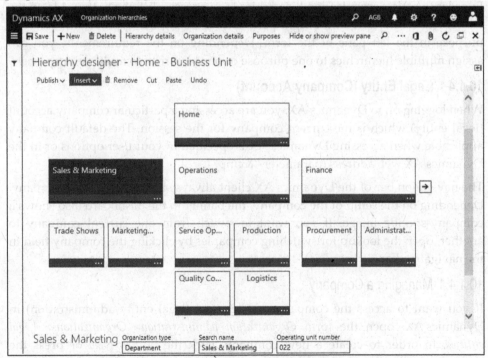

Figure 10-3:   Editing an organization hierarchy in the hierarchy designer

Clicking the button *View* in the action pane provides access to the hierarchy designer for viewing the hierarchy. In the hierarchy designer, you can navigate within the hierarchy, or switch the focus by clicking the button ▦ on the bottom right of the organization unit tiles.

After switching to the edit mode by clicking the button *Edit* in the action pane of the hierarchy designer, you can insert or remove organization units from the hierarchy as applicable by clicking the appropriate button in the toolbar. The buttons *Cut* and *Paste* provide the option to move a unit including subunits within the whole organization hierarchy.

The organization structure applies validity periods, which is why you have to enter an effective date when publishing the hierarchy after editing.

10.1.3.2 Organization Hierarchy Purposes

In case your enterprise requires different hierarchies for different purposes, there are multiple hierarchies in the organization hierarchy form.

Organization hierarchy purposes show in the form *Organization administration> Organizations> Organization hierarchy purposes*. Since hierarchy purposes refer to functional features in Dynamics AX, available purposes (e.g. *Centralized payments* or *Security*) and the allowed organization types per purpose are determined by the application.

In order to assign organization hierarchies to purposes, click the button *Add* on the tab *Assigned hierarchies* in the right pane after selecting the appropriate hierarchy purpose in the left pane of the form. Depending on the requirements, you can assign multiple hierarchies to one purpose or one hierarchy to multiple purposes.

10.1.4   Legal Entity (Company Account)

When logging on to Dynamics AX, you are accessing a particular company account (legal entity) which is the current company for the session. The default company applicable when accessing Dynamics AX is specified in your user options or in the Dynamics AX web address (parameter "&cmp").

The navigation bar of the Dynamics AX client always shows the current company. Depending on the setup of the company, the banner in the dashboard also shows a company-specific image. If you want to switch from one current company to another, open the lookup for switching companies by clicking the company field in the navigation bar.

10.1.4.1 Managing a Company

If you want to access the company management (legal entity administration) in Dynamics AX, open the form *Organization administration> Organizations> Legal entities*. In order to create a new company, click the button *New* or press the shortcut *Alt+N* and enter the company name, the company ID (with up to 4 digits), and the country/region (by default determining applicable country-specific Dynamics AX features) in the *New legal entity* dialog.

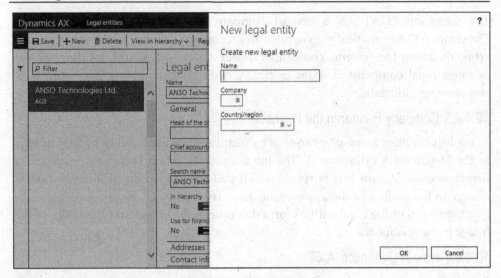

Figure 10-4: Creating a company in the legal entity form

Before you can start entering and posting transactions in the new company, the setup of the company has to be done in all applicable areas and modules (like general ledger, accounts payable, and accounts receivable). A checklist of basic settings is available in the appendix of this book.

Core data in the legal entity form include the company name (which prints on all documents and reports) and further settings like the primary address of the company on the tab *Addresses*. If the company has got additional addresses for purposes like invoicing or delivery, you can add them by clicking the button ⊞ on tab *Addresses*. An example of an additional address is a default delivery address which is different from the primary company address. This delivery address is the default for purchase orders then (if no address from a site or warehouse applies).

The tab *Contact information* contains the contact data of the company. Legal entities in Dynamics AX are covered by the global address book, which is why company addresses and contact data are included there.

Further important settings in the legal entity form include the primary bank account and registration numbers (like the *Routing number* for tax reporting) on the tab *Bank account information*. In a company located in the European Union, enter the VAT registration number (VAT exempt number) on the tab *Foreign trade and logistics*.

10.1.4.2 Companies in the Data Structure

A Dynamics AX database can include multiple company accounts. Except for shared application data (like parties or products), company accounts establish a separate set of data within the application. The key field *DataAreaId* in all relevant Dynamics AX tables determines the company of the particular record.

The company "DAT" is a special company in the Dynamics AX database. Dynamics AX automatically generates this company, which holds system data, when installing the system. You cannot delete it and you should not use it as test or operational company in order to clearly distinguish company data from non-company specific data.

10.1.4.3 Company Banner in the Dashboard

In the legal entities form, you can select a picture to be displayed as banner or logo in the Dynamics AX dashboard. The tab *Images* contains a *Dashboard image* and a *Report company logo* for this purpose, which you can upload by clicking the button *Change* in the toolbar of the appropriate area. The option *Dashboard company image type* tab *Images* of the legal entities form determines the layout and the usage of the image in the dashboard.

10.1.4.4 New in Dynamics 'AX 7'

Based on the browser-based user interface, the layout and option to switch between companies has changed.

10.1.5 Site

Unlike company accounts, which are used for legal entities, sites represent subsidiaries within a company. Since sites are an inventory dimension (storage dimension), they are available in all areas of supply chain management within Dynamics AX.

In order to distinguish between subsidiaries in finance and in cost accounting, you can link the inventory dimension "Site" to a financial dimension. Filtering on the financial dimension then for example provides the option to print an income statement per subsidiary.

10.1.5.1 Multisite Functionality

The multisite functionality for managing subsidiaries in Dynamics AX includes the following options:

➤ **Operations planning** (master planning) – Per site or for the entire company
➤ **Bills of materials** – Per site or for the entire company
➤ **Production control parameters** – Per site or for the entire company
➤ **Item data (Released products)** – Order settings per site or for the entire company
➤ **Transactions** – Sites in all inventory transactions, sales orders, purchase orders and production orders
➤ **Financial reports** – Optionally for sites (if linked to a financial dimension)

10.1.5.2 Setup of Sites

In order to view the sites of the current company, open the form *Inventory management> Setup> Inventory breakdown> Sites*. Apart from the ID, the name, and the address, a site includes the assigned financial dimension on the tab *Financial dimensions*. This setting is mandatory if the dimension link is activated.

The dimension link between the inventory dimension "Site" and a financial dimension is specified in the form *Inventory management> Setup> Posting> Dimension link*. If applicable to your enterprise structure, you can activate and lock the link there. Figure 10-5 for example shows the site form in a company in which sites are linked to the financial dimension "Department".

Since sites are a mandatory storage dimension, they are automatically activated in all storage dimension groups. Every inventory transaction therefore includes a dimension value for the site. In addition, each warehouse has to be linked to a site.

If sites do not apply to the organization of your enterprise, set up Dynamics AX in a way that a single site is the default in all transactions (e.g. applying appropriate defaults in the *Default order settings* of released products). More information on inventory dimensions is available in section 7.2.2.

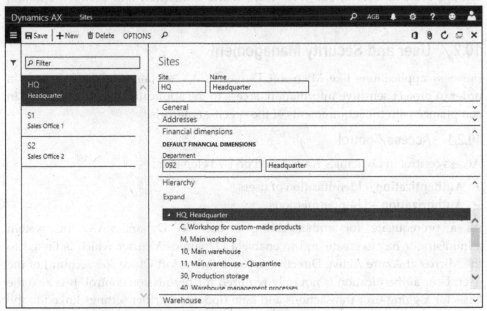

Figure 10-5: Sites in a company (linked to the financial dimension "Department")

10.1.5.3 Production Units

Whereas material management applies *Sites* as a storage dimension for establishing a structure level below legal entities, resource management applies *Production units* for structuring resources and resource groups. Each production unit is linked to a site and represents a plant in operations planning.

10.1.5.4 Linking Sites to the Organization Model

It is not possible to directly include sites in the organization model. But you can link sites to a financial dimension and financial dimensions to organization units, which in the end provides the option to use sites in the organization model.

In order to apply sites to Dynamics AX finance and organization administration, perform following implementation steps:

➤ **Operating units** – Create operating units with a common operating unit type (e.g. *Department* or *Business unit*) for the individual sites
➤ **Financial dimension** – Set up a dimension linked to this organization unit type
➤ **Account structure** – Apply an account structure which contains this dimension
➤ **Dimension link** – Link the storage dimension *Site* to this financial dimension

Choosing the same name for the organization unit and the related site visualizes sites in the organization hierarchy. Through the organization model, security settings are available at site level then. If the dimension link between site and financial dimension is activated, you can perform financial reporting per site.

10.2 User and Security Management

Business applications like Microsoft Dynamics AX contain confidential data. In order to protect sensitive information, access to the application has to be limited in compliance with the requirements of the specific enterprise.

10.2.1 Access Control

Access control in Dynamics AX is based on two elements:

➤ **Authentication** – Identification of users
➤ **Authorization** – User permissions

As a prerequisite for authenticating a user in Dynamics AX, the system administrator has to create and to enable a Dynamics AX user which is linked to the Microsoft Azure Active Directive account (Microsoft Office 365 account) of the user. User authentication is not only required for permission control. It is also the basis for logging user transactions and data updates. Further settings linked to the Dynamics AX user include the favorites, the user options, and the usage data, which enable a personalized workspace in Dynamics AX.

Dynamics AX applies a role-based security model for authorization, which means that security roles control the access to application elements (e.g. menu items). A Dynamics AX user can have one or more roles, which determine his permissions.

Permissions for application elements are not directly assigned to a role, but to duties and privileges. Duties (and privileges below duties) establish a grouping level for permissions in the structure of the security model.

The extensible data security framework in addition provides the option to restrict access based on effective dates or user data, e.g. based on the sales territory.

10.2.2 User Management

Each person accessing Dynamics AX has to be set up as a Dynamics AX user.

10.2.2.1 Creating User Accounts

In order to create a Dynamics AX user, open the list page *System administration> Users> Users* and click the button *New*. After typing a new Dynamics AX *User ID*, enter the Azure Active Directory account of the user in the field *Alias*, and specify the *Domain*. In addition, the slider *Enabled* has to be set to "Yes" in order to enable the user to log on to Dynamics AX.

As an alternative to creating users manually, you can import Dynamics AX users from the Azure Active Directory through the import wizard, which you can access by clicking the button *Import users* in the action pane of the *Users* form.

10.2.2.2 Security Role and Permission Assignment

In order to specify the permissions of the particular user, switch to the tab *User's roles* in the user detail form and assign appropriate security roles. Alternatively, you can use form *System administration> Security> Assign users to roles* to link users to roles. In this form, you can additionally set up rules which assign new users automatically to security roles.

In the *Users* list page, the security roles of a particular user display in the FactBox pane on the right. If a user is assigned to multiple roles, the permissions of all selected roles apply to the user. In case permission settings for an object overlap, the higher access level applies.

After assigning a security role to a user in the user detail form, you can restrict this role at organization level. For this purpose, select the particular role on the tab *User's roles* of the user detail form and click the button *Assign organizations* in the toolbar. In the *Assign organizations* form, you can grant access to the user in the selected role either to all organizations or restricted to specific organizations. If selecting specific organizations, choose either legal entities or elements of organization hierarchies with the purpose *Security*. After selecting an organization in the upper pane of the *Assign organizations* form, click the button *Grant* in the toolbar of the lower pane in order to actually assign the permission.

10.2.2.3 User Options

Clicking the button *User options* in the action pane of the *Users* form provides access to the user options of the selected user. In case the user got appropriate permissions, he or she can also access the personal user options by clicking the button ⚙/*Options* in the navigation bar.

Accessing the user options from the user management applies, if the administrator wants to predefine settings like the language or the start company.

10.2.2.4 Assigning Employees to Users

Apart from being a user, people who are accessing Dynamics AX can be employees, contractors, or contact persons at external parties (e.g. customers). The global address book contains both, master data of workers (employees and contractors) and of external contact persons.

In order to assign a Dynamics AX user to a person in the global address book (worker record or external contact), select the person in the field *Name* of the *User* detail from. The button *Maintain versions* provides the option to enter an effective date and an expiration date.

Worker records are required throughout the whole application of Dynamics AX. Examples of applicable areas are purchase requisitions, sales commissions, project accounting, human resources, case management, and sales prospect management. After linking a user to a worker who is employed in the current company, the worker ID applies to all areas – e.g. automatically inserting it in the field *Employee responsible* when creating a new prospect (*Sales and marketing> Relationships> Prospects> All prospects*).

10.2.2.5 Employee Management

The user form contains general user settings for people accessing Dynamics AX. Independently from the user administration, the worker form is there to manage the enterprise staff.

Workers include employees and contractors, no matter whether they are Dynamics AX users or not. Worker records are shared across companies, and the contact details are included in the global address book. The employment of a worker determines his assignment to one or more companies.

The worker list page (*Human resources> Workers> Workers*) shows all employees and contractors currently employed in any company of the enterprise. In order to view only current employees (workers of the type "Employee") in the current company, open the employee list page (*Human resources> Workers> Employees*). If you want to view the workers employed in the past, or workers with a future employment, click the button *As of date* in the action pane of the worker or employee page.

General worker data are shared across companies, but some data – including the employment – are company-specific. If the employee got a current employment in more than one company, the tab *Employment* in the worker detail form shows company-specific employment data in the current company.

In order to create a new worker, click the button *New* and enter the name, employing company (*Legal entity*), personnel number (if not deriving from a number sequence), worker type (employee or contractor), and employment start date in the *Create new worker* dialog.

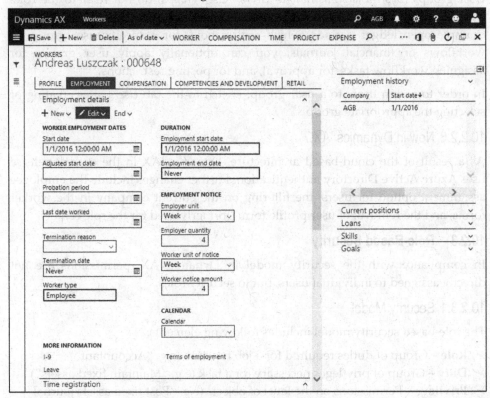

Figure 10-6: Managing employment data in the worker detail form

The default for the employing company is the current company. On the tab *Employment* in the worker detail form, you can edit the employment in the current company or add a new employment if the worker changes from this company to another company of the enterprise, or if he has got a parallel employment in another company.

The detail data which you have to enter in the worker record are primarily depending on the Dynamics AX modules used in your organization. Required details include data for project accounting, human resources, and expense management as applicable.

10.2.2.6 Online Users

If you want to know the users who are currently logged on to Dynamics AX, open the form *System administration> Users> Online users*. The inquiry shows all client sessions connected to the application. If you got appropriate permissions, you can click the button *End sessions* in the toolbar of the tab *Client sessions* to log off a user.

10.2.2.7 User Group

User groups (*System administration> Users> User groups*) do not refer to the role-based security concept, but they are used for some particular settings. You can for example open ledger periods, which are on hold, for a specific user group. In workflows or financial journals, you can optionally apply user groups for assigning workflow tasks, for approval, and for posting restrictions.

In order to assign users to a user group, switch to the tab *Users* after creating or selecting the appropriate group

10.2.2.8 New in Dynamics 'AX 7'

As a result of the cloud-based architecture, Dynamics AX in the current release uses Azure Active Directory authentication. Further changes include the employee assignment option for users, the filtering on the current company in the 'worker forms, and the removal of user profile form (formerly used for the role center).

10.2.3   Role-Based Security

In compliance with the security model in Dynamics AX, permissions are not directly assigned to individual users, but to security roles.

10.2.3.1 Security Model

The role-based security model includes following elements:

➢ **Role** – Group of duties required for a job function (e.g. "Accountant")
➢ **Duty** – Group of privileges necessary for a task (e.g. "Maintain fixed assets")
➢ **Privilege** – Permissions on the level of objects (e.g. "Post fixed assets journal")
➢ **Permission** – Low-level access restriction to securable objects (user interface elements, reports, tables and fields, service operations)

The assignment of a user to one or more roles (depending on his job functions) determines his permissions. In general, roles are linked to duties, and duties in a second level are linked to privileges. But if required, you can also assign a privilege directly to a role.

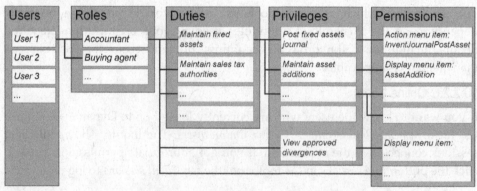

Figure 10-7:   Components of the security model

A role is a set of access permissions required to perform a job function. Apart from functional roles, which refer to the functional tasks, there are additional role types required when setting up a user:

➢ **Functional roles** – For example "Buying agent
➢ **Organizational roles** – For example "Employee"
➢ **Application roles** – For example "System user"

The role "System administrator" has access to all areas of the application. The access settings of this role are not editable.

10.2.3.2 Managing the Security Configuration

In order to manage security roles, duties, and privileges, open the form *System administration> Security> Security configuration*. The security configuration form contains the tabs *Roles*, *Duties* and *Privileges* for managing the different security elements.

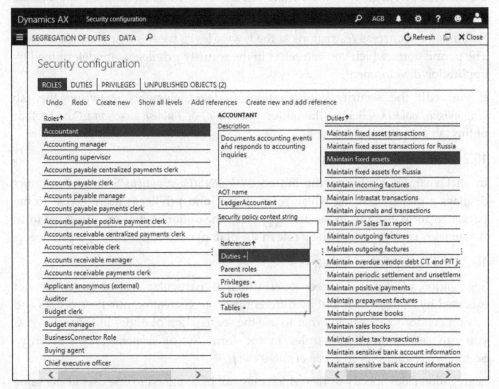

Figure 10-8:   Viewing the duties of the security role "Accountant"

On the tab *Roles*, the left pane shows the roles available in your application. After selecting a role, you can view the related duties and privileges by clicking the appropriate element in the *References* pane in the middle of the form. If you want to add a duty or privilege to the selected role, click the button *Add references* after selecting the appropriate node (e.g. "Duties") in the *References* pane. If you want to create a completely new role, click the button *Create new* (or the button *Copy* which shows after clicking a role).

A duty is a group of privileges required for a particular task, e.g. for maintaining fixed assets. In order to view and edit the duties, switch to the tab *Duties* of the security configuration form. After selecting a duty, you can view the assigned privileges (and roles) by clicking the appropriate element in the *References* pane in the middle of the form. If you want to add a privilege to the selected duty, click the button *Add references* after selecting the node *Privileges* in the *References* pane.

A privilege contains all permissions required for an individual application object. In order to view and edit the security privileges, switch to the tab *Privileges* of the security configuration form. After selecting a privilege, you can view the assigned application objects (e.g. *Action menu items*) by clicking the appropriate element in the *References* pane in the middle of the form. If you want to add a permission to the selected privilege, click the button *Add references* after selecting the appropriate node in the *References* pane.

Permissions set access restrictions at the lowest level, based on application objects. The permissions, which you can select in the security privileges, are determined by application development.

If you edit the security configuration, updated elements show on the tab *Unpublished objects*. Clicking the button *Publish all* or *Publish selection* in the toolbar of this tab activates the changes.

10.2.3.3 Security Diagnostics

In all Dynamics AX forms, the button *OPTIONS/Page options/Security diagnostics* displays a dialog showing which roles, duties, and privileges grant access to the particular form. Buttons in the dialog provide the option to directly access the form *Assign users to roles* (if selecting a role in the dialog) or to add a duty or a privilege.

10.2.3.4 Segregation of Duties

Segregation of duties is used to ensure that particular related tasks are not executed by a single user, but by different users (e.g. creating purchase orders and paying vendor invoices). In order to use the segregation of duties in Dynamics AX, you can set up applicable rules in the form *System administration> Security> Segregation of duties> Segregation of duties rules*.

Segregation rules specify duties which may not be assigned to one user at the same time. They do not prevent permission settings which are in conflict with a rule. But you can validate a segregation rule when setting it up, and you can execute a periodic activity to verify compliance.

10.2.3.5 New in Dynamics 'AX 7'

Changes in the current release include the structure of the security configuration forms and the option to view permission settings through the security diagnostics.

10.3   General Settings

A number of settings is required before an enterprise can start using Dynamics AX. These core settings include:

> **Organization management** – See section 10.1
> **Security management** – See section 10.2
> **Financial management** – See section 9.2

Each module used by your enterprise also needs to be configured according to the specific requirements (e.g. setting up terms of payment in purchasing and sales). In addition, some basic settings apply to all areas of the application. You can find a short description on these settings below.

Explanations regarding the setup of a module are available in the chapter referring to the particular module. An overview of the basic settings for a Dynamics AX implementation is included in the appendix of this book.

10.3.1   Number Sequences

Number sequences control the allocation of numbers throughout the whole application. In particular, number sequences are used in following data areas:

> **Master data** – For example assigning vendor numbers
> **Journals (including orders)** – For example assigning purchase order numbers
> **Posted transactions** – For example assigning invoice numbers

Dynamics AX includes company-specific number sequences and number sequences on enterprise level. The scope parameters of a number sequence control, whether it is shared or specific to a company (or other organization unit).

10.3.1.1 Creating a Number Sequence

In order to edit the number sequences, open the list page *Organization administration> Number sequences> Number sequences*. The FactBox *Number sequence segments* in this page shows the company and other segments of the selected number sequence as applicable. If you want to create a new number sequence, click the button *NUMBER SEQUENCE/New/Number sequence* or press the shortcut key *Alt+N* in the number sequence form. After entering a unique *Number sequence code* and a *Name*, switch to the tab *Scope parameters* of the detail form where you can specify whether the number sequence is shared or restricted to a company or organization unit.

On the tab *Segments* of the detail form, specify the number format for the number sequence. Segments of a number include following types:

> **Alphanumeric** – Number increasing every time the number sequence is used by replacing the number signs (#) in the format with the next number. The length of the alphanumeric segment has to comply with the largest number.

➤ **Constant** – Segments for prefixes (e.g. for a format "INV#####" or "12#####") and for suffixes (e.g. for a format "#####-INV"). In general, prefixes are preferable since they are easier to use (e.g. for filtering).

➤ **Other types** – Segments of the type *Company*, *Legal entity*, *Operating unit* or *Fiscal calendar* are available, if included in the *Scope* of the number sequence.

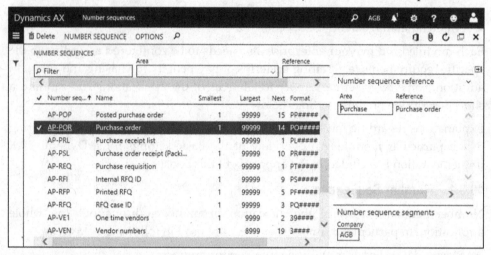

Figure 10-9: The number sequences list page

When setting up the number sequences for document and transaction numbers, it is a good idea to avoid overlapping of number sequences for the different documents in order to facilitate tracking of transactions.

10.3.1.2 Number Sequence References

After setting up the number sequence itself, the number sequence references determine the assignment of a particular number sequence to master data or transactions. In order to edit the number sequence references, switch to the tab *References* in the number sequence detail form, or access the tab *Number sequences* in the parameters of each module.

A single number sequence can be assigned to multiple number sequence references at the same time – for example if you want to apply a common number sequence to invoices and credit notes. This setting does not generate duplicate number, but alternately assigns numbers to invoices and credit notes depending on the chronological order of the transactions.

10.3.1.3 General Settings of a Number Sequence

The numeric first (*Smallest*) and last (*Largest*) number of the number sequence are specified on the tab *General* of the number sequence detail form. The field *Next* shows the number, which the number sequence applies to the next number. You can change the next number, but you have to make sure to avoid duplicate keys and gaps in continuous numbers.

The slider *Manual* controls whether numbers have to be entered completely manually. The sliders *To a lower number* and *To a higher number* specify whether it is possible to change numbers assigned from the number sequence.

The slider finally *Continuous* prevents gaps in a number sequence. Considering server performance, set this slider only in number sequences actually requiring continuous numbers to "Yes". Continuous numbering usually applies to voucher numbers, since it is a statutory requirement in many countries.

10.3.2 Calendars

As a prerequisite for posting any transaction in Dynamics AX, an open ledger period which includes the posting date is required.

10.3.2.1 Ledger Calendar

Ledger calendars (*General ledger> Calendars> Ledger calendars*), which refer to the fiscal calendar associated with your company, determine the open periods in which you can post transactions (see section 9.2.1).

10.3.2.2 Other Calendars

Apart from the calendars in finance, additional period and calendar definitions apply to other areas within Dynamics AX.

The form *Organization administration> Setup> Calendars> Working time templates* (or *Production control> Setup> Calendars> Working time templates*) contains default settings for the weekly working times. Working time templates are a basis for setting up calendars in the form *Organization administration> Setup> Calendars> Calendars* (see section 5.3.1). These calendars apply to supply chain management, including operations planning, production, purchasing, sales, and inventory management.

The project accounting module uses a separate calendar, which you can access in the form *Organization administration> Setup> Calendars> Period types*. This calendar is a basis for project invoicing and is required for estimates, invoice subscriptions, and the project-related employee setup.

10.3.3 Address Setup

The address setup is a prerequisite for entering and printing addresses correctly. In order to access the address setup, which is shared across companies, open in the form *Organization administration> Global address book> Addresses> Address setup*.

On the tab *Country/region* of the address setup, you can view the available countries. Microsoft Dynamics AX provides a standard list of countries but you can enter additional countries by clicking the button *New*.

On the tab *Parameters* of the address setup, sliders specify whether *ZIP/postal code*, *District* or *City* are validated when entering an address. If set to "Yes", you cannot enter an address with – for example – a new ZIP code before inserting the new ZIP code on the tab *ZIP/postal codes* in the address setup.

The address format on the tab *Address format* determines how street, ZIP/postal code, city, and country display in the address field of addresses. In order to comply with the regulations in different countries, an individual format per country is possible. For this purpose, the field *Address format* in the country setup (tab *Country/region* in the address setup) controls the address format per country.

If you want to set up a new format, click the button *New* in the toolbar of the address formats. In the *Configure address component* pane on the right, enter the way address components (including *Street* and *City*) should show on printed documents. The component selection is also used when entering an address: The address only shows fields which included in the address format of the particular country.

When setting up address formats, take into account that Dynamics AX stores the formatted address in addition to the individual fields of the address. If you change the format after entering addresses, you can update existing addresses by clicking the button *Update addresses* in the address format setup.

10.3.4 Parameters

Parameters are basic settings which provide the option to select the business process version, which fits best to your organization, from the options available in Dynamics AX.

Setting correct parameter values is a core task when implementing Dynamics AX. Depending on the individual parameter, you can or cannot easily change a parameter setting at a later date. Before changing any basic setting in an operational environment, make sure that you are aware of all consequences. Depending on the circumstances, read the online help or ask an expert to avoid data inconsistency or other problems.

The system parameters in the form *System administration> Setup> System parameters* contain global parameters like the system language (default language for language texts in shared data, e.g. product descriptions), or the default basic currency.

In addition, a parameters form controlling company-specific settings is available in each module of Dynamics AX. In order to access the parameters of a particular module, open the menu item *Setup> Parameters* – for example the accounts payable parameters in *Accounts payable> Setup> Accounts payable parameters*.

10.4   Workflow Management

A workflow is a sequence of operations in a routine business process, containing the necessary activities for processing a document. Typical examples of workflows are approval processes, e.g. for purchase requisitions.

Microsoft Dynamics AX provides the required functionality for configuring and processing workflows, including the option of automated processes. You can use this functionality for example if you want to automatically approve low-value purchase requisitions while requiring manual approval for high-value requisitions.

10.4.1 Configuring Workflows

Workflows are available in many areas of Microsoft Dynamics AX, including but not limited to:

➤ Purchase requisitions
➤ Purchase orders
➤ Vendor invoices
➤ Free text invoices
➤ Financial journals
➤ Budgeting
➤ Time and attendance

In each applicable menu, the setup folder contains a menu item for the workflows in the particular module. When selecting this menu item, the workflow list page displays the workflows configured in the particular module. The list page *Procurement and sourcing> Setup> Procurement and sourcing workflows* for example contains the workflows in the procurement module.

10.4.1.1 Graphical Workflow Editor

In order to view and to edit a workflow shown in a workflow list page, click the workflow *ID* shown as link in the grid. Dynamics AX then downloads the *Dynamics AX Workflow Editor*, which is a program communicating through services with the cloud-hosted Dynamics AX environment.

After signing in with your Azure Active Directory account, the graphical workflow editor shows the selected workflow with following panes:

➤ **Canvas** – Space for designing the workflow (drag and drop elements and connections)
➤ **Toolbox** – On the left, containing available workflow elements
➤ **Error pane** – Displays error messages and warnings below the canvas (not shown in Figure 10-10, click the button *Error pane* in the action pane to display)

If you want to access the properties of the workflow, do a right-hand click in the empty space of the canvas and select the option *Properties* in the context menu (or click the button *Properties* after selecting an empty space in the canvas). Important workflow settings include the *Owner* of the selected workflow.

In the toolbox on the left pane of the workflow editor, workflow elements are grouped by type (e.g. *Approvals* and *Tasks*). Depending on the selected workflow, the toolbox contains different elements. In order to hide or show the toolbox, you can click the button *Toolbox* in the action pane.

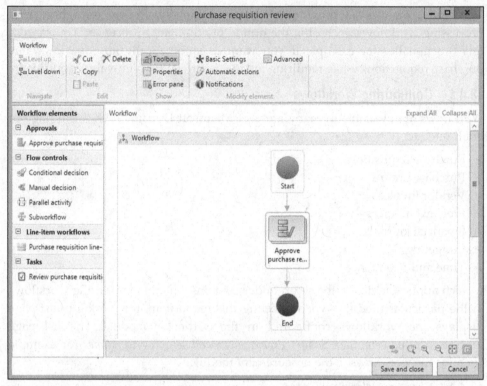

Figure 10-10: Graphical workflow editor showing the purchase requisition workflow

If you want to add a workflow element to the workflow, click it in the toolbox and drag it to the canvas. In order to edit the properties of the element, select the option *Properties* in the context menu (right-hand click on the element) or click the appropriate button in the action pane button group *Modify element*.

The options available for an element are depending on the element type. For elements requiring a manual activity (e.g. *Tasks* or *Manual decision*), the properties include a tab or button *Assignment* for assigning the responsible person. The search path for finding the responsible person is defined through the *Assignment type*. Applicable assignment types include participants (referring to user roles and user groups), hierarchies (referring to the position hierarchy in human resources), workflow users (user starting or owning a workflow), or specific user names.

Workflow elements of the type *Approval* contain a lower workflow level with the approval steps. The assignment of responsible persons for approval is on the level of approval steps. In order to access the approval steps, double-click the particular approval element or click the button *Level down* in the action pane of the workflow editor. In order to view the upper level again, click the button *Level up* or click the link *Workflow* in the path shown in the header line of the canvas.

In the *Escalation* settings, you can set up automatic reassignment of a work item once the time limit for the assigned user is exceeded. On the tab *End action* in the escalation settings, an automatic action is specified in case the escalation path fails.

Settings for *Automatic actions* provide the option to automatically take an action if the condition entered for the automatic action is met – e.g. approving a requisition if the invoice amount is below a particular value.

In order to connect the workflow elements in the canvas, create an arrow between the different elements by clicking on the border of one element and dragging the arrow to the subsequent element (similar to Microsoft Visio). In a valid workflow, all elements between *Start* and *End* have to be linked.

10.4.1.2 Work Item Queues

The option "Queue" for assigning persons to workflow elements is only available for certain workflow element types (e.g. for *Tasks*). As a prerequisite for the queue-based assignment, you set up to work item queues (*Organization administration> Workflow> Work item queues*).

Work item queues are used to pool workflow activities and to assign an activity to a group of people instead of a single person. If a work item is assigned to a work item queue, all members of the queue may claim the work item and work on it.

When setting up a new work item queue, select the workflow type in the lookup field *Document* to specify the workflows in which the work item queue is available. After setting the status of the work item queue to *Active*, it is available for assignment in the appropriate workflows.

Apart from manually adding users to a work item queue, you can apply an automatic assignment based on filter criteria. In order to specify an automatic assignment, click the button *Work item queue assignment* in the work item queue form or access the menu item *Organization administration> Workflow> Work item queue assignment rules*.

10.4.1.3 Workflow Versions

When saving a workflow by clicking the button *Save and close* in the workflow editor, Dynamics AX creates a new version. A dialog asks whether to activate the new version or to keep the previous version activated.

If you want to check and edit the versions of a workflow, click the button *WORKFLOW/Manage/Versions* in the workflow list page. In the workflow versions dialog, you can set a new version or an old version as active if applicable.

The active version applies to workflows submitted after activation. Work items of workflows in progress have to be finished on the original version.

10.4.1.4 Creating Workflows

The button *New* in the workflow list page for creating a workflow opens a dialog, where you have to select the applicable *Workflow type* – e.g. "Purchase requisition review" – before the graphical workflow editor displays as described above.

If there are two workflows of the same type in the workflow list page, specify a default by clicking the button *WORKFLOW/Manage/Set as default* in the action pane of the list page.

10.4.1.5 Basic Settings for Workflows

Processing of workflows is an asynchronous batch job, which is why the next activity in a workflow is not available immediately, but only after Dynamics AX has processed the specific workflow element. Depending on the batch configuration, this can take some time.

In order to initially set up the workflow infrastructure, a wizard is available in the menu item *System administration> Workflow> Workflow infrastructure configuration*. This wizard generates three batch jobs, which show in the form *System administration> Inquiries> Batch jobs*. As a prerequisite for using workflows, these batch jobs have to be processed repeatedly.

10.4.1.6 New in Dynamics 'AX 7'

In order to keep the graphical user experience in the cloud-based architecture, the workflow editor is a separate program downloaded from the workflow list pages.

10.4.2 Working with Workflows

If there is an active approval workflow related to a particular Dynamics AX form, a workflow button displays in the action pane of this form. This button shows that workflow processing is necessary and provides the option to submit the workflow.

When working with workflows, you should keep in mind that the workflow system processes workflow tasks in a batch process. For this reason, work items are not available before the batch process has processed the submitted workflow.

10.4.2.1 Submitting a Workflow

After creating a record which requires workflow processing, submit the workflow by clicking the button *Workflow/Submit* in the action pane (see Figure 10-11). In the *Submit* dialog which shows next, optionally enter a comment and click the button *Submit* at the bottom. Submitting a workflow starts workflow processing and generates work items based on the corresponding workflow elements.

Once the workflow is submitted, the workflow button does not show the option *Submit* any more, but other options depending on workflow settings and on the current status of the workflow. In order to check the current status of workflow processing, click the button *Workflow/View history* in the action pane.

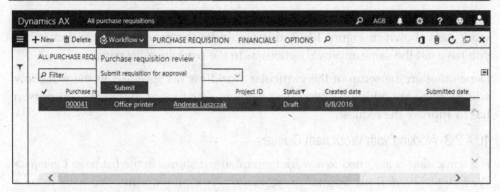

Figure 10-11: Submitting a workflow for a purchase requisition

10.4.2.2 Approving Work Items

Depending on the settings of the related workflow element, work items are either assigned to a work item queue or to individual users (including assignments through settings like participant or workflow user).

The work items assigned to a user show in the left pane of the dashboard (see section 2.1.3) and in his work item list (*Common> Work items> Work items assigned to me*). In the work item list, the available options in the workflow button are depending on the workflow element properties as specified in the workflow editor (*Allowed actions* in *Properties/Advanced settings*). These available options include:

➢ **Approve** – Approving the request
➢ **Reject** – Rejecting the approval finally (which does not prevent re-submitting)
➢ **Request change** – Rejecting, but promising approval if the request is changed
➢ **Delegate** – Transferring the decision to another user

The additional option "Recall" shown in Figure 10-12 (approver and submitter are the same person in this special case) usually is not available for approvers, but for the persons submitting the workflow. Recalling provides the option to stop a workflow before approval (e.g. for changing the request before submitting again).

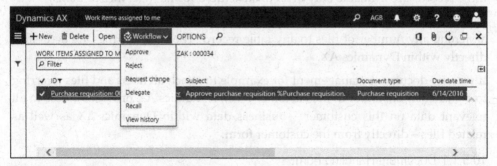

Figure 10-12: Approving a work item

If you want to know more details before deciding on an approval, you can access the original request by clicking the button *Open* in the action pane or clicking the request ID shown as link in the column *ID*. In the original request form (for the work item shown in Figure 10-12, this would be the purchase requisition form), you have got the same approval options as in the work item list page.

Depending on the setup of the particular workflow (as specified in the workflow editor), there are additional workflow element activities or more than one person has to approve the request.

10.4.2.3 Working with Work Item Queues

If a work item is assigned to a work item queue, it shows in the list page *Common> Work items> Work items assigned to my queues*. As a prerequisite, you have to be a member of the work item queue to which the work item is assigned.

In the work item queue, you can claim a work item, on which you want to work, by clicking the button *Workflow/Accept* in the action pane. Accepting a work item moves the item to your work item list (among the other work items directly assigned to you) and prevents other queue members to work on the same item.

In the work item list (*Common> Work items> Work items assigned to me*), you can execute applicable workflow actions (e.g. approving or rejecting) like you do for directly assigned work items. In addition, the workflow button contains the options *Reassign* (for reassigning the work item to other persons) and *Release* (for releasing it back to the queue).

10.5   Other Features

Advanced features, which are available across the whole application, include document management, case management, and the task guides.

10.5.1   Document Management

In daily business, you are working with structured data included as records in your business application (e.g. customers). In parallel, important data referring to these records are available only in an unstructured format (e.g. files or mails).

Document management in Microsoft Dynamics AX supports solving this issue by assigning any number of files to any table record. The attached files are accessible directly within Dynamics AX.

If you use document management for example to attach all notes and files referring to a particular customer in the customer form, Dynamics AX provides access to all relevant data on this customer – business data within Dynamics AX as well as related files – directly from the customer form.

10.5.1.1 Document Handling Form

As a prerequisite for using the document handling form, the slider *Enable document handling* on the tab *Preferences* in your user options has to be set to "Yes".

The document handling form, which you can access in any list page or form by clicking the button 🔳 in the action pane or pressing the shortcut key *Ctrl+Shift+A*, provides access to the document handling form where you can manage notes and documents as applicable. These documents are attached to the record which has been selected in the original form when opening document handling.

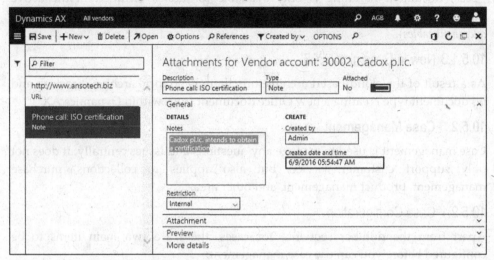

Figure 10-13: Entering a simple note in the document handling form

If you want to create a new document in the document handling form, insert a new record by clicking the button *New* in the action pane or by pressing the shortcut key *Alt+N*. The *Type* selected in the new record determines if the document is a note, a file attachment, or a URL. If the type is a note, you can enter a longer text in the field *Notes* on the tab *General*.

In case the document is an attachment, you can view the attached document later by clicking the button *Open* (which downloads the attachment) or by expanding the tab *Preview* in the document handling form.

10.5.1.2 Document Types and Document Management Setup

In document management, we have to distinguish between following document types:

> **Simple note** – Only including plain text entered in the document handling form
> **File attachment** – Available for attaching files
> **URL** – Used to enter a web link in the field *Description*

In order set up document types, open the form *Organization administration> Document management> Document types*. Each document type refers to a particular class and group (fields *Class* and *Group*), specifying if assigned documents are simple notes, attachments or URLs.

Basic document management parameters (*Organization administration> Document management> Document management parameters*) include the number sequence for documents on the tab *Number sequences* and the file types which are available in document management on the tab *File types* (providing the option to exclude possibly malicious file types like EXE-files).

If the slider *Use active document tables* on the tab *General* in the parameters is set to "Yes", document handling is only available for tables included in the active document tables (*Organization administration> Document management> Active document tables*).

10.5.1.3 New in Dynamics 'AX 7'

As a result of the cloud-based architecture, there is no local archive directory and no document type creating a new Office document from within Dynamics AX

10.5.2 Case Management

Case management is used to manage any questions and issues centrally. It does not only support customer service, but also applies to collections, purchase management, product management, and other areas.

10.5.2.1 Case Configuration

Apart from the number sequence for cases, there are two main items to be configured before you can use case management:

➢ **Case categories** – For grouping purposes
➢ **Case processes** – Specifying the activities for processing a case

Case categories (*Organization management> Setup> Cases> Case categories*) group cases by functional areas in a hierarchical structure. In order to set up a new case category, click the button *New* in the action pane and select the *Category type*. On the tab *General*, you can enter default values for the owner and for the *Case process* which will be used when creating a case with the current category.

Case processes (*Organization management> Setup> Cases> Case processes*) support performing necessary steps when processing a case. Depending on the different types of cases in your enterprise, you can set up one or more case processes. When setting up a new case process, enter the *Name* and *Description* and make sure that the *Type* is "Case process" before saving the record. Then you can access the steps (stages) for case processing by clicking the button *PROCESS/VIEW/Details*. In the process details, you can create a process stage by clicking the button *NEW/Create level*. In the field *Purpose*, enter the name of the stage. If required, you can create a multi-level hierarchy of stages.

For simple case processes, setting up stages may be sufficient. But if applicable, you can enter activities (e.g. *Appointments*) assigned to the stages by clicking the button *New/Create appointment* (or one of the other options in the *New* button). Activities referring to cases, which you can access in the menu folder *Common> Activities*, are in common with the activities in *Sales and marketing* (former CRM activities). If you want to make sure, that a particular activity is executed when working on a case, set the slider *Required* in the activity to "Yes". In addition, the slider *Check for required activities* on the tab *Exit criteria* of the related stage has to be set to "Yes".

10.5.2.2 Processing Cases

If you want to create a new case, click the appropriate button in the action pane of any list page or detail form which refers to case management – e.g. in sales orders (*Sales and marketing> Sales orders> All sales orders*, button *GENERAL/Customer/Cases/ Create case*), customers, collections, vendors, or released products.

Cases created in a sales order are assigned to the order and to the customer. When creating such a case, enter the *Case category* and a *Description* in the *Create* dialog. Defaults for the *Owner*, *Service level agreement* and *Case process* on the tab *Other* of the dialog are retrieved from the selected *Case category*. Clicking the button *Create* in the dialog then creates the case.

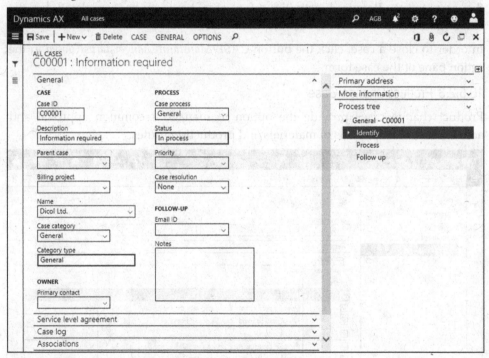

Figure 10-14: Editing details in a case

If you want to follow up on a case, open the list page *Common> Cases> All cases* and switch to the detail form. Assignments of the case (e.g. to a sales order) show on the tab *Associations*. If additional associations apply later, you can add them in the case form (e.g. additionally assigning a return order case to the original sales order). The FactBox *Process tree* shows the process steps as specified in the applicable *Case process*. The current status of the stages shows in the case process form, which you can access by clicking the button *CASE/Process/Case process* in the action pane of the case form.

When starting to work on a case, click the button *CASE/Maintain/Change status/In process* in the action pane of the case form (if this status has not been already selected when creating the case). When proceeding with the case later, click the button *CASE/Process/Case/Change stage* and select the next stage, to which you want to move, in the dialog box.

The tab *Case log* shows all interactions (e.g. receiving a product) referring to the case. Using the case log, other persons looking at a specific case can easily know the status of a case.

If the case is attached to a *Case process* which includes activities (e.g. *Appointments*), you can access the related activities through the menu item *Common> Activities> All activities* (or by clicking the button *GENERAL/Activities/Activities/View activities* in the case form). Required activities of a case have to be completed by the responsible person.

In order to close a case, click the button *CASE/Maintain/Change status/Closed* in the action pane of the case form.

10.5.2.3 Product Change Case

Product change cases provide the option to manage a common approval and activation of multiple bills of materials and production routes.

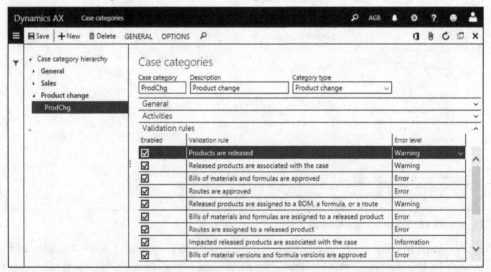

Figure 10-15: Configuring a case category for a product change case

As a prerequisite for product change cases, you must create at least one case category with the *Category type* "Product change". In case categories with this type show the additional tab *Validation rules* in the case category form, where you can enable predefined validation rules to make sure that all conditions for approving a BOM and route are met.

Once the setup is finished, you can create a product change case by clicking the button *ENGINEER/Product change/Create case* in the action pane of the released product form (<u>not</u> the button *GENERAL/Maintain cases/Create case* which does not include the required case category). In the *New case* dialog, enter a *Name* and select a *Case category* for product change cases.

In order to assign bills of materials to the case, open the BOM form and select or create the appropriate BOM. Then click the button *BILL OF MATERIALS/Product change/Associate with case* and select the applicable *Case ID* in the *Associate with case* dialog. Depending on the requirements, you can associate further BOMs and – in a similar way – routes. In addition, you can associate other products (e.g. components) to the case.

If you want to follow up on the change case, view the list *Open cases* in the *Released product maintenance* workspace or the general list page *Common> Cases> All cases* and switch to the detail form. On the tab *Associations* in the case form, you can view all assigned products, BOMs and routes.

Processing the case works the same way as processing a regular case (see above). But in addition to the regular case functionality, the button *CASE/Product change/ Approve and activate changes* is available once the case status in "In process". In the *Approve and activate changes* form, you can set the action *Approve, Activate,* and – for versions – *Expire* individually per line or through the button *Set action* in the toolbar of the *BOMS and routes* and the *BOM versions and route versions* tab. Clicking the button *Apply actions* in the action pane of the form executes the actions selected in the lines.

10.5.3 Task Recorder and Task Guide

Task guides are step-by step instructions explaining how to perform a business process. The task recorder is used to create task guides.

In order to open the task recorder, click the button ⬛/*Task recorder* in the navigation bar. In the *Task recorder* pane on the right-hand side, you can create a recording by clicking the button *Create recording*. Then enter a *Recording name* and click the button *Start* in the next dialog. Once the recording is started, execute the steps which you want to record in the Dynamics AX client. The button ☑ next to each step in the task recorder pane provides the option to add instructions.

Once you have finished the recording, click the button *Stop* in the task recorder banner at the top. The task recorder pane then provides the option to save the recording to your PC, to Lifecycle Services, or to export it as Word document.

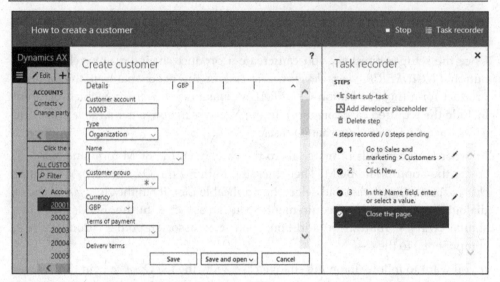

Figure 10-16: Recording a guide in the task recorder

If you want to play a recording as task guide, you can click the button *Play recording as guide* in the task recorder pane and open the recording previously saved to your PC or to Lifecycle Services.

Appendix

Setup Checklist

The checklists below show the most essential steps for setting up Dynamics AX. The section "Basic Setup" contains necessary configuration steps for the functional areas covered by the book. They have to be finished before you can start to use any module. Master data and other essential settings of particular modules are shown in the section afterwards. Depending on the specific requirements of an implementation, additional setup is required in most cases.

Basic Setup

Table A-1: Basic system setup

No.	Name	Menu Item	Section
1.1	Configuration	System administration> Setup> License configuration	
1.2	Parameters	System administration> Setup> System parameters	10.3.4
1.3	Legal entities	Organization administration> Organizations> Legal entities	10.1.4
1.4	Users	System administration> Users> Users	10.2.2

Table A-2: Basic setup of a legal entity

No.	Name	Menu Item	Section
2.1	Operating units	Organization administration> Organizations> Operating units	10.1.2
2.2	Dimensions	General ledger> Chart of accounts> Dimensions> Financial dimensions	9.2.3
2.3	Fiscal calendars	General ledger> Calendars> Fiscal Calendars	9.2.1
2.4	Currencies	General ledger> Currencies> Currencies	9.2.2
2.5	Rate types	General ledger> Currencies> Exchange rate types	9.2.2
2.6	Exchange rates	General ledger> Currencies> Currency exchange rates	9.2.2
2.7	Chart of Accounts	General ledger> Chart of accounts> Accounts> Chart of accounts	9.2.4
2.8	Account structure	General ledger> Chart of accounts> Structures> Configure account structures	9.2.4
2.9	Ledger	General ledger> Ledger setup> Ledger	9.2
2.10	Sites	Inventory management> Setup> Inventory breakdown> Sites	10.1.5
2.11	Warehouses	Inventory management> Setup> Inventory breakdown> Warehouses	7.4.1
2.12	Dimension link	Inventory management> Setup> Posting> Dimension link	10.1.5
2.13	Bank accounts	Cash and bank management> Bank accounts	9.2.5
2.14	Address setup	Organization administration> Global address book> Addresses> Address setup	10.3.3

No.	Name	Menu Item	Section
2.15	Address book parameters	*Organization administration> Global address book> Global address book parameters*	2.4.2
2.16	Number sequences	*Organization administration> Number sequences> Number sequences*	10.3.1
2.17	Units	*Organization administration> Setup> Units> Units*	7.2.1
2.18	Unit conversion	*Organization administration> Setup> Units> Unit conversions*	7.2.1

Table A-3: Basic setup for general ledger and sales tax

No.	Name	Menu Item	Section
3.1	Default descriptions	*Organization administration> Setup> Default descriptions*	9.2.4
3.2	Accounts for aut. transactions	*General ledger> Posting setup> Accounts for automatic transactions*	9.2.4
3.3	Tax posting group	*Tax> Setup> Sales tax> Ledger posting groups*	9.2.6
3.4	Tax authorities	*Tax> Indirect taxes> Sales tax> Sales tax authorities*	9.2.6
3.5	Sales tax settlement periods	*Tax> Indirect taxes> Sales tax> Sales tax settlement periods*	9.2.6
3.6	Sales tax codes	*Tax> Indirect taxes> Sales tax> Sales tax codes*	9.2.6
3.7	Sales tax groups	*Tax> Indirect taxes> Sales tax> Sales tax groups*	9.2.6
3.8	Item sales tax groups	*Tax> Indirect taxes> Sales tax> Item sales tax groups*	9.2.6
3.9	Journal names	*General ledger> Journal setup> Journal names*	9.3.1
3.10	Parameters	*General ledger> Ledger setup> General ledger parameters*	9.3.1

Table A-4: Basic setup for procurement and accounts payable

No.	Name	Menu Item	Section
4.1	Terms of payment	*Accounts payable> Payment setup> Terms of payment*	3.2.2
4.2	Vendor groups	*Accounts payable> Vendors> Vendor groups*	3.2.3
4.3	Posting profiles	*Accounts payable> Setup> Vendor posting profiles*	3.2.3
4.4	Accounts payable parameters	*Accounts payable> Setup> Accounts payable parameters*	
4.5	Procurement parameters	*Procurement and sourcing> Setup> Procurement and sourcing parameters*	

Table A-5: Basic setup for sales and accounts receivable

No.	Name	Menu Item	Section
5.1	Terms of payment	*Accounts receivable> Payment setup>Terms of payment*	3.2.2
5.2	Customer groups	*Accounts receivable> Setup> Customers> Customer groups*	4.2.1
5.3	Posting profiles	*Accounts receivable> Setup> Customer posting profiles*	4.2.1
5.4	Form setup	*Accounts receivable> Setup> Forms> Form setup*	4.2.1

No.	Name	Menu Item	Section
5.5	Accounts receiv. parameters	*Accounts receivable> Setup> Accounts receivable parameters*	
5.6	Sales and markt. parameters	*Sales and marketing> Setup> Sales and marketing parameters*	

Table A-6: Basic setup for product and inventory management

No.	Name	Menu Item	Section
6.1	Storage dimension groups	*Product information management> Setup> Dimension and variant groups> Storage dimension groups*	7.2.2
6.2	Tracking dimension groups	*Product information management> Setup> Dimension and variant groups> Tracking dimension groups*	7.2.2
6.3	Item groups	*Inventory management> Setup> Inventory> Item groups*	7.2.1
6.4	Transaction combinations	*Inventory management> Setup> Posting> Transaction combinations*	9.4.2
6.5	Posting	*Inventory management> Setup> Posting> Posting*	9.4.2
6.6	Item model groups	*Inventory management> Setup> Inventory> Item model groups*	7.2.3
6.7	Costing versions	*Cost management> Predetermined cost policies setup> Costing versions*	7.3.3
6.8	Journal names	*Inventory management> Setup> Journal names> Inventory*	7.4.1
6.9	Warehouse journals	*Inventory management> Setup> Journal names> Warehouse management*	7.4.1
6.10	Parameters	*Inventory management> Setup> Inventory and warehouse management parameters*	

Table A-7: Basic setup for production control

No.	Name	Menu Item	Section
7.1	Production units	*Production control> Setup> Production> Production units*	5.3.1
7.2	Working time templates	*Production control> Setup> Calendars> Working time templates*	5.3.1
7.3	Calendars	*Production control> Setup> Calendars> Calendars*	5.3.1
7.4	Route groups	*Production control> Setup> Routes> Route groups*	5.3.3
7.5	Cost groups	*Production control> Setup> Routes> Cost groups*	7.3.3
7.6	Shared categories	*Production control> Setup> Routes> Shared categories*	5.3.3
7.7	Cost categories	*Production control> Setup> Routes> Cost categories*	5.3.3
7.8	Resource capabilities	*Organization administration> Resources> Resource capabilities*	5.3.2
7.9	Resource groups	*Organization administration> Resources> Resource groups*	5.3.1
7.10	Resources	*Organization administration> Resources> Resources*	5.3.2
7.11	Journal names	*Production control> Setup> Production journal names*	5.5.1

No.	Name	Menu Item	Section
7.12	Calculation groups	*Cost management> Predetermined cost policies setup> Calculation groups*	7.3.3
7.13	Costing sheets	*Cost management> Ledger integration policies setup> Costing sheets*	7.3.3
7.14	Parameters	*Production control> Setup> Production control parameters*	
7.15	Parameters by site	*Production control> Setup> Production control parameters by site*	

Table A-8:   Basic setup for master planning

No.	Name	Menu Item	Section
8.1	Coverage groups	*Master planning> Setup> Coverage> Coverage groups*	6.3.3
8.2	Master plans	*Master planning> Setup> Plans> Master plans*	6.3.2
8.3.	Forecast models	*Master planning> Setup> Demand forecasting> Forecast models*	6.2.2
8.4	Forecast plans	*Master planning> Setup> Plans> Forecast plans*	6.2.2
8.5	Parameters	*Master planning> Setup> Master planning parameters*	6.3.2

Other Key Settings and Master Data

Table A-9:   Other key settings

No.	Name	Menu Item	Section
9.1	Employees	*Human resources> Workers> Workers*	10.2.2
9.2	Terms of delivery	*Sales and marketing> Setup> Distribution> Terms of delivery*	3.2.1
9.3	Modes of delivery	*Sales and marketing> Setup> Distribution> Modes of delivery*	4.4.3
9.4	Cash discounts	*Accounts payable> Payment setup> Cash discounts*	3.2.2
9.5	Payment methods (Purchasing)	*Accounts payable> Payment setup> Methods of payment*	9.3.4
9.6	Activate trade agreements (Purchasing)	*Procurement and sourcing> Setup> Prices and discounts> Activate price/discount*	3.3.3
9.7	Vendor price/ discount groups	*Procurement and sourcing> Prices and discounts> Price/discount groups> Vendor price/discount groups*	3.3.3
9.8	Item discount groups	*Procurement and sourcing> Prices and discounts> Price/discount groups> Item discount groups*	4.3.2
9.9	Trade agreement journal names	*Procurement and sourcing> Setup> Prices and discounts>Trade agreement journal names*	3.3.3
9.10	Price tolerance setup	*Accounts payable> Invoice matching setup> Price tolerances*	3.6.2
9.11	Activate trade agreements (Sales)	*Sales and marketing> Setup> Prices and discounts> Activate price/discount*	4.3.2

No.	Name	Menu Item	Section
9.12	Customer price/ discount groups	*Sales and marketing> Prices and discounts> Customer price/discount groups*	4.3.2
9.13	Charges codes (Purchasing)	*Accounts payable> Charges setup> Charges code*	4.4.5
9.14	Charges codes (Sales)	*Accounts receivable> Charges setup> Charges code*	4.4.5
9.15	Return action (Purchasing)	*Procurement and sourcing> Setup> Purchase orders> Return action*	3.7.1
9.16	Disposition codes (Sales returns)	*Sales and marketing> Setup> Returns> Disposition codes*	4.7.1
9.17	Category hierarchies	*Product information management> Setup> Categories and attributes> Category hierarchies*	3.3.1
9.18	Procurement categories	*Procurement and sourcing> Procurement categories*	3.3.1
9.19	Sales categories	*Sales and marketing> Setup> Categories> Sales categories*	4.3.1
9.20	Document management parameters	*Organization administration> Document management> Document management parameters*	10.5.1
9.21	Document types	*Organization administration> Document management> Document types*	10.5.1
9.22	Workflow configuration	*System administration> Workflow> Workflow infrastructure configuration*	10.4.1

Table A-10: Master data

No.	Name	Menu Item	Section
10.1	Vendors	*Accounts payable> Vendors> All vendors*	3.2.1
10.2	Customers	*Accounts receivable> Customers> All customers*	4.2.1
10.3	Products	*Product information management> Products> All products and product masters*	7.2.1
10.4	Released products	*Product information management> Products> Released products*	7.2.1
10.5	Bills of materials	*Product information management> Bills of materials and formulas> Bills of materials*	5.2.2
10.6	Operations	*Production control> Setup> Routes> Operations*	5.3.3
10.7	Routes	*Production control> All routes*	5.3.3

Commands and Shortcut Keys

Table A-11: Basic commands and shortcut keys

Shortcut Key	Button in the action pane	Description
Alt+N	New	Create a record
Alt+F9	Delete	Delete a record
Alt+S	Save	Save record (in edit mode)
F2	Edit (or OPTIONS/Edit/ Read mode)	Toggle between view and edit mode
Esc		Close form (optionally without saving)
Shift+Esc		Close form and save record
Ctrl+Shift+F5	OPTIONS/Edit/Revert	Restore record (Undo pending changes)
Shift+F5	⟳ (Refresh)	Refresh (Save and synchronize record)
Ctrl+F2	⊞ (top right of the grid)	Show the FactBox pane
Ctrl+Shift+H	Header (in the title line)	Switch to the header view (in transaction forms)
Ctrl+Shift+L	Lines (in the title line)	Switch to the lines view (in transaction forms)
Ctrl+F10	(Right-hand mouse click)	Open the Dynamics AX context menu
Ctrl+G	(Click on the column header)	Open the grid filter for the current column
Ctrl+F3	▼ (on the left-hand side)	Open the filter pane
Ctrl+Shift+F3	OPTIONS/Page options/ Advanced filter/Sort	Open the advanced filter
Ctrl+Shift+A	📎 (Attach)	Document management
Alt+F1	☰ (on the left-hand side)	Navigation pane
Ctrl+?	❓ (Help)	Help on forms

The Dynamics AX online help contains a complete list of all keyboard shortcuts.

Bibliography

Literature

Scott Hamilton: Supply Chain Management using Microsoft Dynamics AX, 2016 Edition (Visions Inc., 2016)

Scott Hamilton: Essential Guide for Discrete Manufacturing using Microsoft Dynamics, 2016 Edition (Visions Inc., 2016)

Murray Fife: 50 Tips & Tricks for the New Dynamics AX (CreateSpace Independent Publishing, 2015)

Keith Dunkinson, Andrew Birch: Implementing Microsoft Dynamics AX 2012 with Sure Step 2012 (Packt Publishing, 2013)

Other Sources

Microsoft: Microsoft Dynamics AX Help Wiki (https://ax.help.dynamics.com/)

Microsoft Dynamics Learning Portal (access is restricted)

Index

Printed in the United States
By Bookmasters